Hawthorne in His Own Time

WRITERS IN THEIR OWN TIME

Joel Myerson, *series editor*

HAWTHORNE
in His Own Time

A BIOGRAPHICAL

CHRONICLE OF HIS LIFE,

DRAWN FROM RECOLLECTIONS,

INTERVIEWS, AND

MEMOIRS BY FAMILY,

FRIENDS, AND

ASSOCIATES

EDITED BY

Ronald A. Bosco and

Jillmarie Murphy

University of Iowa Press
Iowa City

University of Iowa Press, Iowa City 52242
Copyright © 2007 by the University of Iowa Press
www.uiowapress.org
All rights reserved
Printed in the United States of America

The University of Iowa Press is a member of Green Press Initiative and is
committed to preserving natural resources.

Printed on acid-free paper

LCCN: 2006937355
ISBN-10: 1-58729-582-2 cloth; 1-58729-583-0 paper
ISBN-13: 978-1-58729-582-9 cloth; 978-1-58729-583-6 paper

07   08   09   10   11   C   5   4   3   2   1
07   08   09   10   11   P   5   4   3   2   1

Contents

⊰⊱

[v]

Introduction

⇥⊁|⊀⇤

"NATHANIEL HAWTHORNE DEAD!" As obituaries and remembrances appeared in America and England from 19 May 1864 through the ensuing summer months, news of the Great Romancer's quiet transition on 18 May from this world to the next slowly spread. But even as early versions of the story appeared in print, it fell to former President Franklin Pierce to frame a narrative of Hawthorne's final days for the consolation of his family and few close friends. Hawthorne's favorite companion on innumerable outings since their college days at Bowdoin, Pierce had visited Concord in late April and convinced Hawthorne to meet him in Boston on 11 May; proposing that they would set out from there on a leisurely excursion to northern New England, Pierce imagined the trip as an opportunity for the two to greet another spring season together and for Hawthorne to replenish his dwindling strength.

Pierce either spoke or wrote to those he thought deserved firsthand details of Hawthorne's death on the excursion. Writing on 21 May to Horatio Bridge, their lifelong friend from Bowdoin days who was then assigned to the navy department in Washington, he described Hawthorne as "infirm for more than a year[,] . . . particularly within the last three or four months." He said that because William D. Ticknor's sudden death in April had "aggravated" their friend's "enfeebled condition," he thought a journey through New Hampshire, with stops at Franklin, Laconia, and Centre Harbor before arriving at the Pemigewasset House in Plymouth, would be the perfect tonic. Pierce diagnosed Hawthorne's disease as having settled in his "brain or spine, or both," noting, too, that he "walked with difficulty, and the use of his hands was impaired." But, he told Bridge, after arriving in Plymouth on 18 May, "I had decided . . . not to pursue our journey . . . [and] would the next day send for Mrs. Hawthorne and Una to join us there. Alas! there was no next day for our friend." He then provided Bridge with these details of their friend's last hours:

After taking a little tea and toast in his room, and sleeping for nearly an hour upon the sofa, [Hawthorne] retired. A door opened from my room to his, and our beds were not more than five or six feet apart. I remained up an hour or two after he fell asleep. He was apparently less restless than the night before. The light was left burning in my room . . . and I could see him without moving from my bed. I went . . . between one and two o'clock to his bedside, and supposed him to be in a profound slumber. His eyes were closed, his position and face perfectly natural. His face was towards my bed. I awoke again between three and four o'clock, and was surprised—as he had generally been restless—to notice that his position was unchanged—exactly the same that it was two hours before. I went to his bedside, placed my hand upon his forehead and temple, and found that he was dead. He evidently had passed from natural sleep to that sleep from which there is no waking, without suffering, and without the slightest movement.[1]

Pierce's thoughtfulness in writing to friends such as Bridge was commendable, for the public was aware of only the more mundane aspects of Hawthorne's final days and hours, as the press took one of two entirely different approaches to the story. Praising his fictional characters as "much beyond those of Dickens and Thackeray in creative depth," on 19 May the *Boston Daily Evening Transcript* pronounced Hawthorne's passing "a calamity" for the literary world "too great to be expressed in words"; on 20 May, the *Boston Daily Advertiser* predicted his death would "take the public by surprise and cause deep regret" as soon as it became known, the *New York Times* professed relief that his early death "saved" him from "the most awful of miseries that can befall the aspirant for permanent renown—that of seeing the honor and glory of youth extinguished in his own presence," and the *Boston Courier* memorialized him as realizing "our conceptions of a man of genius, in contradistinction to a man of talents, a man of learning, [or] a clever man."[2]

On 20 May, an obituary in the *New-York Tribune* declared Hawthorne's position "as a great and original writer" in the annals of American literature "permanently settled."[3] Far less complimentary obituaries also appeared, however, dredging up his complicated position on slavery and the Civil War as evidenced by his open contempt for Northern as well as Southern mercantile interests, his disrespect for both Abraham Lincoln and the abolitionists in the text and notes accompanying his "Chiefly about War–Matters" essay published in the *Atlantic Monthly* in 1862, and his loyalty to Pierce, whose campaign biography he had written in 1852 and to whom he had dedicated *Our Old Home* despite opposition from his friends and publisher in 1863. For instance, granting that Hawthorne possessed a "subtle and brilliant mind," on 20 May, the *Providence Journal* advised readers that the paper "never had any sympathy with the doctrines of the political party with which [he] acted," and that his position on "our national struggle" disclosed "too deep a sympathy with the sentiments of . . . Pierce"; on the same day, the *Springfield Republican* printed a harsh obituary, stating, "at this time, when all our energies are bending in one direction, the regret and grief of the loyal people of the North is not and cannot be what it would have been, had Mr. Hawthorne ever expressed a word of sympathy for the cause in which we are fighting, or manifested any interest in the preservation of our national integrity."[4] Finally, after assessing Hawthorne's "apostate" character as demonstrated by his critique of America's and his own Calvinist past in his writings, his betrayal of the Socialist ideal represented by Brook Farm through his caricature of the utopian experiment in *The Blithedale Romance,* and his "shameless prostitution of [his] high literary talent" through the services he rendered to Pierce and his party, John Humphrey Noyes, writing for the *Oneida Circular,* concluded, "We have no faith in the permanence of Hawthorne's reputation."[5]

Predictably, Hawthorne's friends ignored the printed guesses—for they were just that—about the impact his friendships and political views would ultimately exert on his reputation. In a eulogy delivered on 23 May at Concord's First Parish Church, the Unitarian minister and Transcendentalist James Freeman Clarke, who had officiated at Nathaniel's marriage to Sophia Amelia Peabody in 1842 and remained close to both throughout the years, mingled traditional Christian consolation with nontraditional literary criticism. Preaching to a congregation that included—among others drawn from New England's literary, academic, and political élite—Henry Wadsworth Longfellow, Louis Agassiz, Oliver Wendell Holmes, James Russell Lowell, Edwin Percy Whipple, John Sullivan Dwight, George Stillman Hillard, Charles Eliot Norton, Ebenezer Rockwood Hoar, James T. and Annie Adams Fields, Bronson Alcott, William Ellery Channing (the younger), Ralph Waldo Emerson, and Pierce, Clarke assured mourners that their "hour of sadness" was an "hour of gladness, too." Although he did not preach from a specific biblical text, Clarke followed basic homiletic form in his eulogy. "In the happiest moments there is some foreboding of loss—an undertone to the joy," he observed, adding that "in the saddest and darkest hours of life there is the presage, the forelooking of the hope which God has planted in all our hearts of the coming of something infinitely higher and better. . . . [W]e may doubt immortality, but not in the presence of death." Then, applying his views to Hawthorne's death, Clarke said,

> Eminently is this the case now. If there ever has been one who was eminently himself, and received, cherished and faithfully fulfilled that which God gave him, it was our friend who has left us. . . . [W]e all knew this of him, and we knew it in his writings, in which he put himself; we know of him that his plan was his own, and that his whole work came according to the law which God had impressed upon it, and that God placed him here to glorify this tame New England life, and to pour over it all that poetry that was in his heart. . . . [N]o other thinker or writer . . . has had such sympathy as he had with that dark shadow which falls over our existence—that shadow which theologians call sin. He seemed to be the friend of sinners in his writings. . . . He entered into [the sinner's] mysterious depths and felt his way through [the] dark passages of the human heart, and always with the tenderest sympathy, always to show us that there is something in our own hearts which might have led us the same way. I think that was a work . . . our friend has done which was never done before as he did it. It was not that he did not recognize all that was right and generous and noble in nature. His books were full of sunshine as well as of shade. They are sunny all through, and the dear mother, Nature, who sympathizes with her children, seems to–day to have bound all the stars of her beauty around her, as a parting tribute to this her son who has been so faithful to her allegiance. All this fragrance and sweetness of the opening of the year which is breathed around us, seems to be the farewell of the mother to her son who has gone on into that higher nature, that nobler work, and that larger life which is ready for us when we have finished our work here.[6]

Writing to her brother Edward Jarvis Bartlett two days after Hawthorne's funeral, young Annie Keyes Bartlett reported that average Concordians were shocked that members of the Saturday Club and the Peabody family insisted that his coffin be opened for a viewing, and that she and others did not appreciate Pierce's attendance at the services. As several narratives in this volume attest, Hawthorne often expressed dread at the prospect of being looked on in death, and his family observed his wish as much for their sake as for his. At the same time Pierce, who along with Daniel Webster supported the notorious Compromise of 1850, had to know that in coming to Concord he was entering an armed camp of unrepentant former abolitionists of the Transcendental stripe. Describing the events of 23 May, Bartlett wrote to brother "Ned,"

. . . Monday was the most beautiful day there ever was[;] the funeral of Mr Hawthorne was at the church and it was beautifully dressed with bouquets of white flowers[;] the coffin had a wreath of lillies of the valley all round it which Una made[.] She was there trimming it in the morning. It was their wish that the coffin should not be opened, but the club of gentlemen to which Mr H belonged wished to see him so the family left the church and it was opened but 'twas closed as soon as they had passed by. Then the Peabody's went round and it was opened again and all the congregation went up so that it was impossible to shut it for a long time. I thought I should fly twas so dreadful to have all the people looking at him when the family were not willing to see him. All the poets were there[:] Holmes, Agassiz, Lowell, Longfellow, Whipple and all the others and "last and least" Franklin Pierce. He is a very fine looking man[,] older than I thought he was. The cemetery was beautiful[.] Mr Clarke made a prayer at the grave. Afterwards we went back to the church to take the flowers down and sent some to the Hawthornes. Cousin Elizabeth [Ripley] saw some people in a chaise apparently looking for the "Old Manse"[;] she went out to meet them and the gentleman put out his hand to shake hands saying he was Gen. Pierce. Of course she was provoked enough to have shaken hands but she invited them in[;] he declined but the lady with him went in[;] he said he would stay to see to his horse. He was cute to shake hands before telling his name.[7]

In the weeks after Hawthorne's death, additional notices of his passing appeared in America and abroad. While none provided the insider's look at the local spectacle that Annie Bartlett conveyed in her letter, Emerson's thoughts on the occasion, which he consigned to the privacy of his journal,[†] and those that Richard Holt Hutton and Edward Dicey wrote for British periodicals[†] and Holmes wrote for the *Atlantic Monthly*[†] disclose a common characteristic: Regardless of the extent to which the authors actually knew him, each tends, as Clarke had in his eulogy, to read Hawthorne's essential character through his writings and concludes that whatever existence he enjoyed in this world, it was a minimal one apart from the life he crafted, expressed, and lived in his fiction. Perhaps anticipating that, if it took hold, such an approach to Hawthorne's life would deprive the world of an excellent chapter in real human history, Bronson Alcott, Hawthorne's Concord neighbor, and Henry A. Bright, one of Hawthorne's closest friends in England, published appreciative accounts of the man as they knew him. Writing in the *Boston Commonwealth*, Alcott drew out his subject's human side by treating his "habitual" reserve and "vast" solitude in ways that nineteenth-century contemporaries, who so prized individualism and privacy, would have appreciated. Alcott's approach to Hawthorne-the-man might have worked had he not squandered its appeal by lapsing into sentimental associations between Hawthorne's fiction and his actual personality. Alluding to his early story "The Gentle Boy" (1832), Hawthorne, he says, "was the Gentle Boy and gentleman all his days, yet lov[ed] the land and landsman, the sailor and the seas"; then, adapting a form of obituary eloquence to his narrative, which Hawthorne would have loathed, Alcott lost track of his subject as he sent him off on a "journey of enchantment[,] . . . from the Gentle Boy setting forth on his pilgrimage, through the inns and customs of the Old Home and the new, to the repose in the Sleepy Hollow for a night, and the awakening to fairer scenes of romance." [8] Although Bright's account appears to have gone largely unnoticed, he fared better than Alcott in expressing the loss that the literary world, and he personally, suffered by Hawthorne's death. Writing in the *London Examiner*, Bright said that the news "came closer home . . . as a cause of grief than the account of many [Civil War] battles." Remarking that with Hawthorne gone, all lovers of the English language had lost one of its "true chiefs," Bright personalized the moment, stating that the grief felt by those who "knew Hawthorne as a friend" eclipsed the regret others might feel over "a great author's death." [9]

The few additional notices of Hawthorne's passing that appeared over the next two years amount to slightly fresher treatments of previously expressed critical positions. In contrast to Emerson, whose passing on 27 April 1882 occasioned more than five hundred printed obituaries, reminiscences, and partial as well as complete biographies in the next two years, Hawthorne seemed fated to premature obscurity. [10] Except for items included in this volume, only a handful of additional pieces from the roughly seventy-five that appeared in print in America or England between July 1864 and September 1866 offered new insights into Hawthorne's life, art, and reputation. Among these were essays by Moncure D. Conway and George William Curtis. Dismissing Hawthorne's association with the Transcendentalists and his commitment to social reform as momentary digressions at best, and labeling his biography of Pierce his best work of fiction, in "The Transcendentalists of Concord," Conway exposed the profound differences between Hawthorne and the persons and movements with which he interacted for much of his active career in the 1840s and 1850s. Although he would publish sympathetic treatments of Hawthorne's life and writings later in the century, here, Conway advanced a claim for greater attention to Emersonian Transcendentalism, but at Hawthorne's expense.[11] By contrast, in two articles that appeared in 1864, Curtis provided far more balanced assessments of Hawthorne's genius and reputation than he had in an earlier sketch collected in *Homes of American Authors* (1853).[†] In his "Editor's Easy Chair" column in *Harper's New Monthly Magazine*, Curtis praised Hawthorne as an American literary genius of the highest order, remarking that his romances were impossible to conceive of elsewhere, since their subjects were so thoroughly American, and in a substantial biographical essay in the *North American Review*, he tempered his earlier criticism of Hawthorne's social isolationism and lack of commitment to the spirit of reform that had inspired his ancestors and continued to inspire his contemporaries with notice of his genuine appeal as an individual and the near perfection of many of his *Twice-Told Tales* and *The Marble Faun*.[12]

In addition to Conway's and Curtis's assessments of Hawthorne's reputation, one other that appeared during this period deserves mention, for inasmuch as it clearly delineates the challenge facing Hawthorne's survivors as to how he ought to be remembered as a person and a writer, it is the one assessment that was truly groundbreaking. Gathering some of his earlier published reviews and biographical essays for a volume he would publish as *Character and Characteristic Men* in 1866, the American critic Edwin Percy Whipple returned to a review he had written for the *Atlantic Monthly* in 1860, just after the publication of *The Marble Faun*. A New Englander born in the seaside village of Gloucester, Massachusetts, in 1819, Whipple had a rare appreciation of the historical and personal past in which Hawthorne intellectually and imaginatively lived and out of which he wrote. He had been an even-handed and favorable reviewer of Hawthorne's writings since the late 1840s, and to judge by all available evidence, the two respected each other's opinions. Unlike most of those who reviewed Hawthorne's writings or attempted to define his character while he was alive, Whipple never blended critical reviews of Hawthorne's work with gratuitous biographical criticism of the sort represented by Curtis's "Hawthorne" to undermine his art or embarrass him. However, in reviewing *The Marble Faun* for the *Atlantic*, he forthrightly illustrated how in Hawthorne's case biography and criticism were inextricably connected.

Whipple's "Nathaniel Hawthorne" in *Character and Characteristic Men* is a virtual reprint of his 1860 review, and its reappearance within two years of Hawthorne's death contributed to the formalization of one of the dominant strains of how he was remembered by those who actually knew him in his time. Taking a retrospective approach to Hawthorne's career, Whipple argued that the paramount strength of *The Marble Faun* is its representation of the brilliance of Hawthorne's art as cumulatively developed over time. "In intellect and imagination, in the faculty of discerning spirits and detecting laws," he wrote, "we doubt if any living novelist is his equal; but his genius, in its creative action, has been heretofore attracted to the dark rather than the bright side of the interior life of humanity, and the geniality which . . . is in him has rarely found adequate expression." Hoping—in 1860—that Hawthorne will eventually write with a mind freed of "sadness" but without the loss of any of its "subtilty and depth," Whipple acknowledged that "he has already done enough to insure him[self] a commanding position in American literature as long as American literature has its existence."[13] But even if Hawthorne's death had not foreclosed Whipple's hope for his future genial treatment of "the bright side of the interior life of humanity," Whipple retained enough of the Calvinist sensibility to recognize that this author could not be other than the person and writer he had already become. In an extremely perceptive overview of Hawthorne's writings through the early 1850s, which demonstrates his facility at psychological—more than mere biographical—criticism but not at the expense of his sympathy for Hawthorne as a person and a writer, Whipple observed,

> There would appear . . . to be no reason for the little notice which Hawthorne's early productions received. The subjects were mostly drawn from . . . New England, and gave the "beautiful strangeness" of imagination to objects, incidents, and characters which were familiar facts in the popular mind. The style . . . had a purity, sweetness, and grace which satisfied the most fastidious and exacting taste. . . . But, though the subjects and the style were thus popular, there was something in the . . . informing spirit which . . . awakened interest without exciting delight. Misanthropy, when it has its source in passion,—when it is fierce, bitter, fiery, and scornful, . . . echoes the aggressive discontent of the world, and furiously tramples on the institutions and the men . . . in the ascendant,—this is always popular; but a misanthropy which springs from insight,—. . . which is lounging, languid, sad, and depressing, . . . has no fanaticism . . . [but] casts the same ominous doubt on subjectively morbid as on subjectively moral action, . . . has no respect for impulses, but has a terrible perception of spiritual laws,—this is a misanthropy which can expect no wide recognition; and it would be vain to deny that traces of this kind of misanthropy are . . . found in Hawthorne's earlier, and are not altogether absent from his later works. He had spiritual insight, but it did not penetrate to the sources of

spiritual joy. . . . A blandly sceptical distrust of human nature was the result of his most piercing glances into the human soul. He had humor, and sometimes . . . of a delicious kind; but this sunshine of the soul was but sunshine breaking through . . . a sombre and ominous cloud. . . . Throughout, the impression is conveyed of a shy recluse, alternately bashful in disposition and bold in thought, gifted with original and various capacities, but capacities which seemed to have been developed in the shade. Shakespeare calls moonlight the sunlight *sick;* and it is in some such moonlight of the mind that the genius of Hawthorne found its first expression. . . . Though dealing largely in description, and with the most accurate perceptions of outward objects, he . . . gives the impression of a man "chiefly accustomed to look inward, and to whom external matters are of little . . . import, unless they bear relation to something within his own mind." But that "something within his own mind" was often an unpleasant something, . . . so that the reader felt a secret dissatisfaction with the disposition which directed the genius, even in the homage he awarded to the genius itself. As psychological portraits of morbid natures, his delineations of character might have given a purely intellectual satisfaction; but there was audible, to the delicate ear, a faint and muffled growl of personal discontent, which showed they were not mere exercises of penetrating imaginative analysis, but had in them the morbid vitality of a despondent mood.[14]

Even before Whipple's insightful *Atlantic Monthly* review of *The Marble Faun* reappeared in his *Character and Characteristic Men* in 1866, Hawthorne's family, close friends, and literary associates had begun discussing the prospects for a biography of him. Appreciating the long-term risk to his personal and literary reputation of allowing the "wrong" person to have the first word, they knew that the time had definitely come. For most of Hawthorne's career, the dominant form for assessing his literary accomplishments was the newspaper or periodical review, and the few that included specific comment on his character or personality hardly advanced his reputation.[15] On the surface, then, Whipple would appear to have been an excellent choice for the honor of writing the first biography of Hawthorne, but if he received serious consideration, no record of the fact has survived. Curtis, Bronson Alcott, Ellery Channing, Emerson, Elizabeth Palmer Peabody (Hawthorne's sister-in-law), Lowell, and Fields may have struck some as reasonable candidates; however, with the exception of Lowell and Fields, most presented certain liabilities.

In the appreciative essays he published in 1864, Curtis had atoned somewhat for his treatment of Hawthorne in 1853, but as numerous citations of that earlier sketch in reminiscences that follow in this volume suggest, the unflattering images he projected there remained fixed in the public's mind for a long time to come. As the first extended consideration of Hawthorne as a man and an artist—as opposed to an author whose writings were under review—Curtis's "Hawthorne" was incredibly influential, and there is no exaggeration in saying that it modeled a type of biographical study of Hawthorne throughout the nineteenth century. Applying his own peculiar version of journalistic license to a reading of *Mosses from an Old Manse* (1846), in "Hawthorne" Curtis blurred the distinction between the refurbished Old Manse in which the Hawthornes lived during the idyllic first years of their marriage and the threadbare historical Old Manse, occupied for the previous fifty years by Ezra Ripley, Concord's "beneficent Pope," Emerson's step-grandfather, and one of the ecclesiastical ghosts who, along with Edward Bliss and William Emerson, haunted the landscape Hawthorne literarily imagined there. Built by Emerson's paternal grandfather, William, in 1770 in a field beside the North Bridge, where on 19 April 1775 the patriots fired "the shot heard 'round the world" that began the American Revolution, in Curtis's hand the Old Manse was transformed into a ramshackle place suitable only for a writer of Hawthorne's silence, reclusiveness, social awkwardness, and gloomy antiquarianism. Pressing forward to the Hawthornes' return to Concord in 1852, when they took up residence in the Wayside, Curtis relentlessly depicted Hawthorne through comparable associations. All of Old Salem's gloom and shadow followed the nomadic writer and his family to their new home, where the fields and woods adjoining the author's property were inhabited by strange forms, where visitors shuddered while in his presence, and where the ghost of Martha Hunt, a suicide by drowning when the Hawthornes lived at the Old Manse, hovered in the mists above the Concord River. Contrite or not for his treatment of Hawthorne in 1853, Curtis was not a plausible candidate to serve as his first biographer.

Although they had known Hawthorne personally and invariably represented themselves as his friends, Alcott, Channing, and Emerson were also possible candidates. Still living at the Wayside in Concord after her husband's death, Sophia Hawthorne had regular contact with all three and occasionally turned to Emerson for advice on financial and publishing matters. But among those who knew them and were capable of being objective, Alcott's and Channing's performance as writers was mixed at best; then—and now, with all we know about the course of their respective careers—there would have been cause to doubt their reliability as recorders of Hawthorne's life and art or as persons who would finally deliver a completed text. A writer of biography, whose *Representative Men* (1850) remained a popular volume years after its publication, even Emerson could not be counted on to prepare a balanced account of Hawthorne's life. Emerson claimed to appreciate Hawthorne, but as his journal entries cited later in this volume reveal, his typical approach to Hawthorne discloses an edge of highly negative literary criticism and a disposition to render his character invisible. To make matters worse—certainly as far as the Boston Brahmin establishment represented by Lowell, Fields, or Holmes would be concerned—Alcott, Channing, and Emerson were Transcendentalists. And the Boston Brahmins would not have been alone in believing that their intellectual affiliation disqualified all three from serving as Hawthorne's biographer. Remembering her visit to Concord in 1862 during which she attended a dinner at the Wayside where Alcott and Emerson were also guests, Rebecca Harding Davis drew a sharp distinction between Hawthorne residing in the nominal seat of Transcendentalism and his being party to the "fraternity" of self-absorbed eccentrics who subscribed to its tenets.[†] Writing nearly forty years after the event, she remarked, "Hawthorne was in this fraternity but not of it. He was an alien among these men, not of their kind. He belonged to no tribe. . . . [H]e was always a foreigner, different from his neighbors. He probably never knew that he was different. He knew and cared little about Nathaniel Hawthorne, nor indeed about the people around him."[16] Edward Dicey, who also visited Hawthorne at the Wayside in the early 1860s, would have agreed with Davis. Alluding to Laurence Sterne's episodic novel *The Life and Opinions of Tristram Shandy, Gentleman* (1759–1767), in a reminiscence published immediately after Hawthorne's death, Dicey offered this observation on the discrepancy between the transient world in which his friend lived and the mundane world that others around him occupied: "[Hawthorne] belonged . . . to [a] scattered Shandean family, who are never in their right places wherever they happen to be born—to that race of Hamlets, to whom the world is always out of joint anywhere."[17]

In the end, Peabody, Lowell, and Fields were the most plausible persons to entrust with Hawthorne's biography. In spite of her closeness to the major Transcendentalists, Peabody had much to recommend her for the role, though in all likelihood she would have declined had she been offered it. Peabody knew Hawthorne far more intimately than either Lowell or Fields

Sophia Amelia Peabody Hawthorne and Nathaniel Hawthorne etchings by
S. A. Schoff, from Julian Hawthorne, *Nathaniel Hawthorne and His Wife:
A Biography* (1884).

had, and she appreciated the unique spiritual and physical relationship her
sister shared with him throughout their marriage, and frequently observed
the warm and rich home life they created for their children; additionally, as
her *Atlantic Monthly* essay on "The Genius of Hawthorne" in 1868 demonstrated, she had been a perceptive reader of her brother-in-law's writings
since the late 1830s.[18] In a letter to Nathaniel's sister Elizabeth, a contemporary whom she had known since their childhood years in Salem, as early as
1838 Peabody professed absolute confidence in the young author's potential. Describing those who had not yet grasped the immensity of his talent—
especially his ability to inspire children through his writings—and predicting
that his art might one day be the salvation of his country, she said,

> . . . [I]t seems to me they live in too gross a region of selfishness to appreciate the
> ambrosial moral aura which floats around our Ariel,—the breath that he respires.
> I . . . would have him help govern this great people; but I would [also] have him
> go to the fountains of greatness and power,—the unsoiled souls,—and weave for
> them his "golden web" as . . . it may be the web of destiny for this country. In every
> country some one man has done what has saved it. It was one Homer that made
> Greece, . . . and one Wordsworth that has created the Poetry of Reflection.[19]

Not knowing the identity of its author, Lowell praised Peabody's *Atlantic Monthly* essay in a letter to Fields: "I love to see [Hawthorne] praised as he deserves"; "I don't think people have any kind of true notion yet what a master he was. . . . Shakespeare, I am sure, was glad to meet him on the other side."[20] "The Genius of Hawthorne" is indeed excellent literary criticism, which equals Whipple's treatment of Hawthorne in *Character and Characteristic Men;* however, unlike Whipple, Peabody virtually ignored Hawthorne's personal history in her examination of his art. At best, she lightly touched on the edges of his life in the essay, preferring instead to demonstrate his genius exclusively through his writings and never through comment on what nineteenth-century readers would have considered his character. Expressing her attitude toward biographical treatments of Hawthorne by George Parsons Lathrop[†] (the Hawthornes' daughter Rose's husband), Julian Hawthorne (their son), and George B. Loring[†] (Nathaniel's friend), which appeared over the ensuing years, Peabody implicitly explained her own decision never to write his life. Repeating privately to her German correspondent, Amelia Boelte, in the 1880s what she had stated publicly for years before, Peabody reported that Hawthorne never wanted a biography to be written of him, and she respected that as well as his preferred form of biographical treatment. "Hawthorne expressed in his lifetime that he hoped his biography would not be written," she told Boelte; he "thought what he had maturely decided to publish would give what was alone valuable in his life."[21] In a subsequent letter to Boelte, Peabody vented her exasperation with the brand of psychological criticism of Hawthorne advanced in Lathrop's *A Study of Hawthorne* (1876) and Julian's wholesale reporting of what she considered privileged letters, conversations, and interactions between his parents, and between them and their friends, in *Nathaniel Hawthorne and His Wife: A Biography* (1884); she approved, however, of Loring's approach to Hawthorne's life in his essay "Nathaniel Hawthorne"[†] (1880) and in his lecture in 1882 on the real and the supernatural in Hawthorne's life and writings, which he drew from the essay. Writing with scientific objectivity garnered from his training, Loring, a physician, mentioned few names besides Hawthorne's in the essay and made the case for his genius with the precision of a logical argument. In an aside to Boelte in 1886, Peabody commented, " 'A Life of Hawthorne translated from the biographies of his son, son-in-law and friend Dr. Loring with omissions of irrelevant matter' would be a splendid book."[22]

Thus, from the perspective of those who may have seriously considered the matter in the mid-1860s, either Lowell or Fields would have seemed a natural choice to serve as Hawthorne's first biographer. Accomplished writers and editors, who between them published every author of note in America as well as many from abroad from the 1840s through the late 1870s, both knew Hawthorne, respected his art, and cherished the literary and personal confidences he shared with them over the years. Peabody may have been the person who, as she liked to say, "discovered" Hawthorne in the late 1830s, but Fields was the one who called on Hawthorne in his Salem garret in 1849, coaxed out of him the manuscript that would become *The Scarlet Letter*, and published the novels that by 1860 had earned him the title "the Great Romancer." Although his vocal and printed contributions to the antislavery movement in New England sharpened the political differences between Hawthorne and himself, Lowell was someone Hawthorne thought he could trust. After the two met when the Hawthornes returned to America from Europe in 1860, Lowell excitedly reported to Grace Norton that Hawthorne said "he was gratified . . . with my little notice of 'The Marble Faun'" in the *Atlantic Monthly* and thought

> it came nearer the kernel than any of them. . . . He told me that his characters always had their own way with him; that they were foredoomed from the first, and that he was only their historian. . . . He said also that it was part of his plan in "The Scarlet Letter" to make Dimmesdale confess himself to a Catholic priest. I, for one, am sorry he didn't. It would have been psychologically admirable.[23]

An appreciative reader of Hawthorne, Lowell invariably grasped "the kernel" of Hawthorne's principal concerns in his writings. Reviewing *The Marble Faun,* Lowell recognized Hawthorne's stature as the nineteenth century's most "purely original writer," saw a kinship between his understanding of human comedy and tragedy and Shakespeare's, and applauded the "psychological and metaphysical" tendencies that informed his romances.[24] Sickened by Hawthorne's death, Lowell exclaimed to William Dean Howells, "Only think of losing Hawthorne! I cannot stomach it!"[25]

When the call to serve finally came, Lowell was the one who first received it. As editor of the *North American Review,* a visible poet and prose writer in his own right, and a longtime associate of most persons to whom he would have to appeal for reminiscences and leads to ungathered Hawthorne material, Lowell knew the projected biography had the potential not only to enhance his own reputation but also to serve Hawthorne's. This was a task to which Lowell was equal in every respect; it was also a task in which, out of respect for Hawthorne, he definitely believed, as may be gleaned from this remark he made in a letter to Hawthorne in February 1863: "You are one of the few men in these later generations whose works are going to *keep*."[26] According to Martin Duberman, Lowell's biographer, shortly after her husband's death, Sophia asked Lowell to write a biography of him, but she then withdrew the offer over a dispute concerning his access to Hawthorne's unpublished writings.[27] Yet, the matter does not appear to have ended there. In late summer 1866, having spoken to Sophia on Lowell's behalf and apparently having smoothed things over, Longfellow approached Lowell to write Hawthorne's life. In a letter to Longfellow dated 14 September 1866, Lowell acknowledged his overture and Sophia's generosity:

> I thank you heartily for the kind things . . . you said to Mrs. Hawthorne about Hawthorne's Life. Of course, I should like to do it very much. Whether I can, is another question. I have never tried my hand at any such thing, and it will take moreover so much time. There are seventeen quartos of "Diary"—a splendid mine . . . but consider the amount of digging. And Mrs. H. tells me there are few letters. If you could find the time to jot down some of your recollections and also the names of anybody you can think of likely to know anything, it would be a great kindness.[28]

In the end, however, Sophia was unwilling to provide Lowell access to either Hawthorne's unpublished notebooks, which she intended to edit for publication herself, or the manuscripts of the four romances left unfinished at the time of her husband's death—"Dr. Grimshawe's Secret," "Septimius Felton," "The Ancestral Footstep," and "The Dolliver Romance," the last of which the family had placed atop his coffin—and so Lowell withdrew from the project.

The biography that Hawthorne's family, close friends, and distant admirers had long awaited finally appeared in four installments printed in the *Atlantic Monthly* between February and May 1871.[†] Approaching retirement, James T. Fields had decided to write Hawthorne's life himself, and it was indeed fortuitous that he emerged as Hawthorne's first significant biographer, albeit seven years after the author's death. Given the vexed public image of Hawthorne that took hold after the appearance of Curtis's sketch in 1853 and the persistent tendency among reviewers even after Hawthorne's death to equate his character and personality with those of his fictional creations, few could have carried off so convincingly and so well the image of Hawthorne as a genuinely charming companion and fellow writer and warm and loving family man as Fields did in the columns of his "Our Whispering Gallery" series. Here, Fields replaced the unearthly ghosts, faint shadows, and human tremblings that haunted Curtis's Hawthorne or shook all who came near him with a portrait of Hawthorne that Fields had himself commissioned from Samuel W. Rowse in 1865: a "golden curl" of Hawthorne's baby hair, poetic lines drawn from Wordsworth, Leigh Hunt, Milton, and others, and testimony from Hawthorne's friends who shared Fields's point of view toward his subject. Citing liberally from Hawthorne's letters to him and others, incorporating almost all the information Elizabeth Manning Hawthorne had supplied at his request about her brother's early history,[†] and featuring rich and witty anecdotes of their personal friendship that began in the late 1840s, in this biography Fields established the standard for the genteel approach to Hawthorne's life for decades to come. Set in "Our Whispering Gallery"— Fields's name for a room above the offices of his publishing house, which was cluttered with mementoes of his numerous literary friendships and where Hawthorne and he sat many an evening, looking out into the twilight and watching the ships dropping down the stream—and narrated by Fields to an eager "nephew" as a reminiscence of his "uncle's" friendship with the author, the four installments of Hawthorne's biography followed a single installment in January on Alexander Pope and William Makepeace Thackeray and preceded six installments on Charles Dickens from June through November and a single one on William Wordsworth and the English writer Mary Russell Mitford in December 1871.

Although Fields modestly revised the "Our Whispering Gallery" narrative for a chapter on Hawthorne in his *Yesterdays with Authors* (1872) and, later, as the basis for *Hawthorne* (1876), a book-length biography, his 1871 series announced not only that Hawthorne had arrived as a serious biographical subject, but also that, flanked by Pope and Thackeray on the one hand and Dickens, Wordsworth, and Mitford on the other, he had arrived in exceptional company. Writing to Fields on 11 February 1871, Lowell congratulated him on the first Hawthorne installment, and noting that a more traditional biography of their friend was unlikely, he urged him to indulge readers with more rather than fewer of the delightful digressions with which he opened the series, and to be generous with the "trifles":

> I am looking forward to your next installment of Hawthorne. I read the first with great interest, and wish you would give us more rather than less—especially in extracts from his letters. We don't seem likely to get a biography, and these in some sort supply it. . . . Be sure and don't leave out anything because it seems trifling, for it is out of these trifles only that it is possible to reconstruct character sometimes, if not always. I think your method is above criticism, and you have hit the true channel between . . . reticence and . . . gossip.[29]

Fields's successful blending of conversational reminiscence with traditional biography, unpublished correspondence, passages from his subject's published writings, anecdotes, and the testimony of others influenced the shape of Hawthorne biographies in the decades that followed. Most appeared as eclectic remembrances in essay form, but early on, two appeared as critical books: Lathrop's *A Study of Nathaniel Hawthorne* (1876) and Henry James's *Hawthorne* (1879).[†] Both were groundbreaking studies of Hawthorne's life and writings; although Julian Hawthorne and Elizabeth Palmer Peabody took exception to these books for different reasons, Lathrop's met with the approval of reviewers, but James's was almost universally panned by them.

By the time Lathrop and James composed their biographies, editions of Hawthorne's notebooks had been available for several years. Edited by Sophia Hawthorne, who censored what went into print, *Passages from the American Note-Books* (1868), *Passages from the English Note-Books* (1870), and *Passages from the French and Italian Notebooks* (1871) provided general readers with a very different view of Hawthorne from the one to which they were accustomed, and Lathrop, James, and all future biographers of Hawthorne made extensive use of them. In Lathrop's case, the notebooks allowed him to negotiate the distance between the "embalming process of biography" and his authorial "intuition," which was "confirmed and seldom confuted by [his] research" into them.[30] Intent on moderating the rush of criticism after Hawthorne's death, which treated his tales and romances as self-exposures, Lathrop argued that Hawthorne disclosed himself not in his fiction but in his notebooks, where he recorded his impressions of people, places, and things and, most important of all, his inner life. "[T]he grossest errors have been committed through the assumption that particular passages in Hawthorne's [fictional] writings apply directly and unqualifiedly to himself," Lathrop wrote, adding, "[t]here is so much imagination interfused with them, that only a reverent and careful imagination can apply them aright." While he, too, would ultimately succumb to a psychological reading of Hawthorne's character through his fiction, Lathrop made a valuable point in his contrast between critics' and general readers' responses to Dickens's characters and the manner in which they typically approached Hawthorne's fiction as a representation of his personal character:

> We don't think of attributing to Dickens the multiform oddities which he pictures with such power, it being manifestly absurd to do so. As Dickens raises the laugh against them, we at once perceive that they are outside of himself. Hawthorne is so serious, that we are absorbed in the sober earnest of the thing, and forget to apply the rule in his case. Dickens's distinct aim is to excite us with something uncommon; Hawthorne's, to show us that the elements of all tragedies lie within our individual natures; therefore we begin to attribute in undue measure to *his* individual nature all the abnormal conditions that he has shown to be potential in any of us.[31]

On its appearance, *A Study of Hawthorne* was for the most part positively received. This was quite a feat for Lathrop, given the fact that, although he admired the author who was his wife's father, Lathrop, a teenager at the time of Hawthorne's death, never met the man and relied completely on family papers, secondhand accounts of Hawthorne, and close readings of his notebooks and fiction for his biography. An anonymous reviewer for the *Boston Daily Advertiser* found it "an interesting book" that would appeal "to all admirers of the wonderful writer of wonderful romances," and in an advertisement in the *New-York Tribune* that culled remarks from various published reviews, *A Study* was praised as a "thoughtful, earnest, sympathetic, well-written and elegantly printed . . . book"—"a labor of love."[32] Julian Hawthorne registered the strongest objections to the biography, stating in a letter printed in the *New-York Tribune* that his brother-in-law had "'composed and published [it] in violation' of a family trust and 'in the face of repeated warning and opposition' from the family."[33] Citing the fact that much of the material from which he quoted was already in print, Lathrop convincingly defended himself in a reply printed in the *Tribune* on 15 July 1876; his position was supported by an anonymous reviewer for *Zion's Herald,* who castigated Julian for his severe, "most bitter, and utterly unwise attack," as well as by most subsequent reviewers.[34] In the family, Rose took her husband's side, as did Elizabeth Palmer Peabody in a letter to Ellen D. Conway dated 21 November 1876:

> Julian doubtless believes he tells the truth but the facts are not quite as would be inferred—Rose never heard that her father's letters were given to Julian exclusively & having them in her possession she retained them to read & nobody hindered or gainsaid till Julian heard of "the Study"—Then he sent for the letters peremptorily & as Rose had read them—she sent them back for Julian & Una whom she recognized as having equal but *not superior* right to hers—Lathrop had not time to read them—& having the materials for his study in printed things he did not need to explore them. . . . Rose who is more like her father in all respects than either of the children—is greatly afflicted—She feels Julian has done more harm to his own than her husband's reputation—. . . & *she sees* that it is he who has violated sacred privacies[.] [35]

Henry James's *Hawthorne* appeared in the middle of that great writer's early period, when novels such as *Roderick Hudson* (1875), *The American* (1877), *The Europeans* (1878), *The Portrait of a Lady* (1881), and *The Bostonians* (1886) represented his impatience with faddish movements such as Transcendentalism, which he thought filled the air with nonsensical propositions as displays of their self-importance, and his doubt whether provincial New England—if not all of provincial America—could ever support a truly literary imagination. In deciding to write *Hawthorne* at this time, James certainly realized that he had selected a figure whose work he confessed to admire, but whose life and art reported so much about human behavior and America that gave him pause. On the opening page of the biography, he admitted as much, stating that "for several reasons" he opted to render his subject's life and art in the form of a "short sketch" that will be more like a "critical essay" than "a biography." [36]

There were very good reasons for James to make the admission, and primary among them was the fact that he lacked data on Hawthorne's personal life to construct the kind of substantive biography he felt his subject deserved. James relentlessly questions *how Hawthorne really lived* and *what Hawthorne really thought* throughout the biography, but soon enough his questioning becomes tiresome and such answers as he offers appear more like acts of literary criticism than of biography. Although he attempted to make up for this deficiency by relying heavily on Fields's reminiscence and Lathrop's *Study* for facts about his subject's day-to-day existence, even these sources were

Nathaniel Hawthorne engraving by R. G. Tietze, from *The Century Magazine* (1894).

insufficient to humanize the particular Hawthorne that James wanted to portray. Additionally, throughout the biography James repeatedly expressed his conviction that to write about Hawthorne was to write about America, a subject without a past and, thus, as far as James was concerned, a subject without a moral or intellectual center. Reviewers, wondering whether the author himself knew the Hawthorne he wished to portray in the biography, were virtually unanimous in expressing their frustration with James's *Hawthorne;* one writing anonymously for the *New York Herald* seemed to speak for all—and perhaps for James as well—when he wrote, "The reader closes [this] book stimulated, but without having made Hawthorne's acquaintance."[37] In fact, James appears to have known the Hawthorne he wished to portray, although he never succinctly expressed his Hawthorne until the final paragraph of the biography:

> He was a beautiful, natural, original genius, and his life had been singularly exempt from worldly preoccupations and vulgar efforts. It had been as pure, as simple, as unsophisticated, as his work. He had lived primarily in his domestic affections, which were of the tenderest kind; and then—without eagerness, without pretension, but with a great deal of quiet devotion—in his charming art. His work will remain; it is too original and exquisite to pass away; among the men of imagination he will always have his niche. No one has had just that vision of life, and no one has had a literary form that more successfully expressed his vision. He was not a moralist, and he was not simply a poet. The moralists are weightier, denser, richer, in a sense; the poets are more purely inconclusive and irresponsible. He combined in a singular degree the spontaneity of the imagination with a haunting care for moral problems. Man's conscience was his theme, but he saw it in the light of a creative fancy which added, out of its own substance, an interest, and, I may almost say, an importance.[38]

Although it is not equal to the depth of information provided in the Fields and Lathrop studies that he mined, James's *Hawthorne* has been generously excerpted in this volume because it shows so clearly the formidable challenges early biographers faced when attempting to capture Hawthorne's life. And, indeed, we would also say that James's effort was not in vain. For instance, he argued far more convincingly than Lathrop had that if they wanted to represent the essence of the man and his art, Hawthorne's future biographers would have to rely on his notebooks; as a means into Hawthorne's mind, they demonstrated that in spite of his reputed withdrawal from society he was a sensitive observer of the people he met, the places he lived in or visited, and all forms of human behavior that at a later date might provide him with the germ of a new story or romance. Remarking that the notebooks "are the exhibition of an unperplexed intellect," James went on to say that their worth was not as an index to Hawthorne's complicated intellect, but to the development of "his imagination—that delicate and penetrating imagination which was always at play, always entertaining itself, always engaged in a game of hide and seek in the region in which it seemed to him that the game could best be played—among the shadows and substructions, the dark-based pillars and supports, of our moral nature." [39]

Among them, Curtis, Fields, and Lathrop and James introduced and defined the three dominant strains of Hawthorne biography that were published through the beginning of the twentieth century by those who knew him quite well or—as in the case of Lathrop and James—knew about him from reliable informants or through access to Hawthorne's private papers, which were gradually appearing in print, though in a highly censored form. Curtis's Hawthorne is represented in this volume only through his caustic 1853 sketch, which, to the extent that it influenced readings of Hawthorne's life and art throughout the nineteenth century, did so primarily in negative reviews of Hawthorne's publications or in critical essays that narrowly constructed his biography through similarly caustic reference to his fiction. In our judgment, Fields's Hawthorne exerted the greatest influence during the nineteenth century on the shaping of his life in reminiscences, memoirs, and critical studies written by those who knew him; in its reliance on amiable reflections on times spent in his company, personal letters exchanged with Hawthorne, and supportive anecdotal asides borrowed from others, Fields's study modeled the genteel form of biography that family, friends, and literary associates emulated in constructing their respective Hawthornes. Fields's influence will be seen in this volume in the reflections on Hawthorne written by Annie Sawyer Downs, Rose Hawthorne Lathrop, Rebecca Harding Davis, George B. Loring, Moncure Daniel Conway, William Dean Howells, and Frank Preston Stearns. Although Fields's approach to Hawthorne also influenced Julian Hawthorne's *Nathaniel Hawthorne and His Wife* (1884) and Horatio Bridge's *Personal Recollections of Nathaniel Hawthorne* (1893), neither is included here. We rejected Julian's study of his parents for inclusion because we concur with the judgment initially expressed by Elizabeth Palmer Peabody and reinforced by subsequent Hawthorne scholarship[40] that he wrote recklessly about the people with whom his parents associated at home and abroad and misrepresented his father's opinions of others in order to sell his book; and while Bridge's study is a valuable representation of his lifetime friendship with Hawthorne, we rejected it, as well, because of its form as a friendship narrated through a collection of correspondence loosely strung together with minimal connective prose. Finally, substantial excerpts from Lathrop's and James's studies of Hawthorne are included here, but since their influence during the nineteenth century is visible primarily in critical treatments by others of Hawthorne's fiction, we have not included these because they are readily available in recent collections of nineteenth-century assessments of Hawthorne's writings.[41]

In approaching the selections that close this introduction, readers might bear in mind Lowell's counsel to Fields after reading his first installment on Hawthorne in "Our Whispering Gallery": incorporate more, not fewer, digressions, and do not overlook the "trifles." Fields was already disposed to follow Lowell's counsel; although it was advice they had not been offered, so too were many whose narratives of their association with Hawthorne follow in this volume, as well as many whose remembrances of him do not occur in sustained narratives but in asides in their correspondence or memoirs, in comparisons they drew between Hawthorne and his contemporaries, or in nostalgic snippets one occasionally finds in archives of nineteenth-century print and manuscript materials. Although digressions and "trifles" will not an entire biographical life make, in a curious way they confirm the American playwright Arthur Miller's justification for his selective appropriation of historical fact to suit his artistic purposes while writing *The Crucible:* "One finds I suppose what one seeks."[42] Miller's comment recognizes the influence that the intellectual and imaginative predispositions of writers and readers exert on historical materials, and it is as instructive for biographical and critical writing as it is for fiction and drama that have their source in history. In Hawthorne's case, digressions and "trifles" such as follow here serve as valuable footnotes to the character featured in many of the remembrances that his contemporaries wrote.

Even before meeting Hawthorne in Italy, Elizabeth Barrett Browning had no difficulty speaking authoritatively about his personality, social manners, and attitude toward Spiritualism; she knew what she considered enough about all three from the expatriate American sculptor William Wetmore Story to pass on the information to Mary Russell Mitford. Hawthorne and Story knew each other in America; after renewing their friendship when the Hawthornes settled in Italy in the late 1850s, Hawthorne featured Story's *Cleopatra,* which was acclaimed at the International Exhibition in London in 1862, in the preface to *The Marble Faun.* Writing from her summer estate in Bagni di Lucca on 20–21 August 1853, Browning told Mitford what she then knew about Hawthorne from Story:

> . . . We were considering your expectations about Mr. Hawthorne—"All right", says Mr. Story . . . "except the rare *half* hours." (of eloquence.) He represents Mr. Hawthorne as not silent only by shyness but by nature & inaptitude. He . . . talks wholly & exclusively with the pen, & . . . does not open out vocally with his most intimate friends any more than with strangers. It is'nt his *way* to converse— That has been a characteristic of some men of genius before him, you know—but you will be nevertheless disappointed. . . . Also, Mr. Story does not imagine that you will get anything from him on the subject of the "manifestations"—You have read the 'Blithesdale Romance' & are aware of his opinion expressed there? He evidently recognized them as a sort of scurvy spirits, good to be slighted because of their disreputableness[.] [43]

Although Hawthorne was critical of the credulity of Spiritualists, including his wife's, after he returned to America in 1860, his reputation in society apparently improved in one surprising respect: Henry James Sr. thought him and Ellery Channing fine specimens of manly Swedenborgians. Writing to Emerson in 1862 the morning after they had both attended a Saturday Club dinner at which Hawthorne and Channing were present, James, who was going to Concord the next day, remarked that even though he would not have time to meet with Emerson, he simply could not "forbear" to report his "impression" of the two. "Hawthorne," he said,

> isn't to me a prepossessing figure, nor apparently at all an *enjoying* person in any way: he has all the while the look—or would have to the unknowing—of a rogue who suddenly finds himself in a company of detectives. But in spite of his rusticity I felt a sympathy for him fairly amounting to anguish, and couldn't take my eyes off him all dinner, nor my rapt attention: as that indecisive little Dr. [Frederic Henry] Hedge found, I am afraid, to his cost, for I hardly heard a word of what he kept on saying to me, and resented his maliciously putting his artificial person between me and the profitable object of study. . . . The thing was that Hawthorne seemed to me to possess human substance and not to have dissipated it all away like that culturally debauched——, or even like good inoffensive comforting Longfellow. . . . [M]y region was a desert with H. for its only oasis. It was so pathetic to see him, contented sprawling Concord owl that he was and always has been, brought blindfold into that brilliant daylight and expected to wink and be lively, like some dapper Tommy Titmouse. I felt him bury his eyes in his plate and eat with such voracity

that no one should dare to speak to him. . . . It was heavenly to see him persist in ignoring the spectral smiles—in eating his dinner and doing nothing *but* that, and then go home to his Concord den to fall upon his knees and ask his heavenly Father why it was that an owl couldn't remain an owl and not be forced into the diversions of a canary. I have no doubt that all the tenderest angels saw to his case that night and poured oil into his wounds more soothing than gentlemen ever know. . . . Channing too seemed so human and good—sweet as summer and fragrant as pinewoods. He is more sophisticated than Hawthorne[,] . . . [but] I felt the world richer by two *men*, who had not yet lost themselves in mere members of society. . . . The old world is breaking up on all hands: the glimpse of the everlasting granite I caught in H. and W. E. shows me that there is stock enough left for fifty better. . . . To the angels, says Swedenborg, death means resurrection to life.[44]

Although Fields and others struggled to obtain information for their reminiscences about Hawthorne's character and appearance in his youth, Horatio Bridge held a perfectly clear image of both in his memory of the friend he made at Bowdoin; however, he did not share it with others until 1893. In his *Personal Recollections of Nathaniel Hawthorne,* he recalled Hawthorne as

a slender lad, having a massive head, with dark, brilliant, and most expressive eyes, heavy eyebrows, and a profusion of dark hair. For his appearance at that time the inquirer must rely wholly upon the testimony of friends; . . . no portrait of him as a lad is extant. On one occasion, in our senior year, the class wished to have their profiles cut in silhouette by a wandering artist of the scissors, and interchanged by all the thirty-eight. Hawthorne disapproved the proposed plan, and steadily refused to go. . . . I joined him in this freak, and so our places were left vacant. I now regret the whim, since even a moderately correct outline of his features as a youth would, at this day, be interesting.

Hawthorne's figure was somewhat singular, owing to his carrying his head a little on one side; but his walk was square and firm, and his manner self-respecting and reserved. A fashionable boy of the present day might have seen something to amuse him in the new student's appearance; but had he indicated this he would have rued it, for Hawthorne's clear appreciation of the social proprieties and his great physical courage would have made it as unsafe to treat him with discourtesy then as at any later time. . . .

Hawthorne, with rare strength of character, had yet a gentleness and an unselfishness which endeared him greatly to his friends. He was a gentleman in the best sense of the word, and he was always manly, cool, self-poised, and brave. He was neither morose nor sentimental; and, though taciturn, was invariably cheerful with

Nathaniel Hawthorne.
Photograph by
W. H. Getchell,
Boston, 1861.
Carte de visite
copy by Case &
Getchell, Boston.

his chosen friends; and there was much more of fun and frolic in his disposition
than his published writings indicate.[45]

Hawthorne was often remembered and measured through comparisons to
various notable contemporaries. For instance, in his *Recollections of a Lifetime* (1857), Samuel Griswold Goodrich, who wrote under the pseudonym
"Peter Parley" and edited *The Token* in which Hawthorne's early stories appeared, reminisced about his publication successes with Nathaniel Parker
Willis, Lydia Maria Child, Lydia Howard Sigourney, and Hawthorne. Goodrich treated Willis and Hawthorne together, but after establishing that the
marked difference between the popularity of their writings corresponded to
that between their temperaments, he concentrated on Hawthorne. Thinking
"N. Hawthorne" a pseudonym at first, Goodrich says that he was pleased in
time to find that it "represent[ed] a very substantial personage"; however, as
the following narrative illustrates, he also feared that, given his despondency,
his almost "fatal rebuff from the reading world," and his tendency to vacil-
late between a literary career and the "mercantile profession," Hawthorne's
success might be a long time coming, if it were to come at all. Of course,
Hawthorne's success did come; summarizing his views, Goodrich states that
Hawthorne finally emerged as "a kind of Wordsworth—less kindly, less genial

toward mankind, but deeper and more philosophical," and, in the end, surrounded by "worshippers":

> It is not easy to conceive of a stronger contrast than ... by comparing ... Hawthorne with ... Willis. The former was ... one of the principal writers for the Token, and his admirable sketches were published side by side with those of the latter. Yet ... everything Willis wrote attracted immediate attention, and excited ready praise, while the productions of Hawthorne were almost entirely unnoticed.
>
> The personal appearance and demeanor of these two ... was also in striking contrast. Willis was slender, his hair sunny and silken, his cheek ruddy, his aspect cheerful and confident. He met society with a ready and welcome hand, and was received readily and with welcome. Hawthorne, on the contrary, was of a rather sturdy form, his hair dark and bushy, his eye steel–gray, his brow thick, his mouth sarcastic, his complexion stony, his whole aspect cold, moody, distrustful. He stood aloof, and surveyed the world from shy and sheltered positions.
>
> There was a corresponding difference in the[ir] writings. . . . Willis was all sunshine and summer, the other chill, dark, and wintry; the one was full of love and hope, the other of doubt and distrust; the one sought the open daylight—sunshine, flowers, music, and found them everywhere—the other plunged into the dim caverns of the mind, and studied the grisly specters of jealousy, remorse, despair. It is ... neither a subject of surprise nor regret, that the larger portion of the world is so happily constituted as to have been more ready to flirt with the gay muse of the one, than to descend into the spiritual charnel-house, and assist at the psychological dissections of the other. . . .
>
> . . . [B]ut, ere long, . . . a large portion of the reading world, obtained a new sense ... which led them to study the mystical, to dive beneath and beyond the senses, and to discern, gather, and cherish ... pearls of price in the hidden depths of the soul. Hawthorne was, in fact, a kind of Wordsworth—less kindly, less genial toward mankind, but deeper and more philosophical. His fate was similar: at first he was neglected, at last he had worshippers.[46]

After Thoreau's death in 1862 and Hawthorne's in 1864, Channing, who had been an intimate friend of both, began to draw extended comparisons in public of their respective character and personality, which he read as far more alike than different. In *Thoreau, The Poet-Naturalist*, which first appeared in 1873, he remarked that the two loved "antithesis in verse" as well as in life. Observing that the "substractive and unsatisfactory" held the greatest attraction for Thoreau, Channing reported that he always stood ready with a challenge for his friends, "[C]ome[,] ... let us see how miserably uncomfortable we can feel," and Hawthorne, who also "enjoyed a grave, and a pocket full of miseries to nibble upon," could be counted on to join in the quest.[47] As he considered their writings, which he treated as a measure of their respective character, Channing drew a telling comparison between the two. Flaunting his knack for obscure allusions as he built up to his most elaborate description of Hawthorne in his study of Thoreau, he said that neither wasted his intellectual or imaginative "moments" of genius on "epistles to Rosa Matilda invalids," "the sugar-gingerbread of Sympathy," or "the boiled maccaroni of pathos." Although he acknowledged that Thoreau's highly descriptive natural history essays were like "fair country invitations to a hospitable house," Channing felt that neither Thoreau's essays nor Hawthorne's fiction, which he saw as "swallowed up in the wretchedness of life, in that sardonic puritan element that drips from the elms of his birthplace," demonstrated that either man possessed sympathy for the human condition. Both, he claimed, "thought it inexpressibly ridiculous that anyone should notice man's miseries, these being his staple product." Channing then offered this description of Hawthorne's character and personality:

> The Concord novelist was a handsome, bulky character, with a soft rolling gait. A wit [Thomas Gold Appleton] said he seemed like a *boned pirate*. Shy and awkward, he dreaded the stranger in his gates; while, as customs-inspector, he was employed to swear the oaths *versus* English colliers. When surveyor, finding the rum sent to the African coast was watered, he vowed he would not ship another gill if it was anything but pure proof spirit. Such was his justice to the oppressed. One of the things he most dreaded was to be looked at after he was dead. Being at a friend's demise, of who[m] . . . he had the care, he enjoyed—as if it had been a scene in some old Spanish novel—his success in keeping the waiters from stealing the costly wines sent in for the sick. Careless of heat and cold indoors, he lived in an Æolian-harp house [the Wayside], that could not be warmed. . . . Lovely, amiable, and charming, his absentmindedness passed for unsocial when he was hatching a new tragedy. As a writer, he loved the morbid and the lame. The "Gentle Boy" and "Scarlet Letter" eloped with the girls' boarding-schools. . . . His characters are not drawn from life; his plots and thoughts are often dreary, as he was himself in some lights.[48]

As neighbors in Concord, and after both had died, Hawthorne and Emerson were often compared to each other, usually to Hawthorne's disadvantage. In his "Tribute" delivered at the Massachusetts Historical Society after Emerson's death, Oliver Wendell Holmes compared the two, and after eulogizing Emerson's intellect, good company, personality, and ability as a lecturer and conversationalist, he paused on the last point to say this about Hawthorne's:

> Speech seemed like a kind of travail to [him]. One must harpoon him like a cetacean with questions to make him talk at all. Then the words came from him at last, with bashful manifestations, like those of a young girl, almost,—words that gasped themselves forth, seeming to leave a great deal more behind them than they told, and died out, discontented with themselves, like the monologue of thunder in the sky, which always goes off mumbling and grumbling as if it had not said half it wanted to, and meant to, and ought to say.[49]

In *Hawthorne and His Circle* (1903), Julian Hawthorne was naturally kinder to his father than Holmes had been, offering this now classic recollection of his interactions with Emerson:

> My father read Emerson with enjoyment[,] though more and more . . . he was disposed to question the expediency of stating truth in a disembodied form; he preferred it incarnate, as it appears in life and in story. But he could not talk to Emerson. . . . Emerson, on the other hand, assiduously cultivated my father's company, and, contrary to his general habit, talked to him continuously; but he could not read his romances; he admitted that he had never been able to finish one of them. He loved to observe him; to watch his silence, which was full of a kind of speech which he was able to appreciate. . . . My father was Gothic; Emerson was Roman and Greek. But each was profoundly original and independent. My father was the shyer and more solitary of the two, and yet persons in need of human sympathy were able to reach a more interior region in him than they could in Emerson. For the latter's thought was concerned with types and classes, while the former had the individual touch. He distrusted rules, but had faith in exceptions and idiosyncrasies. Emerson was nobly and magnanimously public; my father, exquisitely and inevitably private; together they met the needs of nearly all that is worthy in human nature.[50]

Finally, we continue to discover Hawthorne in "trifles" that turn up in unexpected places, and invariably these leave a softer impression of him than mainstream writings do. For instance, as travel writing for newspapers became increasingly popular in the late nineteenth century, Concord became a frequent stop for reporters wending their way through New England. Reporters liked to peep into the private homes (and lives) of Concord celebrities, many of whom, including Emerson, Elizabeth Palmer Peabody, Bronson and Louisa May Alcott, were still alive, or, after visiting Thoreau's and

Hawthorne's graves in Sleepy Hollow Cemetery, meet with individuals who knew them. Ephraim Wales Bull, who had developed the Concord Grape and whose vineyard abutted the common ridge that was shared by the Alcotts' Orchard House and the Hawthornes' Wayside properties, became something of a local hero after 1853, and until his death in 1895 reporters occasionally stopped by for a chat. In 1879, some fifteen years after Hawthorne's death, Bull, who was interviewed by A. B. Harris for an article on Concord, remembered his association with Hawthorne this way:

> He said that when Hawthorne came to the Wayside to live he made up his mind that he would be acquainted with his neighbor. He found him a shy man, who avoided company, who preferred to walk by himself in the retired wood-path rather than mingle with his fellow townsmen, and who chose an unfrequented route to a place if necessity took him forth. "But," said Mr. Bull, "when I become acquainted with him I found him a pleasant companion; if you could once get inside his jacket he was genial. He sometimes came into my house and smoked a cigar—he liked a good cigar[.]"[51]

But not all "trifles" are trifling. In recent years, as acclaimed biographies and critical companions devoted to Hawthorne's life and career have appeared from Edwin Haviland Miller and Brenda Wineapple or been edited by Larry J. Reynolds and Richard H. Millington, other important studies that narrowly concentrate on two aspects of Hawthorne's life have also emerged: studies of his place in Concord history and lore by Philip McFarland and Samuel A. Schreiner Jr. and studies of Sophia Hawthorne, in which Nathaniel plays a featured role, to be sure, but not the primary one, by Megan Marshall and Patricia Dunlavy Valenti.[52] As most narratives printed in this volume attest, Concord was the Hawthornes' home for three crucial periods of Nathaniel's career and throughout those periods, Sophia, an unusually gifted person in her own right, was his wife, confidante, and lover. Nathaniel relied on her judgment in all matters relating to his home life and profession; together, they promised they would never be separated from each other, not even in death.

Sarah Ann Clarke knew the Hawthornes during their lengthy courtship, engagement, and marriage, and in 1894, just after Elizabeth Palmer Peabody's death, she composed a reminiscence of her early friendship with both Elizabeth and her sister, Sophia. In this celebration of Elizabeth's life, Clarke remembered her first introduction to Hawthorne during the winter of

1837/1838, recalling that he appeared "shrouded in a cloak, Byronic and very handsome, . . . gloomy, or perhaps only shy." Sharing common friends and an interest in art, Sarah and Sophia became good friends. When Sophia visited her in Newton in 1839, Sarah had already guessed that Sophia and Nathaniel were secretly engaged, and looking back across the half century that had passed since then, she wrote,

> [When] Sophia [came] to visit me . . . Hawthorne was . . . at Brook Farm, four miles away. . . . He was trying the experiment of living in close connexion with men & women, wh[ich] his reserved nature & habits must have made very difficult for him. He came to Newton to see Sophia Peabody, but would not enter the house and she walked with him in the grounds. After his visit she told me that she was engaged to him, which I had suspected. He decided not to take his wife to Brook Farm but to the old manse in Concord and the same miracle was performed as in the case of Mrs Browning, love conquered neuralgia.[53]

Love may have "conquered [Mrs. Browning's and Sophia's] neuralgia," but what Sarah also knew as she wrote this reminiscence is that Sophia and Nathaniel were, in fact, separated in death; he died and was buried in Concord, while she died in London in 1871 and was buried in the cemetery at Kensal Green. In 1877, when the Hawthornes' daughter Una died, she was buried beside her mother. The Hawthornes' separation in death was widely remarked on by those who knew them. In his reminiscence that follows in this volume, Conway concluded with his memory of standing beside Sophia's open grave in London, while his vision wandered "away to another in that little cemetery at, Concord, . . . and the two, so sundered, seemed to represent a happy tale suddenly broken off, and ending with heaviness and pain."[54] However, in a contemporary instance of life improving art, on 26 June 2006, Sophia and Una were reinterred in Concord's Sleepy Hollow Cemetery. Because their graves in London had fallen into disrepair after, ironically, the branches and roots of an English "common" hawthorn tree cracked their stone surface, the Dominican Sisters of Hawthorne, New York, the religious order founded by the Hawthornes' daughter Rose, arranged for Sophia's and Una's remains to be transferred home and laid beside Nathaniel's. During a ceremony that was marked by a flutist playing tunes from Thoreau's music book and readings from both Nathaniel's and Sophia's writings, Concordians finally achieved, in the words of one reporter, their sense of "completion and enduring romance."[55]

Texts printed in this volume generally have been drawn from their earliest printed version. In all instances, texts drawn from modern editions that print genetic versions of manuscript texts have been silently regularized to show only the author's final level of inscription. Silent emendations have been employed by the editors to provide readers of this volume with as clear and straightforward texts as possible, including, for instance, the insertion of terminal and other necessary forms of punctuation when missing in the source and the correction of obvious typographical errors. Throughout, we have regularized different spellings of Shakespeare's name to "Shakespeare"; however, we have preserved British and archaic spellings of words as found. Throughout, the names of authors and titles of essays and other works have been enclosed in brackets when they have been supplied by the editors, rather than by the authors. Complete bibliographic information on all critical books relating to Hawthorne cited in the introduction or in headnotes to individual selections is provided in Works Cited; bibliographic information for each entry is given in an unnumbered note following the text. Throughout the introduction, an initial superscript dagger ([†]) is used to indicate that a directly or indirectly referenced text is printed in this volume.

We should like to acknowledge Rita K. Gollin, Jayne Gordon, and Joel Myerson for enormously helpful leads and suggestions during our preparation of this volume. We have not included "the sustained but undiscovered contemporary account" of Hawthorne's time at Brook Farm that they trusted we would find, because we have not yet found it; what we have found are numerous brief references to Hawthorne's Brook Farm experience scattered throughout some of the narratives we print here, and along with these, many others that have already been gathered and treated at length by his modern biographers. We also decided against the wholesale printing of scattered and brief observations on Hawthorne by Fuller, Thoreau, Sanborn, and others; these, too, have been treated by his biographers.

We thank Leslie Perrin Wilson, curator of Special Collections in the Concord Free Public Library, for providing us with access to print and manuscript holdings under her charge, and with Ms. Wilson, Joseph C. Wheeler, chair of Town of Concord Historical Commission, for sharing their wealth of Concord fact and lore. Geoffrey P. Williams, University Archivist and Campus Records Officer, Mary Y. Osielski, Special Collections Librarian, M. E. Grenander, Department of Special Collections and Archives, and Winifred Kutchukian of the Interlibrary Loan staff at the University at Albany,

State University of New York, provided courteous and invaluable assistance during the year we worked on this project. Mr. Bosco wishes to express his gratitude to chair of English Stephen M. North, Dean Joan Wick-Pelletier, Provost Susan V. Herbst, and President Kermit L. Hall of the University at Albany for providing him with the intellectual space to work on this volume; he also wishes to thank Matthew Pangborn for a thorough and thoughtful reading of the entire manuscript. Ms. Murphy acknowledges Professor Frances Loeffler, Dean Thomas Nelson, and President Gabriel Basil of Schenectady County Community College for their support of her postdoctoral scholarship. We are both grateful to Holly Carver and the University of Iowa Press for the opportunity to publish this book.

Notes

1. Franklin Pierce to Horatio Bridge, 21 May 1864, printed in Horatio Bridge, *Personal Recollections of Nathaniel Hawthorne* (1893), 176–79. The Works Cited list at the end of this volume provides bibliographic information on all critical books relating to Hawthorne cited in the introduction and in headnotes to individual selections; it also includes abbreviations for works frequently cited. The *Centenary Edition of the Works of Nathaniel Hawthorne* (1962–1997) is the standard edition of Hawthorne's writings; Rita K. Gollin's *Portraits of Nathaniel Hawthorne* (1983) is the definitive iconographic study of Hawthorne.

2. "Death of Nathaniel Hawthorne," *Boston Daily Evening Transcript* (19 May 1864): 2:1; "Death of Hawthorne," *Boston Daily Advertiser* (20 May 1864): 2:1; "Nathaniel Hawthorne," *New York Times* (20 May 1864): 4:5; and [Untitled obituary], *Boston Courier* (20 May 1864): 2:2, respectively; for a listing of known Hawthorne obituaries and related items printed in America and abroad, see Gary Scharnhorst, *Nathaniel Hawthorne* (1988), 185–93.

3. "Obituary," *New-York Tribune* (20 May 1864): 4:6.

4. "The Death of Hawthorne," *Providence Journal* (20 May 1864): 2:1, and "Obituary," *Springfield Republican* (20 May 1864): 2:1, respectively.

5. J[ohn] H[umphrey] N[oyes], "Nathaniel Hawthorne," *Oneida Circular* (30 May 1864): 82.

6. "The Burial of Hawthorne," *Boston Post* (24 May 1864): 2:1. For other—though abridged—accounts of Hawthorne's funeral and burial, see "Funeral of Mr. Hawthorne," *Boston Daily Advertiser* (24 May 1864): 1:3; "Funeral of Mr. Hawthorne," *Boston Daily Evening Transcript* (24 May 1864): 4:4; and "Funeral of Nathaniel Hawthorne," *Albany Argus* (25 May 1864): 2:4.

7. Annie Keyes Bartlett to Edward Jarvis Bartlett, Concord, Massachusetts, 26 May 1864, Concord Free Public Library, Vault A45 Bartlett, Unit 2; quoted with the permission of the Concord Free Public Library.

8. "Hawthorne," *Boston Commonwealth* (3 June 1864): 1:6–7.

9. [Henry A. Bright], "Nathaniel Hawthorne's Death," *London Examiner* (18 June 1864): 387–88.

10. For details, see Robert A. Burkholder and Joel Myerson, *Emerson: An Annotated Secondary Bibliography* (Pittsburgh: University of Pittsburgh Press, 1985), items A1353 through A1875.

11. [Moncure D. Conway], "The Transcendentalists of Concord," *Fraser's Magazine for Town and Country* 70 (August 1864): 245–64. For more sympathetic treatments of his subject, see Conway's "Nathaniel and Sophia Hawthorne" from his *Emerson at Home and Abroad* (1882) in this volume and his *Life of Nathaniel Hawthorne* (1890).

12. Curtis's influential "Hawthorne," which appeared in *Homes of American Authors* (1853), follows in this volume; see also his "Editor's Easy Chair," *Harper's New Monthly Magazine* 29 (August 1864): 405, and "Nathaniel Hawthorne," *North American Review* 99 (October 1864): 539–57.

13. Edwin P. Whipple, "Hawthorne," in *Character and Characteristic Men* (1866), 242. For the original review, see [Edwin Percy Whipple], "Nathaniel Hawthorne," *Atlantic Monthly* 5 (May 1860): 614–22.

14. Whipple, "Hawthorne," in *Character and Characteristic Men*, 220–23.

15. For recent compilations, see Brian Harding, ed., *Nathaniel Hawthorne: Critical Assessments* (1997), and John R. Idol Jr. and Buford Jones, *Nathaniel Hawthorne: The Contemporary Reviews* (1994).

16. Rebecca Harding Davis, "A Little Gossip," *Scribner's Magazine* 28 (November 1900): 568.

17. Edward Dicey, "Nathaniel Hawthorne," *Macmillan's Magazine* 10 (July 1864): 242.

18. [Elizabeth Palmer Peabody], "The Genius of Hawthorne," *Atlantic Monthly* 22 (September 1868): 359–74.

19. Elizabeth Palmer Peabody to Elizabeth Manning Hawthorne, ca. 1838, *Letters EPP*, 224.

20. James Russell Lowell to James T. Fields, 7 September 1868, *Letters JRL*, 1:404–5.

21. Elizabeth Palmer Peabody to Amelia Boelte, 2 May 1886, *Letters EPP*, 424.

22. Peabody to Boelte, May or June 1886, *Letters EPP*, 429. For Loring's address, see "Pictures of Hawthorne. *From an Address by the Hon. G. B. Loring*," *New-York Tribune* (25 April 1882): 6:1.

23. James Russell Lowell to Grace Norton, 12 July 1860, *Letters JRL*, 1:302–3.

24. [James Russell Lowell], "The Marble Faun," *Atlantic Monthly* 5 (April 1860): 509–10.

25. James Russell Lowell to William Dean Howells, 28 July 1864, *Letters JRL*, 1:338.

26. As quoted in Martin Duberman, *James Russell Lowell* (Boston: Houghton Mifflin, 1966), 487–56.

27. Duberman, *James Russell Lowell*, 487–56.

28. James Russell Lowell to Henry Wadsworth Longfellow, 14 September 1866, *Letters JRL*, 1:368.

29. James Russell Lowell to James T. Fields, 11 February 1871, *Letters JRL*, 2:71–72.

30. George Parsons Lathrop, *A Study of Hawthorne* (1876), 14, 7.

31. Lathrop, *A Study of Hawthorne*, 285–86.

32. "Recent Boston Publications," *Boston Daily Advertiser* (30 June 1876): 2:2; *New-York Daily Tribune* (21 July 1876): 6:3.

33. "Nathaniel Hawthorne" (8 July 1876): 2:1–2, as quoted in Scharnhorst, *Nathaniel Hawthorne*, 262.

34. George Parsons Lathrop, "Hawthorne's Letter," *New-York Tribune* (15 July 1876): 2:6; "Our Book Table," *Zion's Herald* (27 July 1876): 234.

35. Elizabeth Palmer Peabody to Ellen D. Conway, 21 November 1876, *Letters EPP,* 380–81.

36. Henry James, *Hawthorne* (London: Macmillan, 1887), 1.

37. "Literature," *New York Herald* (19 January 1880): 5:1.

38. James, *Hawthorne,* 183.

39. James, *Hawthorne,* 28.

40. See Elizabeth Palmer Peabody to Amelia Boelte, 2 May 1886, which follows in this volume.

41. See note 15 above.

42. The Crucible: *Text and Criticism,* ed. Gerald Weales (New York: Viking, 1971), 41.

43. Elizabeth Barrett Browning to Mary Russell Mitford, 20–21 August 1853, *Letters EBB,* 3:391.

44. Henry James Sr. as quoted in Henry James [Jr.], *Notes of a Son and Brother* (1914), 207–9.

45. Bridge, *Personal Recollections of Nathaniel Hawthorne,* 4–6.

46. S. G. Goodrich, *Recollections of a Lifetime* (1857), 2:269–72.

47. William Ellery Channing, *Thoreau, The Poet-Naturalist* (1902), 231.

48. Channing, *Thoreau, The Poet-Naturalist,* 272–74. "Rosa Matilda" is the pseudonym of the English author Charlotte Dacre; the Boston wit Thomas Gold Appleton once remarked that Hawthorne resembled "a *boned pirate*"; and Hawthorne is reputed to have stopped hotel staffers in Philadelphia from stealing the wine used as a palliative during the last hours of his friend Ticknor's life.

49. Oliver Wendell Holmes, "Tribute to Mr. Emerson," *Proceedings of the Massachusetts Historical Society* 19 (May 1882): 308–9.

50. Julian Hawthorne, *Hawthorne and His Circle* (1903), 68.

51. A. B. H[arris], "The Home of the Concord Grape," *New York Evening Post* (14 July 1879): 3:6.

52. See Edwin Haviland Miller, *Salem Is My Dwelling Place* (1991); Brenda Wineapple, *Hawthorne: A Life* (2003); Larry J. Reynolds, ed., *A Historical Guide to Nathaniel Hawthorne* (2001); Richard H. Millington, ed., *Cambridge Companion to Nathaniel Hawthorne* (2004); Philip McFarland, *Hawthorne in Concord* (2004); Samuel A. Schreiner Jr., *The Concord Quartet* (2006); Megan Marshall, *The Peabody Sisters* (2005); and Patricia Dunlavy Valenti, *Sophia Peabody Hawthorne: A Life* (2004).

53. Joel Myerson, "Sarah Clarke's Reminiscences of the Peabodys and Hawthorne," *The Nathaniel Hawthorne Journal 1973,* ed. C. E. Frazer Clark Jr. (Washington, D.C.: NCR Microcard Editions, 1971), 131–32.

54. See Conway, "Nathaniel and Sophia Hawthorne," in *Emerson at Home and Abroad* (1882), 224–25; see also, for example, Annie Sawyer Downs, "Graves of the Hawthornes," *New-York Tribune* (18 April 1880): 9:4.

55. Casey Lyons, "Hawthornes Reunited," *Concord Journal* (29 June 2006): 1, 15.

Chronology

1801	2 August	Nathaniel Hathorne (b. 1775), a sailor's "mate," and Elizabeth "Betsy" Clarke Manning (b. 1780) are married in Salem
1802	7 March	Elizabeth Manning Hathorne born
1804	16 May	Elizabeth Palmer Peabody born
	4 July	Nathaniel Hathorne born at the family residence, 27 Union Street, Salem
1807	16 November	Mary Tyler Peabody born
1808	9 January	Maria Louisa Hathorne born
	March	Nathaniel Hathorne Sr., captain of the brig *Nabby*, which sailed from Salem on 28 December 1807, falls ill with yellow fever in Dutch Guiana (now Suriname)
	April	Word of Captain Hathorne's death arrives in Salem; Betsy Hathorne and her children eventually move in with her parents, Richard and Miriam Lord Manning, at 12 Herbert Street, Salem, where they become part of an extended family that over time includes four unmarried maternal uncles, four unmarried maternal aunts, a great–aunt, occasional servants, and numerous cats
1809	21 September	Sophia Amelia Peabody (SAP), the third daughter of Dr. Nathaniel and Elizabeth Palmer Peabody, born in Salem

1811	Autumn	By this time the Peabody family is living in the "Fontein building" on Union Street, the yard of which backed up to NH's boyhood home on Herbert Street
1813	19 April	Grandfather Richard Manning dies in Raymond, Maine; Uncle Robert Manning assumes guardianship of the Hathorne children
	10 November	NH, injuring his foot while playing at bat and ball, is lame for the next fourteen months; formerly a student at Joseph Emerson Worcester's day school, NH is home-tutored by Worcester in the evenings during his convalescence
1816	Summer	The Hathornes board at a Manning property near Sebago Lake in Raymond, Maine
1818	late October	The Hathornes move to a house on the shore of Sebago Lake
	December	NH boards at the Reverend Caleb Bradley's school in Stroudwater, Maine
1819	January	NH leaves Bradley's school and returns to Raymond
	5 July	NH returns to Salem to prepare for college at a school run by Samuel Archer
1820	by March	In Salem, NH is being tutored in Greek and Latin by Benjamin Lynde Oliver Jr., an attorney, and working in his Uncle William Manning's stagecoach office
1821	early October	NH enters Bowdoin College, Brunswick, Maine, where he establishes lifelong friendships with Horatio Bridge, Jonathan Cilley, Henry Wadsworth Longfellow, and Franklin Pierce
1825	Summer	NH shows his first literary works to his sister Elizabeth
	7 September	NH graduates from Bowdoin and returns to live with his family in the house on Herbert Street, Salem

1828	late October	*Fanshawe* is published anonymously at NH's expense, but soon suppressed by him, it would not be republished until after his death; the Hathornes move into a house on Dearborn Street, Salem, built by Robert Manning; by now NH has added the "w" to the spelling of his name
1832		The Hathornes return to the Herbert Street house
1836	January	NH becomes editor of the *American Magazine of Useful and Entertaining Knowledge* and moves to Hancock Street on Beacon Hill, Boston
	March	First of NH's issues of the *American Magazine* appear in print
	May	With his sister Elizabeth, NH contracts to write *Peter Parley's Universal History, on the Basis of Geography*
	August	NH resigns editorship of the *American Magazine* and returns to Salem
1837	early March	*Twice-Told Tales*, a collection of stories previously published in magazines, appears in print, its publication guaranteed by funding supplied by NH's college friend Horatio Bridge
	late July	*Peter Parley's Universal History, on the Basis of Geography* appears in print
	11 November	In the company of his sisters, NH visits the Peabodys at Elizabeth Palmer Peabody's invitation; shortly thereafter, he meets SAP
1838	November	Through Orestes Brownson, Elizabeth Palmer Peabody persuades George Bancroft, Massachusetts Democratic Party leader and collector of the Port of Boston, to offer NH the post of Boston Custom House inspector, which NH subsequently declines
1839	Winter	NH writes "January Fourth 1839" in large letters in his journal, thus announcing that he and SAP have become secretly engaged

	11 January	NH accepts the position of measurer of coal and salt at the Boston Custom House from Bancroft and begins work on 17 January
	24 July	NH formally proposes marriage to SAP in a letter, and from then on he most often addresses himself to her as "thy husband"
1840	August	The Peabodys move to Boston
	November	NH resigns from the Custom House, effective 1 January 1841, and considers moving to Brook Farm, the utopian experiment that operated in West Roxbury, Massachusetts, from 1841 to 1847
	3 December	*Grandfather's Chair* appears in print
1841	January	NH leaves the Boston Custom House and returns to Salem
	18 January	*Famous Old People* appears in print
	March	*Liberty Tree* appears in print
	12 April	NH arrives at Brook Farm
	late August	NH takes a vacation at the family home in Salem and decides to return to Brook Farm as a paying, rather than a laboring, boarder
	29 September	NH is appointed trustee of Brook Farm and director of finance, and he purchases two shares in the community
	late October	NH leaves Brook Farm for Boston
	December	*Biographical Stories for Children* appears in print
1842	13 January	Second edition of *Twice-Told Tales* appears in print
	9 July	NH and Sophia Amelia Peabody (SAP/SPH) are married by James Freeman Clarke in a room at Elizabeth Palmer Peabody's bookshop, 13 West Street, Boston; on the same day they move into the Old Manse in Concord, which they have rented from Ezra Ripley's heirs and where Henry David Thoreau has dug and planted a garden to welcome the newlyweds; later, they buy from Thoreau "The Rover," the skiff built

and used by him and his brother John during
their excursion on the Concord and Merrimack
Rivers in 1839, and christen it "Water Lily"

1843	February	SPH suffers a miscarriage
	March	NH begins publishing articles in the *United States Magazine and Democratic Review*
	1 May	Mary Tyler Peabody and Horace Mann are married at Elizabeth Palmer Peabody's bookshop in Boston
1844	3 March	Una Hawthorne, NH and SPH's first child, born in Concord
1845	20 June	*Journal of an African Cruiser,* which NH edited for his friend Bridge, appears in print
	September	The Hawthornes are asked to vacate the Old Manse by Samuel Ripley; agreeing to leave by 1 October, they rent a room on Herbert Street, Salem, from Uncle William Manning
	6 September	Represented by his friend George Stillman Hillard, NH sues for the remainder of his investment in Brook Farm
	November	Salem Democrats propose NH for the surveyor of port post in the Custom House
1846	4 February	George Bancroft recommends NH's appointment to President James K. Polk, who nominates him
	7 March	NH awarded $585.70, which he apparently never collects, from his suit against Brook Farm
	9 April	NH sworn in as surveyor of port for the Salem Custom House
	mid-April	SPH moves to Boston; NH follows in May and commutes to the Salem Custom House
	early June	*Mosses from an Old Manse* appears in print
	22 June	Julian Hawthorne, NH and SPH's second child, born in Boston
	August	The Hawthornes move from Boston to Salem, renting a house on Chestnut Street

1847	September	The Hawthornes move to a larger house in Salem, which they have rented on Mall Street; NH's mother and sisters move in with them
	November	Edgar Allan Poe's widely remarked essay "Tale Writing—Nathaniel Hawthorne," in which he mistakenly identifies Hawthorne as a Transcendentalist, appears in *Godey's Lady's Book*
1848	7 November	Zachary Taylor, a Whig, elected president
	November	NH becomes corresponding secretary for the Salem Lyceum and invites Emerson, Thoreau, Mann, Agassiz, and others to lecture
1849	7 June	NH is dismissed from the Salem Custom House, and controversy ensues
	31 July	NH's mother dies
1850	16 March	*The Scarlet Letter* appears in print
	23 May	The Hawthornes arrive in Lenox, Massachusetts, where, after living with Caroline Sturgis and her husband William Tappan for a week, they move into the Red Cottage on the Tappans' Tanglewood estate
	9 July	Zachary Taylor dies; Millard Fillmore becomes president and signs the Compromise of 1850, which Franklin Pierce supports
	August	NH attends picnics with Herman Melville and other literary associates
	17, 24 August	Melville's influential review "Hawthorne and His Mosses" appears in the *Literary World*
	16 November	*True Stories from History and Biography*—collected from *Famous Old People, Liberty Tree, Grandfather's Chair*, and *Biographical Stories for Children*—appears in print
1851	8 March	Third edition of *Twice-Told Tales* appears in print
	9 April	*The House of the Seven Gables* appears in print
	20 May	Rose Hawthorne, NH and SPH's third child, born in Lenox

	8 November	*A Wonder-Book for Boys and Girls* appears in print
	mid-November	*Moby-Dick,* which Melville dedicates to NH, appears in print; the Hawthornes move from Lenox to West Newton, Massachusetts, where they rent rooms from Horace and Mary Peabody Mann
	December	*The Snow-Image and Other Twice-Told Tales* appears in print
1852	2 April	For $1500, NH purchases Bronson Alcott's house, "Hillside," in Concord, and the land across from it from Emerson and Samuel Sewall
	late May	The Hawthornes move to Concord and rename their house—the only one they ever own—"Wayside"
	5 June	Franklin Pierce nominated for president; on 9 June NH volunteers to write Pierce's campaign biography
	14 July	*The Blithedale Romance* appears in print
	27 July	NH's sister Louisa dies following a steamboat explosion on the Hudson River
	11 September	*The Life of Franklin Pierce* appears in print
	2 November	Pierce elected president
1853	11 January	SPH's mother dies
	26 March	U.S. Senate confirms NH's appointment as consul at Liverpool and Manchester
	6 July	The Hawthornes sail from Boston to Liverpool, arriving there on 17 July
	1 August	NH begins consulship
	late August	*Tanglewood Tales* appears in print
1854	8–10 July	NH tours North Wales
	15–29 July	SPH and children vacation at Douglas, Isle of Man, with NH visiting on weekends
	7–20 September	SPH and children vacation at Rhyl, North Wales, with NH visiting 9–11 and 15–19 September
	18 September	Second edition of *Mosses from an Old Manse* appears in print

1855	1 January	SPH's father dies
	1 March	Consular Bill passes, reducing NH's salary effective 1 July
	19 June–2 July	The Hawthorne family vacations at Lansdown Crescent, Leamington
	2–7 July	NH visits Lichfield and Uttoxeter
	9 July	NH leaves for Lake District, returning on 30 July
	23–24 August	NH visits Bolton-le-Moors
	5 September	NH visits London for the first time
	8 October	With Una and Rose, SPH sails for Lisbon; Julian remains with NH
1856	20 March–10 April	NH visits greater London area
	2–8 May	NH visits Scotland
	30 August–4 September	NH and SPH tour Oxford area
1857	13 February	NH writes to President James Buchanan, formally resigning his consulship effective 31 August
	22 May–13 July	NH, SPH, and Julian tour northern England and Scotland
1858	5–14 January	The Hawthorne family travels through Boulogne, Amiens, Paris, Lyons, and Marseilles on their way to Italy
	17–20 January	The Hawthorne family travels through Genoa, Leghorn, and Civita Vecchia on their way to Rome
	23 January	The Hawthornes settle at Via Porta Pinciana
	24–31 May	The Hawthorne family travels from Rome through Spoleto, Assisi, Perugia, and Arezzo on their way to Florence
	1 June	The Hawthornes move into Casa del Bello, Florence
	1 August	The Hawthornes move into Villa Montauto, outside of Florence
	24 October	Una becomes ill with "Roman fever"—malaria
1859	April	Una is severely ill and nearly dies

[1]

	25 May– 24 June	The Hawthorne family travels through Leghorn, Genoa, Marseilles, Avignon, Geneva, Lausanne, Paris, Havre, and Southampton on their way to London
	1–4 July	NH tours Brighton, Arundel, Farnboro, and Aldershott Camp
1860	28 February	*The Marble Faun* appears in print in Britain as *The Transformation*
	7 March	*The Marble Faun* appears in print in America
	22 March	The Hawthorne family moves to Bath
	14–31 May	NH visits London, Cambridge, and Blackheath
	early June	The Hawthorne family moves to Liverpool
	16 June	The Hawthorne family sails to America; James T. Fields is aboard the same ship
	28 June	The Hawthorne family arrives in Boston and goes immediately to Concord
	30 June	NH celebrated at a banquet given by Ticknor and Fields, his publishers
	early August	Renovation and expansion of the Wayside begins, including the addition of a three-story tower attached to the rear of the house, which will serve as NH's study and refuge
	mid-September	Una's illness recurs
1862	6 March	NH travels to Washington, D.C., with William D. Ticknor
	13 March	NH meets Abraham Lincoln at the White House
	15 March	NH visits Harper's Ferry, then leaves for Fortress Monroe and Newport News, Virginia
	28 March	NH tours the Manassas battlefield in Virginia
	10 April	NH arrives home at the Wayside
	5 August– 4 September	NH vacations with Julian in West Gouldsborough, Maine
1863	19 September	*Our Old Home* appears in print; NH dedicates it to Pierce, over opposition from his friends and publisher

1864	29 March	Increasingly debilitated, NH leaves Concord for New York, and possibly Cuba, with William D. Ticknor
	10 April	Ticknor dies in Philadelphia; NH returns home on 14 April
	12 May	Quite ill, NH leaves from Boston on a recuperative journey to northern New England with Pierce
	18 May	NH dies in his sleep at the Pemigewasset House in Plymouth, New Hampshire; on 23 May he is buried in Sleepy Hollow Cemetery, Concord

Hawthorne in His Own Time

[Reminiscences of My Brother from His Childhood through the 1830s] (1870–1871)

ELIZABETH MANNING HAWTHORNE

—)|(—

Elizabeth Manning Hawthorne (1802–1883), Nathaniel's older sister, was his closest companion and confidante during their childhood in Salem and adolescent years in Raymond and Sebago Lake, Maine, and she helped him read for college prior to his admission to Bowdoin. An extremely well-read person, she later supported Nathaniel during his editorship of the *American Magazine of Useful and Entertaining Knowledge* in 1836 by submitting pieces for publication, and she collaborated with him on *Peter Parley's Universal History, on the Basis of Geography* in 1836 and 1837. Writing in *Nathaniel Hawthorne and His Wife* (1884), her nephew Julian remembered her as his father's literary conscience but acknowledged the reclusive disposition that, inherited from their mother, she shared with her brother, in contrast to their younger sister Louisa's sociability:

> [F]rom an exaggerated . . . Hindoo-like construction of . . . seclusion[, their] mother] . . . withdrew entirely from society. . . . Such behavior . . . could not fail to have its effect on the children. They had no opportunity to know what social intercourse meant; their peculiarities and eccentricities were . . . negatively encouraged. . . . It is saying much for the sanity and healthfulness of [their] minds . . . that their loneliness distorted their judgment . . . so little as it did. Elizabeth . . . [had] an understanding in many respects as commanding and penetrating as that of her famous brother; a cold, clear, dispassionate common-sense, softened by a touch of humor. . . . "The only thing I fear," her brother once said, "is the ridicule of Elizabeth." As for Louisa, . . . she was more commonplace than [either] of them; a pleasant, refined, sensible, feminine personage, with considerable innate sociability. (1:4–5)

Elizabeth composed the epistolary reminiscences that follow at the request of James T. Fields, who liberally drew details about her brother's early life from them for his "Our Whispering Gallery" series on Hawthorne in the *Atlantic Monthly* (1871). The value of all her letters at the time was that they provided early personal information her brother had been unwilling to share even with intimates such as Fields. Here Fields learned, for instance, that Hawthorne relished crime stories and was especially fond of the *Newgate Calendar;* delighted in reading through cookbooks for old New England recipes; wanted to join as its resident historian Charles Wilkes's 1830s–1840s naval expedition through the Pacific, to Antarctica, and along the American northwest coast; and extended his loyalty to college friends such as George B. Cheever, whom he visited in jail after Cheever was flogged and sued for libel over a temperance tract he published in 1835. Fields incorporated in his text the two letters Elizabeth enclosed with her letter of 13 December 1870; they deal with Hawthorne's travels with Uncle Samuel Manning through New Hampshire, where they stopped in Farmington and at the Shaker village in Canterbury.

Elizabeth Manning Hawthorne to James T. Fields, 12? December 1870

My dear Mr Fields

The reason I did not write to you immediately is that I sprained my right wrist, a fortnight ago, in getting out of a wagon in the evening; I can hardly hold a pen yet.

In some Portland[, Maine,] newspapers, within a year, some communications, relative to my brother, and purporting to be written by friends of his have appeared. I have not seen any of them, therefore I do not know how much credit they are entitled to. But my cousin Richard C. Manning told me some things that were in them which had been told to him, for he had not seen them himself. One was a letter from an early acquaintance, who had been my brother's companion in many rambles and fishing excursions, and afterwards met him in Europe, where, my brother said that he had hardly been more charmed than when, so many years ago, they sat "looking over Thomas Pond at the slopes of Rattlesnake Mountain" or something to that effect. I believe that to be true, because I remember the place, which was one of his favorites. Perhaps you have seen those newspapers. You know my brother was once an inhabitant of Maine, though but for a short time, except as a student. We lived in Raymond, on one side of the Sebago, then a Pond, now a Lake. We spent one summer there when he was twelve years old, and became permanent residents two years after. It did him a great deal of good, in many ways. It was a new place, with few inhabitants, *far away* "from churches and schools," so of course he was taught nothing; but he became a good shot, and an excellent fisherman, and grew tall and strong. His imagination was stimulated, too, by the scenery and by the strangeness of the people; and by the absolute freedom he enjoyed. One of those newspaper writers says that he was very strictly brought up, and not allowed to form many acquaintances; but I do not remember much constraint, except that we were required to pay some regard to Sunday, which was a day of amusement to most of the people. On Sundays, my Mother was unwilling to have us read any but religious books, but as we grew up, that prohibition was sometimes disregarded. We always had books, perhaps full enough. As soon as we could read with ease, we began to read Shakespeare, which perhaps we should not have done if books of more entertainment had been as plentiful as they are now. My brother studied Shakespeare, Milton and Pope and Thomson. The Castle of Indolence he especially admired. As soon as he was old enough to buy books for himself, he purchased Spenser's Fairy Queen. My Uncle Robert [Manning] was always buying books. I ought to have said in the beginning, that our father died when Nathaniel was four years old, and from that time Uncle Robert took charge of his education, sent him always to the best schools in Salem, and afterwards to College. After the loss of our Father we lived with our Grandfather and Grandmother Manning, where there were four Uncles and four Aunts, all, for many years, unmarried, so that we were welcome in the family. Nathaniel was particularly petted, the more because his health was then delicate and he had frequent illnesses. When he was, I think, about nine years old, he hurt his foot, playing bat and ball, at school, and was lame for more than a year. No injury was discernible, but in a little while his foot ceased to grow like the other. All the Doctors far and near were brought to look at it. Dr Smith of Hanover, then very famous, happening to come to Salem, saw it, among the rest, and he said that Doctor Time would probably help him more than any other. He used two crutches, and wore a wadded boot to sustain the ancle, but it was Doctor Time who cured him at last, and at twelve years old he was perfectly well. People who saw him then asked if this was the little lame boy. Mr. Worcester, the author of the Dictionary, taught a school in Salem when Nathaniel was hurt; and he was one of his pupils. Mr. Worcester was extremely kind, offering to come every day to hear his lessons, so that my brother lost nothing in his studies. He used to lie upon the carpet and read; his chief amusement was playing with kittens, of whom he had always been very fond. He would build houses and covered avenues with books, for the kittens to run through. Of course everything was done that could be thought of for his entertainment, for it was feared that he would be always lame. It was then that he acquired the habit of constant reading. Indeed, all through his boyhood, everything seemed to conspire to unfit him for a life of business, for after he had recovered from this lameness, he had another illness, seeming to lose the use of his limbs, [and was] obliged to resort again to his old crutches, which were pieced at the ends to make them longer. He said, after he began to write, that he had not expected to live to be twenty-five. But at seventeen he was perfectly well and entered college, and after that his health never failed until his long stay in Rome, which, I think, caused his death. He was a very handsome child, the finest boy, many strangers observed, whom they had ever seen. When he was well, Uncle Robert frequently took him into the country, and once at some place in New Hampshire, they met a gentleman and lady who seemed much pleased with him and offered him money, which he refused, because he said he could not spend it there—there were no shops. Another time, in Salem, an old gentleman, a connection of ours, but one whom my brother seldom saw, stopped him in the street and after talking with him a little while, offered him a ten dollar bill, which he also declined to accept, I believe without assigning any reason. The old gentleman was not well pleased, and spoke of it to one of his uncles,—apparently thinking it implied an unfriendly feeling towards himself. My uncle apologized as well as he could, by saying that his Mother disapproved of his having much spending money. I daresay he would have liked the money, in both instances, if it had come from anyone whom he thought nearly enough related to have a right to bestow it.

I cannot write more now, but tomorrow when I hope my hand will be stronger I will begin again. I depend upon your assurance that no one shall know that I write this. If you think it too trivial to be of use pray let me know. . . .

Elizabeth Manning Hawthorne to James T. Fields, 13 December 1870

All the anecdotes that I can remember are too trifling to be told; for instance, he once kicked a little dog that he was fond of, and on being told that the dog would not love him if he treated it so, he said, "Oh, he'll think it is grandmother," who hated a dog, though she would not have kicked it. When he could not speak quite plainly, he used to repeat, with vehement emphasis and gesture, this line, which somebody had taught him, from Richard Third; "My Lord, stand back, and let the coffin pass."[1] It is where Gloster meets the funeral of King Henry the Sixth.

[4]

Pilgrim's Progress was a favorite book of his at six years old. When he went to see his Grandmother Hawthorne he used to sit in a large chair in the corner of the room, near a window, and read it, half the afternoon, without speaking. No one ever thought of asking how much of it he understood. I think it one of the happiest circumstances of his training that nothing was ever explained to him, and that there was no professedly intellectual person in the family to usurp the place of Providence, and supp[l]ement its shortcomings, in order to make him what he was never intended to be. His mind developed itself. Intentional cultivation would have spoiled it. He used to invent long stories, wild and fanciful, and to tell us where he was going when he grew up, and of wonderful adventures he was to meet with, always ending with "and I'm never coming back again." That, perhaps, he said that we might value him the more while he stayed with us.

He inherited much of his temperament—his sensitiveness, and his capacity for placid enjoyment from his mother; and he looked like her.

There was one boy at school with whom he had a regular fight every little while. He said the boy was overbearing and quarrelsome, being a little older than himself.

He often took long walks alone, both before and after his lameness. When we lived in Raymond, I generally went with him, and one cold winter evening when the moon was at the full, we walked out on the frozen Sebago to a point which we were afterwards told was quite three miles from our starting place, and that we were in danger from wild animals. Perhaps we were, for bears were occasionally seen in that vicinity. But Nathaniel said that we would go again the next evening and he would carry his gun. The next evening it fortunately snowed; for we should not have been allowed to go, and there would have been a struggle for liberty. Soon after that he went back to Salem, to go to school. The walks by the Sebago were delightful, especially in a dry season, when the pond was low, and we could follow, as we once did, the windings of the shore, climbing over the rocks until we reached a projecting point, from which there was no resisting the temptation to go on to another, and then still further, until we were stopped by a deep brook impossible to be crossed; though he could swim, but I could not and he would not desert me.

He went for a few months to a school in a neighbouring town, [Stroud-water]. . . . It was kept by the Rev. Mr. Bradley, in whose family he boarded. I do not know whether he learned much, but he had a good time, one night especially, when the barn, close to the house, caught fire; for all his life he enjoyed a fire. On this occasion he said that he helped to dress the children, but there was a complaint made that he snatched up one of them, with a heap of clothes that did not belong to it, and ran to a spot where he could look at the fire; there he put the poor little thing into the trowsers of an older boy, and contrived to fasten them round its neck, and supposed that he had done all that was incumbent upon him. Mrs Bradley said that the child caught a cold, and that Nathaniel was a shockingly awkward boy. In Salem, he always went out when there was a fire; once or twice he was deluded by a false alarm; and after that he used to send me to the top of the house to see if there really was a fire, and if it was well under [way], before he got up. He said that once an old woman who saw him looking at a great fire scolded him in threatening terms, though she forbore from actual violence, in her indignation "at a strong young man's not going to work as other people did." But there was seldom any derangement of the usual routine of things in Salem, and the more people were in any way stirred up, the better he would be pleased.

I cannot write much yet, and I am advised not to write at all at present; so I send you two letters, written in two separate years. The uncle with whom he journeyed was an invalid, and also a Stage Proprietor, travelling at once for health and business. There is nothing remarkable in the letters, but they will show you that he was essentially the same in earlier life as when you knew him. The reason that I have no other letters of his is that he always, when he came home, burned all he had written. . . .

Elizabeth Manning Hawthorne to James T. Fields, 16 December 1870

. . . Soon after Nathaniel left College he wrote some tales "Seven Tales of My Native Land," with the motto from Wordsworth "We are Seven." I think it was before Wordsworth's Poems were re-published here. I read the Tales in Manuscript; some of them were very striking, particularly one or two Witch Stories. . . .

Elizabeth Manning Hawthorne to James T. Fields, 26 December 1870

When my brother was about fourteen he wrote me a list of the books he had been reading. There were a good many of them; but I only remember such of the Waverl[e]y Novels as he had not previously read, and as were then published, and Rousseau's Heloise and his Confessions (both of which were considered by his friends extremely improper) and the Newgate Calendar, which he persisted in going through to the end, though I believe there are several volumes, in spite of serious remonstrances. But every book he read was good for him, whatever it would have been for other boys. I do not think he ever opened one, except in the course of his education, because it was recommended as useful, and to be true was sometimes an objection in his eyes. In one of Miss Edgeworth's Tales a novel written by Bishop Berkeley—*Gaudentio di Lucca*—is mentioned; and, as it happened to be in a Circulating Library, I got it for him to read; but he said that it was *true,* and he would not even look it over. The printing and binding were unlike those of novels, and it was not particularly entertaining, but there was much in it that would have suited him. After he left College, he depended for books principally upon the Salem Athenaeum and a Circulating Library, the latter of which supplied him with most of the novels then published. The Athenaeum was very defective; and it was one of my brother's peculiarities that he never would visit it himself, nor look over the Catalogue to select a book, nor indeed do anything but find fault with it; so that it was left entirely to me to provide him with reading, and I am sure nobody else would have got half so much out of such a dreary old library as I did. There were some valuable works; The Gentlemen's Magazine, from the beginning of its publication, containing many curious things, and 6 vols. folio, of Howell's State Trials, he preferred to any others. There was also much that related to the early History of New England, with which I think he became pretty well acquainted, aided, no doubt, by the Puritan instinct that was in him. He was not very fond of history in general. He read Froissart with interest, and his love of Scott's novels led him, when very young, to read Clarendon, and other English historics of that period, and earlier; of which there were several very curious ones in the Athenaeum. He said that he did not care much for the world before the fourteenth century. He read such French books as the Library contained, there were not many except Voltaire's and Rousseau's. There was one long series of Volumes, the Records of some learned society, the Academie des Inscriptions, I think, which contained a good deal that was readable. It was his custom to write in the forenoon, and usually in the afternoon, unless the weather was especially fine, when he often took a long walk; but the evenings he spent in reading, going out for about half an hour, however, after tea. If there was any gathering of people in the town he always went out; he liked a crowd. When General Jackson, of whom he professed himself a partizan, visited Salem, in 1833, he walked out to the boundaries of the town to meet him, not to speak to him—only to look at him; and found only a few men and boys collected, not enough, without the assistance that he rendered, to welcome the General with a good cheer. It is hard to fancy him doing such a thing as shouting.

When he was a boy of fifteen he was not so very shy; he was too young to go into society, but he went to dancing school balls, for he was a good dancer, and he never avoided company, and talked as much as others of his age. I think, too, that his boyhood was very happy, for his imagination was agreeably occupied, and his feelings were in all things considered, and, though he was lame and sometimes otherwise ill, he suffered but little actual pain. And I know his college life was pleasant, and that he had many friends. It was only after his return to Salem and when he felt as if he could not get away from there and yet was conscious of being utterly unlike every one else in the place, that he began to withdraw into himself; though even then, when there were visitors in the family, he was always social. But he never liked to have his writings spoken of; he knew their merit, and was weary of obscurity, but yet he shrank from observation. Once in a while, every summer if he could, he went out of town for four or five weeks; he went to Niagara, to Nantucket, and Martha's Vineyard and other places. Once he spent two months at Swampscot[t]. You remember Susan in *The Village Uncle*, one of the Twice Told Tales. She was not quite the creation of fancy. He called her the Mermaid and was perpetually telling us how charming she was. He said she had a great deal of what the French call *espieglerie*[2]— describing her just as she is represented in the Village Uncle. She kept a little shop, too, and her father was a fisherman, who brought fish to Salem to sell. I should have feared that he was really in love with her, if he had not talked so much about her; and besides, she was not the first one of whom I had heard. There was a girl in the interior of Massachusetts, as captivating, in a different style, as the Mermaid. In his youth, beauty was the great attraction to him, and one which he declared he never could dispense with in a wife. Where there was beauty, he fancied other good gifts. In his childhood homeliness was repulsive to him. While he was lame, a good, kindhearted woman used to come to see him, and wanted to carry him about, in her arms, as he was fond of being carried; but he seemed to feel as if she were an Ogress, and hated to have her look at him, only because she was ugly, and fat, and had a loud voice. The woman who made his clothes, before his lameness, was also extremely plain, and it was very difficult to persuade him to go to her to be measured. As to clothes, it was one of his whims to dislike to put on new ones.

When the Exploring Expedition under Commodore Wilkes was sent out, he endeavoured, through Franklin Pierce and others of his political friends, to obtain the office of Historiographer. On some accounts it would have been a good thing for him, but he never would have written The Scarlet Letter, if he had succeeded in getting that appointment. If he had gone out into the world, he would have hardened his heart, as I suppose most men do, and his novels are the result of the most exquisite susceptibility. And if he had been happily married in his early manhood, it would not have been so well for the world. The mingling of another mind with his would have spoiled the flavor of his genius. (This is *your* remark, Mr Fields, nobody's else, certainly not mine; it is something that the keenness of your insight shows you, and you will never discern a more absolute truth.) Goethe said, in reference to Byron, that ennui was the true source of inspiration. Ennui may perhaps be defined as the feeling that a square peg has when he is put into, and kept in, the round hole. Then, if the peg could relate its feelings and its thoughts, they would be better worth hearing than any it would have in a more congenial position. Now my brother was all his life just so misplaced, as far as his inclinations were concerned. He wished to travel, and he desired every advantage that prosperity can bestow. One odd, but characteristic notion of his was that he should like a competent income that would neither increase nor diminish. I said, that it might be well to have it increase, but he replied, "No, because then it would engross too much of his attention." Afterwards, when he lived more in the world, he must have felt that an increasing income could in no circumstances be objectionable. There is a little poem of Lord Surrey's, called "The Mean[e]s to Attain[e] Happy Life," which expresses what my brother's ideas of happiness were; probably he had never read it, at that time; but the author must have been of a mind kindred with his.

In 1836, I think, he went to Boston to edit the American Magazine of Useful Knowledge. He was to be paid $600 a year, but probably he was not paid anything; for the proprietors became insolvent, or were already so before they engaged him, when a few numbers had appeared. I believe Mr Alden Bradford had been the Editor, and Nathaniel did not change the plan that he had pursued, admitting no fiction into its pages. It was printed on coarse paper, with wood engravings that it was a pain to look at. There were no contributors; he had to write it all himself, and he was furnished with no facilities for collecting the useful knowledge that it was his business to send forth to the world. He wrote short biographical sketches of eminent men, and other articles of a similar kind; and when I met with anything that might pass for *useful,* I copied it and sent him,—extracts from books, such as people who subscribed for that Magazine would be likely to comprehend. He wrote a Narrative of Mrs. Dust[o]n's Captivity—you know she was carried off by the Indians—in which he does not much commiserate the hardships that Mrs. Dust[o]n endured, but reserves his sympathy for her husband, who suffered nothing at all, who was not carried captive, but who, he says, was a tender-hearted man, who took care of the children, and probably knew that his wife would be a match for a whole tribe of Indians. Mrs Dust[o]n when she escaped killed as many of her Captors as she could, boys among others, which seemed unfeminine to my brother. It was told in a very entertaining manner, and the narrative ought not to be lost; indeed all that he wrote for the Magazine did him great credit, evincing not only much miscellaneous information, but a power of adapting himself to the minds of others whose culture and pursuits were unlike his own.

He wrote a good deal for The Token—some Tales which I believe were not published; besides the "Seven Tales of My Native Land," which he ought not to have burned; I should have been very glad to have them now.

When the Rev. Mr. Cheever, who was in College at the same time with my brother, though not in the same class, nor the same set, was knocked down and flogged in the streets in Salem, and then imprisoned, Nathaniel visited him in Jail; this showed great sympathy and strong indignation.

I am sorry that I have had nothing more important to tell you, his life was so monotonous that if I could recall every event of it I could hardly record more than a list of the books that he read. . . .

I have just received a letter from a gentleman who wishes to prepare something about my brother for publication. I have had many such applications, but I have always declined supplying more than dates and places of residence, and I shall of course decline now, because I have told you all there is to be told. Will you oblige me by burning what I have written when you have done with it. . . .

Say that you had your information from a friend of his, older than himself, who had known him all his life.

Elizabeth Manning Hawthorne to James T. Fields, 28 January 1871

My dear Mr Fields

I received the Atlantic Monthly and read it with much pleasure. I am quite satisfied with what you say about my brother, which I have never been before with anything that I have read about him. You ask me if there is anything to correct; except that Fanshawe was published at least four years before 1832, I observe nothing. Before 1832 he had become thoroughly ashamed of it. Perhaps I made the mistake when I wrote to you; but I am sure that I am right now, because I remember the date of the occasion on which my copy of the book fell into his hands, and I never saw it again; it was in Dec. 1832 and I think it was published in 1828.

Will you tell me who the old lady is who remembers my brother in his cradle? Most of the families who lived in that neighborhood then were fixtures, and I recollect them twenty years after. There is (if she is living now) a Mrs Oliver, who was a Miss Briggs; if it is not she, I am at a loss to guess who it can be. Or it might be Mrs. Barstow, my father's niece; but she was not exactly a neighbor. It is her daughter Elinor, now Mrs. Condit, who was the original little Annie; my brother was fond of her. He liked little girls, but he said he did not think boys worth raising. Elinor was a very affectionate child. She was almost the only person out of his immediate family who knew my brother; and I believe people liked to tease her about him—to say something to his disadvantage, in order to see her kindle into wrath in his defense. She told me about it the last time I saw her. She said that she was a perfect little tempest. Once she came to him, crying, because somebody had told her that he was an infidel—he must be, as he never went to church. He took her on his knee and comforted her—told her that he was not an infidel, and that he did go to church whenever he happened to be elsewhere than in Salem, on a Sunday. Then he talked very seriously with her. Speaking of The Scarlet Letter, she said that he must have intended to represent Hester as unrepentant; else her peace of mind would have been restored, and above all, she would not have been ready to fall into the same sin again.

I think if you looked over a file of old Colonial Newspapers you would not be surprised at the fascination my brother found in them. There were a few volumes in the Salem Athenaeum; he always complained because there were no more. Cookery-Books, especially old ones, were another odd fancy of his. He sometimes talked of compiling one;—not for the concoction of luxurious dishes, but of the homely, New England dainties to which he had been accustomed in his childhood—not even dainties, indeed, but such plain things as Apple-Dumplings, of which he was fond all his life; and Squash Pies, and such Indian Cakes as Phebe made, in the House of the Seven Gables. He said he thought all the old New England dishes were good, but that a professed cook always spoiled them.

[11]

Una has written to ask me if I have any articles of his in any old Magazines which might be inserted in a new edition of his works. I have nothing at all—no Magazines—though I think that there must be papers of his in some Magazines or Annuals, for I remember tales which I thought admirable; but it may be that they were never published; for he was very impatient and if there was any delay, he would have them returned to him if he could, and I suppose put them in the fire. He wrote two or three New Years' Addresses for the Salem Gazette. In the Twice Told Tales there is only one republished—The Sister Years. I suppose the others might be found. For the Democratic Review he wrote a biography of Cilley, who was killed in a duel; it was quite long and would help to fill up the volume, but it was mostly political. Some portions of it, however, might be worth republishing. There was, in The New England Magazine, I think, an article called "My Visit to Niagara." I do not know why that was not inserted in the complete edition. He wrote several things for the Knickerbocker Magazine, which was sent to him for three years. It was among his books in Concord. If Mrs Hawthorne has it in England, perhaps she will find something there.

When my brother was young he covered the margins and the fly leaves of every book in the house with lines of poetry and other quotations, and 'with his own name, and other names.' Nothing brings him back to me so vividly as looking at those old books. . . .

Notes

1. William Shakespeare, *Richard III*, 1.2.38.
2. "Espieglerie": mischievousness.

Randall Stewart, "Recollections of Hawthorne by His Sister Elizabeth," *American Literature* 16 (January 1945): 318–31.

[Childhood Encounters with Hawthorne in Salem] (1887)

[LUCY ANN SUTTON BRADLEY]

The reminiscence that follows, which describes Hawthorne's early years in the Salem home of his maternal grandmother, Miriam Lord Manning, first appeared in the *New York Observer* on 4 August 1887, where it was signed "Vieja"—"Old Woman." The authenticity of the reminiscence and the identity of Lucy Ann Sutton Bradley as its author were established by Manning Hawthorne in a study that appeared in the *Essex Institute Historical Collections* in 1947. According to Manning Hawthorne's reconstruction of events related in the piece, Bradley, who was Grandmother Manning's great-grand niece and roughly the same age as the Hawthorne children, first visited the Manning home with her mother in 1812–1813. The text of Bradley's reminiscence is taken from Manning Hawthorne's study, but biographical facts about Bradley provided by Hawthorne are supplemented here by information reported in the genealogical files of the Thomas Osgood Bradley Foundation (www.bradleyfoundation.org).

Lucy Ann Sutton Bradley was born in Portland, Maine, in 1804 and died in Buenos Aires, Argentina, in 1888, the year after her reminiscence appeared in the *Observer*. In 1827, she married Thomas Osgood Bradley, a dry goods merchant, in Portsmouth, New Hampshire, and in 1829, they left America for Argentina, where Thomas established a wool brokerage in Buenos Aires. Bradley describes herself as "nearly ten years of age" when she first met Nathaniel, which suggests that the visit occurred late in 1813 or early in 1814; since her narrative abruptly ends with the statement, "Nathaniel entered college [in 1821] and I left the States [in 1829]," it is unclear on the point of how many additional times they may have met.

Even though more than seventy years had passed since her first meeting with Nathaniel, Bradley appears to have a clear recollection of all the persons she encountered and a good memory for incidents that brought her into contact with Nathaniel. Her account describes his day-to-day life as a young boy and his generally otherwise unrecorded playful nature. Although she notes with pleasure that they enjoyed reading many of the same authors, she cannot resist reporting his boyish taunts about whether she had seen any witches near

Salem's Gallows Hill or how she managed to read fine literature in Portland, where the conservative Congregational minister Edward Payson presided. Manning Hawthorne makes much of Bradley's remark that the widow Hathorne was not quite the odd, reclusive figure following her husband's death that contemporary and later accounts often depict, and he claims that Elizabeth Palmer Peabody was the one who promoted this version of her character (see 178, 182n5). However, as the evidence gathered throughout this volume suggests, contemporary descriptions of Betsy Hathorne's character are remarkably consistent, so that in this instance, at least, Bradley is either painting a more rosy picture of Hathorne's character than others saw or just happened to visit during her good days. Living in the house at the time of Bradley's first visit to the Mannings were the elder Mrs. Manning, Betsy and her three children, and Betsy's siblings: Mary, Priscilla, Robert, Samuel, and William Manning. John Dike, who is also mentioned in Bradley's reminiscence, did not live in the house, though he later married Priscilla Manning.

THE REMINISCENCES OF MY early life recall distinctly my first acquaintance with Nathaniel Hawthorne. When I was nearly ten years of age, my mother took me on a visit to her Aunt Manning in Salem. This aunt was grandmother to Nathaniel. His mother, Mrs. Hawthorne, was formerly Betsey Manning; she was now a widow with her three children living with Mrs. Manning. The two unmarried daughters, Mary and Priscilla, with the brothers Robert and Samuel, composed the family living in Herbert Street.

On the day of our arrival, and while my mother was resting, Aunt Mary took me by the hand and led me to the sitting room, where Nathaniel was standing by the side of his mother and reading aloud. Mrs. Hawthorne kindly noticed me, and then Aunt Mary said to Nathaniel: "This is your cousin, and I want you to be very polite to her." He extended his hand with the book in it toward the table and said: "She can play with my dominoes"—the blocks for the game were scattered about the table. His mother said something in a low voice about "brushing up." In leaving the room with his Aunt Mary, I heard him say: "I wish she were a boy." His mother said to me: "Never mind, my dear, he is rather shy of little girls; but he will play with you by and by."

I did not see him again until the next morning after breakfast, when he said to me, "If you want to ride, come with me to the carriage house." I looked for my bonnet. "No matter for that, it's right out here," said he, and I followed him into an old building and a room, the sides of which were filled with carriages and coaches of all description—broken, worn and mouldy. This was a surprise to me, and I was asking whose are they, and what are they here for? when he climbed into one and said, "Come." There were no steps, but with his help I succeeded in mounting, and I found very comfortable seats. "This is what I like," he said, as he began rocking so furiously that I begged him to stop. He did so, and then answered some of my questions.

His Uncle Sam had a livery stable, and these carriages belonged to him, but all the people who used to ride in them were dead, and now their ghosts came and peeped out at him when he was riding; but he was not afraid of them, because his mother said he must have exercise, and she would not allow him to go out with the horses. "Don't you like to rock so?" he asked. "Yes, but slowly," I replied.

I made several visits after that to the carriages, for I was spending a year with my uncle in Danvers, and I went often to Salem. In doing so, I had to pass "Gallows Hill," where the witches were hanged, and the graveyard where they were buried. Nathaniel would inquire, "Did you see a witch?" and tell me of those he had read about. When he found that I was not frightened, he drew out his book and began to read from "Childe Harold." "Why Nathaniel," I asked, "do you read Byron?" "Why not?" asked he. "I don't know, only my mother would not allow me to read it." "Well," he asked, "what do you read down-East?"

He always spoke of Portland with contempt of the dear old town. I mentioned "Miss Edgeworth," "Pilgrim's Progress," "The American Museum," and that I read Shakespeare with my father. "Shakespeare!" he exclaimed; do they read plays down there? I thought Mr. Payson would not have his people go to the theatre or dances." Dr. Payson had not been long settled in Portland, but there had been a great revival there. Nathaniel must have heard this talked about by some who were not Christians. I told him I thought Mr. Payson was right, and then we repeated some sentences from plays, and he told me the story of the "Merchant of Venice."

In returning to the house we found his mother waiting, for he had exceeded his time nearly an hour. "Oh, mother!" was his first salutation, "this downeaster knows Shakespeare." I felt a little indignant that he felt so meanly of Portland and retorted, "I would rather be a down-easter than live in Salem witchcraft." This produced a smile from his mother, but he never called me "down-easter" after that, and the next morning we read from "The Tempest" and he was quite amiable for the remainder of my visit. I had learned to understand him; when he was quiet or disinclined to play, he was thinking over his lesson, or preparing little surprises for his mother. I depended upon him for amusement, and the house seemed dreary without him.

It was a cheerless home. The rooms had but little furniture of the plainest kind. No carpets or curtains. Mrs. Hawthorne and her family lived upstairs, practising the greatest economy by taking their meals up there. I was always pleased to go up into "grandma's room." She was always in bed, her room was carpeted, and more like my own home than any other part of the house. To sit in her easy chair at the side of her bed and listen to her stories of my mother when she was a little girl, and the time she was nearly lost in a snowstorm in Ipswich, was a delight to me. She was always ready to listen to my questions, but answered very few.

Aunt Mary was the only cheerful one in the family; she was nurse as well as housekeeper, and when she came to wait upon her mother, I always said "good-by" and left the room. The last time I thus took my leave, she said to Aunt Mary, "Don't let the child be harmed."

A few months after that my mother was in Danvers, and took me with her to spend a few days in Salem. Nathaniel did not go to the carriage house now, but went daily to the roof of the house to read aloud and to declaim. On the last day of the visit, I heard Nathaniel call me; I went to the skylight opening on the roof, and looking out, saw him with his back braced against the chimney, book in hand. He called me to come; I told him I was afraid because the roof was sloping. He called back, "Just like girls."

That evening I was taken to Danvers and did not visit Salem for many years. Nathaniel was preparing for college, and his sister Elizabeth was assisting him. He had a room in the third story, and she in the second story directly under his, the window of each opening into a garden, or what had once been a garden; it was now a tangled mass of vines, herbs and weeds, a few feet of grassy turf here and there discernible.

I have thought, when reading some of his works, that he might have drawn weird images from these shadowed vacancies. The brother and sister communicated with each other by means of a small basket, in which they put their papers, let down from Nathaniel's window and drawn up again.

Some changes had been made after the grandmother's death. Mrs. Hawthorne took her meals with the family. I did not meet Nathaniel at the table,

[16]

and from some remarks learned that he did not wish to meet his Uncle Robert, as he was dissatisfied with his arrangement for his collegiate course. This uncle was his guardian, and he had proved a generous, noble-hearted brother to Mrs. Hawthorne, and a kind friend to the family. As Nathaniel went to college, I knew that all was amicably settled with his uncle.

I never heard him allude to school life, or mention any boy companions. In neither of my visits did I meet a boy or girl of our own age. His aunt Priscilla married a widower, Mr. Dike, who had a son and daughter, and he must have had some intimacy with them; but I never met them together. I believe that his surroundings favored his love of isolation, and made him the author of "The Marble Faun."

He loved to tease his aunt Mary. On one occasion, a relative of the servant, Jane, was visiting her and taken sick. Their family physician was called, but a young assistant came; he was gentlemanly, understood the case, gave her medicine, and when he came the next day, he inquired, "How many times did she cascade?" This was heard by the family, and caused general amusement. It was talked about at the table, and the young man was called such names as are bestowed upon ignoramuses. Aunt Mary defended him, called him "a nice young man."

Nathaniel and Elizabeth were very busy talking it over, and soon showed a letter they had been writing to Aunt Mary, professing admiration and asking permission to call upon her, and signed it "from one who met you in the sick room." Jane was to come to the front door and knock while we were at supper. Nathaniel was to go to the door and bring the letter to Aunt Mary. This was all done as planned.

Nathaniel took the letter to the candle, and reading the direction, handed it to his Aunt Mary. She took her glasses, read it, and rising, was about to leave the table. We all sat silent, but observant, when Nathaniel asked, "Who is it from, Aunt Mary?" "From you, I think," answered she, "and now you may wait on the table, while I prepare to receive your visit."

We felt that the laugh was upon the plotters. Nathaniel went straight to her, took her arm in his and walked to the sitting room, where he nobly confessed his part, and all was forgiven. This was my last visit to the home in Herbert Street. Nathaniel entered college and I left the States.

[Lucy Ann Sutton Bradley, "Nathaniel Hawthorne's Boyhood,"] in Manning Hawthorne, "A Glimpse of Hawthorne's Boyhood," *Essex Institute Historical Collections* 83 (1947): 179–84.

[Epistolary Thoughts on Hawthorne, 1838–1886]

Elizabeth Palmer Peabody

⸜⸝⸜⸝

An education and social reformer, Elizabeth Palmer Peabody (1804–1894) was the oldest of the dynamic Peabody sisters. She assisted Bronson Alcott in the Temple School in Boston in the 1830s, operated a bookshop and circulating library on West Street in Boston in the 1840s, and published several of her brother-in-law Nathaniel Hawthorne's works under her own imprint. Peabody became active in the Transcendentalist movement in the late 1830s, joining the Transcendentalist Club, publishing the *Dial* between 1841 and 1843, developing friendships with George and Sophia Ripley and with Margaret Fuller (who conducted several "Conversations" at Peabody's bookshop), and bringing promising individuals such as Jones Very and Hawthorne to the attention of Emerson and his circle. In her middle and later years, Peabody continued to experiment with new pedagogical practices, opening America's first English-speaking kindergarten in Boston in 1860. She also lectured at Alcott's Concord School of Philosophy in the 1880s; the "Conversation" on Hawthorne that occurred there in 1880 and in which she participated appears later in this volume.

Although Peabody and Hawthorne were not formally acquainted until November 1837, when he and his sisters visited the Peabodys, as children growing up in Salem, they had lived for a time only a few yards from each other. Reading *Twice-Told Tales* (1837) on its publication, Peabody assumed that Hawthorne's sister Elizabeth was the author, an error that his sister Louisa quickly corrected. After their initial meeting, which was then followed by Hawthorne's introduction to Sophia, who had been away when the Hawthornes first called, Peabody and Hawthorne struck up a lasting friendship based on mutual respect for each other's talents. Knowing that Hawthorne lacked the kind of financial security required for him to write, through Orestes Brownson, Peabody approached George Bancroft, then a Massachusetts Democratic Party leader and collector of the Port of Boston, to offer Hawthorne the post of Boston Custom House inspector; although he declined that position, in January 1839 he accepted the post of measurer of coal and salt at the Boston Custom House.

Labeled Transcendentalism's "Boswell" by Theodore Parker, Peabody occupied a central position in the movement, which has been slow to be acknowledged. For almost a century, until new historical and feminist scholarship emerged to set the record straight, she—like Margaret Fuller, Lidian Jackson Emerson, Mary Moody Emerson, Caroline Healey Dall, and other women of the time—seemed fated to the periphery of the great men with whom she associated. Yet, as Bruce A. Ronda's *Elizabeth Palmer Peabody: A Reformer on Her Own Terms* (1999) and Megan Marshall's *The Peabody Sisters: Three Women Who Ignited American Romanticism* (2005) have persuasively shown, Peabody was an intellectual of considerable depth. She had everyone's ear, especially Emerson's. Her bookshop was a meeting place and informal library that served Boston's élite and major literati; outliving all first generation members, she possessed Transcendentalism's and a fair share of American Romanticism's longest-lived institutional memory.

Parker did not exaggerate Peabody's knack for detail, some of it remembered long after the fact. As the first two epistolary excerpts that follow indicate, which are the only letters included here contemporaneous with the impressions they relate, Peabody was quick to recognize talent and make a cause of struggling artists such as Hawthorne. In her letter to fellow education reformer Horace Mann, who would marry her sister Mary in 1843, she appealed for help in securing reliable booksellers for Hawthorne's works, especially those written for children, while in her letter to Elizabeth Hawthorne, she expressed her fear that, having finally emerged from familial seclusion, her brother might return to it and fail "to weave . . . his 'golden web' " for America's "unsoiled souls" (224). In her letter to the Salem antiquarian Francis Henry Lee, Peabody elaborately reprises the story she told Horace Mann almost a half century earlier of her discovery of Hawthorne, but one of the letter's more interesting details is her description of how "mercury being given even to babies for every little ail" (418) likely accounted for her sister Sophia's early onset of frailty. Finally, in the first of two letters to her German correspondent, Amelia Boelte, who had written that a friend of hers intended to prepare a biography of Hawthorne for European readers, Peabody is brutally candid on the shortcomings of nephew Julian's biography of his parents, *Nathaniel Hawthorne and His Wife* (1884), especially his speaking of people with whom his parents were associated "in the most careless and reckless manner" and his constant "misrepresenting Hawthorne with respect to others" (425). In the second of her two letters to Boelte, Peabody vehemently denies any early romantic attachment to Hawthorne and confirms the sense among their contemporaries of the ideal, exclusive love shared between Hawthorne and Sophia. This letter would appear to settle once and for all the nature of the relationship between Peabody and Hawthorne prior to his falling in love with her sister; yet, given her own statement in the letter—"I am free to say that had Hawthorne wanted to marry me he would probably not have found much difficulty in getting my consent;—but it is very clear to me now, that I was not the person to make *him* happy or to be made happy *by* him, and Sophia *was*" (431)—Peabody may not have settled the matter as neatly as she thought. Less than a decade later, Caroline Healey Dall wrote to Thomas Niles, "Sophia never knew of her sister's engagement to N.H., but Hawthorne lived in terror less E.P.P. should tell her. Many an hour of bitter weeping has she passed in my house because of his insulting letters about it—after he was married" (Dall to Niles, 1894, as quoted in *Letters EPP*, 431n1).

Elizabeth Palmer Peabody to Horace Mann, 3 March 1838

My dear friend,—

. . . There is a young man in this town—not so very young either—(he is between thirty &: forty years old)—of whom you have heard—the Author of the "Twice told Tales." He is I think a man of first rate genius.—To my mind he . . . surpasses *Irving* even—in the picturesque beauty of his style—& certainly in the purity—elevation—and justness of his conscience—An extreme shyness of disposition—and a passionate love of nature—together with some peculiar circumstances have made him live a life of extraordinary seclusion. When he left college he did not fancy one of the three professions—but preferred that the literary part of his life should be *voluntary*.—In study and thought many years have passed—and occasionally he has dropped a gem into the passing periodicals. . . . His time of study however has a[t] length passed—and he is now turning his attention to taking up some serious business for his life—Authorship does not seem to offer a means of living—He has not thriven with the booksellers. His book [*Twice-Told Tales*] which sold so quick has yielded him nothing . . . at length [by the] failure of the stationers company. But he had in his mind one great moral enterprise as I think it & you will agree—to make an attempt at creating a new literature for the young—as he has a deep dislike to the character of the shoals of books poured out from the press—If you will take the trouble to read "The Gentle boy"—& "little Annie's Ramble" & "The Gray Champion" & "the Maypole of Merry

Mount" you will I think see indications of a genius for such an enterprise that could not fail to make a *fortune* at last that would satisfy so very moderate desires as his—He told me of this scheme only to say he thought he should be obliged to give it up—But I think he has no genius for negotiation with booksellers—& moreover . . . he seemed inclined to *reconsider* when he found that I too thought this reform necessary & feasible.—He has deep views—thinks society in this country is only to be controlled in its *fountain of youth*—has a natural religion that overflows in silent worship—& the delicacy of his morality is I think beautifully indicated in "Fancy's Showbox—" another of those "Twice told Tales" which were not written for the young—but have merely been the amusement of his leisure hours.—He says that were he embarked in this undertaking he should feel as if he had a right to live—he desired no higher vocation—he considered it the highest.—Now you will agree with me in thinking this indicates a pure & noble mind—for he has political friends who have been offering him government offices & every temptation had he any low ambition—

I am quite acquainted with a sister of his [Elizabeth]—a remarkable person who has a great influence over him—when she pleases to exert it—And I see him a good deal myself & find him deeply interested in such things as interest my mind—& you know what they are—Now I wish you would say something in your next about this—Whether you do not believe that *hereafter* such labours will be more appreciated than at present—Capen is a bookseller of *principle*—the only man I know in that line capable of being liberal.—If you have leisure—I think a suggestion from you to *Capen*—who thinks every thing of you—to endeavour to enlist Hawthorne by good offers to write for the young—would perhaps secure him to this work—. . .

Elizabeth Palmer Peabody to Elizabeth Manning Hawthorne, ca. 1838

My Dear Miss Hawthorne,

I saw how much your brother was suffering on Thursday evening, and am glad you think it was not a trial, but rather the contrary, to hear my loquaciousness. I talked because I thought it was better than to seem to claim entertainment from him, whose thoughts must be wandering to the so frightfully bereaved. . . . If, as you say, he has been so long uneasy—however, perhaps he had better go; only, may he not bind himself long, only be free to return to freedom. In general, I think it is better for a man to be harnessed to a draycart to do his part in transporting "the commodity of the world"; for man is weak, and needs labor to tame his passions and train his mind to order and method. But the most perilous season is past for him. If, in the first ten years after leaving college, a man has followed his own fancies, without being driven by the iron whip of duty, and yet has not lost his moral or intellectual dignity, but rather consolidated them, there is good reason for believing that he is one of Nature's ordained priests, who is consecrated to her higher biddings. I see that you both think me rather enthusiastic; but I believe I say the truth when I say that I do not often overrate, and I feel sure that this brother of yours has been gifted and kept so choice in her secret places by Nature thus far, that he may do a great thing for his country. And let me tell him what a wise man said to me once (that Mr. J. Phillips of whom I once spoke to you): "The perilous time for the most highly gifted is not youth. The holy sensibilities of genius—for all the sensibilities of genius are holy—keep their possessor essentially unhurt as long as animal spirits and the idea of being young last; but the perilous season is middle age, when a false wisdom tempts them to doubt the divine origin of the dreams of their youth; when the world comes to them, not with the song of the siren, against which all books warn us, but as a wise old man counselling acquiescence in what is below them." I have no idea that any such temptation has come by your brother yet; but no being of a social nature can be entirely beyond the tendency to fall to the level of his associates. And I have felt more melancholy still at the thought of his owing anything to the patronage of men of such thoughtless character as has lately been made notorious. And it seems to me they live in too gross a region of selfishness to appreciate the ambrosial moral aura which floats around our Ariel,—the breath that he respires. I, too, would have him help govern this great people; but I would have him go to the fountains of greatness and power,—the unsoiled souls,—and weave for them his "golden web" as Miss Burley calls it,—it may be the web of destiny for this country. In every country some one man has done what has saved it. It was one Homer that made Greece, . . . and one Wordsworth that has created the Poetry of Reflection. How my pen runs on,—but I can write better than I can speak.

Elizabeth Palmer Peabody to Francis Henry Lee, 1885

Dear Mr. Lee,

I am writing Reminiscences of my Life & times for posthumous publication but I think I can make a few extracts from the part which tells of my earliest recollections of Salem of which I was not a native but went there in 1808 on my 4th birthday, for it is one of my earliest recollections that my father told me when we were driving thither from Lynn in a carriage to remember that I went to live in Salem on my 4th birthday. My sister Sophia who married Mr. Hawthorne was born in Salem, in a house in Summer Street in September 1809, and when she was two years old it is a curious coincidence that we lived in the Fontein building in Union Street very near the house in which Hawthorne was born. But his mother in her widowhood moved into a house belonging to her brother in Herbert Street the next street east.—My sister Mary who used to play out doors with the neighbor's children remembers playing with Hawthorne, and his sisters, for there was communication through the (back) yards of the houses of both streets—But I was a less playful child and I only remember his eldest sister Elizabeth who was a year older than I and he, who were of the same age within six weeks. . . . The circumstances were these[.] My mother had given up keeping school to her sister Amelia who with her adopted mother Mrs. Cranch had taken it into Mall Street, that my mother might devote herself to the care of Sophia who had a terrible time in getting her teeth, aggravated undoubtedly by the medication in the heroic method which was at its height, at that time mercury being given even to babies for every little ail, & my poor sister who was made a sufferer for life by her loss of blood in a most frightful [?].—I remember mother always sitting with Sophia on a pillow in her lap—and she had me there endeavouring to teach me who at six years old could hardly read intelligibly though I had been taught for two years.—But though backward in perception I was precocious in reflection & remember how warmly used to be discussed the peculiarity of the widow Hawthorne who had shut herself up after her husbands death & made it the habit of her life never to sit down at a table but always eat her meals above in the chamber she never left. For this, she was constantly criticized & condemned by the neighbours, including connections of the family, whom she would not see but my mother's sensibility & imagination were touched by what she heard; and being told that the smart little Elizabeth, was a bookworm, she took the occasion to write to Mrs. Hawthorne a note, to ask her if she would allow Elizabeth to come to our house to be taught an hour or two a day, because she wanted a companion to stimulate a dull little girl of her own by example—My mother had a wonderful epistolary power, & I dare say she made Mrs. Hawthorne feel her respect & sympathy. At all events Mrs. Hawthorne was so much touched by the note, that she not only complied with her request, but sent through Elizabeth an invitation to mother to call & see her, which she did, and found her a most intelligent, well read, and lively woman. (But my youthful admiration for the astonishing learning of Elizabeth reacted to discourage me who had no power of utterancy at all—at that time[.])

We soon moved away to the corner of Cambridge & Essex St to a house owned by Miss Susy Hawthorne . . . and the other acquaintance was dropped. Some eight or ten years after when Mrs. Hawthorne was living at Sebago Pond in Maine . . . I saw a letter written by Elizabeth Hawthorne to one of her schoolmates in the beauty of whose composition was so great and the subject matter so interesting, that I obtained permission to copy it off—and planned to write & ask her for correspondence, on the pretext of our childish intimacy. But I had not quite courage to do this & in 1820 left Salem for residence in Lancaster Massachusetts. When however some 15 years later, I heard after years of wondering who was the author of certain tales in the Tokens & New England Magazine among the rest "the Gentle Boy" I learned on returning to Salem to live in 1836, that they attributed to a son of the widow Hawthorne. Now I did not remember any son only Elizabeth, & I concluded at once that the stories were written by Elizabeth for I argued that a man who could write so would be very distinguished, & of this man I had never heard & nobody in Salem seemed to know any thing about him.

And so I determined to call on her and attempt to renew our intimacy, altho I heard that ever since Mrs. Hawthornes return to Herbert Street about 15 years before, Elizabeth had shut herself up; & refused to see any body, lying in bed all day and reading, and like her mother refusing to see any visitors whatever.

Nevertheless I called, and was told, by an old aunt who also had a domicile of her own in the house that though Mrs. Hawthorne & Elizabeth never saw visitors—there was another sister Louisa who was more like ordinary people. I was ushered by her into a neat little parlour on the second floor where Miss Louisa received me. When I told her of my early acquaintance with Elizabeth, and my desire to renew the acquaintance she said, But Lizzie never sees any body; I know it but thought she might make an exception of me, who never had forgotten her, and who felt acquainted with her from the Gentle Boy & other tales that I named[.]

She replied—But it was not Lizzie but my brother who wrote those tales—

I had been so certain & had maintained to Miss Susan Burley & others who like me had long wondered after the author, that I was silenced—

All right I said—If your brother wrote those stories he has no right to be idle—He never is idle, she said; then rising, added I will go & tell Lizzie of y[ou]r call—she soon came back laughing and said Lizzie says that if you will come some evening she will come out and see you[.]

But she did not say *what* evening, and in vain [I] waited for weeks for the special invitation I expected. But not long after this the first edition of the Twice Told Tales was printed, and a copy was sent to me "With the respects of Nathaniel Hawthorne" and soon after I wrote a note to Miss Elizabeth & told her I wanted to ask of her brother what were the steps to take to get an article into the Democratic Review . . . and won't all three of you put aside ceremony & come & pass *this* evening with me? It was Saturday noon & my idea was that this invitation which I knew would be a most unexpected surprise might succeed—if there was not too much time given for them to deliberate, and my device succeeded. . . .

But this [is] a long enough article for your little paper. . . . He often told me that that invitation of mine made an era in his life. . . .

Elizabeth Palmer Peabody to Amelia Boelte, 2 May 1886

My dear Miss Boelte,

I hope . . . that your friend who is going to write a book about Hawthorne has not hurried through the work. It is a great opportunity to do a thing that I hope greatly at heart, and that is that Hawthornes life should be properly presented to the continent of Europe and not under the shadow of some mistakes that have been made by his principal and greatest biographer, his son Julian.

Hawthorne expressed in his lifetime that he hoped his biography would not be written. He thought what he had maturely decided to publish would give what was alone valuable in his life. But of course people wrote about him and finally his son-in-law Lathrop, who had been brought up as it were on his books, of which he was personally fond, but who had never seen the man being only eleven years old when he died and living away in the Sandwich Islands, but who met his youngest daughter in Boston in 1868 and married her in 1871, published 'a Study of Hawthorne' collecting all that was extant about him from his friends and myself, of which he made good sale and produced a lovely little book. A year or two ago a Boston publisher wanted to publish a Life of Hawthorne and engaged Julian to write it. But the circumstances were peculiar and unfavourable. Julian, who had married at 21 (in 1870), had been driving the quill like mad *ever since* for daily bread for himself and growing family and had had eight children losing only a baby in 12 years, and was utterly run down in health and in means and was paid beforehand for his work on the condition of its being written at once. He was at the time with his large family in a cheap town to live in on the extremity of Long-Island. . . . I knew nothing but that the book was written—none of the unfavourable conditions—he did not tell me his plan or ask for my help, who had all his mothers early journals, [and] had been the confidante of Hawthorne for nearly a year before he became intimate with Sophia. . . . At the time he first saw her we all and she herself considered her a hopeless invalid and not a subject for marriage. I sent to Julian her letters to me during the summer that she became intimate with [Hawthorne] with no tho't on her part of marriage to any body, and when he thought, as he once expressed it to me, that she was "a flower not to be worn in any man's bosom but lent from Heaven." I knew the history of the three years engagement when it was kept secret from almost everybody else, even in the two families. But he never came and asked me anything. His sister Rose was in New York, he never asked her anything or showed her the book. We saw it first when it was printed. He was especially intent on showing what his father was in his own family, what the marriage was. He calls it in his preface the annals of a happy marriage. But it speaks of other people in the most careless and reckless manner, on stating the hospitalities the family received in England, and misrepresenting Hawthorne with respect to others.

There never was a person more careful of others feelings and personalities in what he put [down; Hawthorne] never . . . noted anything except after looking at it in all moods, and his genius led him to look at things in their eternal relations as it were, and to let the circumstantial go after it had done its work. In his private journals however he as far as possible put down in all its rare ugliness the mere fact—or the passing mood—not for other people who he never expected would see it, but for his own cool consideration, for he did not want to be the fool of his own ideality. Well! Julian has violated these private papers and published some things especially about persons that Hawthorne would never have let any mortal eye see. He destroyed quantities of these private journals in which all the ups and downs of his early and earlier life were written down. And I think it was only the accident of his death away from home that caused any to be left. We cannot regret that they were left. My sister called one of them the American, the English and the Italian note-books. He had to make up for his publisher two large volumes and I could have given him most precious matter, but he filled up by putting in other people's letters to his father without their leave, and which were mostly not worth publishing, and which involved a good deal of false statement. So that when it came out, there was quite a burst of resentment by friends of persons spoken of, and Julian who was all worn out nervous with his dozen years of book work, and full of neuralgia, replied angrily and made bad worse by insulting all the best friends of his father and both families.

Well, now I am going to send the book by mail in sheets and mark on the margin all that I do hope his German biographer will *leave out,* and which, if all of it is left out, will give a much more just and truthful picture of the man. Then I shall send to Lathrop and ask him to send his 'Study' . . . and to a certain Dr Loring who will send a copy of a lecture in which he does justice to other aspects of Hawthorne touched on neither by Julian or Lathrop. I should not wonder, if such a book were written in Germany, it would be translated into English, there are so many people who feel so much regret at Julians mistakes, which seem likely to be immortalised with those parts of the book which are most exquisitely done, and which show what some people doubt, that genius and culture in *both* parties to a marriage do not spoil but may make perfect a marriage. I think his German biographer has a great opportunity to do a most beautiful and truthful thing. . . .

You will observe . . . that I have been very frank with respect to my nephew's faults[;] . . . I beg you will never speak of it to anybody and *destroy this letter* after it has served its purpose, though . . . you may *read it* to the lady who is to be the biographer, putting her under bonds to be also reticent. Julian is a splendid fellow but could not understand how I should say what I have.

Elizabeth Palmer Peabody to Amelia Boelte, 30 June 1886

Dear Miss Boelte.

Today I received a card from you on which was written what I hope has not been read at any post office, especially the one in Jamaica Plain—that *some*body has told you that Hawthorne was first engaged to be married to *me!* and that I magnanimously gave him up to my sister Sophia, because I found she had given her heart to him, and that you have told this story to sundry other persons!—

I must hasten to tell you that it is all a mistake.—It is true that for the first three years after Hawthorne became known to and a *visitor* in our family, it was *rumoured,* that there was *probably* an engagement between him and *me* for we were manifestly very intimate *friends* and Sophia was considered so much of an invalid as not to be marriageable by any of us, including *herself* and Hawthorne, and as my sister Mary for two years of this time was living in Boston and keeping school there, *I* seemed to be the only one of the three to whom he *could* be engaged.

But *I* was aware, from the first week of our acquaintance with Hawthorne, that *he* was so much in love with Sophia—at first sight—that he would probably never marry any *other* woman.

At that time (from 1837 to 1840) a great change took place in Sophia,— which we all (myself, Sophia, and Hawthorne) did ascribe to his intimacy with her, which worked like animal magnetism upon her, suspending, when he was *walking* with her, the chronic pain in her head, that she had had, from the time she was 12 years old to thirty, and for the *next* three years 1839 to 1842 she *was* engaged to him, which was not made known however even to his own sister, nor to our acquaintance, till they concluded to be married and go to the old Manse in Concord *to live* in July 1842.—And by that time the rumour had (I thought) entirely died out,—for during those three years (when I was keeping my circulating foreign library and importing book-store in West Street)—Boston, he came to spend the evening whenever he was in Boston, and saw her in her own parlour, to which was never admitted any other of our guests.—She had made her marriage conditional on her perfect recovery,—and besides, not until that date had he the pecuniary where withal to be married. You can easily understand that under such exceptional circumstances of our acquaintance, there *might* be a misunderstanding, and *false impressions* and also that the *imagination* of people would be *piqued* to *create stories.* But the truth is that Hawthorne *never* had the idea of marrying any other woman than my sister Sophia.

But I was the *confidante* of this determination of his, even before Sophia was;—and, while he still thought (to use his own exquisite words in a letter to me), "She was a flower never destined to be worn in any man's bosom, but lent from Heaven for a *season* to mortals, to show the possibilities of human purity and womanliness." In a subsequent letter, he said, (referring to her *conditions*)—"Far be it from me to snatch the boon from Providence before it is granted." She, in her perfect piety having said that "if God willed to grant them the *boon,* He would make her well." And she believed He would.

An engagement like *this* was too sacred a thing to be exposed to the pitiless gossip of society and *hence* the secrecy of it, and *you know* when society's curiosity is excited and not gratified,—it will *make up* and then believe its *own* conjectures.—

There is *generally* conjured up some romantic story about any woman who is never married. But I have escaped rumours of being engaged pretty well—especially considering that in the case of the husbands of both my sisters, it was manifest that they were very intimate and cherished *friends of mine,* before they were engaged to my sisters. And to have known two such men intimately as friends might very well account for *my* not marrying *at all,* for a third—equal to either—was not likely to turn up.—But I was endowed by Heavenly Grace with such a power of imaginative sympathy, that I have known and understood married love in the persons of my sisters, and also of several other friends. I believe *matches* are made in Heaven[.] . . . And it is from the *mismatched* that most of the social evils of life arise,—and the Millenium will not come til there is a reform of this matter. It is *because* I believe marriage is a sacrament, and nothing *less,* that I am dying as an old Maid.—I have had too much respect for marriage to make a conventional one in my own case.—I am free to say that had Hawthorne wanted to marry me he would probably not have found much difficulty in getting my consent;—but it is very clear to me now, that I was not the person to make *him* happy or to be made happy *by* him, and Sophia *was.*—If there was ever a "match made in Heaven" it was *that.* . . .

Letters of Elizabeth Palmer Peabody: American Renaissance Woman, ed. Bruce A. Ronda (Middletown, CT: Wesleyan University Press, 1984), 199–201, 223–24, 417–21, 424–27, 430–32.

[Journal Thoughts on Hawthorne, 1838–1864]

Ralph Waldo Emerson

If pressed for the truth, the authors of many of the narratives collected in this volume would likely confess that the person they most often came to see in Concord was Ralph Waldo Emerson (1803–1882), not Hawthorne—and certainly not Bronson Alcott, Ellery Channing, or Thoreau. Yet, even if Emerson was not the primary object of their visit, as the acknowledged leader of the Transcendentalist movement from the 1830s onward, and as Concord's only true international celebrity from the 1840s until his death, he cast a long and enduring shadow over the presence and reputations of all who gathered in the town during the mid-nineteenth century.

It is difficult to imagine two persons more different in temperament and outlook than Emerson and Hawthorne. A member of the latest generation of descendants of New England's first settlers who for more than two centuries had supplied clergymen for her most distinguished pulpits, a public intellectual who transformed the speaker's platform into a pulpit where he preached a new gospel of the individual's personal relation to nature and the divine and of social reform to America's post-Revolution generations, and sufficiently cosmopolitan to be at ease in large or small companies, by lineage and personal disposition Emerson was everything that Hawthorne was not—or, at least, that Hawthorne chose not to be. Hawthorne was compared to Emerson more often than to any other of his contemporaries; even the quality of his character and personality and the degree of his worldly success were measured against Emerson's. However one assesses the justice of the comparisons, there is little doubt that Hawthorne always suffered by them. More painful yet, on reading the journals of both men, it is apparent that they were each conscious of the public's inclination to "size them up" in this way. In an uncharacteristic act of apologetic self-effacement, Emerson admitted as much to Sophia after Hawthorne's death and in the second of two journal passages printed below. Writing to Sophia on 11 July 1864, he said, "I have had my own pain in the loss of your husband. He was always a mine of hope to me, and I promised myself a rich future in achieving at some day, when we should both be less engaged to tyrannical studies & habitudes, an unreserved intercourse with him. I thought I could well wait his time & mine for what was so well worth waiting" (*Letters RWE*, 9:147–48). This letter echoes the sentiment Emerson had earlier expressed in his journal, on the day after he served as a pallbearer at Hawthorne's funeral; there, confessing Hawthorne's death "a surprise & disappointment," he wrote that it deprived both men of the "happiness" to one day "conquer a friendship" (*JMN*, 15:59–60).

Hawthorne was brought to Emerson's attention by Elizabeth Palmer Peabody, who in 1837–1838 claimed the obscure writer from Salem and the ecstatic poet Jones Very as her latest discoveries. In June 1838, she gave Emerson a copy of "Foot-prints on the Sea-shore," which had appeared in January in the *Democratic Review*; after reading it, he quipped in his journal, "E. P. P. brought me yesterday Hawthorne's Footprints. . . . I complained that there was no inside to it. Alcott & he together would make a man" (*JMN*, 7:21). As disparaging of Hawthorne's fiction as Hawthorne was of Emersonian idealism with its Platonic and Swedenborgian tinges, Emerson never fully appreciated Hawthorne's talent. In 1839, after commenting that it was "no easy matter to write a dialogue," he linked Hawthorne to Cooper and Dickens as examples of writers who definitely could not (*JMN*, 7:242). Indeed, there is always an edge to Emerson's judgments on Hawthorne's literary ability. For instance, after noting in 1842 that Hawthorne's growing "reputation as a writer is a very pleasing fact," Emerson says that "this is a tribute to the man," "because his writing is not good for anything" (*JMN*, 7:465). By 1846, he appears completely out of patience with Hawthorne as an imaginative artist, remarking that he "invites his readers too much into his study, opens the process before them. As if the confectioner should say to his customers[,] Now let us make the cake" (*JMN*, 9:405). And as harsh as he was about Hawthorne's writings, Emerson could be harsher yet about Hawthorne's loyalty to his friends, especially Franklin Pierce. Writing shortly after Hawthorne's death, Emerson observed, "Hawthorne [was] unlucky in having for a friend a man who cannot be befriended; whose miserable administration admits but of one excuse, imbecility. Pierce was either the worst, or he the weakest of all our Presidents" (*JMN*, 15:361).

When the newlyweds Nathaniel and Sophia moved into the Old Manse in July 1842, Emerson paid them a welcoming visit. One might imagine the two men eying each other at the time and wondering what writings Hawthorne would produce in the house where Emerson had earlier composed *Nature* (1836). Although Emerson complained in his journal, "I fancied that I needed society & that it would help me much if fine persons were near . . . but now that

C[hanning]. & H[awthorne]. are here, and A[lcott soon returns] . . . I look with a sort of terror at my gate" (September 1842; *JMN*, 8:261), he invited Hawthorne on a two-day saunter out to the Shaker community in Harvard, Massachusetts, the town in which as newlyweds Emerson's own parents had settled prior to the Reverend William Emerson's call in 1799 to serve as pastor of Boston's prestigious First Church. Emerson always remembered the walk as a fine occasion for the two to get to know each other, but Hawthorne did not, and his reason is not too difficult to see. In his account that follows of the roughly forty-mile walk that began on 27 September, which took the two from Concord through Stow on their way to Harvard, where they spent the night, then back to Concord by way of Littleton and Acton the next day, Emerson appears completely self-absorbed, so much so that Hawthorne's most visible moment occurs literally outside of the narrative, when he wanders off to smoke a cigar.

SEPT[EMBER]. 27 [1842] WAS a fine day, and Hawthorne & I set forth on a walk. We went first to the Factory where [Damon] makes Domett cloths, but his mills were standing still, his houses empty. Nothing so small but comes to honour & has its shining moment somewhere; & so was it here with our little Assabet [River] or North Branch; it was falling over the rocks into silver, & above was expanded into this tranquil lake. After looking about us a few moments we took the road to Stow. The day was full of sunshine and it was a luxury to walk in the midst of all this warm & coloured light. The days of September are so rich that it seems natural to walk to the end of one's strength, & then fall prostrate saturated with the fine floods. . . . Fringed gentians, a thornbush with red fruit, wild apple trees whose fruit hung like berries, and grapevines were the decorations of the path. We scarcely encountered man or boy in our road nor saw any in the fields. This depopulation lasted all day. But the outlines of the landscape were so gentle that it seemed as if we were in a very cultivated country, and elegant persons must be living just over yonder hills. Three or four times . . . we saw the entrance to their lordly park. But nothing in the farms or in the houses made this good. And it is to be considered that when any large brain is born in these towns it is sent, at sixteen or twenty years, to Boston or New York, and the country is tilled only by the inferior class of the people, by the second crop . . . of the men. Hence all these shiftless poverty-struck pig-farms. . . . Our walk had no incidents. It needed none, for we were in excellent spirits, had much conversation, for we were both old collectors [of thoughts] who had never had opportunity before to show each other our cabinets, so that we could have filled with matter much longer days. We agreed that it needed a little dash of humor or extravagance in the traveller to give occasion to incident in his journey. Here we sober men easily pleased kept on the outside of the land & did not by so much as a request for a cup of milk creep into any farmhouse. If want of pence in our pocket or some vagary in our brain drove us into these "huts where poor men lie"[1] to crave dinner or night's lodging, it would be so easy to break into some mesh of domestic romance, learn so much pathetic private history, perchance see the first blush mantle on the cheek of the young girl when the mail stage came or did not come, or even get entangled ourselves in some thread of gold or grey. Then again the opportunities which the taverns once offered the traveller of witnessing & even sharing in the joke & the politics of the teamster & farmers on the road, are now no more. The Temperance Society emptied the bar-room; it is a cold place. H. tried to smoke a cigar, but I observed he was soon out on the piazza. After noon we reached Stow, and dined, then continued our journey towards Harvard, making our day's walk . . . about 20 miles. The last mile, however, we rode in a wagon, having been challenged by a friendly fatherly gentleman, who knew my name, & my father's name & history, & who insisted on doing the honours of his town to us, & of us to his townsmen; for he fairly installed us at the tavern, introduced us to the Doctor, & to General——, & bespoke the landlord's best attention to our wants. We get the view of the Nashua River valley from the top of Oak-Hill, as we enter Harvard village. Next morning, we begun our walk at 6 1/2 o'clock for the Shaker Village distant 3 1/2 miles. Whilst the good Sisters were getting ready our breakfast, we had a conversation with Seth Blanchard & Cloutman of the Brethren, who gave an honest account by yea & by nay of their faith & practice. They were not stupid like some whom I have seen of their society, & not worldly like others. The conversation on both parts was frank enough; with the downright I will be downright, thought I, and Seth showed some humour. I doubt not we should have had our own way with them to a good extent . . . if we could have staid twenty four hours. . . . After breakfast Cloutman showed us the farm, vineyard, orchard, barn, herb room, pressing room &c. The vineyard contained two noble arcades of grapes . . . full of fruit; the orchard fine varieties of pears, & peaches & apples.

They have . . . enough to supply the wants of the 200 souls in this family. . . . Moreover, this settlement is of great value in the heart of the country as a model farm, in the absence of that rural nobility we talked of yesterday. Here are improvements invented or adopted from the other Shaker Communities which the neighboring farmers see & copy. From the Shaker Village we came to Littleton, & thence to Acton, still in the same redundance of splendour. It was like a day of July, and from Acton we sauntered leisurely homeward to finish the nineteen miles of our second day before four in the afternoon.

[24 May 1864] Yesterday . . . we buried Hawthorne in Sleepy Hollow, in a pomp of sunshine & verdure, & gentle winds. James F. Clarke read the service in the Church & at the grave. Longfellow, Lowell, Holmes, Agassiz, Hoar, Dwight, Whipple, Norton, Alcott, Hillard, Fields, Judge Thomas, & I, attended the hearse as pall bearers. Franklin Pierce was with the family. The church was copiously decorated with white flowers delicately arranged. The corpse was unwillingly shown—only a few moments to this company of his friends. But it was noble & serene in its aspect—nothing amiss—a calm & powerful head. A large company filled the church, & the grounds of the cemetery. All was so bright & quiet, that pain or mourning was hardly suggested, & Holmes said to me, that it looked like a happy meeting.

Clarke in the church said, that Hawthorne had done more justice than any other to the shades of life, shown a sympathy with the crime in our nature, &, like Jesus, was the friend of sinners.

I thought there was a tragic element in the event, that might be more fully rendered—in the painful solitude of the man—which, I suppose, could not longer be endured, & he died of it.

I have found in his death a surprise & disappointment. I thought him a greater man than any of his works betray, that there was still a great deal of work in him, & that he might one day show a purer power.

Moreover I have felt sure of him in his neighborhood, & in his necessities of sympathy & intelligence, that I could well wait his time—his unwillingness & caprice—and might one day conquer a friendship. It would have been a happiness, doubtless to both of us, to have come into habits of unreserved intercourse. It was easy to talk with him—there were no barriers—only, he said so little, that I talked too much, & stopped only because—as he gave no indications—I feared to exceed. He showed no egotism or self-assertion, rather a humility, &, at one time, a fear that he had written himself out. One day, when I found him on the top of his hill, in the woods, he paced back the path to his house, & said, "*this path is the only remembrance of me that will remain.*" Now it appears that I waited too long.

Lately, he had removed himself the more by the indignation his perverse politics & unfortunate friendship for that paltry Franklin Pierce awaked—though it rather moved pity for Hawthorne, & the assured belief that he would outlive it, & come right at last.

I have forgotten in what year . . . but it was whilst he lived in the Manse, soon after his marriage, that I said to him, "I shall never see you in this hazardous way; we must take a long walk together. Will you go to Harvard & visit the Shakers?" He agreed, & we took a [September] day, & walked[,] . . . got our dinner from the Brethren, slept at the Harvard Inn, & returned home by another road the next day. It was a satisfactory tramp; we had good talk on the way. . . .

Note

1. William Wordsworth, "Song at the Feast of Brougham Castle," 1. 161.

The Journals and Miscellaneous Notebooks of Ralph Waldo Emerson, ed. William H. Gilman, Ralph H. Orth, et al., 16 vols. (Cambridge and London: Harvard University Press, 1960–1982), 8:271–75, 15:59–60.

[First Years of Marriage at the Old Manse, 1842–1845]

[Sophia Amelia Peabody Hawthorne]

⇥※⇤

After nearly a century-and-a-half of being overshadowed by the reputation of her illustrious husband, Sophia Amelia Peabody Hawthorne (1809–1871) may be finally coming into her own. An artist, author, editor of her husband's unpublished writings after his death, Transcendental thinker, and devout person, Sophia was an unusually gifted woman of her time. She overcame the invalidism of her childhood and an enforced exile to Cuba for her health from 1833 to 1835, developed into an accomplished artist, encouraged her husband's literary career and served as the couple's social front from the time they began courting in 1838 until Nathaniel's death in 1864, bore and raised three children, patiently endured financial hardship for much of her married life, and followed her husband wherever he found opportunities to produce income. The first serious—though flawed—portrayal of her character appeared in son Julian Hawthorne's *Nathaniel Hawthorne and His Wife* (1884); the next occurred in 1950, when Louise Hall Tharp published *The Peabody Sisters of Salem*. More recently, Megan Marshall's *The Peabody Sisters* (2005) has restored Sophia's position as an intellectual and artistic force who, along with her sisters Elizabeth and Mary, ignited the Romantic and Transcendental impulses of their time, and in *Sophia Peabody Hawthorne: A Life* (2004), Patricia Dunlavy Valenti has paid Sophia the ultimate tribute: she has treated her as a serious subject in the initial volume of a biography that takes her life up to 1847. Because groundbreaking treatments of the Peabody sisters generally and Sophia specifically are just now appearing, there is every reason to expect that future studies will restore them fully to the history that each of them participated in making.

The selection that follows was edited from the manuscript by Valenti in 1996. Valenti drew the text from Sophia's entries in Nathaniel's notebooks, where they initially served as her private reflections on the first months of their marriage but quickly became the basis to a journal conversation between husband and wife. The passages printed here are limited to those that Sophia began to write within days of her wedding in July 1842, continued through the birth of daughter Una in March 1844, and ended in October 1845, when the couple vacated the Old Manse. Although Sophia's prose has bothered some readers as overly sentimental, we include it here as a means to allow her a voice of her own in this volume. For while Sophia is a presence in many of the selections we print, her voice is ultimately silent in them.

Here, Sophia comes alive as an unexpectedly passionate woman who is very much in love. Her literary art transforms the Manse and the larger Concord community of her first three years of marriage into a personal, enchanting Eden, where Nathaniel is "Adam," "The Bright One," who lights her life as well as her way on their frequent walks together. If Sophia appears too passionate, so does Nathaniel, and he perhaps exceeds his wife's passion—at least in her eyes—as he daily collects flowers to freshen the house she is decorating with her paintings, rows her on the Concord River in the skiff they purchased from Thoreau and christened the "Water Lily," tends their vegetable and fruit gardens, reads to her every afternoon or evening, and writes to her almost daily whenever he is absent from home. What follows, then, is a unique idyll of one nineteenth-century marriage in which the honeymoon, as Nathaniel and Sophia's friends acknowledge, never really ended.

Among those mentioned in the circle of family members, friends, and acquaintances are a number of the Hawthornes' old friends and newer Transcendentalist acquaintances, including Cornelia Romana Hall Park, the Peabody sisters' friend; Abigail (Abba) May Alcott, Anna and Louisa May Alcott, and Junius Alcott, Bronson's wife, daughters, and younger brother, respectively; Samuel Gray Ward, a friend of Emerson and Fuller, who was married to Anna Hazard Barker Ward; Maria Louisa Hawthorne, Nathaniel's younger sister; Jack Flint, who worked the farm to the north of the Old Manse; Maria King Prescott, Timothy Prescott's widow, who lived across from the Old Manse with her daughter, Abby (Abba) Prescott; Martha Lawrence Prescott, Timothy Prescott's daughter by a previous marriage, and John Shepard Keyes, a Concord attorney and Emerson's close friend, who married in 1844; Charles Lane, cofounder with Alcott and others of Fruitlands; George Partridge Bradford, a Brook Farm member and close friend of the Hawthornes, Emerson, and Thoreau; Ellen Kilshaw Fuller, Margaret's younger sister, who married Ellery Channing in 1842 and moved to a house near Emerson's; Mary Bryan, the Hawthornes' housekeeper at the Old Manse; Anna Blake Shaw, another of Sophia's close friends, and her sister Sarah Blake Sturgis Shaw, who was Francis (Frank) George Shaw's wife; Caroline Sturgis, a Transcendentalist poet, close friend of Fuller and Emerson, and from 1836 a frequent visitor to Concord;

Lidian Jackson Emerson, Emerson's second wife, and Ruth Haskins Emerson—
"Madam Emerson"—his mother; Mary Hosmer, the daughter of Edmund and
Sally Pierce Hosmer, and Elizabeth J. Weir, later the Emerson children's gov-
erness and Emerson's copyist; John Louis O'Sullivan, founder of the *Democratic Review* and Una's godfather; Sarah Sherman Hoar—"Mrs. Hoar"—the
wife of Samuel Hoar, one of Concord's most prominent citizens, and Elizabeth
Sherman Hoar's mother; Ruth Hathorne, Nathaniel's paternal aunt; Sophia
Palmer Pickman, Sophia's maternal aunt; Mary Wilder White Foote, Sophia's
lifelong friend; and Ellen Sturgis Hooper, Caroline's sister and the wife of
Robert William Hooper. Context makes clear that "Plato" is the Hawthornes'
private name for Emerson.

[CONCORD, JULY 1842] . . . When I came to [Nathaniel], he told me I had
transgressed the law of right in trampling down the unmown grass, & he tried
to induce me to come back, that he might not have to violate his conscience by
doing the same thing. And I was very naughty & would not obey, & therefore
he punished me by staying behind. This I did not like very well, & I climbed
the hill alone. We penetrated the pleasant gloom & sat down upon the carpet
of dried pine leaves. Then I clasped him in my arms in the lovely shade, & we
laid down a few moments on the bosom of dear mother Earth. Oh how sweet
it was! And I told him I would not be so naughty again, & there was a very
slight diamond shower without any thunder or lightening, & we were happiest. We walked through the forest, & came forth into an open space, whence
a fair broad landscape could be seen, our old Manse holding a respectable
place in the plain, the river opening its blue eyes here & there, & waving
mountainous ridges closing in the horizon. There we plucked whortleberries
& then sat down[.] There was no wind & the stillness was profound. There
seemed no movement in the world but that of our pulses. The Earth was still
before us. It was very lovely but the rapture of my spirit was caused more by
knowing that my own husband was at my side than by all the rich variety of
plain, river, forest & mountain around & at my feet.

[10 August] Yesterday was the monthlyversary of our wedding day, & quite
worthy to be so, for it was one of the loveliest days that ever enriched the
earth. The bridal was on the 9th of July, which dawned fair after a long season of clouds & rain just as yesterday was born of shadows and gloom—for it
had rained nearly a week, & the sun . . . shines this morning—. . . I waked

at light & sprang up to note the promise of the heavens[;] . . . the rising sun dispersed mists, & the heavenly blue appeared. . . . Sarah Clarke arranged my bridal robe & dressed my hair with pond lilies & Cornelia braided it— [A]t half past eleven . . . James Clarke pronounced us husband & wife before God & Man. There were present besides the family Cornelia, and Sarah & the cook Bridget. While [our anniversary] ceremony was proceeding, the sun shone forth with great splendor, as no adventure, except that my love dropped some of his berries, because I had so carelessly fastened the string of the basket, & I threw myself upon a haystack & shocked his conscience very much. He prayed Heaven for a pitchfork to put it up again. . . . I am very naughty. It is inexcusable for he is the loveliest being who ever breathed life—Yes—with all his strength & spirit & power, he has the most perfect loveliness of nature I ever witnessed or imagined. He is a true Seraph. . . .

This morning my darling husband brought from the river some pond lilies, pickerel weed, cardinal flowers & one spike of arrowhead, & I put them all into our alabaster fountain. One could scarcely see a fairer sight—All these are river plants & become each other wonderfully—. . .

[20 August] This week the weather has been very gloomy until yesterday— Though I think I should not have known it, had not Adam daily lamented the injury which continued dampness caused his garden. For I care very little what guise the heavens wear, whether it be sunny or shadowy abroad, so complete and sufficient is my inward happiness, so effectual a sun of my system is my dearest lord. I have not been well in the body, so that I could not be so demonstrative as usual, but there is never any variation in my felicity, while I recognize my position, & know that I am indeed his wife for the first time since we came to Paradise. It was also the first time that I had left my beloved in our Eden alone, though he has often gone from me for a season. He accompanied me down the avenue & along the road a short space, but would not go with me because he was in undress. . . .

[24 August] Monday morning I walked to Mrs Alcotts. . . . After a very pleasant call at the cottage, Mrs Alcott proposed that Junius should row me home in the boat, instead of my returning through the dusty road. So Anna & Louisa & Junius & I proceeded to the river, & Mrs Alcott had a crimson cushion placed on my seat, & Mr. Junius scattered twigs of trees beneath my feet to shield me from the dust or damp of the boat, & away we floated down the shining stream. It was utterly still[.] . . . The purple pickerel flower & the gorgeous cardinals & spirea of all colors, & arrowhead & pond lilies all seemed rejoiced to be in that faery world beneath the earth—. . . Once in a while a troop of birds flew along in the remote heaven below & vanished like spirits. Oh who would ever imagine that there was mud & fire & rock under our little boat instead of that rare picture! It was perfectly bewitching with one great want. My noble & kingly husband should have been sitting before me with oars in hand instead of some Junius Alcott who had no place in my regard. Presently we anchored in a baylet & Junius sprang out & pulled up a "conclave of cardinals" (as my dear husband felicitously calls a group of these flowers) & presented them to me—. . . But what Roman Cardinal ever wore such a cloak as these imperial yankee dignitaries? . . . God paints better than man can imitate. I was landed on a rock at the foot of our orchard & arrived at dinner just after my husband & Louisa had seated themselves, feeling like a water-nymph fresh from jewelled caves & reedy depths. In the afternoon we went to our wooded hill to gather whortleberries. . . . Then we began our labors, & most silently, like three dumb Dryads, filled our baskets. . . . After tea, Louisa & I winnowed our berries of all unworthiness, while my beloved husband sat opposite me, showing like a star. Ah now I have thought. The sun set in his eyes & they rayed out the lost splendor upon me & into my heart. . . .

Yesterday, . . . we went to seek Cardinals on the riverbanks—& we found two hundred and ninety potentates standing ankle deep in water, & pulled them out. I do not believe there was ever such a resplendent sight seen before—as two hundred and ninety cardinals in a compact group, as they hung over my husbands shoulder coming home. I arranged them all in the flower table after tea in the evening.

[8 September] My dearest husband has gone to sail on the river. . . . The sun has not risen above our opposite hill & I think I will record a little of my beautiful life, my happiest, most enchanting life. . . . Those visitors who interrupted my dear husband [on 24 August] . . . (O that they had come later) were Margaret [Fuller] and Mr Sam Ward. We had an exceedingly pleasant visit from them. Mr Ward was greatly delighted with the house & its environs[.] He seemed to think Boston could not afford so charming a drawing room as our quaint old parlor. . . . We went down the orchard to the rivers banks, & my husband & Mr W laid down upon the grass while Margaret & I sat on the rocks: Margaret was very brilliant & while she talked to my husband, Mr Ward addressed himself to me, whom he apparently thought a kind of enchanted mortal, in an earthly Elysium[.] He wanted to know what we did, & I told him we did nothing to describe, yet very much in reality—that we did not intend to accomplish any thing that could be told of, these lovely summer days. He said he was idle two months after his marriage, . . . & he seemed to think we must begin to work now, as our two months had passed[.] He said the honeymoon never would end, which I could have assured him of—. . . [H]e thought my husband was a kingly man far surpassing all he had anticipated, for who can prefigure him? I cannot even, from day to day. Tuesday the day dawned lustrously without a cloud. Our sister Louisa [Hawthorne] went away in the stage at 1/2 past six. I like Louisa very much, she is so sincere & true & disinterested, & I am glad she has been to see us, because I wanted her to know that her worshipped brother is not very miserable with me & that he lives in a sweet retirement. . . .

[Mid-September?] . . . The earth . . . looked fresh & green & autumn had hung out one or two gorgeous banners as a token. . . . The river was perfectly still & soft, taking all the trees and the heavens captive in its depths, where we decided that they were more real than those we could touch & see above; at least *as* real—why not? All men seemed asleep, except in a neighboring farmyard, but . . . we discerned good Mr Jack Flint with two shining tin-pails, about to milk his cows. . . . We left the river & wended through a short lane in which grow the blue gentian with closed bells . . . & my dearest love gathered all there was. It is very beautiful to see him plucking flowers with so much interest. It adds such a grace to his kingliness.

[11 December] It is nearly three months since I have recorded my life & love in this journal. We have had many visitors, & have been to Boston & Salem meanwhile & various things have prevented my writing here. Last week we took our first walk together since the snow fell. The afternoon commenced with being rather dim, with pale blue sky beautified with very soft delicate clouds of faint purple—This dimness was to me very beautiful, but my dearest husband said he preferred broad sunshine. We went towards Peters lane, but finding an inland sea that covers a meadow . . . quite frozen over, & boys skating upon it, we concluded to walk across it. This was very pleasant— Little islands of trees & bushes were scattered about in the icy arms of the tiny sea, clasped with immitigable force. . . . We soon crossed the frozen lake & then the snow was not hard enough to uphold us & at nearly every step an evil jinnee seemed to pull our heels down as if to weary us out, but we did not heed it & proceeded on over another meadow & entered Sleepy Hollow by a very pretty winding ascent between the trees. On the summit my dear lord threw himself down on the fair snow. . . .

[41]

[April? 1843] . . . It is the inward thought alone that renders the body either material or angelical. . . . Before our marriage I knew nothing of its capacities & the truly married alone can know what a wondrous instrument it is for the purpose of the heart—. . . The unholiness of a union on any other ground than *entire* oneness of spirit, immediately & eternally causes the sword of the flaming cherubim to wave before this tree of life—The profane never can taste the joys of Elysium—because it is a spiritual joy, & they cannot percieve it.

. . . On Thursday 13th [April] my darling husband took me out in the boat. It was charming to be again on the water. We went to the red bridge, but the tide was so high & the stream so rapid beneath it, that we could not go under. The counter currents held our waterlily almost still, but finally we turned & gave it to the care of the downward flow without using the paddle much. We floated over the meadows where in the summer we walk upon the grass, & the trees seemed growing directly from the rivers depths. . . .

I never was in the country before at the opening of spring that I recollect. . . . This sense of newcoming life from sympathy with the deliverance of earth from winter is a novel experience. My soul is a mighty river also, breaking free from frost & ice—no—not frost & ice neither; for I have been free & unshackled all through the cold weather in the heavenly summer of my husbands heart—but still it breaks forth. I have a new hope, partly from the sun of joy in my dear loves eyes, for he has sighed much for warm days & flowers & green grass, & now he is very glad—& partly I suppose from involuntary response to the budding trees & rushing waters & birds wings & voices. But I could not be satisfied in feeling this mighty springing upwards & forwards unless I were in love. I am thankful that I first know Spring after I am married. My heart is so full—it rises to so high a mark—. . . I myself am Spring with all its birds, its rivers, its buds, singing, rushing, blooming in his arms. I feel new as the Earth which is just born again—I rejoice that I am, because I am his, wholly, unreservedly his—Therefore is my life beautiful & gracious. Therefore is the world pleasant as roses. . . .

[23 April] It is far different to day from last Sunday. Then it was soft & sunny after a misty dawn, & the birds sang on every twig—They sang without an end—I felt inclined to respond "Yes, yes, yes—I know it I know it! There never was such a sun, such an air, such a sky, such a God! I know it, dear little fellow worshippers!" My heart said this but they were not content to stop. . . . Last Sunday evening Ellery Channing made us his first visit—He looked brighter & was more sociable than he used to be last summer. I think perhaps he will prove more worthy & interesting a companion than thou supposest, dearest husband. He has to me a pleasanter way of saying things than Mr Thoreau, because wholly without the air of saying anything of consequence. Monday he dined & took tea with us & I enjoyed his visit better than any from him before. His complexion seems several shades lighter & he smiles oftener. . . . Ellery came again this week & went out in the boat & took tea on his return—

[28 April] Friday afternoon—my dearest husband took me out in the boat. We went aground on the meadows, were nearly upset in a maelstrom beneath the red bridge, beating up against the rocks, & attempting to go ashore at the foot of the orchard, were stuck fast between the stones of the wall & narrowly escaped destruction! My sweetest love seemed discouraged at once before all these mishaps & obstacles, while I could only laugh; for I cannot feel fear; & danger I do not mind with him: but I found out a solution of this mystery when we were landed. Thou wast discouraged for my sake only, thou tender hero. Alone thou never feelest alarm. Can I love or admire thee most?

I called at Mrs Prescotts after we came back & found only the blooming Miss Abba—blooming & stalwart. But I must not forget to mention that we floated on the river by a small snake, who evidently set sail by accident & was vainly attempting to keep his head & white throat above the water. My husband tried to lift him out on his paddle, but he wriggled off, not knowing friends from enemies. We passed an even row of young willows upon which were many chattering blackbirds with agitated tails—I think they are probably the gossips & scandal mongers among the birds & also contrivers of mischief & therefore wear the livery of his sable majesty[.] Across the river we saw the greenest slope which yet had refreshed [our] eyes. . . .

I had a new pleasure last week in raking up dry leaves & twigs in the avenue—It was rural calisthenics—It was a rich delight for not only I was making the avenue nice, but I was giving the new grass air & light, & was myself breathing pure nectar & tides of music from the birds above & around sweetly mad, with rapture—quakes gently shocked the air.

[9 May] Dearest husband thou shouldst not have to labour, especially with the hands, & thou hatest it rightfully. Thou art a seraph come to observe Nature & men in a still repose, without being obliged to exert thyself in reproduction or in clearing away old rubbish. Apollo among his herds could not have looked so out of place as thou with saw & axe & rake in hand. The Flower of Time should only unfold—It should be put to no Use. I wish I

could be Midas long enough to turn into sufficient gold for thy lifes sustenance & embellishment. . . .

Last Thursday [May] 4th I took the first walk into the woods with my
Phoebas Apollo—There was no sunshine & the wind was determinately east
& strong so that we were chilled *to* our hearts, but not *through* those warm
tropics of love; for no wind could chill the airs there. . . . We visited the ru-
ined cottage & moralized a little over its hearthstone & then descended into
a vale by the water[.] . . . We continued to follow the woodland aisle & I was
very much attracted by the pale-green moss that hung from the trees like long
hoary hair. It was beautiful to examine, like the sea moss—& I gathered some
to make a wreath. The ground was flaked with the white everlasting, springing up in great abundance every where as if to write Immortality all over the
earth. My darling husband finally saw a cliff in the wood & we went in &
climbed it, & there we found were many columbine plants. . . . Coming home
we were arrested by an orchestra of blackbirds upon a leafless tree. My opinion of white birds has changed very much upon farther acquaintance. They
have evidently settled all their domestic & political affairs & left off gossip,
& now in bands of forties & fifties they perform wonderful symphonies. One
might shut his eyes & dream he had caught the music of the spheres in his
ear, or that through the gate of Heaven . . . a mingled strain of . . . psaltery,
dulcimer & harp touched by angels, had strayed to Earth to reclaim man to
harmony. . . .

The next afternoon 5th May, Friday we walked to the wood crowned hill
Barretts Hill. We as yet had seen no flowers, but I felt sure that some lovely
violets were blooming on that sunny declivity—So as we strayed along earnestly looking, I finally caught the blue eye of the first violet! I threw myself
down & kissed the precious little stranger. . . . Then we climbed the hill & sat
quietly beneath the pine trees a short time. Descending again what should I
behold beneath some bushes but a fair white anemone, bending its lily head
like an ivory bell. I shouted aloud & we found more & more till finally we
gathered as very large bunch of these most graceful flowers. So we returned
very rich that memorable day.

On Saturday [May] 6th we went to Sleepy Hollow by way of the village[.] . . . On a hill at the right entering the Hollow we found a few of the
first Pedate violets. . . . But after leaving Sleepy Hollow, & crossing a narrow
brook, thousands of wood anemones greeted our vision on the bank, & the

white violet in purple brocade. I sat down & gathered as many as I could hold. Miss Martha Prescott & her lover Mr John Keyes sat on the hill-top meanwhile. On this day we had a visit from Ellery Channing who had arrived to take up his residence in Concord. On . . . [the] 7th Mr Lane . . . called to see us. . . . [He] was very genial & agreable & full of sense, & decidedly Alcotty in countenance. . . . Ellery came to tea in the afternoon, to escape a great talk at Mr Emersons. . . . And in the evening we were delighted to recieve George Bradford, as pure a spirit as God ever made. . . . About the first of May the cherry trees began to bloom & now (19th) pear, apple & peach are all in full glory. I never before saw peach trees in blossom. Two in our large orchard . . . look like fountains of flower-wreaths, throwing out their long branches in noble curves—& snowy white blooms—. . .

. . . On Thursday afternoon my beloved went with me to call on Ellen and Ellery Channing at their funny little red house. Ellen . . . is enchanted with her home entirely & looked very happy, though weary, for she is not quite arranged. My dear husband went out to see the chief of the domain, who was at work on his acre, & as I saw him from the window, very much of a brownie in his appearance. I was delighted with the view from Ellens chamber window. A broad, level, tranquil plain skirted by low hills & woods—Its effect was most reposeful & swect. . . . In that direction they have the unobstructed rising sun—From the other chamber they have the setting sun & Mr Emersons house—Ellen said she had seen no columbines nor Thalectroides anemones! & as we proposed to go home through the woods, I determined to gather her some. My dearest love had discovered a bank of the last mentioned, & we came that way . . . [and] found ourselves on quite an eminence from which was a fine view. A friendly hospitable broad stump invited us to sit & . . . we accepted the invitation—. . . I was particularly struck with the beauty of the young oaks—Their new leaves were of crimson—& pale yellow, & beautiful blossoms—. . . The new foliage of the birches also was very beautiful—. . . They look like little pyramids on the wing in etherial dance. While we sat on the good old stump, a mocking bird entertained us by means of his single throat, with the notes of all the birds & sounds in Nature, even the frogs croak. He sat alone on a tree & amused himself apparently as well as us. Finally we descended the hill & went through Sleepy Hollow & visited the bank of Thalectroides. . . . When we gave up the harvesting, we met an apple tree . . . & we purloined the rosy blossoms. . . . Then we climbed the hill opposite our house, & came home. I put . . . all the [flowers] I had into a tin basket & sent them to Ellen that night, greatly to her joy, as she said by Mary [Bryan]. . . .

This week I have planted my flower garden. It is the first time I ever put any seeds into the earth—. . . I have China Astors, Gilly Flower, Amaranths gold & white, Lavateras, Columbines, Scholchis, Lycnis, Musk plant, Marble Perns, Foxgloves, white & purple candytufts, dahlias, nasturtiums, morning glories, snap dragons, mourning brides, & many others—My dear husband has also about finished planting his garden this week. For more than a fortnight we have had asparagus on the table—He has planted potatoes, corn, squashes, peas, beans, tomatos, cucumbers, melons, turnips, carrots, radishes, sweet herbs.

I find that the humming bird, that most exquisite of Gods creations, frequents the cherry trees, & upon those near our chamber window I have often seen them this month. They are a type of fine fancy, & perhaps suggested Ariel to the imagination of Shakespeare. . . .

It has been an inexpressible happiness to watch the coming of summer & spring step by step with such a synonym & harmony of Nature as my husband. . . . I could never have appreciated it with half a soul as I once possessed. Now it seems as if indeed we were first born & saw the world fresh from Gods hand as on the morning of Creation.

[23 May] This morning we found upon awakening that there was falling a blessed rain. It has not rained before since Mayday when it poured in the morning & cleared up in the afternoon[.] On that day at 1/2 past 11 my sister Mary was married to Mr Horace Mann, & went directly to England an hour after the ceremony. This marriage was a sudden conclusion & they had but a month to prepare for a six months tour in Europe. It was a most happy event in my life as well as the crowning joy of hers, for I never could be reconciled to her hard labor for others, & her sad countenance. Now she is entirely content. . . . The aspect of every green thing is superb now & how the new seeds & young plants rejoice—! Very early while we were still in bed, my dear husband announced a bird in the gallery. . . . He flew backwards & forwards, & I opened the window for him to go out if he liked. How he got in is a mystery—On Sunday afternoon Ellery & Ellen Channing came to tea. We had a very pleasant visit. Ellery shines, & he seems perfectly to idolize my darling husband. Monday morning I began the bust of the noblest head in Christendom or Heathenesse, that of my own dear Lord.

[6 June] My beloved has gone to fish—. . .

We have heard from Mary Mann just a month from her departure—She says she feels "perfect satisfaction." This is to hear rich music. Beethoven could not surpass that strain for my heart. . . . I was the first to part off from the family in this way with a fine sound of cymbals, called spherical harmony, & now Mary has shot into her orbit, having found the other half of her globe. . . . To her as to me nothing is wanting but that those left behind should also roll in full circles through the blue depths of joy. I wish [our sister] Elizabeth could take up the wondrous tale & echo "And I as you!" . . .

[Mid-June?] God gives us all that is of eternal worth—consummate Love—perfect health even a lovely home—& in still addition—the power to recieve friends & make them happy—Sweetest husband—. . .

On the 22nd of this month the first roses bloomed. The sweet briar bush on the southern side of our house first unfolded its flowers. It was the day that golden Anna Shaw, & her sister Sarah—the Rose of Sharon, came to see us—& it was a very fit time. We had a most charming visit from them, dearest, did we not? They arrived at nine oclk on the loveliest day we had had, a true midsummer day. . . . Thou, beloved, didst greet them at the door of thy study with the most celestial smile & gleam that *they* ever beheld, though it is *my* daily privilege—

. . . [W]e stayed in the parlor a while & they were charmed with the room—the curtains, the couch & all—Golden Anna threw herself on the flowered carpet, a more splendid flower than all—& the Rose of Sharon half reclined on the Ottoman—beautiful ornaments for my parlor! . . . Sarah wanted to hear Marys letters from London & so I read aloud—Annas attention wandered, . . . for she said she felt on enchanted ground & kept falling into trances. In the midst my dearest husband came out of his study & thou didst look most lovely, beloved, & thou wentst to the village & to Mr Emersons to find if he would return for our dinner. After thou hadst gone, Anna went into our chamber & took a nap. . . . Before Anna awoke, thou didst return bringing those velvet roses. Thou didst present one to Sarah with a smile that might have created light—. . . Thou didst disappear into thy study till Mr. Emerson came for lo! as I was looking down the avenue, who should appear at the gate but Plato himself. . . . Anna & Sarah descended into the parlor to see him & I requested thee to come too, dearest. Our dinner was very pleasant—Mary Bryan prepared it excellently—lamb, our own asparagus maccaroni & potatoe—& for the second course a custard pudding. . . . Mr Emerson was very agreable & talked a great deal. He remained after dinner a long time, holding vivid discourse with Anna—

. . . Thou, dearest husband, didst thy part & more, considering thy inclinations, & Anna asked afterwards whether thou wast not unusually sociable, for from what she had heard, she did not expect so much intercourse with thee. She said it was beautiful to meet thine eyes, because there was such a friendly glance in them—I should think it was about five when Mr E. took leave & thou didst accompany him[.] . . . Thou dost fulfil all my dreams of beautiful hostship as well as of every thing else desirable. . . .

Today bloomed the first damask rose (24th June)—. . . It is of a pink-purple with five curved petals of exquisite form—It was about the first of June that thou didst bring some home to me, beloved. . . .

My garden does not entirely succeed. Not all the seeds I planted have come up & but one dahlia of the five which [my] Father put in the ground when he was here. . . . [O]n the 21st [June], the longest day of the year, thou tookst me out in the boat: We saw many green headed, orange throated frogs sprawled upon the water with their noses out, looking imperturbably grave. We saw an Iris too (Irises have just come) but could not pluck it with safety. I paddled a little to help thee when the tide & wind were strong against us.

[9 July] This is the anniversary of our wedding day. . . . It is the loveliest weather & the moon is about full. What a sweet return of that happy hour. But I think that we of all persons make small account of dates & anniversaries & all outward marks of life. I doubt if ever there were lovers who thought less of gifts & visible tokens of united spirits. It is because we trulyest love & therefore live in the spirit & need no appurtenances to testify perfect accord. We have been in the free ranges of Eternity ever since we first recognized each other & Time is beneath our feet. How can we bestow anything upon each other when we are an indivisible soul? What note should we take of set times and seasons when there are no such measures in Eternity, but only successions of States. Our state is now one of far deeper felicity than last 9th of July. Then we had visions & dreamed of Paradise—Now Paradise is here & our fairest visions stand realized before us. . . . I have not felt very well for two weeks; but it is the very poetry of discomfort, for I rejoice at every smallest proof that I am as ladies wish to be who love their lords—& thou are so tender & indulgent to all my whims & moans & thou dost look so radiant with satisfaction & content, that I feel as if I could bear joyfully any amount of pain or unease for thy sake. Thou never wast so sweet & lovely as now—So I think

[48]

as the days pass & so beautiful! Now as thou sittest before me I think thou art of peerless beauty—Ah may our little dovelet look like thee!

. . . Every beautiful morning I have felt a sense of suffocation when Thou hast shut thyself into this study to toil & spin intellectual yarn for the benefit of nations. Yet beloved, I cannot quite regret that there is some necessity for thee to write sometime because so much wealth of wisdom & delicate reprehension of folly & wrong would be lost to the world, wert thou quite silent. . . .

[29 August] . . . Sweetest love, I recieved thy dearest letter yesterday morning & there art no words to express my joy. Thou wast best & tenderest to write so soon. Thou didst know that though I resigned thee pretty heroically, & smiled at the last, that my heart was divided & bereaved by thy absence[.] . . . Over & over & over again I read the beloved words. . . . I wonder I am not wholly transfigured by such deep & heavenly love. My soul *is* transfigured & has been ever since thou first toldest me that I was dearer to thee than all else. I am happy beyond the reach of circumstance for this reason. This makes me laugh at all kind of outward mishaps. They cannot invade me, for I am bulwarked & sheilded by the consciousness of thy precious love. . . .

I am glad thou wilt stay till Saturday for thy sake. I trust thou wilt bring me many tales of the sea when thou comest. Oh thou will feel so well & refreshed. My pulses bound to think of it. . . . After dinner Ellery Channing came to talk with me about Mr Allston[,] . . . stayed a great time & was very agreeable. . . . A shabby gentleman came just now for the boat. I never saw such a strange man. He was either crazy, drunk or a knave—His face prevented all confidence & his manner equally—I do not know as we shall ever see our Water lily again. He was dressed in a worn black velvet frock coat[.] He made me shudder.

[30 August] Best beloved—The hero of the velvet coat brought back the boat safely . . . so that whatever else bad he may do, he does not steal boats. Sweetest, I love thee! What a heavenly lot it is to be loved through all height & depths, infinitely, by *thee*! . . . I feel the enchantment of thy loving more now than ever before. It can no more be worn than the face of the sun which for uncounted years has kindled the world with light every morning. This will outlast all suns & vivify us with life & warmth through vanishing eternities. We are far more comprehensively *lovers* than ever. . . . The word "forever" is much desecrated—

We know how to use it with sacred reverence[.] . . . Oh dearest it is true indeed that thou with thy gorgeous & profound nature art half my soul! my own husband forever.—

. . . After breakfast I arranged my flowers & solar lamp, & partly mended thy russia gown—Ellery Channing came to say Caroline Sturgis was at Mr Emersons & he wished to go out with her in the boat this afternoon. So he went to see whether it would do. He sat down awhile & talked of Mr Thoreaus fathers lead pencils, as being as good as the English & he wished they might be used instead. . . .

[1 September] Sweetest husband I sent thee a letter yesterday instead of writing here. . . . Ellery & Caroline did not come to go in the boat. . . . As I sat in the Hall, in the profound solitude & silence, I hear the apples drop one by one in the orchard—It was a sound of the fullness of time—I thought of Bryant

When the sound of falling nuts is heard.[1]

But above all, I thought of thee. No one was here & I wanted thee with my whole soul—

After tea I went to see Mrs Prescott & found only Miss Abby at home—We sat in the Hall in the evening without a light & "wholly destroyed—" as Mary said, with "muskitties." . . .

[19 November] This Indian summer is very beautiful[.] . . . This morning we watched the opal dawn & stars becoming pale before it, as also the old moon, which rose between five & six & in the form of a boat of pure silvery gold, floated up the sea of rosy air. Our bed now stands so that we can command a view of the eastern heaven & part of the avenue—I am so early a riser . . . but this morning I lay & watched the coming of the day with my lord.

. . . My dearest love is reading Shakespeare aloud to me this winter, & I can truly say I never had an idea of it before. As made apparent by his voice, it is a magnificent gallery of pictures, illustrated by noble sentiments. . . . Can there be a happier life? The rich intellectual feasts, & the perpetual joy of this new hope in my bosom for both of us, & the . . . penetrating love which makes illustrious every moment, & the quiet of Eternity & its permanence superadded. . . . [M]y reality has proved wholly ideal & will ever, for the sacredness, the loftiness, the etherial delicacy of such a soul as my husbands, will keep Heaven about us through the long blue vistas of futurity. My thought does not yet compass him. He rises upon me daily like a new sun. It is so refreshing to find one person without theories of any kind, without party or sectarian tendency, free from earthly clogs, & floating like a star on its own way, without rule except Gods hand. This is one secret of his perennial charm & newness. He lives, transparent to Heaven & pure Thought, & can Thought be exhausted? He does not meddle with Truth & it lays upon him like the blessed sunshine, full & broad. No microscopes[,] no burning glasses, nor any of those impertinent littler dividers & dissectors nor large magnifiers disturb its serene wholeness & greatness. I hourly thank God that he is my husband—all nature in a man! . . .

[3 April 1844] A month ago to-day, our little daughter was born, at 1/4 past nine, one pleasant Sunday morning[.] . . . We were very glad to have her a spring-flower, blooming at the time of the coming of birds. . . . Our babys vigorous cries at the moment of birth told well for her strength, & the Doctor pronounced her a healthy, perfect child. In about two hours I first looked upon her, with emotions that a mother only can have—I was glad to see that she was . . . quite fair—. . . [T]he beauty of her hand was very uncommon from the first—with long, taper fingers, & exquisitely shaped nails—exactly like Endymions. I was very glad for this as she was a little lady. For a boy, it is not of consequence. She developed very fast & . . . her face had an expression of hope & trust. . . . [H]er cheeks round & her eyes larger & larger—They are dark blue & clear & bright, but I suppose they will change. I hoped they would be like her fathers, & I still hope they will, at least that they will have his long fine eyelashes, if not the depth & expression of his eyes. Her eyebrows seem not formed at all like his, but the brow is a little similar—. . . She promises to be of beautiful form & very graceful. . . .

[7 April] Baby is five weeks old today—Within two days her hair has grown perceptibly. . . . It is of a golden brown or auburn, & I trust will curl as her fathers & mothers did. Her brow grows more & more like her fathers, & Mrs Emerson, who came to see me on Friday *5th* said she resembled her father in all respects very much. It rejoiced my heart to hear her. Both she & Madam Emerson . . . thought her a fine babe. She grows fairer every moment & lovelier & her smile is very sweet. . . . It is beyond exception enchanting to watch her fulfilling. . . . Many months before she was born, we anticipated a daughter, & named her Una—. . . If she be like her father, as well in mind as face, she will be rightly named—of most delicate spirit, impatient of wrong & ugliness—demanding beauty of all things & persons—& like the "heavenly Una" of Spenser[.] . . .

[9 April] Yesterday morning I was waked as usual by Unas little sounds & I bent over her & said—"Darling baby!" She responded to my greeting by the sweetest smile immediately. . . . And now she begins to make conversations with musical tones—. . . I took her out in the avenue yesterday morning,—& she liked it very well. Two little girls, Mary Hosmer and Elizabeth Weir, came to see her & were greatly delighted. Mr & Mrs Alcott called in the afternoon & Mr Alcott thought her eyes were like mine—Mrs Alcott said she looked neither like her father nor mother nor any of the family, & was a remarkable looking child with her dark blue eyes & light hair—Afterwards she shocked me by saying she resembled a very ordinaryly faced lady[.] . . .

[8 May] On Mayday we had quite a splendid levee of Margaret, Sarah, Caroline, [and] Plato[.] . . . It was a truly poetic May-day, such as Margaret said she had never known in her life—Since Una was Queen of the May, should it not be a lovelier day than has been known within the memory of man? Sarah Clarke came first & Una was beautiful. She smiled & talked to her & Sarah was charmed with her appearance—& manners & so were all. . . . Mary Hosmer brought Una a little basket of wild flowers in the morning which she had gathered—But I cannot yet induce her to smile at flowers. . . . She will smile in the midst of some of her speeches as if it were a pleasant thought—She now smiles when she meets her fathers eyes, whether he speaks or not.

On the eve of the 3rd day of May . . . arrived her godfather, Count Louis O[']Sullivan—She was awake, & her father took her downstairs to see him. He was delighted with her, & she looked very lovely & tranquil. He brought her an exquisite silver cup, shaped like a lily-bell, with her name engraved upon it, & a Newfoundland dog, now in his baby hood, whose name is Leo. So the lady Una already has her Lion to guard her from all peril, & to crouch at her feet & kiss her lily white hand. . . . Her little soul shines brighter & brighter out of her eyes, & she often looks as if she would wing upwards through fulness & ecstasy of life. This morning I carried her to the looking glass & when she met her own glance . . . [s]he was well pleased—. . . Afterwards her father tried, but she would not meet her own eyes so fully—. . .

[24 September] I have had no time to record of the beautiful life of our child[.] . . . She is now nearly seven months old. Towards the last of May (21st) her grandmother came to see us & on the 24th, we all went to Boston . . . [where] our little Una was vastly admired & pronounced the most beautiful, majestic, queen like reposeful of babies—a picture—a statue—a born lady—a princess—a dream baby—a book baby—an ideal child—& every fine name that could be applied. . . .

. . . [W]e returned to Concord—. . . She was very quiet during the ride & Mrs Hoar, who was in the stage, said she looked as if she were meditating

Tales—to write some day. On the 3rd July . . . Sarah Clarke came to make a visit & upon the 9th, our wedding day, came Margaret Fuller. . . . She smiled upon Sarah the first glance. Being a discerner of spirits, she percieved at once the clear infinitude, truth fulness & simplicity of her nature—At Margaret she gazed with earnest & even frowning brow for a long time without recognizing her. Here she found a complex being, rich & magnificent but difficult to comprehend & of a peculiar kind, perhaps unique—But when Margaret next took her, after another examination she smiled approvingly & from that moment distinguished her by the gladdest welcomes whenever she appeared, & sat in her arms with full content by the hour—She detected at last her greatness & real sweetness & love & trusted in her wholly.

[25 January 1845] . . . We all went to Boston on the 14th November [1844]—& I took Una to Salem for ten days. Her Grandmother Hawthorne was entirely satisfied . . . & Aunt Ruth thought her charming—. . . We spent a few days with Aunt Pickman, & two or three with Mary Foote—Then Una & I returned to Boston & staid four weeks longer. She was prodigiously admired. . . . One pronounced her a very deep baby, because she has such a profound look with her eyes—Mr Frank Shaw said she was an angel of light[.] . . . But Ellen Hooper seemed fully to appreciate her surpassing loveliness. She said she had an ineffable expression & was a perfect gem—that she felt wholly satisfied when looking at her—& quoted Mr. Emersons essays where he speaks of knowing a god by the content one felt at looking upon him—

Note

1. Cf. William Cullen Bryant, "The Death of the Flowers," l. 21.

Patricia Dunlavy Valenti, "Sophia Peabody Hawthorne's *American Notebooks*," in *Studies in the American Renaissance 1996,* ed. Joel Myerson (Charlottesville: University Press of Virginia, 1996), 129–50.

[Reminiscences of a Childhood in Concord in the 1840s] (1891)

[Annie Sawyer Downs]

>)|(<

Born in Manchester, New Hampshire, before 1840, Annie Sawyer Downs (ca. 1836–1901) settled with her family in Concord, where they stayed until 1852, when they moved to Haverhill, Massachusetts. Downs's father, Dr. Benjamin Sawyer, practiced homeopathic medicine and occasionally treated Sophia Hawthorne and Lidian Emerson. Because Downs did not compose them until 1891, her reminiscences interweave distant childhood memories with facts and anecdotes that did not emerge until midcentury or later about relations among the Hawthornes, Margaret Fuller, the Alcotts, Henry Thoreau, and the Emersons. Like most nineteenth-century writers who commented on Concord's attraction, Downs states that its idyllic atmosphere made "heroic examples" out of the everyday lives of these figures, but she is more unguarded in her enthusiasm than most, exclaiming that the mere mention of the figures' names "bear[s] for me a conjuror's spell" (103). At times, however, Downs assumes the role of small-town gossip, as when she reports that "the Concord ladies" never appreciated Fuller's modernity or "fine sentiments," and quotes Thoreau's unmarried Aunt Maria's dismissal of Fuller's charm: "All bosh, my dear! . . . [W]hen a woman does not know herself what she wants to say, how can she expect anybody else to find out?" (97). Similarly, though she reports the apocryphal tale about an exchange between Emerson and Thoreau during Henry's famous night in jail—"Henry," asked Emerson, "why are you here?" "Waldo," replied Thoreau, "why are you not here?"—Downs says the community's sympathy was not with either of them but with Sam Staples, "the irate sheriff who declared in season and out . . . that 'he'd a let [Thoreau] stay until he got enough of it'" (100).

. . . [T]O THOSE ACQUAINTED with the circumstances, it does not appear surprising that so many remarkable persons were attracted to Concord, Massachusetts, between 1830 and 1880. The name of the town is itself significant of the character and aim of its founders. What appears to have been the most important factor in the fashioning of Concord character was the presence in the settlement from a very early period of an unusual number of books. The fact that there were so many books is probably due to the liberal education and easy circumstances of the founders, and the wide and constant use of the books themselves, to the sheltered situation of the town, and that it never offered any inducements to trade or manufacturers. Mr. Hawthorne used to say Concord character was like the Concord river,—so slow that even Henry Thoreau never was quite certain it had any current!

However that may be, it is undoubtedly true that there never has been in Concord any sympathy with the hurry, distraction, and never-ending whirl characterizing adjacent towns and cities. On the contrary, circumstances have always favored plain living, honest speech, and a singular quality of condition which may have existed in Utopia, but I know not where else.

And what more could be desired to render a beautiful village fit residence for poets, orators, and genius generally than ... proximity to Boston and Harvard College, an appreciative constituency, a history of two hundred years, and numerous woods, fields, and thickets wherein to roam at will? Only one thing more, that this paradise should be inexpensive, even cheap, which was exactly what it was when in 1835 Ralph Waldo Emerson made his home in the "Old Manse," which has been for more than a hundred years the harbor where the whole Emerson family have put in when they needed repairs in mind, body, or estate. . . .

But when I first remember the Old Manse, Mr. Hawthorne, not Mr. Emerson, was living in it. . . . Hawthorne's reason for coming to the Old Manse was very much what Emerson's had been. He was just married, had nothing to live on, and desired a cheap rent as well as congenial society for his wife, himself being not only indifferent but intolerant of society. Margaret Fuller, the Channings, George William Curtis, the Thoreaus . . . and Alcotts were names I oftenest heard when a child. Another family exercised perhaps even more direct influence upon our own household. . . . This was the family of Mr. Minot Pratt, who had been among the most enthusiastic and persevering of the Brook Farm community, and who when forced to acquiesce in its abandonment, continued to practice through a long life the self-denial and ascetic simplicity there demanded. . . .

Once a year the Pratts gave a picnic to which all Concord high and low, rich and poor, old and young, wise and foolish, trooped in a long procession. Probably the only time I ever saw Margaret Fuller was at one of these gatherings. She sat under a great tree with a little girl in her arms. Her long hair was loose and hung about her like a garment. As at that time it was very unusual to see flowing hair, it made a deep impression upon my mind.... [She] ... must have been a very noticeable figure in Concord society and I well remember hearing the village Doctor say he had just met Mr. Hawthorne who told him all the song-birds must be abroad that afternoon, for first he met Margaret Fuller and soon after Mr. Emerson, both in Sleepy Hollow! A little rustic seat used to indicate the spot where Mr. Hawthorne met these rare and delightful visitants....

A child has no chronology and many occurrences crowd my mind which may be synchronous and may be years apart. A glimpse of Hawthorne that I once enjoyed at his home in the Old Manse is, however, just as delightful as if capable of date and verification. I was sent to the Manse with a package of medicine for Mrs. Hawthorne and told to repeat exactly the minute directions I had received. I stood on tip-toe before the ancient door at the end of the long avenue of half-dead ash trees and just managed to reach the ponderous iron knocker. This knocker with the head of an Egyptian sphinx, I have since heard, is said to rise and fall three times when a death is to take place in the family, although at that time I knew nothing half so interesting about it. Mr. Hawthorne himself opened the door and I did my errand and delivered my message. Suddenly he said, "Wouldn't the Doctor's little girl like to see the new baby?" Of course the Doctor's little girl was eager to see anything which was new, and he led me up the aged stairs, then, asking me to wait a moment, disappeared through a partially opened door. Before long he reappeared with the tiniest morsel of humanity [Una] I had ever seen in his long, strong arms. He was singularly handsome, of great height, and corresponding breadth, and as he stood there with his raven hair and brilliant dark eyes, I was certain he looked exactly like Prince Charming who aroused the sleeping beauty in the enchanted forest....

Concord gossips of that day called Mrs. Hawthorne "homely, plain," but certainly her room was not. Being an artist she had done what, common enough now, was then very rare—painted her furniture herself. On the head of the bed she had copied Guido's Aurora and at its foot what she called one of Raphael's Hours, while on the wash-stand was Venus rising from the sea, and on the dressing table Correggio's Cupid. It was my first acquaintance with art, and instead of walking home, I appeared to be floating on the clouds.

Mr. Hawthorne cared little for Concord and I fancy at that time Concord returned the sentiment with usury. Mr. Emerson told me not long before his death that he never knew Mr. Hawthorne, but felt always as if there was an impassable gulf between them. Once determined to bridge it, he invited him to accompany him upon a long walking tour. When he left him at his own gate after several days' constant intercourse, he fancied he had succeeded. But the next time they met the gulf had opened wider than ever. They may have read each other's writings, although personally I recall no such statement on the part of Mr. Emerson, who indeed read very few of the books written by his contemporaries. . . .

Hawthorne was the least known, least accessible of all the Concord notables. He passed whole days on the river in a rough boat he bought of Henry Thoreau and called the [Water] Lily, went to the post office after dark through woods and fields instead of along the street and as if he dreaded salutation from the moon and stars, muffled himself in an old broadcloth cloak whose rusty black velvet collar completely covered the lower part of his face. Unlike Mr. Emerson he read everything. The librarian of the Concord Athenaeum said he changed his books every evening and after asking for this and for that, would say, "Never mind, just give me another volume of the *Spectator*."

But Concord and Concord conditions must have made a deep impression upon his mind, for persons as well known as its minister and its doctor are immortalized upon his pages. From Brook Farm he drew many incidents as well as the setting of *The Blithedale Romance,* but the tragic though fitting ending of Zenobia was incident for incident a Concord occurrence. Not far from the "Old Manse" lived Miss Martha Hunt, the daughter of a farmer. The family, a little outside the village circle, and somewhat straitened in money matters, were of unquestioned respectability and innate refinement. This daughter, under twenty, became interested in Margaret Fuller, the Channings and Emersons, while they in turn lent her books and endeavored to brighten her somewhat monotonous life. But she became discouraged and one summer morning walked down to the Concord river and ended her misery in its sluggish bosom.

Hawthorne took the "[Water] Lily" and, accompanied by Ellery Channing, assisted the other neighbors in looking for her body. After hours of search they found her just as Miles Coverdale, by which name Hawthorne was often called, and Hollingsworth, always supposed to be Ellery Channing, discovered Zenobia. I have been told, for this happened before my day, that Martha Hunt's death cast a shadow upon the Concord philosophy which time alone dispelled. It was said, despairing of reconciling its fascinating ideals with the sombre realities of life, she sought in suicide relief from struggle.

In after years when a sister of Martha Hunt's, only a baby at the time of her death, committed suicide at the same place and hour, and in almost exactly the same manner, it was acknowledged that the taint must have been in the blood and not in the Concord philosophy.

When the owners of the "Old Manse" . . . wished to occupy it themselves, Mr. and Mrs. Hawthorne returned to Salem. But Mr. Hawthorne had lived there long enough to double its fame, for in the same upper chamber where Mr. Emerson had written "Nature" he wrote *Mosses from an Old Manse*. When he came back with his family to Concord, he bought of Mr. Alcott the house now known as "The Wayside" . . . below Mr. Emerson's on the Boston road. Our family left Concord while the Hawthornes were away and I remember "The Wayside" only as the home of the Alcotts. I saw Mr. and Mrs. Hawthorne at a summer fete on the Concord river after their return from Europe when praises of *The Marble Faun* were in everybody's mouth. Many old acquaintances present that afternoon remarked the great change which had taken place in the personal appearance of both Mr. and Mrs. Hawthorne. When they left America Mr. Hawthorne's hair was black as night, while Mrs. Hawthorne's was the tawny red which Titian loved. At the festivity in Concord both their heads were silver white!

Mr. Hawthorne had a great dread of living to be old. It is a Concord tale that he said to Miss Elizabeth Peabody, his sister-in-law, "A man ought never to live beyond sixty." "But Nathaniel, how can a man help it? A man must live out his days." For answer he looked steadily out of the window and after a long silence said under his breath, "A man's days are in a man's hands." The answer was remembered when without warning he died at sixty.

Another Concord story is that, for . . . months before his death [in 1864], whenever he tried a pen or made a mark idly with pencil he wrote 1864, which he told some friend he had always written unconsciously whenever the thought of his own death passed through his mind.

Still another Concord tale is that he requested his family not to look upon his face after death, and Mrs. Hawthorne, whose will throughout their mutual life seems to have been entirely lost in his, was so afraid her yearning to see him once more would prevail that she dared not allow his body to be brought home, but desired that it might remain in the church until the funeral.

Annie Sawyer Downs, "Mr. Hawthorne, Mr. Thoreau, Miss Alcott, Mr. Emerson, and Me," ed. Walter Harding, *American Heritage* 30 (December 1978): 95–99.

[On First Meeting Hawthorne in America, 1852]

[Henry Arthur Bright]

-)|(-

Hawthorne credited Henry Arthur Bright (1830–1884), a businessman and man of letters from Liverpool, and Francis Bennoch as the two best friends he made in England. The year before Hawthorne's appointment as U.S. consul to Liverpool and Manchester, Bright, accompanied by his Cambridge (UK) friend, Thomas Burder, spent five months in America, in part as a representative of Gibbs, Bright, and Company, his father's shipping firm, but mostly as a tourist. Bright's travels took him up and down the eastern seaboard, west to the Ohio and Mississippi Rivers, and north to Quebec and Montreal. As he would say for the rest of his life—but especially after renewing acquaintances with him in England in 1853—the highpoint of his travels was the opportunity to meet Hawthorne in Concord. Armed with a letter of introduction to Hawthorne from Longfellow, Bright and his companion first called on Emerson, who on Saturday, 25 September 1852 walked them over to the Wayside, where they met Hawthorne.

The amount of attention Bright devotes to Emerson throughout his travel diary suggests that he, rather than Hawthorne, had been the real object of his visit to Concord. As Bright's narrative unfolds, it seems clear that Longfellow and Thomas Gold Appleton had forewarned him about some of the characters he would meet there, especially Bronson Alcott. Here, Alcott is referred to as "Emerson's 'Skimpole Plato'" (397), a label—based on a character in Charles Dickens's *Bleak House* who hides his innate selfishness under the guise of childishness—that was given to him by Longfellow's wife, Fanny. As characterized by Bright, Hawthorne's embarrassment over his exchange with Fredrika Bremer was undoubtedly genuine, not only because the exchange had obviously become a subject of local gossip, but also because the gossip was true. In the selection that follows next in this volume, Bremer reports her frustration at being unable to engage Hawthorne in a meaningful conversation when she called on him in Lenox in September 1850.

ON THURSDAY [23 SEPTEMBER 1852] at twelve we three started for Concord to see Emerson and Hawthorne. We got there in about an hour. It was a beautiful day, and I felt in particular good spirits and health. It was a bright early Autumn day, a light fresh wind played among the trees and blew away a leaf here and there, and reddened the tints on the maples and the oaks, as we walked along the broad lanes of Concord. Like an English village is the Concord of Massachusetts and of Emerson. Huge trees stand singly out between the footpath and the road, and most of all the drooping elms bend over us as we pass. White houses with gardens before them are on each side of the way. A little girl with straw hat and clever face, and school book under her arm is standing on our track, and we ask her where Emerson is living. "Watch," she replied, "keep down the road and past the meeting house, and when you've turned to the right you'll see his house amidst a grove of pines."

There it is! the door is standing wide open, and the girl who answers our bell shows us into his study. The study is surrounded with well-filled and badly arranged book-cases, the table is covered with well read and badly bound books. Over the chimney-piece is a picture of the Three Fates, in an open drawer is a collection of ripening pears.

But here is Emerson;—a tall, thin, angular figure, with quiet gentlemanly manner, unaffected look and pleasant voice. He's by no means awful or incomprehensible. . . . We walked in his garden with him; he is interested in pear-trees and pumpkins, and told us of one of the early settlers who asserted that "in America God Almighty feeds His people with pumpkins."

He took us to see Hawthorne, and as we went along, talked pleasantly all the way. Hawthorne's house is an old one—100 years old—and a hill rises pleasantly behind it. Hawthorne leads an almost hermit life; he's a strange man, so shy and retiring that he is rarely seen, and hardly speaks when he is seen. He is so gentle and mild that you feel as if speaking to a girl, said Emerson, when speaking to him. "Yet there is a pang of bitterness which is most plainly visible in everything he writes. Sometimes too, he comes out with truths which show so great a worldly knowledge, that involuntarily you say, where did the man learn all this."

Here however is Hawthorne—a man with an eye so black and piercing you shrink away as he fixes it steadily upon you, with a brow so grand and massive, that had you not seen Webster you'd say it was the most wonderful you ever saw; yet with awkward gait and manner, and a shyness which oppresses you as much as himself, yet he asks us in, and talks slightly in answer to questions and so forth. Emerson does most of the conversation, and we go deeply into the mysteries of the heathen and Christian Socialism. When we rise to go, Hawthorne promises Emerson to join us at dinner at four, and we bid him goodbye. E[merson] and B[urder] had already left the garden when the hermit novelist asked us to come and see his view from the hill, and an old summer-house built by a man called Alcott, a man Longfellow told me of, as Emerson's "Skimpole Plato," and the man whom Carlyle abused to Tom Appleton [as] . . . "The man who came here with his potatoe gospel, and at last I said to him, 'Sir, I'd rather talk to any old woman, or child, or lunatic, or donkey than to you, let us never meet again,' and he replied, 'Mr. Carlyle, you've exactly expressed my sentiments with regard to you.' And so we parted."

Back to the arbour in Hawthorne's garden. It is now tumbling to decay, but he seems very fond of it, and told us he would not have it touched. It commands a good view, and from the hill top is a better view still. Hawthorne tells me he likes it better than his view at Lenox—"that mountain scenery was stereotyped in my mind, this never wearies me." He spoke of England, and how he longed to see it, and how deeply he and all New Englanders felt towards it. The asters were growing all over the hill top. . . .

Hawthorne arrived [for dinner at Emerson's], and seemed in decent spirits and all right. Unluckily, a moment or two before dinner Emerson maliciously said "I hear Hawthorne that Miss Bremer makes honourable mention of you." "Where?" asked Hawthorne; Emerson appealed to Burder who had mentioned to Emerson the story I had told him about Miss Bremer: Burder threw the onus of it all on me, and I had to blurt out that I didn't know that anything was printed, Miss B. had mentioned Mr. H. in private conversation. "My interview with Miss Bremer was not a very successful one," said Hawthorne, and, dinner being announced, he said he could not stay, and vanished, to my annoyance and Emerson's amusement.

Before dismissing Hawthorne, I must mention his children,—a long-haired red-haired Una, and a beautiful glorious boy called Julian. Hawthorne is a democrat and will be promoted by his friend Pierce, perhaps (as T. Appleton says) "as Minister to some aesthetic Court."

[Henry Arthur Bright, On First Meeting Hawthorne in America, 1852], in *Happy Country This America: The Travel Diary of Henry Arthur Bright,* ed. Anne Henry Ehrenpreis (Columbus: Ohio State University Press, 1978), 395–400.

From *The Homes of the New World;*
Impressions of America (1853)

FREDRIKA BREMER

>-)|(-

Born in Finland, the popular novelist and travel writer Fredrika Bremer (1801–
1865) spent most of her life in Sweden. Mingling Old World prejudices with extensive firsthand commentary on American culture at midcentury, her *Homes
of the New World; Impressions of America* ranks among the best produced in
the genre during this period. Based upon Bremer's visit to America in the late
1840s and early 1850s during which she had access to leading literary and intellectual figures of the day, *Homes of the New World* appealed to both European
and American readers and provided American writers with an introduction to
audiences abroad. Although Bremer writes at length about the literary figures
she encountered, the following account of her evening visit to Hawthorne in
Lenox in September 1850 is noteworthy for both its brevity and the contrast she
creates between that visit and the enjoyable full day she had spent earlier in
the company of Catharine Maria Sedgwick and the accomplished women who
gathered around her. As the preceding reminiscence by Bright indicates, Hawthorne was embarrassed by the awkward quiet of his meeting with Bremer,
which had become the stuff of Boston gossip even before her book appeared
in print.

THE COUNTRY AROUND LENOX is romantically lovely, inspired with wood-
covered hills, and the prettiest little lakes. Amid this scenery have Catharine
Sedgwick and Nathaniel Hawthorne their rural homes. I had been invited
to both. . . . I spent four-and-twenty hours with the excellent and amiable
Catharine Sedgwick and her family, enjoying her company and that of several
agreeable ladies. There were no gentlemen—gentlemen, indeed, seemed to
be rare in social circles of this neighborhood. But they were less missed here
than is generally the case in society, because the women of this little circle are
possessed of unusual intellectual cultivation—several of them endowed with
genius and talent of a high order. Fanny Kemble has her home here when
she resides in America; at the present time she is in England. The scenery is

beautiful; these ladies enjoy it and each other's society, and life lacks nothing to the greater number.

I am, in a general way, struck with the number of ladies, and the scarcity of gentlemen in the homes of the lesser cities in the Eastern States. The gentlemen run over to the larger cities, or to the Great West, to carry on business, to construct rail-ways, or to acquire wealth in one way or another. . . .

I spent an extremely agreeable day with Miss Sedgwick, and one evening with Hawthorne, in an endeavor in converse. But, whether it was his fault or mine, I can not say, but it did not succeed. I had to talk by myself, and at length became quite dejected, and felt I know not how. Nevertheless, Hawthorne was evidently kind, and wished to make me comfortable—but we could not get on together in conversation. It was, however, a pleasure to me to see his beautiful, significant, though not perfectly harmonious head. The forehead is capacious and serene as the arch of heaven, and a thick mass of soft dark brown hair beautifully clustered around it; the fine, deep-set eyes glance from beneath well-arched eyebrows like the dark but clear lakes of the neighborhood, lying in the sombre bosom of mountain and forest; the nose is refined and regular in form; the smile, like that of the sun smiling over the summer woods; nevertheless, it has a bitter expression. The whole upper part of the countenance is classically beautiful, but the lower part does not perfectly correspond, and is deficient in decided character.

Immediately in front of Hawthorne's house lies one of those small clear lakes, with its sombre margin of forest, which characterize this district, and Hawthorne seems greatly to enjoy the view of it, and the wildly wooded country. His amiable wife is inexpressibly happy to see him so happy here. A smile, a word from him conveys more to her than long speeches from other people. She reads his very soul, and—"he is the best of husbands." Rose, the youngest child, is still on the mother's breast. Hawthorne's house is a happy, quiet little abode, embracing a beautiful family life.

From *The Homes of the New World; Impressions of America,* trans. Mary Howitt, 2 vols. (New York: Harper & Brothers, 1853), 2:596–97.

"Hawthorne" (1853)

GEORGE WILLIAM CURTIS

>|<

A prolific author, travel writer, critic, and political journalist, George William Curtis (1824–1892) knew most of the major figures associated with New England Transcendentalism and was particularly taken with Emerson. Curtis and his brother James Burrill Curtis joined the Brook Farm community in 1842 and lived there as boarders for nearly a year and a half. Following a brief stint in New York, Curtis joined his brother in Concord in 1844, where they stayed with a farmer's family for most of the next two years. He spent from 1846 to 1850 abroad, living in Europe, Egypt, and Syria. On his return to America, Curtis became one of the editors of *Putnam's Monthly Magazine* when it began in 1852, and the following year he inaugurated a series of columns known as the "Editor's Easy Chair" for *Harper's New Monthly Magazine*, which he continued for many years.

The sketch that follows, which was quite influential in shaping Hawthorne's personal reputation in the nineteenth century, is discussed at length in the introduction to this volume.

HAWTHORNE HAS HIMSELF DRAWN the picture of the "Old Manse" in Concord. He has given to it that quiet richness of coloring which ideally belongs to an old country mansion. It seems so fitting a residence for one who loves to explore the twilight of antiquity—and the gloomier the better—that the visitor, among the felicities of whose life was included the freedom of the Manse, could not but fancy that our author's eyes first saw the daylight enchanted by the slumberous orchard behind the house, or tranquillized into twilight by the spacious avenue in front. The character of his imagination, and the golden gloom of its blossoming, completely harmonize with the rusty, gable-roofed old house upon the river side, and the reader of his books would be sure that his boyhood and youth knew no other friends than the dreaming river, and the melancholy meadows and drooping foliage of its vicinity.

Since the reader, however, would greatly mistake if he fancied this, in good sooth, the ancestral halls of the Hawthornes,—the genuine Hawthornden,—he will be glad to save the credit of his fancy by knowing that it was here our author's bridal tour,—which commenced in Boston, then three hours away,—ended, and his married life began. Here, also, his first child was born, and here those sad and silver mosses accumulated upon his fancy, from which he heaped so soft a bed for our dreaming. "Between two tall gate-posts of rough hewn stone (the gate itself having fallen from its hinges at some unknown epoch) we beheld the gray front of the old parsonage, terminating the vista of an avenue of black ash trees." It was a pleasant spring day in the year 1842, and as they entered the house, nosegays of fresh flowers, arranged by friendly hands, welcomed them to Concord and summer.

The dark-haired man, who led his wife along the avenue that afternoon, had been recently an officer of the customs in Boston, before which he had led a solitary life in Salem. Graduated with Longfellow at Bowdoin College, in Maine, he had lived a hermit in respectable Salem, an absolute recluse even from his own family, walking out by night and writing wild tales by day, most of which were burnt in his bachelor fire, and some of which, in newspapers, magazines, and annuals, led a wandering, uncertain, and mostly unnoticed life. Those tales, among this class, which were attainable, he collected into a small volume, and apprising the world that they were "twice-told," sent them forth anew to make their own way, in the year 1837. But he piped to the world, and it did not dance. He wept to it, and it did not mourn. The book, however, as all good books do, made its way into various hearts. Yet the few penetrant minds which recognized a remarkable power and a method of strange fascination in the stories, did not make the public, nor influence the public mind. "I was," he says in the last edition of these tales, "the most unknown author in America." Full of glancing wit, of tender satire, of exquisite natural deception, of subtle and strange analysis of human life, darkly passionate and weird, they yet floated unhailed barques upon the sea of publicity,—unhailed, but laden and gleaming at every crevice with the true treasure of Cathay.

Bancroft, then Collector in Boston, prompt to recognize and to honor talent, made the dreaming story-teller a surveyor in the custom-house, thus opening to him a new range of experience. From the society of phantoms he stepped upon Long Wharf and plumply confronted Captain Cuttle and Dirck Hatteraick. It was no less romance to our author. There is no greater error of those who are called "practical men," than the supposition that life is, or can be, other than a dream to a dreamer. Shut him up in a counting-room, barricade him with bales of merchandise and limit his library to the leger and cashbook, and his prospect to the neighboring signs; talk "Bills receivable" and

"Sundries Dr. to Cash" to him forever, and you are only a very amusing or very annoying phantom to him. The merchant prince might as well hope to make himself a poet, as the poet a practical or practicable man. He has laws to obey not at all the less stringent because men of a different temperament refuse to acknowledge them, and he is held to a loyalty quite beyond their conceptions.

So Captain Cuttle and Dirk Hatteraick were as pleasant figures to our author in the picture of life, as any others. He went daily upon the vessels, looked, and listened, and learned; was a favorite of the sailors, as such men always are,—did his work faithfully, and having dreamed his dream upon Long Wharf, was married and slipped up to the Old Manse, and a new chapter in the romance. It opened in "the most delightful little nook of a study that ever offered its snug seclusion to a scholar." Of the three years in the Old Manse the prelude to the *Mosses* is the most perfect history, and of the quality of those years the "Mosses" themselves are sufficient proof. They were mostly written in the little study, and originally published in the *Democratic Review,* then edited by Hawthorne's friend O'Sullivan.

To the inhabitants of Concord, however, our author was as much a phantom and a fable as the old Pastor of the parish, dead half a century before, and whose faded portrait in the attic was gradually rejoining its original in native dust. The gate, fallen from its hinges in a remote antiquity, was never re-hung. The wheel-track leading to the door remained still overgrown with grass. No bold villager ever invaded the sleep of the glimmering shadows in the avenue. At evening no lights gleamed from the windows. Scarce once in many months did the single old knobby-faced coachman at the railroad bring a fare to "Mr. Hawthorne's." "*Is* there anybody in the old house?" sobbed the old ladies in despair, imbibing tea of a livid green. The knocker, which everybody had enjoyed the right of lifting to summon the good old Pastor, no temerity now dared touch. Heavens! what if the figure in the mouldy portrait should peer, in answer, over the eaves, and shake solemnly his decaying surplice! Nay, what if the mysterious man himself should answer the summons and come to the door! It is easy to summon spirits,—but if they come? Collective Concord, mowing in the river meadows, embraced the better part of valor and left the knocker untouched. A cloud of romance suddenly fell out of the heaven of fancy and enveloped the Old Manse:

> In among the bearded barley
> The reaper reaping late and early [1]

did not glance more wistfully toward the island of Shalott and its mysterious lady than the reapers of Concord rye looked at the Old Manse and wondered over its inmate.

Sometimes, in the forenoon, a darkly clad figure was seen in the little garden plot putting in corn or melon seed, and gravely hoeing. It was a brief apparition. The farmer passing toward town and seeing the solitary cultivator, lost his faith in the fact and believed he had dreamed, when, upon returning, he saw no sign of life, except, possibly, upon some Monday, the ghostly skirt of a shirt flapping spectrally in the distant orchard. Day dawned and darkened over the lonely house. Summer with "buds and bird-voices" came singing in from the South, and clad the old ash trees in deeper green, the Old Manse, in profounder mystery. Gorgeous autumn came to visit the story-teller in his little western study, and departing, wept rainbows among his trees. Winter impatiently swept down the hill opposite, rifling the trees of each last clinging bit of Summer, as if thrusting aside opposing barriers and determined to search the mystery. But his white robes floated around the Old Manse, ghostly as the decaying surplice of the old Pastor's portrait, and in the snowy seclusion of Winter the mystery was as mysterious as ever.

Occasionally Emerson, or Ellery Channing, or Henry Thoreau,—some Poet, as once Whittier, journeying to the Merrimac, or an old Brook Farmer who remembered Miles Coverdale, with Arcadian sympathy,—went down the avenue and disappeared in the house. Sometimes a close observer, had he been ambushed among the long grasses of the orchard, might have seen the host and one of his guests emerging at the back door, and sauntering to the river-side, step into the boat, and float off until they faded in the shadow. The spectacle would not have lessened the romance. If it were afternoon,— one of the spectrally sunny afternoons which often bewitch that region,—he would be only the more convinced that there was something inexplicable in the whole matter of this man whom nobody knew, who was never once seen at town-meeting, and concerning whom it was whispered that he did not constantly attend church all day, although he occupied the reverend parsonage of the village, and had unmeasured acres of manuscript sermons in his attic, beside the nearly extinct portrait of an utterly extinct clergyman. Mrs. Radcliffe and Monk Lewis were nothing to this; and the awe-stricken observer, if he could creep safely out of the long grass, he did not fail to do so quietly, fortifying his courage by remembering stories of the genial humanity of the last old Pastor who inhabited the Manse, and who for fifty years was the bland and beneficent Pope of Concord. A genial, gracious old man, whose memory is yet sweet in the village, and who, wedded to the grave traditions of New England theology, believed of his young relative, Waldo Emerson, as Miss Flite, touching her forehead, said of her landlord, that he was "—M—quite—M—," but was proud to love in him the hereditary integrity of noble ancestors.

This old gentleman,—an eminent figure in the history of the Manse, and in all reminiscences of Concord,—partook sufficiently of mundane weaknesses to betray his mortality. Hawthorne describes him watching the battle of Concord, from his study window. But when the uncertainty of that dark moment had so happily resulted, and the first battle-ground of the Revolution had become a spot of hallowed and patriotic consideration, it was a pardonable pride in the good old man to order his servant, whenever there was company, to assist him in reaping the glory due to the owner of a spot so sacred. Accordingly, when some reverend or distinguished guest sat with the Pastor in his little parlor, or, of a summer evening, at the hospitable door under the trees, Jeremiah or Nicodemus, the cow-boy, would deferentially approach and inquire:

> "Into what pasture shall I turn the cow to-night, Sir?"
> And the old gentleman would audibly reply:
> "Into the battle-field, Nicodemus, into the battle-field!"

Then naturally followed wonder, inquiry, a walk in the twilight to the riverbank, the old gentleman's story, the corresponding respect of the listening visitor, and the consequent quiet complacency and harmless satisfaction in the clergyman's bosom. That throb of pride was the one drop of peculiar advantage which the Pastor distilled from the revolution. He could not but fancy that he had a hand in so famous a deed accomplished upon land now his own, and demeaned himself, accordingly, with continental dignity.

The pulpit, however, was his especial sphere. There he reigned supreme; there he exhorted, rebuked, and advised, as in the days of Mather. There he inspired that profound reverence, of which he was so proud, and which induced the matrons of the village, when he was coming to make a visit, to bedizen the children in their Sunday suits, to parade the best tea-pot, and to offer the most capacious chair. In the pulpit he delivered everything with the pompous cadence of the elder New England clergy, and a sly joke is told at the expense of his even temper, that on one occasion, when loftily reading the hymn, he encountered a blot upon the page quite obliterating the word, but without losing the cadence, although in a very vindictive tone at the truant word, or the culprit who erased it,—he finished the reading as follows:

> He sits upon the throne above,
>   Attending angels bless.
> While Justice, Mercy, Truth, and—(another word which is blotted out)
>   Compose his princely dress.

We linger around the old Manse and its occupants as fondly as Hawthorne, but no more fondly than all who have been once within the influence of its spell. There glimmers in my memory a few hazy days, of a tranquil and half-pensive character, which I am conscious were passed in and around the house, and their pensiveness I know to be only that touch of twilight which inhered in the house and its associations. Beside the few chance visitors I have named, there were city friends, occasionally, figures quite unknown to the village, who came preceded by the steam-shriek of the locomotive, were dropped at the gate-posts, and were seen no more. The owner was as much a vague name to me as anyone.

During Hawthorne's first year's residence in Concord, I had driven up with some friends to an aesthetic tea at Mr. Emerson's. It was in the winter and a great wood-fire blazed upon the hospitable hearth. There were various men and women of note assembled, and I, who listened attentively to all the fine things that were said, was for some time scarcely aware of a man who sat upon the edge of the circle, a little withdrawn, his head slightly thrown forward upon his breast, and his bright eyes clearly burning under his black brow. As I drifted down the stream of talk, this person, who sat silent as a shadow, looked to me, as Webster might have looked had he been a poet,—a kind of poetic Webster. He rose and walked to the window, and stood quietly there for a long time, watching the dead white landscape. No appeal was made to him, nobody looked after him, the conversation flowed steadily on as if everyone understood that his silence was to be respected. It was the same thing at table. In vain the silent man imbibed aesthetic tea. Whatever fancies it inspired did not flower at his lips. But there was a light in his eye which assured me that nothing was lost. So supreme was his silence that it presently engrossed me to the exclusion of everything else. There was very brilliant discourse, but this silence was much more poetic and fascinating. Fine things were said by the philosophers, but much finer things were implied by the dumbness of this gentleman with heavy brows and black hair. When he presently rose and went, Emerson, with the "slow, wise smile" that breaks over his face like day over the sky, said: "Hawthorne rides well his horse of the night."

Thus he remained in my memory, a shadow, a phantom, until more than a year afterward. Then I came to live in Concord. Every day I passed his house, but when the villagers, thinking that perhaps I had some clue to the mystery, said: "Do you know this Mr. Hawthorne?" I said: "No," and trusted to Time.

Time justified my confidence and one day I, too, went down the avenue, and disappeared in the house. I mounted those mysterious stairs to that apocryphal study. I saw "the cheerful coat of paint, and golden-tinted paper-hangings, lighting up the small apartment; while the shadow of a willow tree, that swept against the overhanging eaves, atempered the cheery western sunshine." I looked from the little northern window whence the old Pastor watched the battle, and in the small dining-room beneath it, upon the first floor there were "Dainty chicken, snow-white bread," and the golden juices of Italian vineyards, which still feast insatiable memory.

Our author occupied the Old Manse for three years. During that time he was not seen probably, by more than a dozen of the villagers. His walks could easily avoid the town, and upon the river he was always sure of solitude. It was his favorite habit to bathe every evening in the river, after nightfall, and in that part of it over which the old bridge stood, at which the battle was fought. Sometimes, but rarely, his boat accompanied another up the stream, and I recall the silent and preternatural vigor with which, on one occasion, he wielded his paddle to counteract the bad rowing of a friend who conscientiously considered it his duty to do something and not let Hawthorne work alone; but who, with every stroke, neutralized all Hawthorne's efforts. I suppose he would have struggled until he fell senseless rather than ask his friend to desist. His principle seemed to be, if a man cannot understand without talking to him, it is quite useless to talk, because it is immaterial whether such a man understands or not. His own sympathy was so broad and sure, that although nothing had been said for hours, his companion knew that not a thing had escaped his eye, nor had a single pulse of beauty in the day, or scene, or society, failed to thrill his heart. In this way his silence was most social. Everything seemed to have been said. It was a Barmecide feast of discourse, from which a greater satisfaction resulted than from an actual banquet.

When a formal attempt was made to desert this style of conversation, the result was ludicrous. Once Emerson and Thoreau arrived to pay a call. They were shown into the little parlor upon the avenue, and Hawthorne presently entered. Each of the guests sat upright in his chair like a Roman senator; to them, Hawthorne, like a Dacian king. The call went on, but in a most melancholy manner. The host sat perfectly still, or occasionally propounded a question which Thoreau answered accurately, and there the thread broke short off. Emerson delivered sentences that only needed the setting of an essay to charm the world; but the whole visit was a vague ghost of the Monday Evening Club at Mr. Emerson's,—it was a great failure. Had they all been lying idly upon the river brink, or strolling in Thoreau's blackberry pastures, the result would have been utterly different. But imprisoned in the proprieties of a parlor, each a wild man in his way, with a necessity of talking inherent in the nature of the occasion, there was only a waste of treasure. This was the only "call" in which I ever knew Hawthorne to be involved.

In Mr. Emerson's house, I said it seemed always morning. But Hawthorne's black-ash trees and scraggy apple-boughs shaded "A land in which it seemed always afternoon."[2] I do not doubt that the lotus grew along the grassy marge of the Concord [River] behind his house, and that it was served, subtly concealed, to all his guests. The house, its inmates, and its life, lay, dream-like, upon the edge of the little village. You fancied that they all came together, and were glad that at length some idol of your imagination, some poet whose spell had held you, and would hold you, forever, was housed as such a poet should be.

During the lapse of the three years since the bridal tour of twenty miles ended at the "two tall gate-posts of rough hewn stone," a little wicker wagon had appeared at intervals upon the avenue, and a placid babe, whose eyes the soft Concord day had touched with the blue of its beauty, lay looking tranquilly up at the grave old trees, which sighed lofty lullabies over her sleep. The tranquility of the golden-haired Una was the living and breathing type of the dreamy life of the old Manse. Perhaps, that being attained, it was as well to go. Perhaps our author was not surprised nor displeased when the hints came, "growing more and more distinct, that the owner of the old house was pining for his native air." One afternoon I entered the study, and learned from its occupant that the last story he should ever write there was written. The son of the old pastor yearned for his homestead. The light of another summer would seek its poet in the Old Manse, but in vain.

While Hawthorne had been quietly writing in the "most delightful nook of a study," Mr. Polk had been elected President, and Mr. Bancroft in the Cabinet did not forget his old friend the surveyor in the custom-house. There came suggestions and offers of various attractions. Still loving New England, would he tarry there, or, as inspector of woods and forests in some far-away island of the Southern Sea, some hazy strip of distance seen from Florida, would he taste the tropics? He meditated all the chances, without immediately deciding. Gathering up his household gods, he passed out of the Old Manse as its heir entered, and before the end of summer was domesticated in the custom-house of his native town of Salem. This was in the year 1845.

Upon leaving the Old Manse he published the *Mosses,* announcing that it was the last collection of tales he should put forth. Those who knew him and recognized his value to our literature, trembled lest this was the last word from one who spoke only pearls and rubies. It was a foolish fear. The sun must shine—the sea must roll—the bird must sing, and the poet write. During his life in Salem, of which the introduction to the *Scarlet Letter* describes the official aspect, he wrote that romance. It is inspired by the spirit of the place. It presents more vividly than any history the gloomy picturesqueness of early New England life. There is no strain in our literature so characteristic or more real than that which Hawthorne had successfully attempted in several of his earlier sketches, and of which the *Scarlet Letter* is the great triumph. It became immediately popular, and directly placed the writer of stories for a small circle among the world's masters of romance.

Times meanwhile changed, and Presidents with them. General Tyler was elected, and the Salem Collector retired. It is one of the romantic points of Hawthorne's quiet life, that its changes have been so frequently determined by political events, which, of all others, are the most entirely foreign to his tastes and habits. He retired to the hills of Berkshire, the eye of the world now regarding his movements. There he lived a year or two in a little red cottage upon the "Stockbridge Bowl," as a small lake near that town is called. In this retreat he wrote the *House of the Seven Gables,* which more deeply confirmed the literary position already acquired for him by the first romance. The scene is laid in Salem, as if he could not escape a strange fascination in the witch-haunted town of our early history. It is the same black canvas upon which plays the rainbow-flash of his fancy, never, in its brightest moment, more than illuminating the gloom. This marks all his writings. They have a terrible beauty, like the Siren, and their fascination is sure. After six years of absence, Hawthorne has returned to Concord, where he has purchased a small house formerly occupied by Orphic Alcott. When that philosopher came into possession, it was a miserable house of two peaked gables. But the genius which recreated itself in devising graceful summer-houses, like that for Mr. Emerson, . . . soon smoothed the new residence into some kind of comeliness. It was an old house when Mr. Alcott entered it, but his tasteful finger touched it with picturesque grace. Not like a tired old drudge of a house, rusting into unhonored decay, but with a modest freshness that does not belie the innate sobriety of a venerable New England farm-house, the present residence of our author stands withdrawn a few yards from the high road to Boston, along which marched the British soldiers to Concord bridge. It lies at the foot of a wooded hill, a neat house of a "rusty olive hue," with a porch in front, and a central peak and a piazza at each end. The genius for summer-houses has had full play upon the hill behind. Here, upon the homely steppes of Concord, is a strain of Persia. Mr. Alcott built terraces, and arbors, and pavilions, of boughs and rough stems of trees, revealing—somewhat inadequately, perhaps—the hanging gardens of delight that adorn the Babylon of his Orphic imagination. The hill-side is no unapt emblem of his intellectual habit, which garnishes the arid commonplaces of life with a cold poetic aurora, forgetting that it is the inexorable law of light to deform as well as adorn. Treating life as a grand epic poem, the philosopher Alcott forgets that Homer must nod, or we should all fall asleep. The world would not be very beautiful nor interesting, if it were all one huge summit of Mont Blanc.

Unhappily, the terraced hill-side, like the summer-house upon Mr. Emerson's lawn, "lacks technical arrangement," and the wild winds play with these architectural toys of fancy, like lions with humming-birds. They are gradually falling, shattered,—and disappearing. Fine locust-trees shade them, and ornament the hill with perennial beauty. The hanging gardens of Semiramis were not more fragrant than Hawthorne's hill-side during the June blossoming of the locusts. A few young elms, some white pines and young oaks complete the catalogue of trees. A light breeze constantly fans the brow of the hill, making harps of the tree-tops, and singing to our author, who "with a book in my hand, or an unwritten book in my thoughts," lies stretched beneath them in the shade.

From the height of the hill the eye courses, unrestrained, over the solitary landscape of Concord, broad and still, broken only by the slight wooded undulations of insignificant hillocks. The river is not visible, nor any gleam of lake. Walden Pond is just behind the wood in front, and not far away over the meadows sluggishly steals the river. It is the most quiet of prospects. Eight acres of good land lie in front of the house, across the road, and in the rear the estate extends a little distance over the brow of the hill.

This latter is not good garden-ground, but it yields that other crop which the poet "gathers in a song." Perhaps the world will forgive our author that he is not a prize farmer, and makes but an indifferent figure at the annual cattle-show. We have seen that he is more nomadic than agricultural. He has wandered from spot to spot, pitching a temporary tent, then striking it for "fresh fields and pastures new." It is natural, therefore, that he should call his house "The Wayside,"—a bench upon the road where he sits for a while before passing on. If the wayfarer finds him upon that bench he shall have rare pleasure in sitting with him, yet shudder while he stays. For the pictures of our poet have more than the shadows of Rembrandt. If you listen to his story, the lonely pastures and dull towns of our dear old homely New England shall become suddenly as radiant with grace and terrible with tragedy as any country and any time. The waning afternoon in Concord, in which the blue-frocked farmers are reaping and hoeing, shall set in pensive glory. The woods will forever after be haunted with strange forms. You will hear whispers, and music "i' the air." In the softest morning you will suspect sadness; in the most fervent noon, a nameless terror. It is because the imagination of our author treads the almost imperceptible line between the natural and the supernatural. We are all conscious of striking it sometimes. But we avoid it. We recoil and hurry away, nor dare to glance over our shoulders lest we should see phantoms. What are these tales of supernatural appearances, as well authenticated as any news of the day,—and what is the sphere which they imply? What is the more subtle intellectual apprehension of fate and its influence upon imagination and life? Whatever it is, it is the mystery of the fascination of these tales. They converse with that dreadful realm as with our real world. The light of our sun is poured by genius upon the phantoms we did not dare to contemplate, and lo they are ourselves, unmasked, and playing our many parts. An unutterable sadness seizes the reader, as the inevitable black thread appears. For here Genius assures us what we trembled to suspect, but could not avoid suspecting, that the black thread is inwoven with all forms of life, with all development of character.

It is for this peculiarity, which harmonizes so well with ancient places, whose pensive silence seems the trance of memory musing over the young and lovely life that illuminated its lost years,—that Hawthorne is so intimately associated with the "Old Manse." Yet that was but the tent of a night for him. Already with the *Blithedale Romance,* which is dated from Concord, a new interest begins to cluster around "The Wayside."

I know not how I can more fitly conclude these reminiscences of Concord and Hawthorne, whose own stories have always a saddening close, than by relating an occurrence which blighted to many hearts the beauty of the quiet Concord river, and seemed not inconsonant with its lonely landscape. It has the further fitness of typifying the operation of our author's imagination: a tranquil stream, clear and bright with sunny gleams, crowned with lilies and graceful with swaying grass, yet doing terrible deeds inexorably, and therefore forever after, of a shadowed beauty.

Martha was the daughter of a plain Concord farmer, a girl of delicate and shy temperament, who excelled so much in study that she was sent to a fine academy in a neighboring town, and won all the honors of the course. She met at the school, and in the society of the place, a refinement and cultivation, a social gayety and grace, which were entirely unknown in the hard life she had led at home, and which by their very novelty, as well as because they harmonized with her own nature and dreams, were doubly beautiful and fascinating. She enjoyed this life to the full, while her timidity kept her only a spectator; and she ornamented it with a fresher grace, suggestive of the woods and fields, when she ventured to engage in the airy game. It was a sphere for her capacities and talents. She shone in it, and the consciousness of a true position and genial appreciation gave her the full use of all her powers. She admired and was admired. She was surrounded by gratifications of taste, by the stimulants and rewards of ambition. The world was happy, and she was worthy to live in it. But at times a cloud suddenly dashed athwart the sun—a shadow stole, dark and chill, to the very edge of the charmed circle in which she stood. She knew well what it was, and what it foretold, but she would not pause nor heed. The sun shone again; the future smiled; youth, beauty, and all gentle hopes and thoughts bathed the moment in lambent light.

But school-days ended at last, and with the receding town in which they had been passed, the bright days of life disappeared, and forever. It is probable that the girl's fancy had been fed, perhaps indiscreetly pampered, by her experience there. But it was no fairy-land. It was an academy town in New England, and the fact that it was so alluring is a fair indication of the kind of life from which she had emerged, and to which she now returned. What could she do? In the dreary round of petty details, in the incessant drudgery of a poor farmer's household, with no companions of any sympathy—for the family of a hard-working New England farmer are not the Chloes and Clarissas of pastoral poetry, nor are cow-boys Corydons,—with no opportunity of retirement and cultivation, for reading and studying, which is always voted "stuff" under such circumstances,—the light suddenly quenched out of life, what was she to do?

"Adapt herself to her circumstances. Why had she shot from her sphere in this silly way?" demands unanimous common sense in valiant heroics.

The simple answer is, that she had only used all her opportunities, and that, although it was no fault of hers that the routine of her life was in every way repulsive, she did struggle to accommodate herself to it,—and failed. When she found it impossible to drag on at home, she became an inmate of a refined and cultivated household in the village, where she had opportunity to follow her own fancies, and to associate with educated and attractive persons. But even here she could not escape the feeling that it was all temporary, that her position was one of dependence; and her pride, now grown morbid often drove her from the very society which alone was agreeable to her. This was all genuine. There was not the slightest strain of the *femme incomprise* in her demeanor. She was always shy and silent, with a touching reserve which won interest and confidence, but left also a vague sadness in the mind of the observer. After a few months she made another effort to rend the cloud which was gradually darkening around her, and opened a school for young children. But although the interest of friends secured for her a partial success, her gravity and sadness failed to excite the sympathy of her pupils, who missed in her the playful gayety always most winning to children. Martha, however, pushed bravely on, a figure of tragic sobriety to all who watched her course. The farmers thought her a strange girl, and wondered at the ways of a farmer's daughter who was not content to milk cows, and churn butter, and fry pork, without further hope or thought. The good clergyman of the town, interested in her situation, sought a confidence she did not care to bestow, and so, doling out *a, b, c,* to a wild group of boys and girls, she found that she could not untie the Gordian knot of her life, and felt, with terror, that it must be cut.

[76]

One summer evening she left her father's house and walked into the fields alone. Night came, but Martha did not return. The family became anxious, inquired if anyone had noticed the direction in which she went, learned from the neighbors that she was not visiting, that there was no lecture nor meeting to detain her, and wonder passed into apprehension. Neighbors went into the adjacent woods and called, but received no answer. Every instant the awful shadow of some dread event solemnized the gathering groups. Everyone thought what no one dared to whisper, until a low voice suggested "the river." Then, with the swiftness of certainty, all friends, far and near, were roused, and thronged along the banks of the stream. Torches flashed in boats that put off in the terrible search. Hawthorne, then living in the Old Manse, was summoned, and the man whom the villagers had only seen at morning as a musing spectre in his garden, now appeared among them at night to devote his strong arm and steady heart to their service. The boats drifted slowly down the stream—the torches flared strangely upon the black repose of the water, and upon the long, slim grasses that, weeping, fringed the marge. Upon banks, silent and awe-stricken crowds hastened along, eager and dreading to find the slightest trace of what they sought. Suddenly they came upon a few articles of dress, heavy with the night dew. No one spoke, for no one had doubted the result. It was clear that Martha had strayed to the river, and quietly gained the repose she sought. The boats gathered round the spot. With every implement that could be of service the melancholy task began. Long intervals of fearful silence ensued, but at length, toward midnight, the sweet face of the dead girl was raised more placidly to the stars than ever it had been to the sun.

> Oh! is it weed, or fish, or floating hair,—
>> A tress o' golden hair,
>> O' drownèd maiden's hair,
>> Above the nets at sea?
> Was never salmon yet that shone so fair
>> Among the stakes on Dee.[3]

So ended the village tragedy. The reader may possibly find in it the original of the thrilling conclusion of the *Blithedale Romance,* and learn anew that dark as is the thread with which Hawthorne weaves his spells, it is no darker than those with which tragedies are spun, even in regions apparently so torpid as Concord.

Notes

1. Cf. Alfred, Lord Tennyson, "The Lady of Shalott," ll. 28–29.
2. Tennyson, "The Lotos-Eaters," l. 4.
3. Charles Kingsley, "The Sands of Dee," ll. 13–18.

George William Curtis, "Hawthorne," in *Homes of American Authors* (New York: G. P. Putnam, [1853]), 291–313.

[Vagabondizing with Hawthorne in England in 1856]

[FRANCIS BENNOCH]

> Hawthorne considered the London businessman, politician, and poet Francis Bennoch (1812–1890) and Henry Bright the two best friends he made in England. Bennoch and Bright facilitated the Hawthorne family's transition from American to English life, introducing them to an ever-widening circle of acquaintances drawn from English high society, politics, and the arts; they each also delighted in showing the family their respective versions of "old" England and "new" by taking them from the storied sites of London's great halls, cathedrals, and museums to the rural haunts made famous by Wordsworth and Coleridge. Bennoch frequently accompanied the Hawthorne family on their travels and, much as Franklin Pierce did in America, in England he always stood ready to spirit Nathaniel away on a day- or week-long jaunt through the countryside for relief from the drudgery of his consulship. In the selection that follows, Bennoch describes one of their more memorable excursions; here, the two leave from London's Waterloo Station, "rely[ing only] upon Providence" for the necessities to sustain them on a tour that would take them to Aldershot, Albury, Tunbridge Wells, Battle, and Hastings. As a tribute to his enduring friendship toward her husband and her family, Sophia dedicated her edition of *Passages from the English Note-Books of Nathaniel Hawthorne* (1870) "To Francis Bennoch, . . . who, by his generous and genial hospitality and unfailing sympathy, contributed so largely . . . to render Mr. Hawthorne's residence in England agreeable and homelike."

THE FULL PARTICULARS OF my first brief vagabondizing with Hawthorne began in this wise: I had seen him at his house at Rock Ferry, Birkenhead, he had dined with me at Manchester, and we had passed a few notes of acquaintance. Some months afterwards he came to see London, and after spending a week or so with an agreeable young man, who, however, knew little or nothing of London society, he made a formal call upon me late one afternoon, intending to return to Liverpool the next day. I never saw a man more miserable: he was hipped, depressed, and found fault with everything;

London was detestable; it had but one merit—it was not so bad as Liverpool! I soon learned that he was not obliged to return at once, so I proposed that at two o'clock the next afternoon he should meet me at Waterloo Station, and rely upon Providence for the rest! He did not quite see the good of that, but nevertheless agreed to come. It happened that my friend of several years, Captain Shaw, now of the Fire Brigade, was then at Aldershot, attached to, and one of the captains of, the North Cork Rifles. He had often asked me to visit him a few days, and now there seemed a chance. So I wrote to tell him I was coming and who would accompany me, also the train by which he might expect us. True to time Hawthorne and I met, and away we whirled, he never asking where to!

The fresh air seemed to revive him. When we reached Farnboro' Shaw was on the platform, his carriage and servants outside, so I said, "Come along, Hawthorne! There's a fellow I know, and we may as well stop here as go farther, and I know we shall be treated well!" A single word gave Shaw the cue, and off we drove. As we entered the camp, Hawthorne opened his eyes in amazement; soon we pulled up at an officers' hut, which, with a servant for each, was placed at our disposal. After wandering about for an hour or so, he manifestly wondering still, we returned to dress for dinner, which was lavish in every respect, and the wine superb. Hawthorne was placed on the right of the Colonel, a jovial Irishman, while Shaw and I sat opposite. The anecdotes were numerous and racy; Hawthorne's health was drank, being introduced in a manner most gratifying by one of the officers familiar with all his works, and who quoted some of the powerful sentences of *The Scarlet Letter*. Hawthorne was in ecstasy, and the smallest hour of the morning had come and been followed by its neighbor before we retired. We remained at Aldershot three days, driving around the beautiful neighborhood and finishing up by witnessing a field day, or grand inspection of the entire force in camp, by the Duke of Cambridge. All this was so entirely new, that in the modest, retiring man it set working an entirely new set of ideas. Whilst there, I had time to communicate with Tupper, and set him on the *qui vive*. Now Hawthorne became eager to know whither we were bound. I told him as Providence had been tolerably good so far, we would trust in Providence still.

Captain Shaw having driven us to the station, we left him with regret, and off we started. The scenery around Guildford greatly pleased Hawthorne, and when we found ourselves among the swelling hills that lie between Guildford and Dorking, he became quite excited. As we approached the station nearest Albury, I saw Tupper on the platform, and accordingly suggested to Hawthorne that as he liked the neighborhood so well we would better remain there a few hours, to which he assented. Scarcely had we set foot upon the platform when forth sprang Tupper, welcoming me with out-stretched hands; then turning to Hawthorne, accosted him in grandiloquent terms as the mighty author of *The Scarlet Letter,* and announced that he himself was the Lord of the House of Seven Gables! Which was quite true. After walking over some of the charming hills, visiting Mr. Drummond's beautiful place, and peeping into his Irvingite church, smoking and dim with incense, we returned to luncheon, driving afterward to Wotton, the charming residence and exquisite domain of Mr. Evelyn, where his ancestor wrote his famous Diary. Unhappily he was not at home so we returned to dinner which was served early, as I had resolved to reach Tunbridge Wells that Saturday night. We were hardly seated when Mr. Evelyn was announced: he had returned soon after our visit, and seeing our cards resolved to return the call at once. Assuming that Hawthorne would delight in the opportunity to see anything rare, especially so if unique, he brought with him the original manuscript of Evelyn's famous Diary: anything more beautiful, even as to penmanship, it would be difficult to conceive.

But above and beyond this he brought with him the identical prayer-book used on the scaffold when Charles I was beheaded—a book having an intense interest from the fact that when the blow was struck and the blood spurted, several drops fell upon its open pages where is printed the service read on such occasions, the stains being still quite distinct. This circumstance gave to Hawthorne's peculiar temperament an intensity of satisfaction,—not pleasure, not delight, but— a sort of thrilling excitement, because he had never before been so near to anything kingly, and the curiosity lost none of its horrors—rather were these increased—because of the fact of its being the evidence of a kingly death. Of this scene and circumstance Hawthorne frequently spoke, dwelling upon it as one of the facts far exceeding any he had ever imagined. After a pressing invitation to revisit the locality, we departed for Tunbridge Wells; here we visited the high rocks and other places of interest, and on the Monday left for Battle, with the view of seeing the Abbey. But, at the bookseller's, the only place in the small town, so we were informed, where cards to view the Abbey could be obtained, we were met with the prompt reply to our question, "Impossible. [T]he only day for visitors to be admitted is [such and such a day,] therefore I cannot give you cards." I asked for a piece of paper, scribbled a few lines, inclosed the cards of Hawthorne and myself, and desired the man of books to kindly have it delivered, the messenger to await the reply. He argued that to send it would be only a waste of time, and moreover for him to send such a missive might bring him into trouble, as it was well known the request would be refused. I persisted: the note was sent, and in ten minutes came an order from Lady Vane to admit the strangers. The stationer himself became stationary and half bewildered—he absolutely glared with wonder—but I did not reveal the mystery, nor explain the magic used—the talismanic characters which had worked such wonders.

I trusted that Hawthorne's name was one to conjure with, and happily was not deceived. At the private entrance to this most interesting of all the historical abodes of England, we were met by Lady Vane herself, now Duchess of Cleveland, who personally conducted us over the family apartments, and then handed us over the head gardener, with special instructions to point out everything calculated to interest us. Many of the chief facts of this visit will be found recorded in Hawthorne's published Note-Books, and also in *Our Old Home,* but the precise circumstances of how he came there have never before been told. When he stood upon the spot where the body of Harold is believed to have been buried—the spot which formed the centre of the High Altar of the church subsequently erected, it may be conceived, though I am utterly unable to describe, the intensity of feeling, the quivering nervous emotion that agitated Hawthorne. It was the defeat of the Saxon, but nevertheless the triumph of England, as it laid the foundation of all her future greatness, and became the example that led to all her subsequent achievements. After having the battle-field carefully described and an hour of meditation, we drove on to Hastings. Our first visit was of course to the ruins of the grand old castle, which, although in a shattered condition, still frowns with contempt, as it were, on the angry sea which chafes unceasingly its rocky base. Here I turned the conversation on the occasional escapades of authors, and the different views expressed by them as to the various peculiarities in national life, mentioning Irving and Willis on one hand, and Mrs. Trollope and Dickens on the other: incidentally, but with an object, I asked his opinion of the Bon Gaultier Ballads, and what he thought of the authors. In language more emphatic than was his wont he denounced the rhymes as detestable, and as for the authors, were they present he would rejoice in kicking them over the precipice, with the hope that if their necks were not broken, "the multitudinous sea" might complete the work of destruction on their miserable carcasses!

Upon the utterance of this delightful sentiment, I proposed a bath for each, so that whatever might be our spiritual condition, our bodies might at least be refreshed and purified.

This accomplished, I thought we should further strengthen ourselves by partaking of a luncheon. The question as to which of the numerous excellent hostelries in the town should have the honor of our patronage was settled by my stating that some old and dear friends were sojourning at this fashionable watering place, on whom I should like to call early in the afternoon (Knowing the while that luncheon would be there awaiting us). On our arrival, the host and hostess greeted us with a warm and cordial welcome. The charming lady, all grace and kindness, devoted herself to Hawthorne, while our host and myself discussed familiar topics, of necessity referring to our early associations. Romance and poetry were discussed; the drama, with its famous exponents; art and literature in their higher developments; the famous men on both sides of the Atlantic;—all came in for a share of our diversified talk. After a fascinating interview of a few hours, the time came for our departure, and our liberal entertainers insisted upon accompanying us to the railway station, the lady taking Hawthorne's arm. We were just in time, adieux were made, the whistle screamed, and almost instantly we entered the tunnel. On emerging from the darkness I found Hawthorne quite excited, and, expressing his great admiration of the delightful persons whom it had been indeed a joy to meet and from whom it was verily a pain to part, he quickly asked, "Who are they? I did not quite catch their names." I replied, "I hardly dare reveal absolutely who they are, and what they are, but I may tell you that our host is Theodore Martin a poet of no small eminence, whose translations from the German and Danish poets are of surpassing excellence, and his fascinating wife is Helen Faucit, in every sense the best of all existing English actresses." "Ah!" exclaimed Hawthorne, "I felt I was in the presence of superior intelligence, but why, my dear friend, did you not tell me who your friends were, that I might have been prepared to meet them properly? I fear I made myself appear like an ass." I assured him that I had never seen him more at his ease, nor altogether more like himself in his best form—that I kept him in the dark for fear that, with full knowledge, he might have become abashed and silently hid himself in the farthest corner of the room. Besides, after your energetic remarks up at the old castle, "How could I?" "Why not!" "Because Theodore Martin is one of the authors of the Bon Gaultier's Ballads!" The expression on Hawthorne was most comical;—first, one of doubt, then almost dismay; but becoming settled and serious, he said, "This is an experience I shall never forget, and from this time I will never condemn any man before I know him, however much I may disagree with his opinions."

This is of necessity a very brief epitome of our brief and singular tour. In its recital I feel that my own personality is too pronounced, but that could not be avoided. I found Hawthorne utterly prostrated by depression; I hoped to lift him out of himself and think that I succeeded. From that time, his Note Books which truthfully pictured his life, for he was most honest in his pencillings, reveal that everything relating to his Old Home and its people was seen by him through a medium perfectly natural, and unclouded by any film of prejudice.

[Francis Bennoch, "A Week's Vagabondage,"] in T. A. J. Burnett, "A Week's Vagabondage with Nathaniel Hawthorne," *The Nathaniel Hawthorne Journal 1971,* ed. C. E. Frazer Clark Jr. (Washington, D.C.: NCR Microcard Editions, 1971), 33, 35, 37, 39, 41, 43, 45.

[My Earliest Memories of Father: Italy, 1858–1859] (1897)

Rose Hawthorne Lathrop

>|<

Nicknamed "Rosebud" by her parents, Rose Hawthorne Lathrop (1851–1926), the youngest of Nathaniel and Sophia's three children, was born in Lenox, Massachusetts, where the Hawthornes lived in the Red Cottage they rented from Caroline Sturgis and her husband, William Tappan. Barely two years old when her father's appointment as consul to Liverpool and Manchester was confirmed by the U.S. Senate, Rose had no memory of her parents' relocation from Lenox to Concord's Wayside in 1852, nor of the early years the family spent in the British Isles. Although she wrote authoritatively in *Memories of Hawthorne* (1897) about the time spent in Portugal with her mother and her sister, Una, in 1856–1857 and the family's journey from London through France before their arrival in Italy in 1858, her authority derives entirely from her mother's diary and letters as well as from letters in her possession that were exchanged between her parents. As she admits in the following selection from *Memories of Hawthorne,* which details the family's sojourn in Italy, her first sustained recollections of her father date from the family's arrival in Rome during the papacy of Pius IX (Giovanni Maria Mastri-Ferretti) and their eventual settlement in Florence. Remembering the many friends her parents made or renewed acquaintances with among the Anglo-American communities in Rome and Florence, Rose identifies three as her favorites: George Partridge Bradford, "who always reminded me of a priest of the true type"; Elizabeth Sherman Hoar, "whose vestal soul, celebrating constant rites over the memory of her dead betrothed [Charles Chauncy Emerson], made her the image of a nun"; and the Brownings, especially Robert, who "was a perfection which *looked at me,* and moved vigorously," and for "many years . . . associated himself in my mind with the blessed visions that had enriched my soul in Italy" (391, 402).

Two days shy of thirteen years at the time of her father's death in 1864, Rose remained in Concord with her mother, sister, and brother, Julian, until they moved to Germany, where Julian pursued his studies, and afterwards to England, where Sophia continued to edit Nathaniel's notebooks until her death in February 1871. On 11 September 1871, Rose and George Parsons Lathrop, whom she had earlier met in America, were married in London. Their marriage was not a happy one. Lathrop's publication of *A Study of Hawthorne* (1876), which caused a near-fatal rift between the Lathrops and Julian, their purchase of the Wayside in 1879, which was marred by the death there of their only child, Francis (1876–1881), and Lathrop's alcoholism took a terrible toll on their relationship. They sold the Wayside in 1883, struggled through most of the 1880s in an increasingly vexed marriage in which neither felt fulfilled, converted to Roman Catholicism in 1891, and permanently separated in 1895. By the time Lathrop died in 1898, Rose, in spite of her father's injunction against her youthful enthusiasm for writing, had produced a number of short stories and poems and moved to New York City. There, she trained as a nurse and opened a refuge for cancer patients in a tenement on the Lower East Side; she wrote *Memories of Hawthorne* partly to support her work on behalf of the terminally ill. On 8 December 1900, Rose professed vows as a Dominican nun; in 1901, as Mother Alphonsa, she opened Rosary Hill, a home for incurables, in Hawthorne, New York.

MY FIRST FREQUENT COMPANIONSHIP with my father began in Italy, when I was seven years old. We entered Rome after a long, wet, cold carriage journey that would have disillusionized a Doré. As we jolted along, my mother held me in her arms, while I slept as much as I could. . . . It was a solemn-faced load of Americans which shook and shivered into the city of memories that night. In "Monte Beni," as he preferred to call "The Marble Faun," my father speaks of Rome with mingled contempt for its discomforts and delighted heartiness for its outshining fascinations. "The desolation of her ruin" does not prevent her from being "more intimately our home than even the spot where we were born." A ruin or a picture could not satisfy his heart, which accepted no yoke less strong than spiritual power. Rome supplies the most telling evidence of human failure, because she is the theatre of the greatest human effort, both in the ranks of Satan and of God; and she visibly mourns her sins of mistake at the feet of spiritual victory, Saints Peter and Paul. . . . And while the observer in Rome may well feel sad in the midst of reminders of the enormous sins of the past, there is an uplifting, for the soul eager to perceive the truth, in all her assurances of that mercy which is the cause of religion. If the Holy See was established in Rome because it was the city where the worst wickedness upon earth, because the most intelligent, was to be found, we may conclude that the old emperors, stormy and grotesque, are responsible for its melancholy "atmosphere of sin," to which Hilda alludes as a condition of the whole planet; and not the popes who have prayed in Rome, nor the people who believe there. In printed remarks about Italy both my parents say that she most reminds them of what is highest.

But, whether chilly or warm, the Eternal City did not at once make a conquest of my father's allegiance, though before he bade it farewell, it had painted itself upon his mind as sometimes the sunniest and most splendid habitation for a populace, that he knew. In the spring my sister wrote:—

"We are having perfectly splendid weather now,—unclouded Italian skies, blazing sun, everything warm and glorious. But the sky is too blue, the sun is too blazing, everything is too vivid. Often I long for the more cloudy skies and peace of that dear, beautiful England. Rome makes us all languid. We have to pay a fearful price for the supreme enjoyment there is in standing on the very spots made interesting by poetry or by prose, imagination, or . . . truth. Sometimes I wish there had never been anything done or written in the world! My father and I seem to feel in this way more than the rest. We agree about Rome as we did about England." . . .

We were not able to seize upon the choicest luxuries of living, as our accommodations, even such as they were, proved to be expensive enough to hamper us. We had all expected to be blissful in Italy, and so the inartistic and inhuman accessories of life were harder to bear there than elsewhere. I remember a perpetual rice pudding . . . of which the almost daily sight maddened us, and threw us into a Burton's melancholy of silence, for nothing could prevent it from appearing. We all know what such simple despairs can do. . . . But spring was faithful, and at its return we began to enjoy the scenes of most note within and beyond the walls: the gleaming ruins, and fresh, uncontaminated daisies that trustfully throve beside some of them; the little fountains, with their one-legged or flat-nosed statues strutting ineffectually above them,—fountains either dry as dead revelers or tinkling a pathetic sob into a stone trough; the open views where the colors of sunlit marble and the motions of dancing light surrounded the peasants who sprang up from the ground like belated actors in a drama we only keep with us out of childish delight.

My father had never looked so serious as he did now, and he was more slim than in England. He impressed me as permeated by an atmosphere of perception. A magnetic current of sympathy with the city rendered him contemplative and absorbent as a cloud. He was everywhere, but only looked in silence, so far as I was aware. "The Marble Faun" shows what he thought in sentences that reveal, like mineral specimens, strata of ideas stretching far beyond the confines of the novel. While he observed Rome . . . he felt the sadness of the problems of the race which there were brought to a focus. Yet it is a singular fact that, notwithstanding this regret for her human pathos, perhaps the best book he ever wrote was created among the suggestive qualities of this haven of faith,—the book which inculcates the most sterling hope of any of his works. I saw in my walks with him how much he enjoyed the salable treasures and humble diversions of the thoroughfare. . . . Ingenuous simplicity, freedom from self-consciousness and whitewash, frank selfishness on a plane so humble that it can do little harm,—all this is amusing and restful after long hours with transcendental folk. . . .

My father looked in good spirits as we moved along. When he trafficked with an Italian fruit-vender, and put a few big hot chestnuts into his pocket, with a smile for me, I (who found his smile the greatest joy in the world) was persuaded that really fine things were being done. The slender copper piece which was all-sufficient for the transaction not only thrilled the huckster with delight, but became precious to me as my father's supple, broad fingers held it, dark, thin, small, in a respectful manner. He caressed it for a moment with his large thumb,—he who was liberal as nature in June,—and when the fruit-vender was wrought up to the proper point of ecstasy he was allowed to receive the money, which he did with a smile of Italian gracefulness and sparkle, while my father looked conscious of the mirthfulness of the situation with as lofty a manner as you please. As for the peasant women we met, under their little light-stands of head-drapery, they were easily comprehensible, and expressed without a shadow of reserve their vanity and tiger blood by an openly proud smile and a swing of the brilliantly striped skirt. The handsomest men and women possible, elaborately dressed, shone beside tiers of the sweetest bunches of pale violets, or a solitary boy, so beautiful that his human splendor scintillated, small as he was, sat in the pose and apparel that the world knows through pictures, and which pigment can never well render any more than it can catch the power of a sunset or an American autumn. The marble-shops were very pleasant places. A whirring sound lulled the senses into dreamy receptiveness, as the stone wheel heavily turned with soft swiftness, giving the impression that here hard matter was controlled to a nicety by airy forces; and a fragrance floated from the wet marble lather, while the polishing of our newly picked up mementos from the ruins went on, which was as subtle as that of flowers. A man or two, hoary with marble-dust and ennobled by the "bloom" of it, stood tall and sad about the wheel, and we handed to these refined creatures our treasures of . . . porphyry and other marbles picked up "for remembrance" (and no doubt once pressed by a Caesar's foot or met by a Caesar's glance), in order to observe the fresh color leap to the surface,— yellow, red, black, or green. Far more were we thrilled at finding scraps of iridescent glass lachrymals, containing all the glories of Persian magnificence, while pathetically hinting of the tears of a Roman woman two thousand years ago.

The heart of Rome was . . . St. Peter's, and its pulse the Pope. The most striking effect the Holy Father produced upon me, standing at gaze before him with my parents, was when he appeared, in Holy Week, high up in the balcony before the mountainous dome, looking off over the great multitude of people gathered to receive his blessing. . . . He was clothed in white not whiter than his wonderful pallor. My father implie[d] in a remark that Pio Nono impressed him by a becoming sincerity of countenance, and this was so entirely my infantile opinion that I became eloquent about the Pope, and was rewarded by a gift from my mother of a little medallion of him and a gold scudo with an excellent likeness thereon. . . .

Going to the Pincian Hill on Sunday afternoons, when my father quite regularly made me his companion, was the event of my week which entertained me best of all. To play a simple game of stones on one of the gray benches in the late afternoon sunshine, with him for courteous opponent, was to feel my eyes, lips, hands, all my being, glow with the fullest human happiness. When he threw down a pebble upon one of the squares which he had marked with chalk, I was enchanted. When one game was finished, I trembled lest he would not go on with another. He was never fatigued or annoyed—outwardly. He had as much control over the man we saw in him as a sentinel on duty. Therefore he proceeded with the tossing of pebbles, genially though quietly, not exhibiting the least reluctance, and uttering a few amused sounds, like mellow wood-notes. Between the buxom groups of luxuriant foliage the great stream of fashion rolled by in carriages, the music of the well-trained band pealing forth upon the breeze; and in the tinted distance, beyond the wall of the high-perched garden which surrounded us, the sunset shook out its pennons. Through the glinting bustle of the crowd and the richness of nature my father peacefully breathed, in half-withdrawn brooding, either pursuing our pebble warfare with kindest stateliness, or strolling beside lovely plots of shadowed grass, fragrant from lofty trees of box. An element by no means slight in the rejoicing of my mind, when I was with him of a Sunday afternoon, was his cigar, which he puffed at very deliberately, as if smoking were a rite. The aroma was wonderful. The classicism which followed my parents about in everything of course connected itself with my father's chief luxury, in the form of a bronze match-box, given him in Rome by my sister, upon which an autumn scene of harvest figures was modeled with Greek elegance, and to this we turned our eyes admiringly during the lighting of the cigar. There was a hunter returning to a home draped with the grape, bringing still more of that fruit, and a rabbit and bird, hung upon a pole, while his wife and child were ever so comfortably disposed upon the threshold, and the hunting-dog affectionately lapped the young matron's hand. An autumn was also depicted on the reverse, presumably a year earlier than the one just described, where two lovers stood among sheaves of wheat, their sickles in hand, and the youth held up a bunch of grapes which the maiden, down-looking, gently raised her arm to receive. At last it would grow too late to play another game, and my father's darkly clothed form would be drawn up, and his strongly beautiful face lifted ominously. Before leaving the hill we went to look over the parapet to the west, where stood, according to "Monte Beni," "the grandest edifice ever built by man, painted against God's loveliest sky." . . .

Among the friends much with us was the astronomer, Miss Maria Mitchell, whom we had long known intimately. She smiled blissfully in Rome, as if really visiting a constellation; flashing her eyes with silent laughter, and curling her soft, full, splendid lips with fascinating expressions of satisfaction. I loved her for this, but principally because, while with us in Paris, it was she who had with delicious comradeship introduced me to that perfection of all infantile taste—French gingerbread, warm (on an outdoor counter) with the sunshine of the skies! She had the long list of churches and ruins and pictures catalogued upon her efficient tongue, and she and my mother ran together like sisters to see the sights of beauty and reminiscence; neither of them ever tired, and never disappointed. Her voice was richly mellow, like my father's, and her wit was the merry spray of deep waves of thought. The sculptor, Miss Harriet Hosmer . . . charmed the romancer. She was cheerfulness itself, touched off with a jaunty cap. Her smile I remember as one of those very precious gleams that make us forget everything but the present moment. She could be wittily gay; but there was plenty of brain power behind the clever *mot,* as immensities are at the source of the sun-ray. There was a blessing in the presence of Miss Elizabeth Hoar, once engaged to that beloved brother of Mr. Emerson whom death had taken. She seemed to me . . . like a tall, speaking monument, composed of diamonds and pearls. She talked a great deal, gently, with a penetrating sweetness of voice, and looking some-what down, as those do who have just received the news of a bitter sorrow. She knew everything that was fine in history and poetry and art; and to be near her, and to catch at moments the clear unfaltering challenge of her sad but brave eyes, was to live a little nobler one's self. . . .

Many friends were in Rome, both as residents and as tourists, and in all my after-life our two winters there were the richest of memories, in regard both to personalities and exquisite objects, and to scenes of artistic charm. Yet . . . if the tall, slender figure of my father were not at hand, even my mother's con-stantly cheering presence and a talkative group of people could not warm the imagination quite enough. He says, in speaking of the Carnival, "For my part, though I pretended to take no interest in the matter, I could have bandied *confetti* and nosegays as readily and riotously as any urchin there." These few words explain his magnetism. The decorous pretense of his observant calm could not make us forget the bursts of mirth and vigorous abandon which now and then revealed the flame of unstinted life in his heart. . . .

I went with my father and mother to several painters' and sculptors' stu-dios (besides innumerable visits to churches and galleries), all filling my mind with unfailing riches of memory. I hope I shall be pardoned for giving the general effect of this companionship and sight-seeing upon many years of reflection in a strain that is autobiographical. The studio which I best remem-ber was Mr. Thompson's, he who had painted the portrait of my father used in the editions of "Twice-Told Tales." The room was very large, but not very high, and it had a great deal of shadow in it. I did not think he painted as well as Raphael; but I delighted in the smell of his pigments, which were intensely fragrant. I thought his still moist canvas upon the easel, of a little Peter and a well-groomed angel, infinitely amusing. It was history scrubbed, and rather reduced in size. I was half appalled, half fascinated, by my temerity in having such frivolous private opinions of a picture that my mother and father felt the excellence of with reverence and praise. A minute portrait of me was painted by Mr. Thompson; one for which I did not find it at all amusing to sit, as I had to occupy a stiff chair . . . without any of the family to keep me in heart, although I had almost never been left with friends in that way, and although I was by that time a perfect recluse in disposition. So I was under the impression that I was being punished by the invisible powers....

I wondered, even at seven years of age, how sculptors in the flesh could come and carve original conceptions among the unspeakably successful attempts of those who were already thinnest dust, yet whose names have so much personality in them that a sovereign presence fills the place where they are spoken,—sculptors whose statues step as it were unexpectedly (themselves surprised) into sight, with none of the avoirdupois of later stone-work; that heaviness which, in some of the finest of these modern figures, causes them to pause involuntarily, as if snowed upon.... Story's Cleopatra is smooth, close-fibred as glass, and the snowstorm has not been allowed to drift upon the folds of her robe, the interstices of her modeling. She, with a few others of still later date, comes near to the old art, which has as much possibility for our imaginative survey as the plot of "The Marble Faun," so marvelously, so intricately, so unslavishly finished. In looking at the Dying Gladiator, we wonder whether he has already passed on from mastering the thought of his approaching death to the remembrance of his wife and children; or whether upon the agony of the physical pang and the insult to courage, which his wound has brought him to endure, is yet to break the pathos of a hero's regret for the relinquished sweetness of love and home.

The Marble Faun suggests the problem as to whether he has for an instant stopped laughing, or will not immediately laugh; and what has a little while ago, or will suddenly cause, the animal fury of gladness to turn this jocund athlete into a dancing, bewilderingly enticing companion, chiming with guffaws and songs. Cleopatra's watchful melancholy partook also of classic momentariness, and I hoped she would spring to her feet. I liked very much to go to Mr. Story's studio, and I thought that for so slight a figure he was remarkably fearless.

The arches of triumph, which my mother studied reverently, seemed to me too premeditated and unnecessary; although an architect could no doubt have explained why, even to the present day, the little door for the little cat should supplement the big door of all space, which one would at first take to be a hero's best environment. Not thus unnecessary appeared the Coliseum; haunted by wild beasts, especially lions, leaping ... in hobgoblin array from the cavernous entrances which were pointed out to me as connected in the days of triumphant tyranny with their donjons. Many tender thoughts filled my reflections as I saw pilgrims visiting, and kneeling before, the black cross in the centre, and the altars around the walls. I delighted to muse within the circular ruin, upon whose upper rim, jagged but sunlit, delicate vegetation found a repentant welcome. The circular form of the ruin is full of eloquence, as one approaches from the Forum. What would be grace in a smaller structure is tragedy in so immense a sweep, which melts into vagueness ... or swirls before you in a retreating curve that figures the never-changing change of eternity.

The tomb of Cecilia Metella, and other successive tombs of the Appian Way beyond the walls, gave me my first impression of death that really was death. There could be, I reflected, looking at the sepulchres of these old Romans, no pretty story about the poor folk having gone to heaven comfortably from their apparent bodies. Here were the ashes of them, after a thousand years, in contemptible little urns; and they were expected to enjoy, in that much impaired state, sundry rusty bric-à-brac, dolls, and tear-vials of spookish iridescence, until, in the vast lapse of time, even a ghost must have got tired. Unaided by the right comment, I was dragged down considerably by those pagan tombs; and as an antidote, the unexplained catacombs were not sufficiently elevating. I did not read the signs of the subterranean churches aright, any more than the uncultivated Yankee reads aright an Egyptian portraiture. Monkish skulls and other unburied bones, seen by the light of *moccoletti,* were to me nothing but forms of folly. . . .

In the square beneath our windows, during Lent, booths were set, and countless flat pancake-looking pieces of dough were caught up by a white-capped and aproned cook, with a long-handled spoon, and fried in olive oil placed in a caldron at the booth's door, to be served to passers in the twinkling of an eye. I watched this process until I grew to regard Lent as a tiresome custom. Having tested the cakes, I found them to be indistinct in taste, for all their pretty buff tint, and the dexterous twist of the cook's wrist as he dumped them and picked them up. If they had been appetizing I should have been sharply interested in the idea of becoming a Catholic, but their entire absence of relish convinced me that the Italians lacked mental grasp and salvation at a single swoop: and this in spite of the fact that one of my mother's most valued friends, Mrs. Ward, had lately joined the Church. It was her husband who said of her, "Whatever church has Anna, has St. Anna!" . . .

Before this serious season of pancakes ... the Carnival had rushed upon my sight, carrying all our friends through its whirlpool. Every gay cloth, shawl, and mat that could be brought into service I had rejoiced to see displayed upon the balconies. . . . Sudden descents of flowers upon one's shoulders and lap in the carriage, from a window or a passer, or a kindly feeling stranger in another carriage, made one start in mirthful response. Sudden meetings with dear friends, or friends who seemed almost dear in the cheerful hurly-burly, became part of the funny scrimmage. . . .

To stand or sit at the windows beside the show was an experience full of pleasure; and if the window was on a level with the heads of the huddling passers, one could be in all the merriment yet not jostled; one could easily pick out a pretty woman or a handsome man to whom to throw a bouquet; and one could see energetic revelers, already well supplied with flowers, reaching high windows with bouquets by means of those wooden contrivances which . . . look like impracticable ladders. The fair recipient at the lattice never failed to respond with an ecstatic smile if this Jacob's ladder had been sufficiently long to reach her welcoming hand. Meantime, many bunches of flowers, some large and elegant, some small and merely gay of color, were being thrown aloft or flung downward, making fountains and cataracts of flowers. . . . There was an intoxicating enjoyment in being singled out as the recipient of fragrant flowers, sent with a laugh of the eyes; or of a handful of sugared almonds, tossed with a gay shout of compliment. If the passer who thus honored us was a complete stranger . . . we felt the untrammeled bonhomie which . . . we were expected to feel as a matter of course not for a moment only, but for life.

Upon all these things I delighted to think and afterwards to ponder, because I realized that they were of vital interest to the intelligence which was to me greatest and dearest.

Between our two winters in Rome we spent the summer in Florence, to which we journeyed by carriage over a road that was hung like a rare gallery with landscapes of the most picturesque description, and bordered close at hand by many a blue or crimson or yellow Italian anemone with its black centre. This experience was all sunshine, all pastime. . . .

We were hot in the city of Florence. My only consolation was to eat unnumbered cherries and apricots, for I did not as yet like the figs. My brother and I sometimes had a lurid delight in cracking the cherry and apricot stones and devouring the bitter contents, with the dreadful expectation of soon dying from the effects. Altogether I considered our sojourn in the town house, Casa del Bello, a morose experience; but it was, fortunately, short. My mother had a different feeling: she wrote home to America, "It is a delightful residence."

Without doubt it contained much engaging finery. Three parlors, giving upon a garden, were absorbed into the "study" for my father alone; and my mother was greatly pleased to find that fifteen easy-chairs were within reach of any whim for momentary rest between the campaigns of sight-seeing. To add to my own arbitrary shadow and regret of that time, the garden at the rear of the house was to me damp; full of green things and gracefully drooping trees, doubtless, but never embracing a ray of sunshine. Yet it was hot; all was relaxing; summer prevailed in one of its ill-humored moods. To make matters worse, my brother had caught in this Dantesque garden a brown bird, whether because sick or lame I know not. But an imprisoned bird it certainly was; and its prison consisted of a small, cell-like room, bare of anything but the heart-broken glances of its occupant. My father objected to the capture and caging of birds, and looked with cold disapproval upon the hospitable endeavor of my brother to lengthen the existence of a little creature that was really safer in the hands of Dame Nature. Presently the bird from the sad garden died, and then indeed Florence became intolerable to me! I wandered through the long, darkish hall that penetrated our edifice from front to back, and I sometimes emerged into the garden's bosky sullenness in my unsmiling misery. Again my mother's testimony proves my mind to have been strangely influenced by what to her was "a garden full of roses, jessamine, orange and lemon trees, and a large willow-tree drooping over a fountain in its midst," with a row of marble busts along a terrace: altogether a place that should have filled me with kittenish glee. The "Note-Books" . . . suggest that it harbored malaria. I looked with painful disappointment upon the unceasing dishes of fresh purple figs, which everybody else seemed to enjoy. I saw pale golden wine poured from poetic bottles braided with strands of straw, like pretty girls' heads of flaxen hair; and I was surprised that my father had the joyousness to smile, though sipping what he was later to call "Monte Beni Sunshine."

That nothing of misery might be excluded from my dismal round of woe, the only people whom I could go to see were the Powers family, living opposite to us. Mr. Powers petrified me by the *sang-froid* with which he turned out, and pointed out, his statues. Great artists are apt to be like reflections from a greater light, . . . but Mr. Powers seemed to me to defy art to lord it over his splendid mechanical genius, the self he managed so well. To prove beyond a doubt that material could not resist him, he would step from the studio into an adjoining apartment, and strike off button-like bits of metal from an iron apparatus which he had invented. It was either buttons or Venuses with him, indifferently, as I supposed. . . .

A morning dawned when the interest in living again became vigorous. A delicate-looking, essentially dignified young gentleman, the Count da Montaüto, seeming considerably starved, but fascinatingly blue-blooded, appeared in our tiresome house. I heard that we were to remove to a villa at Bellosguardo, a hill distant fifteen minutes' drive from the city, where the summer was reasonable[.] . . .

One . . . happy day, we toiled by carriage, between light-colored walls, sometimes too high for any view,—that once caused my mother a three hours' walk, because of a misturn,—over little hot, dusty roads, out and up to the villa. My father and brother had already walked thither; and my brother's spirits, as he stood beside the high iron gateway, in front of the gray tower which was the . . . chief outline of the old country-seat, were pleasant to witness, and illustrated my own pent-up feelings. He shouted and danced before the iron bars of the gate like a humanized note of music, uncertain where it belonged, and glad of it.

Our very first knowledge of Montaüto was rich and varied, with the relief from pretentiousness which all ancient things enjoy, and with the appealing sweetness of time-worn shabbiness. The walls of the hall and staircase were of gray stone, as were the steps which led echoingly up to the second story of the house. . . . The tower and the adjacent loggia were the features that preëminently sated our thirst for suggestive charm, and they became our proud boast and the chief precincts of our daily life and social intercourse. The ragged gray giant looked over the road-walls at its foot, and beyond and below them over the Arno valley, rimmed atop with azure distance, and touched with the delicate dark of trees. Internally, the tower . . . was dusty, broken, and somewhat dangerous of ascent. Owls that knew every wrinkle of despair and hoot-toot of pessimism clung to narrow crevices in the deserted rooms, where the skeleton-like prison frameworks at the unglazed windows were in keeping with the dreadful spirits of these unregenerate anchorites. The forlorn apartments were piled one above the other until the historic cylinder of stone opened to the sky. In contrast to the barrenness of the gray inclosures, through the squares of the windows throbbed the blue and gold, green and lilac, of Italian heavens and countryside.

At the dangers of the stairway my father laughed, with flashing glances. He always laughed (it was a sound peculiarly passionate and low, full, yet unobtrusive) at dangers in which he could share himself, although so grave when, in the moral turmoil, he was obliged to stand and watch uneven battle; not the less sorry for human nature because weakness comes from our ignoring the weapons we might have used. But on those trembling stairs he approved of the risk we ran, while cautioning me not to drop through one of the holes, and then stumbled within an inch of breaking his own neck, and laughed again.

"While gropingly descending these crazy steps one dusky evening, I grati-fied Julian exceedingly by hitting my nose against the wall," he admits in the "Note-Books." Who would not enjoy seeing a monarch come to so humble a contact with the bulwarks of his tower? Especially if he were royal enough not to take offense at one's mirth, as this one never did. Reaching the topmost heights of the stone pile, shaggy with yellow moss, we eagerly pressed to the battlements and drank in the view, finding all Florence spread out before us, far down from the breeze and light and prospect of our perch,—understand-ing the joy of falcons that are long hooded, and then finally *look*.

On one side of the tower was the lawn, hemmed round by a somewhat high semicircular stone wall. In front of it was Florence, pinnacled and roof-crowded, across the gentle valley. Not far away rose Galileo's rival tower, and the habitations of one or two friends. On another side of the keep the valley dipped more decidedly; and in the foreground clustered a collection of trees upon a grassy slope, divided from the villa lawn by a low wall, over which my father and mother sometimes bought grapes, figs, pomegranates, and peaches grown upon the place, which were smilingly offered by the count's *contadini*. These from their numbers were unrecognizable, while their prices for the exquisite fruit were so small that it was a pleasure to be cheated. Behind the tower stretched lengthily the house, its large arched doorway looking upon all comers with a frown of shadow. Still further behind basked a bevy of fruit gardens and olive-tree dotted hillsides with their vines of the grape. We used to sit on the lawn in the evenings, and sometimes received guests there; look-ing at the sky, moon, comet, and stars ("flowers of light," my mother called them) as if they were new. Any mortal might have been forgiven for so regard-ing them, in the sapphire glory of an Italian night. My mother's untiring voice of melodious enthusiasm echoed about the group in ejaculations of praise.

. . . There was a sadness about Italy, although it lay under "the smile of God," as my father calls its sunshine. He and my mother often mention this shadow . . . in their records. At times the cause seems to them to come from the "incubus" of the Catholic religion. . . . Glorious scenes were constantly soothing this sense of human sorrow, scenes such as cannot be found in regions outside the Church. . . .

Some of the rooms at Montaüto I studiously avoided. The forlorn cavern of a parlor, or ballroom, I remember to have seen only once. There was a painful vacuum where good spirits ought to have been. Along the walls were fixed seats, like those in the apse of some morally fallen cathedral, and they were covered with blue threadbare magnificence that told the secrets of vanity. Heavy tables crowded down the centre of the room. I came, saw, and fled. The oratory was the most thrilling place of all. It opened out of my sister's room, which was a large, sombre apartment. It was said to attract a frequently seen ghost by the force of its profound twilight and historic sorrows; and my sister, who was courageous enough to startle a ghost, highly approved of this corner of her domain. But she suddenly lost her buoyant taste for disembodied spirits, and a rumor floated mistily about that Una had seen the wretched woman who could not forget her woes in death. . . .

The roads going to and fro between the cream-colored stone walls of the surrounding country were unsparingly hot. I can feel now the flash of sunbeams that made me expect to curl up and die like a bit of vegetation in a flame. I tried to feel cooler when I saw the peasant women approaching, bent under their loads of wheat or of brush. . . . It seemed to be no end of a walk to Florence, and the drive thither was also detestable,—all from the heat and dust, and probably only at that time of year. The views of many-colored landscape, hazy with steaming fields, were lovely if you could once muster the energy to gaze across the high road-walls when the thoroughfare sank down a declivity. After a while there were cottages, outside of which ancient crones sat knitting like the wind, or spinning as smoothly as machines, by the aid of a distaff. Little girls, who were full-fledged peasant women in everything but size, pecked away at their knitting[,] . . . proud of their lately won skill and patient of the undesired toil. They were so small and comely and conformable, and yet conveyed such an idea of volcanic force ready to rebel, that they entranced me. Further inside the heart of the city upstarted the intoxications of sin and the terrible beggars with their maimed children. I never lost the impressions of human wrong there gathered into a telling argument. . . .

I sometimes went with my mother when she called at Casa Guidi, where the Brownings lived. . . . The house . . . seemed to have a network of second-story piazzas, and the rooms were very much shadowed and delightfully cool. Mr. Browning was shining in the shadow, by the temperate brightness of mind

alone, and ever talking merrily. . . . Mrs. Browning was there: so you knew by
her heavy dark curls and white cheeks, but doubted, nevertheless, when you
came to meet her great eyes, so dreamy that you wondered which was alive,
you or she. Her hand, usually held up to her cheek, was absolutely ghostlike.
Her form was so small, and deeply imbedded in a reclining-chair . . . that it
amounted to nothing. The dead Galileo could not possibly have had a wiser
or more doubtfully attested being as a neighbor. If the poor scientist had
been there to assert that Mrs. Browning breathed, he would probably have
been imprisoned forthwith by another incredulous generation. My mother
speaks . . . of the refreshment of Mr. Browning's calls [in Rome], and says that
the sudden meetings with him gave her weary nerves rest during the strain of
my sister's illness. . . . But Mr. Browning was a perfection which *looked at me,*
and moved vigorously! For many years he associated himself in my mind with
the blessed visions that had enriched my soul in Italy, and continued to give
it sustenance . . . when we again threw ourselves upon the inartistic mercies
of a New England village. . . .

. . . I have wondered whether the Faun would have sprung with such un-
tainted jollity into the sorrows of to-day if Mr. Browning had not leaped so
blithely before my father's eyes. "Browning's nonsense," he writes, "is of a
very genuine and excellent quality, the true babble and effervescence of a
bright and powerful mind; and he lets it play among his friends with the faith
and simplicity of a child."

I think I must be right in tracing one of the chief enchantments of the story
of Dr. Grimshawe to these months upon the hill of Bellosguardo. For at Montaüto one of the terrors was the cohort of great spiders. There is no word in
the dictionary so large or so menacing as a large spider of the Dr. Grimshawe
kind. Such appear, like exclamations, all over the world. I saw one as huge
and thrilling as these Italian monsters on the Larch Path at the Wayside, a few
years later; but at Montaüto they really swaggered and remained. We perceive
such things from a great distance, as all disaster may be perceived if we are not
more usefully employed. A presentiment whispers, "There he is!" and looking unswervingly in the right direction, there he is, to be sure. I could easily
have written a poor story . . . upon the effectiveness of these spiders, glaring in
the chinks of bed-curtains, or moving like shadows upon the chamber wall or
around the windows, and I can guess my father's amusement over them. They
were as large as plums, with numerous legs that spread and brought their personality out to the verge of impossibility. I suppose they stopped there, but I

am not sure. No wonder the romancer humorously added a touch that made a spider of the doctor himself, with his vast web of pipe-smoke! . . .

Of the discussions about "Monte Beni" I remember hearing a good deal, as my mother laughingly rehearsed passages in letters and reviews which scolded about Hawthorne's tantalizing vagueness and conscienceless Catholicity. My parents tried to be lenient towards the public, whose excitement was so complimentary, if its usually heavy inability to analyze its best intellectual wine was fatiguing. My father never for a moment expected to be widely understood[, . . . but he] must have . . . deduced something in the way of chances for appreciative analysis from prevalent literature. He struck me as a good deal like an innocent prisoner at the bar, and if I had not been a member of his family I might have been sorry for him. As it was, I felt convinced that he could afford to be silent, patient, indifferent, now that his work was perfected. My mother put into words all that was necessary of indignation at people's desire for a romance or a "penny dreadful" that would have been temporary and ineffective.

From *Memories of Hawthorne* (Boston and New York: Houghton, Mifflin, 1897), 352–54, 356–62, 365–66, 368–69, 371–81, 382–89, 392, 400–4, 410.

[Memories of the Hawthornes at the Wayside in 1862] (1900)

Rebecca Harding Davis

⇥|⇤

In this reminiscence of her first journey to New England, the pioneering literary and journalistic realist Rebecca Harding Davis (1831–1910) describes her early desire to become a writer and her first meeting with the Hawthornes, Bronson and Louisa May Alcott, Elizabeth Palmer Peabody, and Emerson, among others, in 1862. Since she hailed from Wheeling, Virginia (later West Virginia), Davis's experience of the Civil War was a topic of interest wherever she went. Visiting Concord at Nathaniel's invitation after her "Life in the Iron Mills" appeared in the *Atlantic Monthly* in April 1861, Davis was impressed with the character and friendliness of some of her new acquaintances. She was especially fond of Louisa May Alcott, whom she describes as writing books that were "true and fine", yet as incapable of imagining "a life as noble as her own" (565), and of Peabody, whom she credits as "a woman of wide research and a really fine intelligence" but, given the anecdote she relates here, as sometimes possessing "the discretion of a six-year-old child" (569). By contrast, Davis was impatient with the "seers": Bronson Alcott and Emerson. In this piece written forty years after first meeting them, Davis remembers Alcott as an "awkward . . . old man, absolutely ignorant of the world, but with an obstinate faith in himself" (564), and she remains completely resistant to Emerson, ridiculing him throughout for his aloofness, egotism, and tendency to use people, including his friends, as objects of study. Hawthorne, however, endures as her favorite. Vividly recalling her last day in Concord, she recounts a morning walk with Nathaniel and Sophia to the Old Manse and Sleepy Hollow, the idyllic haunts of their early married life. She reports that as he reclined on the grass at Sleepy Hollow, which had been consecrated as a cemetery in 1855, Nathaniel looked up with a laugh and uttered what has since become one of his most quoted lines: "'Yes,' he said, 'we New Englanders begin to enjoy ourselves—when we are dead.'" "Of the many pleasant things which have come into my life," Davis concludes, this visit to Concord "was one of the pleasantest and best" (570).

IN THE GARDEN OF the old house in Virginia where we lived, there were some huge cherry-trees, with low growing branches, and in one of them our nurse, Barbara, having an architectural turn of mind, once built me a house. Really, even now, old as I am, and after I have seen St. James's and the Vatican, I can't imagine any house as satisfactory as Barbara's. . . .

One day I climbed up with a new book, the first cheap book by the way that I ever saw. It was in two volumes; the cover was of yellow paper and the name was "Moral Tales." The tales, for the most part, were thin and cheap as the paper; they commanded no enchanted company bad or good into the cherry-tree.

But among them were two or three unsigned stories which I read over so often that I almost know every line of them by heart now. One was a story told by a town-pump, and another the account of the rambles of a little girl like myself, and still another a description of a Sunday morning in a quiet town like our sleepy village. There was no talk of enchantment in them. But in these papers the commonplace folk and things which I saw every day took on a sudden mystery and charm, and for the first time I found that they, too, belonged to the magic world of knights and pilgrims and fiends.

The publisher of "Moral Tales," whoever he was, had probably stolen these anonymous papers from the annuals in which they had appeared. Nobody called him to account. Their author was then, as he tells us somewhere, the "obscurest man of letters in America."

Years afterward, when he was known as the greatest of living romancers, I opened his "Twice-Told Tales" and found there my old friends with a shock of delight as keen as if I had met one of my own kinsfolk in the streets of a foreign city. In the first heat of my discovery I wrote to Mr. Hawthorne and told him about Barbara's house and of what he had done for the child who used to hide there. The little story coming from the backwoods touched his fancy, . . . for I presently received a note from him saying that he was then at Washington, and was coming on to Harper's Ferry, where John Brown had died, and still farther to see the cherry-trees and . . . *Me*. . . .

I wish he had come to the old town. It would have seemed a different place forever after to many people. But we were in the midst of the Civil War and the western end of the Baltimore & Ohio Railroad was seized just then by the Confederates and he turned back.

A year later I saw him. It was during my first visit to New England, at the time when certain men and women were earning for Boston its claim to be called the modern Athens.

I wish I could summon these memorable ghosts before you as I saw them then and afterward. To the eyes of an observer, belonging to the common-place world, they did not appear precisely as they do in the portraits drawn of them for posterity by their companions . . . who walked and talked with them apart—always apart from humanity.

That was the first peculiarity which struck an outsider in Emerson, Haw-thorne, and the other members of the *Atlantic* [*Monthly*] coterie; that while they thought they were guiding the real world they stood quite outside of it, and never would see it as it was. . . .

I remember listening during one long summer morning to Louisa Alcott's father as he chanted pæans to the war, the "armed angel which was wakening the nation to a lofty life unknown before."

We were in the little parlor of the Wayside, Mr. Hawthorne's house in Con-cord. Mr. Alcott stood in front of the fireplace, his long gray hair streaming over his collar, his pale eyes turning quickly from one listener to another to hold them quiet, his hands waving to keep time with the orotund sentences which had a stale, familiar ring as if often repeated before. Mr. Emerson stood listening, his head sunk on his breast, with profound submissive atten-tion, but Hawthorne sat astride of a chair, his arms folded on the back, his chin dropped on them, and his laughing, sagacious eyes watching us, full of mockery.

I had just come up from a border State where I had seen the actual war: the filthy spewings of it; the political jobbery in Union and Confederate camps; the malignant personal hatreds wearing patriotic masks, and glutted by burn-ing homes and outraged women; the chances in it, well improved on both sides, for brutish men to grow more brutish, and for honorable gentlemen to degenerate into thieves and sots. War may be an armed angel with a mission, but she has the personal habits of the slums. This would-be Seer who was talking of it, and the real Seer who listened, knew no more of war as it was than I had done in my cherry-tree when I dreamed of bannered legions of crusaders *debouching* in the misty fields.

Mr. Hawthorne at last gathered himself up lazily to his feet and said, qui-etly: "We cannot see that thing at so long a range. Let us go to dinner," and Mr. Alcott suddenly checked the droning flow of his prophecy and quickly led the way to the dining-room.

Early that morning when his lank, gray figure had first appeared at the gate, Mr. Hawthorne said: "Here comes [Emerson,] the Sage of Concord. He is anxious to know what kind of human beings come up from the back hills in Virginia. Now I will tell you," his eyes gleaming with fun, "what he will talk to you about. Pears. Yes. You may begin at Plato or the day's news, and he will come around to pears. He is now convinced that a vegetable diet affects both the body and soul, and that pears exercise a more direct and ennobling influence on us than any other vegetable or fruit. Wait. You'll hear presently."

When we went in to dinner, therefore, I was surprised to see the Sage eat heartily of the fine sirloin of beef set before us. But with the dessert he began to advocate a vegetable diet and at last announced the spiritual influence of pears, to the great delight of his host, who laughed like a boy and was humored like one by the gentle old man.

Whether Alcott, Emerson, and their disciples discussed pears or the war their views gave you the same sense of unreality, of having been taken, as Hawthorne said, at too long a range. You heard much sound philosophy and many sublime guesses at the Eternal Verities; in fact, never were the eternal verities so dissected and pawed over and turned inside out as they were about that time. . . . But the discussion left you with a vague, uneasy sense that something was lacking, some back-bone of fact. Their theories were like beautiful bubbles blown from a child's pipe, floating overhead, with queer reflections on them of sky and earth and human beings, all in a glow of fairy color and all a little distorted.

Mr. Alcott once showed me an arbor which he had built with great pains and skill for Mr. Emerson to "do his thinking in." It was made of unbarked saplings and boughs, a tiny round temple, two storied, with chambers in which were seats, a desk, etc., all very artistic and complete, except that he had forgotten to make any door. You could look at it and admire it, but nobody could go in or use it. It seemed to me a very fitting symbol for this guild of prophets and their scheme of life. . . .

Of the group of famous people in Concord . . . Emerson was best known to the country at large. . . . The tall, gaunt man with the watchful, patient face and slightly dazed eyes, his hands clasped behind his back, that came slowly down . . . that summer day was Uncle Sam himself in ill-fitting brown clothes. . . . Voice and look and manner were full of the most exquisite courtesy, yet I doubt whether he was conscious of his courtesy or meant to be deferential. Emerson . . . was a student of man, an explorer into the dim, obscure regions of human intelligence. He studied souls as a philologist does words or an entomologist beetles. He approached each man with bent head and eager eyes. "What new thing shall I find here?" they said. . . .

When I heard him coming into the parlor at the Wayside my body literally grew stiff and my tongue dry with awe. And in ten minutes I was telling him all that I had seen of the war, the words tumbling over each other, so convinced was I of his eagerness to hear. He was eager. If Edison had been there he would have been just as eager to wrench out of him the secret of electricity, or if it had been a freed slave he would have compelled him to show the scars on his back and lay bare his rejoicing, ignorant, half-animal soul, and an hour later he would have forgotten that Edison or the negro or I were in the world—having taken from each what he wanted.

Naturally Mr. Emerson valued the abnormal freaks among human souls most highly, just as the unclassable word or the mongrel beetle are dearest to the grammarian or the naturalist. The only man to whose authority he bowed was Alcott, the vague, would-be prophet, whose ravings he did not pretend to fathom. He apparently shared in the popular belief that eccentricity was genius. . . .

Outside of [this circle] of disciples there was then throughout the country a certain vague pride in Emerson as an American prophet. We were in the first flush of our triumph in the beginnings of a national literature. We talked much of it. Irving, Prescott, and Longfellow had been English, we said, but these new men—Holmes and Lowell and Hawthorne were our own, the indigenous growth of the soil. In the West and South there was no definite idea as to what truth this Concord man had brought into the world. But in any case it was American truth and not English. Emerson's popularity . . . outside of New England was wide, but vague and impersonal. . . .

Hawthorne was in this fraternity but not of it. He was an alien among these men, not of their kind. He belonged to no tribe. I am sure that wherever he went during his whole life, from the grassy streets of Salem to the docks of Liverpool, on Parisian boulevards or in the olive groves of Bellosguardo, he was always a foreigner, different from his neighbors. He probably never knew that he was different. He knew and cared little about Nathaniel Hawthorne, nor indeed about the people around him. The man next door interested him no more than the man in Mozambique. He walked through life, talking and thinking to himself in a language which we do not understand.

It has happened to me to meet many of the men of my day, whom the world agreed to call great. I have found that most of these royalties seem to sink into ordinary citizens at close approach.

The poet who wrings the heart of the world or the foremost captain of his time you find driving a bargain or paring a potato, just as you would do. You are disappointed at every turn. You expect to see the divine light shining through their talk to the office-boy or the trainman, and you never catch a glimmer of it; you are aggrieved because their coats and trousers have not something of the cut of kingly robes.

Hawthorne only, of them all, always stood aloof. Even in his own house he was like Banquo's ghost among the thanes at the banquet.

There is an old Cornish legend that a certain tribe of mountain spirits were once destroyed by the Trolls, all except one, who still wanders through the earth looking for his own people and never finding them. I never looked at Hawthorne without remembering the old story.

Personally he was a rather short, powerfully built man, gentle and low voiced, with a sly, elusive humor gleaming sometimes in his watchful gray eyes. The portrait with which we all are familiar—a curled barber-shop head—gives no idea of the singular melancholy charm of his face. There was a mysterious power in it which I never have seen elsewhere in picture, statue, or human being.

Wayside, the home of the Hawthornes in Concord, was a comfortable little house on a shady, grassy road. To please his wife he had built an addition to it, a tower into which he could climb, locking out the world below, and underneath, a little parlor, in whose dainty new furnishings Mrs. Hawthorne took a womanish delight. Yet, somehow, gay Brussels rugs and gilded frames were not the background for the morbid, silent recluse.

Mrs. Hawthorne, however, made few such mistakes. She was a soft, affectionate, feminine little woman, with intuitions subtle enough to follow her husband into his darkest moods, but with, too, a cheerful, practical Yankee "capacity" with which to meet baker and butcher. Nobody could have been better fitted to stand between Hawthorne and the world. She did it effectively. When I was at Wayside, they had been living there for two years—ever since their return from Europe, and I was told that in that time he had never once been seen on the village street.

This habit of seclusion was a family trait. Hawthorne's mother had managed to live the life of a hermit in busy Salem, and his sister, meeting a disappointment in early life, had gone into her chamber, and for more than twenty years shut herself up from her kind, and dug into her own soul to find there what truth and life she could. During the years in which Nathaniel, then a young man, lived with these two women, he, too, chose to be alone, going out of the house only at night, and finding his food on a plate left at his locked door. Sometimes weeks passed during which the three inmates of the little gray wooden house never saw each other's faces.

Hawthorne was the product of generations of solitude and silence. No wonder that he had the second sight and was naturalized into the world of ghosts and could interpret for us their speech.

America may have great poets and novelists, but she never will have but one necromancer.

The natural feeling among healthy, commonplace people toward the solitary man was a tender sympathy such as they would give to a sick child. "Nathaniel," an old blacksmith in Salem once said to me, "was queer even as a boy. He certainly was queer. But you humored him. You *wanted* to humor him."

One person, however, had no mind to humor him. This was Miss Elizabeth Peabody, Mrs. Hawthorne's sister. She was the mother of the kindergarten in this country, and gave to its cause, which seemed to her first in importance, a long and patient life of noble self-sacrifice. She was a woman of wide research and a really fine intelligence, but she had the discretion of a six-year-old child. She loved to tell the details of Hawthorne's courtship of her sister, and of how she herself had unearthed him from the tomb of the little gray house in Salem, and "brought him into Sophia's presence." She still regarded him as a demi-god, but a demi-god who required to be fed, tutored, and kept in order. It was her mission, she felt, to bring him out from solitudes where he walked apart, to the broad ways of common-sense.

I happened to be present at her grand and last *coup* to this end. One evening I was with Mrs. Hawthorne in the little parlor when the children brought in their father. The windows were open, and we sat in the warm twilight quietly talking or silent as we chose. Suddenly Miss Peabody appeared in the doorway. She was a short, stout little woman, with her white stockinged feet thrust into slippers, her hoop skirt swaying from side to side, and her gray hair flying to the winds.

She lighted the lamp, went out and brought in more lamps, and then sat down and waited with an air of stern resolution.

Presently Mr. Emerson and his daughter appeared, then Louisa Alcott and her father, then two gray old clergymen who were formally presented to Mr. Hawthorne, who now looked about him with terrified dismay. We saw other figures approaching in the road outside.

"What does this mean, Elizabeth?" Mrs. Hawthorne asked.

"I did it. I went around and asked a few people in to meet our friend here. I ordered some cake and lemonade, too."

Her blue eyes glittered with triumph as Mrs. Hawthorne turned away. "They've been here two years," she whispered, "and nobody has met Mr. Hawthorne. People talk. It's ridiculous! There's no reason why Sophia should not go into society. So I just made an excuse of your visit to bring them in."

Miss Elizabeth has been for many years among the sages and saints on the heavenly hills, but I have not yet quite forgiven her the misery of that moment.

The little room was quite full when there rustled in a woman who came straight to Mr. Hawthorne, as a vulture to its prey. I never heard her name, but I knew her at sight as the intellectual woman of the village, the Intelligent Questioner who cows you into idiocy by her fluent cleverness.

"So delighted to meet you *at last!*" she said, seating herself beside him. "I have always admired your books, Mr. Hawthorne. I was one of the very first to recognize your power. And now I want you to tell me about your methods of work. I want to hear all about it."

But at that moment his wife came up and said that he was wanted outside, and he escaped. A few moments later I heard his steps on the floor overhead, and knew that he was safe in the tower for the night.

He did not hold me guilty in the matter, for the next morning he joined his wife and me in a walk through the fields. We went to the old manse where they had lived when they were first married, and then wandered on to the wooded slopes of the Sleepy Hollow Valley in which the Concord people had begun to lay away their dead.

It was a cool morning with soft mists rolling up the hills, and flashes between of sudden sunlight. The air was full of pungent woody smells, and the undergrowth blushed pink with blossoms. There was no look of a cemetery about the place. Here and there, in a shady nook, was a green hillock like a bed, as if some tired traveller had chosen a quiet place for himself and laid down to sleep.

Mr. Hawthorne sat down in the deep grass and then, clasping his hands about his knees, looked up laughing.

"Yes," he said, "we New Englanders begin to enjoy ourselves—when we are dead."

As we walked back the mists gathered and the day darkened overhead. Hawthorne, who had been joking like a boy, grew suddenly silent, and before we reached home the cloud had settled down again upon him, and his steps lagged heavily.

Even the faithful woman who kept always close to his side with her laughing words and anxious eyes did not know that day how fast the last shadows were closing in upon him.

In a few months he was lying under the deep grass, at rest, near the very spot where he sat and laughed, looking up at us.[1]

I left Concord that evening and never saw him again. He said good-by, hesitated shyly, and then, holding out his hand, said: "I am sorry you are going away. It seems as if we had known you always."

The words were nothing. I suppose he forgot them and me as soon as he turned into the house. And yet, because perhaps of the child in the cherry-tree, and the touch which the Enchanter laid upon her, I never have forgotten them. They seemed to take me, too, for one moment, into his enchanted country.

Et in Arcadia, ego.[2]

Of the many pleasant things which have come into my life, this was one of the pleasantest and best.

Notes

1. Davis here collapses the span between her visit to Concord in 1862 and Hawthorne's death in 1864.

2. "*Et in Arcadia, ego*" loosely translates as, "I too have once been in Arcadia," with Arcadia suggesting a land of enchantment.

"A Little Gossip," *Scribner's Magazine* 28 (November 1900): 562–66, 568–70.

"Nathaniel Hawthorne" (1864)

[RICHARD HOLT HUTTON]

⟫|⟪

The English writer and theologian Richard Holt Hutton (1826–1897) was among the first to publish a retrospective obituary of Hawthorne in which the specifics of his life were secondary to their fictional representation in his art. In this respect, Hutton's essay that follows is an important variation on the dominant strain of personal accounts and literary reviews of Hawthorne that were published during his life. Educated in London, Heidelberg, and Berlin, Hutton held editorial positions on the *London Inquirer,* a Unitarian publication, the *National Review,* and the *Spectator.* In this sympathetic essay, Hutton claims that Hawthorne's entire literary subject was himself; taking a psychological approach, he argues that the genius reflected in Hawthorne's art was his own "ghostly half appeal for sympathy, half offer of counsel on the diseases latent in New England nature," so that it can only be appreciated by readers who, like Hawthorne, have lived "behind the veil" (706). In an interesting twist on what other accounts collected in this volume characterize as his pathology, Hutton concludes that Hawthorne's aloofness and isolation were actually his personal and aesthetic salvation: "What gave him [his] pure style, . . . fine taste, . . . delicate humor, . . . touching pathos, in a great degree even [his] radiant imagination and . . . consummate ingenuity, was the consciously separate . . . life which he lived. Without it he might have been merely a shrewd, hard, sensible, conservative, success-worshipping, business-loving, Yankee democrat" (706).

THE GHOSTLY GENIUS OF Hawthorne is a great loss to the American people. He has been called a mystic, which he was not,—and a psychological dreamer, which he was in very slight degree. He was really the ghost of New England,—we do not mean the "spirit," nor the "phantom," but the ghost in the older sense in which that term is used as the thin, rarefied essence which is to be found somewhere behind the physical organization,—embodied, indeed, and not by any means in a shadowy or diminutive earthly tabernacle, but yet only half embodied in it, endowed with a certain painful sense of the gulf between his nature and its organization, always recognizing the gulf, always trying to bridge it over, and always more or less unsuccessful in the attempt. His writings are not exactly spiritual writings; for there is no dominating spirit in them. They are ghostly writings. He was, to our minds, a sort of sign to New England of the divorce that has been going on there . . . between its people's spiritual and earthly nature, and of the impotence which they will soon feel, if they are to be absorbed more and more in that shrewd, hard earthly sense which is one of their most striking characteristics, in *communicating* even with the ghost of their former self. Hawthorne, with all his shyness and tenderness, and literary reticence, shows very distinct traces also of understanding well the cold, curious, and shrewd spirit which besets the Yankees even more than other commercial peoples. His heroes have usually not a little of this hardness in them. Coverdale, for instance, in the "Blithedale Romance," confesses that "that cold tendency between instinct and intellect which made me pry with a speculative interest into people's passions and impulses appeared to have gone far towards unhumanizing my heart." Holgrave, in the "House of the Seven Gables," is one of the same class of shrewd, cold curious heroes. Indeed, there are few of the tales without a character of this type. But though Hawthorne had a deep sympathy with the practical as well as the literary genius of New England, it is always in a far-removed and ghostly kind of way, as though he were stricken by some spell which half-paralyzed him from communicating with the life around him, as though he saw it only by a reflected light. His spirit haunted rather than ruled his body; his body hampered his spirit. Yet his external career was not only not romantic, but identified with all the dullest routine of commercial duties. That a man who consciously *telegraphed,* as it were, with the world, transmitting meagre messages through his material organization, should have been first a Custom-house officer in Massachusetts, and then the Consul in Liverpool, brings out into the strongest possible relief the curiously representative character in which he stood to New England as its literary or intellectual ghost. . . .

Hawthorne, who was a delicate critic of himself, was well aware of the shadowy character of his own genius, though not aware that precisely here lay its curious and thrilling power. In the preface to "Twice-Told Tales" he tells us frankly, "The book, if you would see anything in it, requires to be read in the clear brown twilight atmosphere in which it was written; if opened in the sunshine, it is apt to look exceedingly like a volume of blank pages." And then he adds, coming still nearer to the mark, "They are not the talk of a secluded man with his own mind and heart, *but his attempts, and very imperfectly successful ones, to open an intercourse with the world."* That is, he thinks, the secret of his weakness; but it is also the secret of his power. He carries with him always the air of trying to manifest himself; and the words come faintly, not like whispers so much as like sounds lost in the distance they have traversed. A common reader of Mr. Hawthorne would say that he took a pleasure in mystifying his readers, or weaving cobweb threads, not to bind their curiosity, but to startle and chill them, so gravely does he tell you in many of his tales that he could not quite make out the details of a fictitious conversation, and that he can only at best hint its purport. . . . This is a favourite device of Mr. Hawthorne's, and does not . . . proceed from the wish to mystify, so much as from the refusal of his own imagination so to embody his own conception as to make it clearly conceivable to the mind of his readers. He had a clear conception of his own design, and a conception, too, of the world for which he was writing, and was ever afraid of not conveying his own conception, but some other distinct from it and inconsistent with it, to the world, if he expressed it in his own way. He felt that he could not reproduce in others his own idea, but should only succeed in spoiling the effect he had already, by great labor, produced. He had manifested himself partially, but the next stroke, if he made it at all, would spoil everything, mistranslate him, and reverse the impression he hoped to produce. It was the timidity of an artist who felt that he had, as it were, to translate all his symbols from a language he knew thoroughly into one he knew less perfectly, but still so perfectly as to be nervously sensible to the slightest fault. . . . [L]ike a ghost that moves its lips but cannot be heard, he simply acquiesced in the incapacity, only using expressive gestures and vague beckonings to indicate generally a subject for awe or fear. . . . Hawthorne was continually expressing his regret that his native country has as yet no Past, and he seems always to have been endeavoring to supply the want by peopling his pictures of life with shadowy presences, which give them some of the eerie effect of a haunted house or a mediæval castle. We doubt much, however, whether it was really a Past after which he yearned. When he laid his scene in Italy or wrote about England he certainly made little or no use of their Past in his art, and, we imagine, that all he really craved for was that interposing film of thought between himself and the scene or characters he was delineating, which spared his isolated imagination the necessity of trying to paint in the exact style of the people he was addressing. He wanted an apparent excuse for the far-off and distant tone of thought and feeling which was most natural to him.

And when we turn from the manner to the thoughts of this weird New England genius, we find the subjects on which Hawthorne tries to "open intercourse" with the world are just the subjects on which the ghost of New England would like to converse with New England,—the workings of guilt, remorse, and shame in the old Puritan times, as in the "Scarlet Letter;" the morbid thirst to discover and to sin the unpardonable sin, as in the very striking little fragment called "Ethan Brand"[;] . . . the eternal solitude of every individual spirit, and the terror with which people realize that solitude, if they ever do completely realize it, as in the extraordinary tale of the awe inspired by a mild and even tender-hearted man, who has made a vow which puts a black veil forever between his face and that of all other human beings, and called the "Minister's Black Veil;"—the mode in which sin may develop the intellect treated imaginatively both in "Ethan Brand," and at greater length and with even more power in "Transformation;"—the mysterious links between the flesh and the spirit, the physical and the spiritual nature, a subject on which all original New England writers have displayed a singular and almost morbid interest, and which Hawthorne has touched more or less in very many of his tales, especially in the strange and lurid fancy called "Rappaccini's Daughter," where Hawthorne conceives a girl accustomed by her father's chemical skill to the use of the most deadly poisons, whose beauty of mind and body is equal and perfect, but who, like deadly nightshade or the beautiful purple flowers whose fragrance she inhales, breathes out a poison which destroys every insect that floats near her mouth, shudders at her own malign influence on everything she touches, and gives rise, of course, to the most deadly conflict of emotions in those who love her;—these and subjects like these, indigenous in a mind steeped in the metaphysical and moral lore of New England, endowed with much of the cold simplicity of the Puritan nature, and yet insulated from the world for which he wished to write, and too shy to press into it, are the favourite themes of Hawthorne's brooding and shadowy moods.

His power over his readers arises from much the same cause as that of his own fanciful creation,—the minister who wore the black veil as a symbol . . . and who startled men less because he was hidden from their view than because he made them aware of their own solitude. . . . Hawthorne, with the pale melancholy smile that seems ever to be always on his lips seems to speak from a somewhat similar solitude. Indeed, we suspect the story was a kind of parable of his own experience. Edgar Poe, though by no means a poor critic, made one great blunder, when he said of Hawthorne, he has not half the material for the exclusiveness of authorship that he has for its universality. He has the purest style, the finest taste, the most available scholarship, the most delicate humor, the most touching pathos, the most radiant imagination, the most consummate ingenuity, and with these varied good qualities he has done *well* as a mystic. But is there any one of these qualities which should prevent his doing doubly well in a career of honest, upright, sensible, prehensible, and comprehensible literature? Let him mend his pen, get a bottle of visible ink, come out from the Old Manse, cut Mr. Alcott, hang (if possible) the editor of the *Dial*, and throw out of window to the pigs all his old numbers of the *North American Review.*

The difficulty did not lie in these sacrifices, but in the greater feat of escaping from himself, and could he have done so, of course he would as much have lost his imaginative spell as a ghost would do who really returned into the body. That pallid, tender, solitary, imaginative treatment of characteristics and problems which have lain, and still lie, very close to the heart of New England,—that power of exhibiting them lit up by the moonlight of a melancholy imagination,—that ghostly half appeal for sympathy, half offer of counsel on the diseases latent in the New England nature,—were no eccentricity, but of the essence of his literary power. What gave him that pure style, that fine taste, that delicate humor, that touching pathos, in a great degree even that radiant imagination and that consummate ingenuity, was the consciously separate and aloof life which he lived. Without it he might have been merely a shrewd, hard, sensible, conservative, success-worshipping, business-loving, Yankee democrat, like the intimate College friend, Ex-President Pierce, whom he helped to raise to a somewhat ignominious term of power, and who was one of the mourners beside his death-bed. Hawthorne had power to *haunt* such men as these because he had nursed many of their qualities, thoughts, and difficulties, in a ghostly solitude, and could so make them feel, as the poor folks said figuratively of themselves after communing with the veiled minister, that "they had been with him behind the veil."

[Richard Holt Hutton], "Nathaniel Hawthorne," *Spectator* 37 (18 June 1864): 705–6.

"Nathaniel Hawthorne" (1864)

EDWARD DICEY

﹥❘❬

The English writer Edward Dicey (1832–1911) was educated at Trinity College, Cambridge, where, after taking honors in mathematics and classics, he decided to pursue a career as a journalist, reviewer, and political commentator. His publications appeared in *Macmillan's Magazine,* the London *Daily Telegraph,* the London *Daily News,* and the *Observer;* he served as the editor of the *Observer* from 1870 to 1889. Dicey's interest in international affairs led him to write several books, including *England and Egypt* (1884), *The Story of the Khedivate* (1902), and *The Egypt of the Future* (1907), and it also led him to Washington, D.C., in the early 1860s, where he first met Hawthorne. In the obituary reminiscence that follows, Dicey draws a perceptive contrast between Hawthorne's seemingly dispassionate attitude toward the Civil War and his friend William D. Ticknor's pragmatic, if not capitalistic, view of the conflict. But the high point of this reminiscence is its account of the several days Dicey spent alone with Hawthorne at the Wayside. If the description of that visit is to be believed, Hawthorne might well have included Dicey with Bright and Bennoch in his short list of the best Englishmen he ever met.

ALL PERSONS, I FANCY, who have lived for a period in America must, at times, feel a sort of strange doubt as to whether their recollections are not creations of their own fancy. My life in the United States often seems to me, on looking back, like a stray chapter interleaved by mistake into the book of my existence. I have lived longer in other foreign countries, but in them I was always a stranger, and knew that I should remain so to the end. In the Northern States, I was, for the time, at home. I lived the life of the people amongst whom I was thrown. I learnt to know their family histories, the details of their household existence, the little cares and pleasures which make up the sum of daily life all the world over. For a time I was a sharer in this life, and then, with the sailing of the packet from the shores of the New World, the whole of this existence came to an abrupt close. So I often catch myself thinking about some home far away in that distant country, and wondering whether it looks the same as when I saw it last; and then, when the recollection comes that time has gone by, and that the children are growing up and have forgotten me, doubtless, long ago, the whole scene becomes so confused and hazy that I begin to doubt whether I have ever seen it or only have dreamed it. It is so hard to realize that if I returned I should not find things exactly as I left them: that, for instance, if I went back I should no longer find a welcome in the house of Hawthorne. Let me write of him as I knew him. Let me say a few words in recollection of a man of genius, whom it was my fortune to know somewhat intimately.

My acquaintance with Hawthorne was not one of long duration. I first shook hands with him one Sunday evening, at a Washington party, in the month of March, 1861. I shook hands with him for the last time in parting at the door of his own house, at Concord, some three months later. Circumstances, however, rendered this acquaintance of a more intimate character than that which usually springs up from a chance letter of introduction; and I fancy that knowledge I thus gained enabled me to understand something of the true nature of a man little understood in [my country (England)], and much misunderstood in his own. I need hardly say that the winter of 1862 was the first of the great civil war. McClellan was then in his glory as the young Napoleon; the grand army of the Potomac was just leaving its winter-quarters to commence what was regarded as a triumphal progress, and Washington was filled with travellers of all classes and all nations, gathered to witness the aspects of this vast struggle. Amongst others, Hawthorne had come there, in company with the late Mr. Ticknor, the well-known Boston publisher. It was at a reception . . . that I met Hawthorne. I fancy that I had once seen him before in Rome. At any rate, his face seemed strangely familiar to me. He was utterly un-American in look—unlike, that is, the normal Yankee type, as we picture it to ourselves. As I write, I can see him now, with that grand, broad forehead, fringed scantily by the loose worn wavy hair, passing from black to gray, with the deep-sunk flashing eyes—sometimes bright, sometimes sad, and always "distrait"-looking—as if they saw something beyond what common eyes could see, and with the soft feminine mouth, what, at its master's bidding—or, rather, at the bidding of some thought over which its master had no control—could smile so wondrous pleasantly. It was not a weak face—far from it. A child . . . might have cheated Hawthorne; but there were few men who could have cheated him without his knowing that he was being cheated. He was not English-looking except in as far as he was not American. When you had once gazed at his face or heard him speak, the very idea that he ever could have gone a-head in any way, or ever talked bunkum of any kind seemed an absurdity in itself. How he ever came to have been born in that bustling New World became, from the first moment I knew him, an increasing mystery to me. If ever a man was out of his right element it was Hawthorne in America. He belonged, indeed, to that scattered Shandean family, who are never in their right places wherever they happen to be born—to that race of Hamlets, to whom the world is always out of joint anywhere. His keen poetic instinct taught him to appreciate the latent poetry lying hid dimly in the great present and the greater future of the country in which his lot was thrown; and, though keenly, almost morbidly, sensitive to the faults and absurdities of his countrymen, he appreciated their high sterling merit with that instinctive justice which was the most remarkable attribute of his mind. England itself suited him but little better than the States—more especially that part of England with which his travels had made him most familiar. To have been a happy man, he should . . . have been born in some southern land, where life goes onward without changing, where social problems are unknown, and what has been yesterday is to-day, and which will be to-morrow. Never was a man less fitted to buffet out the battle of life amidst our Anglo-Saxon race. He held his own . . . manfully, and kept his head above those waters in which so many men of genius have sunk. But the struggle was too much for him, and left him worn-out and weary. Had . . . the conditions of his life been more suited to his nature, he would, I suspect, have dreamed the long years away—and what he gained the world would have lost.

Before I met him for the first time, I was warned not to be surprised at his extreme shyness. The caution was not unneeded. There was something almost painful in the nervous timidity of his manner when a stranger first addressed him. My impression was that he meant to say, The kindest thing you can do is not to speak to me at all; and so, after a few formal phrases, of which I can recall nothing, our conversation ended, and, as I thought, our acquaintance also. Circumstances, however, threw us gradually together. There were . . . in Washington, numerous expeditions to the different localities of the war, to which we both were invited. The list of my acquaintances was necessarily small, as I was a stranger; and it so happened that persons with whom I was most intimate were also old friends of Hawthorne. Moreover—I say this out of no personal feeling, but in order to illustrate the character of the man of whom I write—he felt himself more at his ease with me than with his own countrymen at that particular crisis. The American mind, being of our own nature, is not a many-sided one. It grasps one idea, or rather one side of an idea, and holds it with a sublime and implicit confidence in the justice of its views. That McClellan was a heaven-born general, that the army of the Potomac must take Richmond, that the rebellion was nearly crushed, that the rebels were, one and all, villains of the deepest dye, that the North was wholly and altogether in the right, and the South wholly and altogether in the wrong, were axioms held in Washington, during the spring of 1862, as confidently and as unhesitatingly as we held an analogous belief during our wars with the Great Napoleon. Now, it was impossible for a man like Hawthorne to be an enthusiastic partisan. When Goethe was attacked, because he took no part in the patriotic movement which led to the war of German independence, he replied, "I love my country, but I cannot hate the French." So Hawthorne, loving the North, but not hating the South, felt himself altogether out of harmony with the passion of the hour. If he spoke his own mind freely, he was thought by those around him to be wanting in attachment to his country. And therefore, seeing that I—though sympathizing with the cause which at least was his cause also—could not look upon it after the fashion of Americans, he seemed to take a pleasure in talking to me about his views. Many are the conversations that I have had with him, both about the war and about slavery. To make his position intelligible, let me repeat an anecdote which was told me by a very near friend of his and mine, who had heard it from President Pierce himself. Frank Pierce had been, and was to the day of Hawthorne's death, one of the oldest of his friends. At the time of the Presidential election of 1856, Hawthorne, for once, took part in politics, wrote a pamphlet in favour of his friend, and took a most unusual interest in his success. When the result of the nomination was known, and Pierce was president-elect, Hawthorne was among the first to come and wish him joy. He sat down in the room moodily and silently, as was his wont when anything troubled him; then, without speaking a word, he shook Pierce warmly by the hand, and at last remarked, "Ah, Frank, what a pity!" The moment the victory was won, that timid, hesitating mind saw the evils of the successful course—the advantages of the one which had not been followed. So it was always. Of two lines of action, he was perpetually in doubt which was the best; and so, between the two, he always inclined to letting things remain as they are. Nobody disliked slavery more cordially than he did; and yet the difficulty of what was to be done with the slaves weighed constantly upon his mind. He told me once, that, while he had been consul at Liverpool, a vessel arrived there with a number of negro

[118]

sailors, who had been brought from slave-states and would, of course, be enslaved again on their return. He fancied that he ought to inform the men of the fact, but then he was stopped by the reflection—who was to provide for them if they became free; and, as he said, with a sigh, "while I was think-ing the vessel sailed." So I recollect, on the old battle-field of Manassas, in which I strolled in company with Hawthorne, meeting a batch of runaway slaves—weary, footsore, wretched, and helpless beyond conception; we gave them food and wine, some small sums of money, and got them a lift upon a train going Northwards; but not long afterwards, Hawthorne turned to me with the remark, "I am not sure we were doing right after all. How can those poor beings find food and shelter away from home?" Thus this ingrained and inherent doubt incapacitated him from following any course vigorously. He thought, on the whole, that Wendell Phillips and Lloyd Garrison and the Abolitionists were in the right, but then he was never quite certain that they were not in the wrong after all; so that his advocacy of their cause was of a very uncertain character. He saw the best, to alter slightly the famous Hora-tian line, but he never could quite make up his mind whether he altogether approved of its wisdom, and therefore followed it but falteringly;

> Better to bear those ills we have
> Than fly to others that we know not of,[1]

expressed the philosophy to which Hawthorne was thus borne impercepti-bly. Unjustly, but yet not unreasonably, he was looked upon as a pro-slavery man, and suspected of Southern sympathies. In politics he was always halting between two opinions; or, rather, holding one opinion, he could never sum-mon up his courage to adhere to it and it only. Moreover, if I am to speak the truth, the whole nature of Hawthorne shrank from the rough wear and tear inseparable from great popular movements of any kind. His keen observant intellect served to show him the weaknesses and vanities and vulgarities of the whole class of reformers. He recognised that their work was good; he admired the thoroughness he could not imitate; but somehow the details of popular agitation were strangely offensive to him. On one occasion I was pres-ent with Hawthorne at a great picnic, where the chief celebrities of the then new Republican Congress were assembled. Many of them were men who had come raw from the Western States, with all the manners and customs of those half-civilized communities. There was a good deal of horse-play and rough joking and good-humoured vulgarity, sufficient to amuse, without annoying, anyone who liked to observe eccentricity of character. But to Hawthorne the whole scene seemed inexpressively disagreeable and repulsive, and I shall never forget the expression of intense disgust with which he turned to me, after a leading senator had enlivened the day by telling a very broad story in front of a bar where we all were liquoring, and whispered, "How would *you* like to see the Lord Chancellor of England making a fool of himself in a pot-house?" And so this fastidiousness often . . . obscured the usual accuracy of his judgment. The impression, for instance, made upon him by the personal manner and behaviour of President Lincoln was so inconsistent with his own ideas of dignity, that he longed . . . to describe him as he really appeared, and only failed to do so, in his "Sketches of the War," in consequence of the representations of his friends. Still, I can recall how, after he had been describing to me the impression left upon him by his visit to the White House, an eminently characteristic doubt crossed his mind as to whether he was not in the wrong. "Somehow," he said, "though why I could never discern, I have always observed that the popular instinct chooses the right man at the right time. But then," he added, "as you have seen Lincoln, I wish you could have seen, Pierce too; you would have seen a real gentleman."

Thus, about the whole question of the war, Hawthorne's mind was . . . always hovering between two views. He sympathised with the war in principle; but its inevitable accessories—the bloodshed, the bustle, and, above all perhaps, the bunkum which accompanied it—were to him absolutely hateful. Never was a man more strangely misplaced by fate than Hawthorne in that revolutionary war-time. His clear powerful intellect dragged him one way, and his delicate sensitive taste the other. That he was not in harmony with the tone of his countrymen was to him a real trouble, and he envied keenly the undoubting faith in the justice of their cause . . . possessed by the brother men-of-letters among whom he lived. To any one who knew the man, the mere fact that Hawthorne should have been able to make up his mind to the righteousness and expediency of the war at all, is evidence of the strength of that popular passion which has driven the North into conflict with the South. It was curious to me at that time to see how universal this conviction of the justice of the war was amongst the American people. A man less like Hawthorne than his friend and companion Ticknor cannot well be conceived. A shrewd, kindly man of business, with little sentiment in his disposition, he valued, and was valued by, Hawthorne—exactly because each possessed the qualities in which the other was deficient. In a different war, and on different grounds, he was, perhaps, naturally more adverse to the war than even Hawthorne himself. Ticknor . . . always seemed to me a man who took life very pleasantly—eminently not a reformer; ready enough, after a kindly fashion, to think that everything was for the best in the best possible of worlds; and well inclined towards the Southerners, with whom he had had business and personal relations of old standing date. . . .

But I wish not to wander into politics. I am thinking now rather of the contrast between those two friends—one so shrewd, the other so simple—both so kind. Their relation was more like that of old school-boy friends than the ordinary one of author and publisher. Ticknor was so proud of Hawthorne, and Hawthorne was so fond of Ticknor; and yet in a relationship of this kind there was absolutely no loss of dignity on either side. When I was in Boston, Hawthorne was going to write—or, rather, was thinking of writing—a novel, to be brought out in England simultaneously with its production in America; and it was arranged, at Hawthorne's request, that Ticknor was to accompany him over to England to make the arrangements for the sale of his copyright. I can recall now the plans we made for meeting and dining together in London, and how both the men, each after his own fashion, seemed to enjoy the prospect of coming over to the old country, which they loved so well. Here, in England, people accused Hawthorne, as I think, unfairly, for the criticisms contained in his last book upon our national habits and character. The abuse was exaggerated, after our wont; but I admit, freely, that there were things in the "Old Home" which I think its author would not have written if his mind had not been embittered by the harsh and unsparing attacks that, ever since the outbreak of the war, have been poured upon everything and everybody in the North. With all his sensitiveness, and all his refinement, and all his world-culture, Hawthorne was still a Yankee in heart. He saw the defects of his own countrymen only too clearly; he was willing enough to speak of them unsparingly; but, when others abused his country, then the native New England blood was roused within that thoughtful nature. . . .

. . . I, for one, should find it difficult to have anything but the kindliest memories of Nathaniel Hawthorne. The days that I spent in his house at Concord are recorded in my memory as among the pleasantest of a wandering life. Most of the family happened to be away from home, so that our company was a very small one. It was in the first blush of early summer, and the little New England village was at the height of its quiet beauty. The house itself, lying beyond the village, at the foot of a low hill, buried almost in trees, was a fitting home for

the author of the "Scarlet Letter." In his own home, the shyness which often
rendered it difficult to get on with him seemed to fall away. To me . . . he was
the most courteous and kindly of hosts; and I think, before the end of my visit,
he had overcome the nervous doubt which always oppressed him, whether it
was possible for anybody not to get bored in his company. As I write, I recall,
one by one, all the incidents of that visit—the strolls in the pine wood above
the house, where the leaves fluttered to and fro, and the wind sighed fitfully;
the lounges on the hot summer afternoons, on the banks of the torpid Concord stream, watching the fish dart in and out underneath the rushes; the row
upon the little lake, with visits to the neighbours' houses, in that genial, kindly
community; and, above all, the long talks at night, when everybody else was
asleep, and when over the cigars and whisky Hawthorne would chat on in
that low musical voice I found such a charm in listening to. He was not a brilliant talker; there are not many sayings of his I can recollect, worth repeating
in themselves as disjointed fragments. It is difficult to analyse the charm of
anything which pleases you; but if I were obliged to try to explain the attraction of Hawthorne's talk, I should say it lay in the odd combination of clear,
hard-headed sense and dreamy fancy. Cynical he was not; his mind was too
large a one for anything small or mean; but he was tolerant of everything to a
marvellous degree; catholic in all his judgments; skeptical because he saw any
question from so many points of view. In truth, at the time I often fancied that
Shakespeare's conversation in private life must have been akin to that I heard
on those evenings spent in Hawthorne's study. On the last evening I passed
there I remember that our talk rambled, after many things, as men's talk often
will, to the question of what was to happen to us when life is over. We were
speaking of the spiritualist creed, that existence recommences, under another
form, the moment after death. "Ah," said Hawthorne, half laughing, half seriously, "I hope there will be a break. A couple of thousand years or so of sleep
is the least that I can do with before I begin life again."

These few words which I have written I have written frankly, knowing, or at
any rate believing, that Hawthorne himself would prefer to be so written of. I
think he knew and judged himself with the same measure as he judged others.
I recollect, as we shook hands for the last time, at the door of his house, he
said to me, in parting, "I am glad for once to have met an Englishman who can
see there are two sides to every question." The compliment was undeserved
enough, but I have sought to merit it in saying something of him who made it.

And those who knew him best, and therefore loved him best, will not, I think, be angry with me for so doing.

Note

1. William Shakespeare, *Hamlet*, 3.1.80.

Macmillan's Magazine 10 (July 1864): 241–46.

"Hawthorne" (1864)

Oliver Wendell Holmes

Oliver Wendell Holmes (1809–1894) was among the few people who saw Hawthorne on the day he left Boston for his final journey with Franklin Pierce. A Harvard graduate, practicing physician, Unitarian reformer, New England's resident autocrat, professor, and poet "at the breakfast-table," and a Boston Brahmin of the first order, Holmes enjoyed a cordial relationship with Hawthorne—far more cordial, in fact, than either might have imagined at first glance. Whether occasionally meeting at the Saturday Club or among a few of their mutual friends, such as Emerson, Longfellow, Fields, and James Russell Lowell, Holmes seemed more than willing to leave Hawthorne to his silences, and he never probed too deeply into the "calm despondency" or "backwardness and hesitancy" that gave hint of Hawthorne's troubled inner life and family history (99). Although they disagreed over the Civil War, Holmes knew that Hawthorne was opposed to slavery, and while they may not have discussed it in person, their writings disclose that they came fairly close to being of one mind on the behavior and ideas of many of their Transcendental acquaintances, whose excesses and eccentricities had been encouraged by their beliefs. As a distant sequel to the sympathetic obituary reminiscence that follows, in his "At the Saturday Club" (*Atlantic Monthly* 53 [January 1884]: 68–71), Holmes remembered Hawthorne twenty years after his death. Among the versified ghosts of Longfellow, Agassiz, and Emerson gathered in the club's old meeting room at the Parker House, Hawthorne suddenly appears:

> But who is he whose massive frame belies
> The maiden shyness of his downcast eyes?
> Who broods in silence till, by questions pressed,
> Some answer struggles from his laboring breast?
> An artist Nature meant to dwell apart,
> Locked in his studio with a human heart,
> Tracking its caverned passions to their lair,
> And all its throbbing mysteries laying bare.

> Count it no marvel that he broods alone
> Over the heart he studies—'t is his own;
> So in his page whatever shape it wear,
> The Essex wizard's shadowed self is there,
> The great Romancer, hid beneath his veil
> Like the stern preacher of his sombre tale;
> Virile in strength, yet bashful as a girl,
> Prouder than Hester, sensitive as Pearl. (70)

IT IS WITH A SAD PLEASURE that the readers of this magazine will see in its pages the first chapter of "The Dolliver Romance," the latest record of Nathaniel Hawthorne meant for the public eye. The charm of his description and the sweet flow of his style will lead all who open upon it to read on to the closing paragraph. With its harmonious cadences the music of this quaint, mystic overture is suddenly hushed, and we seem to hear instead the tolling of a bell in the far distance. The procession of shadowy characters which was gathering in our imaginations about the ancient man and the little child who come so clearly before our sight seems to fade away, and in its place a slow-pacing train winds through the village-road and up the wooded hillside until it stops at a little opening among the tall trees. There the bed is made in which he whose dreams had peopled our common life with shapes and thoughts of beauty and wonder is to take his rest. This is the end of the first chapter we have been reading, and of that other first chapter in the life of an Immortal, whose folded pages will be opened, we trust, in the light of a brighter day.

It was my fortune to be among the last of the friends who looked upon Hawthorne's living face. Late in the afternoon of the day before he left Boston on his last journey I called upon him at the hotel where he was staying. He had gone out but a moment before. Looking along the street, I saw a figure at some distance in advance which could only be his,—but how changed from his former port and figure! There was no mistaking the long iron-gray locks, the carriage of the head, and the general look of the natural outlines and movement; but he seemed to have shrunken in all his dimensions, and faltered along with an uncertain, feeble step, as if every movement were an effort. I joined him, and we walked together half an hour, during which time

I learned so much of his state of mind and body as could be got at without worrying him with suggestive questions,—my object being to form an opinion of his condition, as I had been requested to do, and to give him some hints that might be useful to him on his journey.

His aspect, medically considered, was very unfavorable. There were persistent local symptoms, referred especially to the stomach,—"boring pain," distension, difficult digestion, with great wasting of flesh and strength. He was very gentle, very willing to answer questions, very docile to such counsel as I offered him, but evidently had no hope of recovering his health. He spoke as if his work were done, and he should write no more.

With all his obvious depression, there was no failing noticeable in his conversational powers. There was the same backwardness and hesitancy which in his best days it was hard for him to overcome, so that talking with him was almost like love-making, and his shy, beautiful soul had to be wooed from its bashful prudency like an unschooled maiden. The calm despondency with which he spoke about himself confirmed the unfavorable opinion suggested by his look and history.

The journey on which Mr. Hawthorne was setting out, when I saw him, was undertaken for the benefit of his health. A few weeks earlier he had left Boston on a similar errand in company with Mr. William D. Ticknor, who had kindly volunteered to be his companion in a trip which promised to be of some extent and duration, and from which this faithful friend, whose generous devotion deserves the most grateful remembrance, hoped to bring him back restored, or at least made stronger. Death joined the travellers, but it was not the invalid whom he selected as his victim. The strong man was taken, and the suffering valetudinarian found himself charged with those last duties which he was so soon to need at the hands of others. The fatigue of mind and body thus substituted for the recreation which he greatly needed must have hastened the course of his disease, or at least have weakened his powers of resistance to no small extent.

Once more, however, in company with his old college-friend and classmate, Ex-President Pierce, he made the attempt to recover his lost health by this second journey. My visit to him on the day before his departure was a somewhat peculiar one, partly of friendship, but partly also in compliance with the request I have referred to.

I asked only such questions as were like to afford practical hints as to the way in which he should manage himself on his journey. It was more impor-

tant that he should go away as hopeful as might be than that a searching examination should point him to the precise part diseased, condemning him
to a forlorn self-knowledge such as the masters of the art of diagnosis sometimes rashly substitute for the ignorance which is comparative happiness.
Being supposed to remember something of the craft pleasantly satirized in
the chapter before us, I volunteered, not "an infallible panacea of my own
distillation," but some familiar palliatives which I hoped might relieve the
symptoms of which he complained most. The history of his disease must,
I suppose, remain unwritten, and perhaps it is just as well that it should be
so. Men of sensibility and genius hate to have their infirmities dragged out of
them by the roots in exhaustive series of cross-questionings and harassing
physical explorations, and he who has enlarged the domain of the human
soul may perhaps be spared his contribution to the pathology of the human
body. At least, I was thankful that it was not my duty to sound all the jarring
chords of this sensitive organism, and that a few cheering words and the pre-
scription of a not ungrateful sedative and cordial or two could not lay on me
the reproach of having given him his "final bitter taste of this world, perhaps
doomed to be a recollected nauseousness in the next."

There was nothing in Mr. Hawthorne's aspect that gave warning of so sudden an end as that which startled us all. It seems probable that he died by the
gentlest of all modes of release, fainting, without the trouble and confusion of
coming back to life,—a way of ending liable to happen in any disease attended
with much debility.

Mr. Hawthorne died in the town of Plymouth, New Hampshire, on the
nineteenth of May. The moment, and even the hour, could not be told, for
he had passed away without giving any sign of suffering, such as might call
the attention of the friend near him. On Monday, the twenty-third of May, his
body was given back to earth in the place where he had long lived, and which
he had helped to make widely known,—the ancient town of Concord.

The day of his burial will always live in the memory of all who shared in its
solemn, grateful duties. All the fair sights and sweet sounds of the opening
season mingled their enchantments as if in homage to the dead master, who,
as a lover of Nature and a student of life, had given such wealth of poetry to
our New-England home, and invested the stern outlines of Puritan character
with the colors of romance. It was the bridal day of the season, perfect in light
as if heaven were looking on, perfect in air as if Nature herself were sighing for
our loss. The orchards were all in fresh flower,—

> One boundless blush, one white-empurpled shower
> Of mingled blossoms,[1]—

the banks were literally blue with violets; the elms were putting out their tender leaves, just in that passing aspect which Raphael loved to pencil in the backgrounds of his holy pictures, not as yet printing deep shadows, but only mottling the sunshine at their feet. The birds were in full song; the pines were musical with the soft winds they sweetened. All was in faultless accord, and every heart was filled with the beauty that flooded the landscape.

The church where the funeral services were performed was luminous with the whitest blossoms of the luxuriant spring. A great throng of those who loved him, of those who honored his genius, of those who held him in kindly esteem as a neighbor and friend, filled the edifice. Most of those who were present wished to look once more at the features which they remembered with the lights and shadows of life's sunshine upon them. The cold moonbeam of death lay white on the noble forehead and still, placid features; but they never looked fuller of power than in this last aspect with which they met the eyes that were turned upon them.

In a patch of sunlight, flecked by the shade of tall, murmuring pines, at the summit of a gently swelling mound where the wild-flowers had climbed to find the light and the stirring of fresh breezes, the tired poet was laid beneath the green turf. Poet let us call him, though his chants were not modulated in the rhythm of verse. The element of poetry is air; we know the poet by his atmospheric effects, by the blue of his distances, by the softening of every hard outline he touches, by the silvery mist in which he veils deformity and clothes what is common so that it changes to awe-inspiring mystery, by the clouds of gold and purple which are the drapery of his dreams. And surely we have had but one prose-writer who could be compared with him in aërial perspective, if we may use the painter's term. If Irving is the Claude of our unrhymed poetry, Hawthorne is its Poussin.

This is not the occasion for the analysis and valuation of Hawthorne's genius. . . . The last effort of Hawthorne's creative mind is before him in the chapter here printed. The hand of the dead master shows itself in every line. The shapes and scenes he pictures slide at once into our consciousness, as if they belonged there as much as our own homes and relatives. That limpid flow of expression, never laboring, never shallow, never hurried nor uneven nor turbid, but moving on with tranquil force, clear to the depths of its profoundest thought, shows itself with all its consummate perfections. Our literature could ill spare the rich ripe autumn of such a life as Hawthorne's, but he has left enough to keep his name in remembrance as long as the language in which he shaped his deep imaginations is spoken by human lips.

Note

1. James Thomson, "Spring," from *The Seasons,* ll. 110–11.

Atlantic Monthly 14 (July 1864): 98–101.

From "Our Whispering Gallery" (1871)

[JAMES T. FIELDS]

\>|<

One of mid-nineteenth-century America's most influential publishers, James Thomas Fields (1817–1881) began his career at seventeen as a clerk in Boston's Old Corner Bookstore. In 1843, he became junior partner in Ticknor and Fields, as the firm was generally known after 1846; Ticknor and Fields evolved into Fields, Osgood and Company in 1868 and eventually into Houghton Mifflin. Fields published the foremost contemporary American and British writers, many of whom considered him a personal friend on whose business sense and aesthetic taste they were more than willing to stake their fortunes and literary reputations. Succeeding James Russell Lowell as editor of the *Atlantic Monthly* in 1862, Fields held that position until 1870. He retired from publishing in 1871 to concentrate on lecturing and writing; his major writings include *Yesterdays with Authors* (1872), in which he collected his reminiscences of Wordsworth, Dickens, Thackeray, and Hawthorne, among others, and *Underbrush* (1877), a collection of personal sketches and essays. With his wife, Annie Adams Fields, Fields hosted a popular literary salon; for many years their home on Boston's Beacon Street served as an "American Mecca" for international guests such as Dickens and as a congenial setting where American luminaries such as Holmes and Emerson held intellectual conversations with a select company.

The selection that follows, which was enormously influential in shaping Hawthorne's personal reputation in the nineteenth century, is discussed at length in the introduction to this volume.

. . . To-day we will sit opposite the likeness of the rarest genius America has given to literature,—a man who lately sojourned in this busy world of ours, but during many years of his life

Wandered lonely as a cloud,[1]

a man who had, so to speak, a physical affinity with solitude. I hope you have read and enjoyed . . . the writings of this author, who has never soiled the public mind with one unlovely image. His men and women have a magic of their own, and we shall wait a long time before another arises among us to take his place. Indeed, it is highly probable no one will ever walk precisely the same round of fiction which he traversed with so free and firm a step.

The portrait we are looking at was made by Rowse . . . and is a very truthful representation of the head of Nathaniel Hawthorne. He was several times painted and photographed, but it was impossible for art to give the light and beauty of his wonderful eyes. I remember to have heard, in the literary circles of London, that, since Burns, no author had appeared there with so fine a face as Hawthorne. Old Mrs. Basil Montagu told me, many years ago, that she sat next to Burns at dinner, when he appeared in society in the first flush of his fame. . . . She said . . . that, although the company consisted of some of the best bred men of England, Burns seemed to her the most perfect gentleman among them. She noticed, particularly, his genuine grace and deferential manner toward women, and I was interested to hear Mrs. Montagu's brilliant daughter, when speaking of Hawthorne's advent in English society, describe him in almost the same terms as I had heard her mother . . . describe the Scottish poet. I happened to be in London with Hawthorne during his consular residence in England, and I was always greatly delighted at the rustle of admiration his personal appearance excited when he entered a room. His bearing was modestly grand, and his voice touched the ear like a melody. . . .

Here is a golden curl which adorned the head of Nathaniel Hawthorne when he lay a little child in his cradle. It was given to me many years ago by one near and dear to him. I have two other similar "blossoms," which I keep pressed in the same book of remembrance. One is from the head of John Keats, and was given to me by Charles Cowden Clarke, and the other graced the head of Mary Mitford, and was sent to me after her death by her friendly physician, who watched over her in her last hours. Leigh Hunt says,

> There seems a love in hair, though it be dead.
> It is the gentlest, yet the strongest thread
> Of our frail plant,—a blossom from the tree
> Surviving the proud trunk;—as though it said,
> Patience and Gentleness is Power. In me
> Behold affectionate eternity.[2]

There is a charming old lady, now living two doors from me, who dwelt in Salem when Hawthorne was born, and, being his mother's neighbor at that time . . . there came a message to her intimating that the baby could be seen by calling. So my friend tells me she went in, and saw the little winking thing in its mother's arms. She is very clear as to the beauty of the infant, even when only a week old, and remembers that "he was a pleasant child, quite handsome, with golden curls." She also tells me that Hawthorne's mother was a beautiful woman, with remarkable eyes, full of sensibility and expression, and that she was a person of singular purity of mind. Hawthorne's father . . . she describes as a warm-hearted and kindly man, very fond of children. He was somewhat inclined to melancholy, and of a reticent disposition. He was a great reader, employing all his leisure time at sea over books. . . .

When Hawthorne was a little more than twelve, the family moved to Raymond; here his out-of-door life did him great service, for he grew tall and strong, and became a good shot and an excellent fisherman. Here also his imagination was first stimulated, the wild scenery and the primitive manners of the people contributing greatly to awaken his thought. At seventeen he entered Bowdoin College, and after his graduation returned again to live in Salem. . . .

When a youth he made a journey into New Hampshire with one of his relatives. They travelled by wagon, and met with many adventures which the young man chronicled in his letters home. Some of the touches in these epistles were very characteristic and amusing, and they showed in those early years his quick observation and descriptive power. The travellers "put up" at Farmington, in order to rest over Sunday. Hawthorne writes to a member of the family in Salem: "As we were wearied with rapid travelling, we found it impossible to attend divine service, which was, of course, very grievous to us both. In the evening, however, I went to a Bible class, with a very polite and agreeable gentleman, whom I afterwards discovered to be a strolling tailor, of very questionable habits."

When the travellers arrived in the Shaker village of Canterbury, Hawthorne at once made the acquaintance of the Community there, and the account which he sent home was to the effect that the brothers and sisters lead a good and comfortable life, and he wrote "If it were not for the ridiculous ceremonies, a man might do a worse thing than to join them." Indeed, he spoke to them about becoming a member of the Society, and was evidently much impressed with the thrift and peace of the establishment. . . .

The traits of the Hawthorne character were stern probity and truthfulness. Hawthorne's mother had many characteristics in common with her distinguished son, she also being a reserved and thoughtful person. Those who knew the family describe the son's affection for her as of the deepest and tenderest nature, and they remember that when she died his grief was almost insupportable. . . .

I first saw Hawthorne when he was about thirty-five years old. He had then published a collection of his sketches, the now famous "Twice-Told Tales." Longfellow, ever alert for what is excellent, and eager to do a brother author opportune and substantial service, at once came before the public with a generous estimate of the work in the North American Review; but the choice little volume, the most promising addition to American literature that had appeared for many years, made little impression on the public mind. Discerning readers, however, recognized the supreme beauty in this new writer, and they never afterwards lost sight of him. . . .

I came to know Hawthorne very intimately after the Whigs displaced the Democratic romancer from office. In my ardent desire to have him retained in the public service, his salary at that time being his sole dependence,—not foreseeing that his withdrawal from that sort of employment would be the best thing for American letters that could possibly happen,—I called, in his behalf, on several influential politicians of the day, and I well remember the rebuffs I received in my enthusiasm for the author of the "Twice-Told Tales." One pompous little gentleman in authority, after hearing my appeal, quite astounded me by his ignorance of the claims of a literary man on his country. "Yes, yes," he sarcastically croaked down his public turtle-fed throat, "I see through it all, I see through it; this Hawthorne is one of them 'ere visionists, and we don't want no such a man as him round." So the "visionist" was not allowed to remain in office, and the country was better served by him in another way. In the winter of 1849, after he had been ejected from the customhouse, I went down to Salem to see him and inquire after his health. . . . He was then living in a modest wooden house. . . . I found him alone in a chamber over the sitting-room of the dwelling; and as the day was cold, he was hovering near a stove. We fell into talk about his future prospects, and he was, as I feared I should find him, in a very desponding mood. "Now," said I, "is the time for you to publish, for I know during these years in Salem you must have got something ready for the press." "Nonsense," said he; "what heart had I to write anything, when my publishers . . . have been so many years trying to sell a small edition of the 'Twice-Told Tales'?" I still pressed upon him the good chances he would have now with something new. "Who would risk publishing a book for *me,* the most unpopular writer in America?" "I would," said I, "and would start with an edition of two thousand copies of anything you write." "What madness!" he exclaimed; "your friendship for me gets the better of your judgment. No, no," he continued; "I have no money to indemnify a publisher's losses on my account." I looked at my watch and found that the train would soon be starting for Boston, and I knew there was not much time to lose in trying to discover what had been his literary work during these last few years in Salem. . . . I pressed him to reveal to me what he had been writing. He shook his head and gave me to understand he had produced nothing. At that moment I caught sight of a bureau . . . near where we were sitting; and immediately it occurred to me that hidden away somewhere in that article of furniture was a story or stories . . . and I charged him vehemently with the fact. He seemed surprised, I thought, but shook his head again; and I rose to take my leave, begging him not to come into the cold entry, saying I would come back and see him again in a few days. I was hurrying down the stairs when he called after me from the chamber, asking me to stop a moment. Then quickly stepping into the entry with a roll of manuscript in his hands he said: "How in Heaven's name did you know this thing was there? As you have found me out, take what I have written, and tell me, after you get home and have time to read it, if it is good for anything." . . . On my way up to Boston I read the germ of "The Scarlet Letter"; before I slept that night I wrote him a note all aglow with admiration of the marvellous story he had put into my hands, and telling him that I would come again to Salem the next day and arrange for its publication. . . .

One beautiful summer day, twenty years ago, I found Hawthorne in his little red cottage at Lenox, surrounded by his happy young family. His boy and girl were swinging on the gate as we drove up to his door, and with their sunny curls formed a beautiful feature in the landscape. As the afternoon was cool and delightful, we proposed a drive over to Pittsfield to see Holmes, who was then living on his ancestral farm. Hawthorne was in a cheerful condition and seemed to enjoy the beauty of the day to the utmost. Next morning we were all invited by Mr. Dudley Field, then living at Stockbridge, to ascend Monument Mountain. Holmes, Hawthorne, Duyckinck, Herman Melville, Headley, Sedgwick, Matthews, and several ladies, were of the party. We scrambled to the top with great spirit, and when we arrived, Melville, I remember, bestrode a peaked rock, which ran out like a bowsprit, and pulled and hauled imaginary ropes for our delectation. Then we all assembled in a shady spot, and one of the party read to us Bryant's beautiful poem commemorating Monument Mountain. Then we lunched among the rocks, and somebody proposed Bryant's health, and "long life to the dear old poet." This was the most popular toast of the day, and it took . . . a considerable quantity of Heidsieck to do it justice. In the afternoon . . . we made our way, with merry shouts and laughter, through the Ice-Glen. Hawthorne was among the most enterprising of the merry-makers; and being in the dark much of the time, he ventured to call out lustily, and pretend that certain destruction was inevitable to all of us. After this extemporaneous jollity, we all dined together . . . and Hawthorne rayed out in a sparkling and unwonted manner. I remember the conversation at table chiefly ran on the physical differences between the present American and English men, Hawthorne stoutly taking part in favor of the American. This . . . was a happy day throughout, and I never saw Hawthorne in better spirits.

Often . . . I have seen him sitting in the chair you are now occupying by the window, looking out into the twilight. He liked to watch the vessels dropping down the stream, and nothing pleased him more than to go on board a newly arrived bark from Down East, as she was just moored at the wharf. One night we made the acquaintance of a cabin-boy on board a brig, whom we found off duty and reading a large subscription volume, which proved, on inquiry, to be a Commentary on the Bible. When Hawthorne questioned him why he was reading, then and there, that particular book, he replied with a knowing wink at both of us, "There's consider'ble her'sy in our place, and I'm a studying up for 'em."

He liked on Sunday to mouse about among the books, and there are few volumes in this room that he has not handled or read. He knew he could have unmolested habitation here, whenever he chose to come, and he was never allowed to be annoyed by intrusion of any kind. He always slept in the same room,—the one looking on the water; and many a night I have heard his solemn footsteps over my head, long after the rest of the house had gone to sleep. Like many other nervous men of genius, he was a light sleeper, and he liked to be up and about early; but it was only for a ramble among the books again. One summer morning I found him as early as four o'clock reading a favorite poem, Grainger's "Ode on Solitude," a piece he very much admired. That morning I shall not soon forget, for he was in the vein for autobiographical talk, and he gave me a most interesting account of his father, the sea-captain, who died of the yellow-fever, and of his beautiful mother, who dwelt a secluded mourner ever after the death of her husband. Then he drew a picture of his college life, and of his one sole intimate, Franklin Pierce, whom he loved devotedly his life long.

[135]

In the early period of our acquaintance he much affected the old Exchange Coffee-House in Devonshire Street, and once I remember to have found him shut up there before a blazing coal-fire, in the "tumultuous privacy" of a great snow-storm, reading with apparent interest an obsolete copy of the "Old Farmers Almanac," which he had picked up about the house.... After he was chosen a member of the Saturday Club he came frequently to dinner with Felton, Longfellow, Holmes, and the rest of his friends, who assembled once a month to dine together. At the table, on these occasions, he was rather reticent than conversational, but when he chose to talk it was observed that the best things said that day came from him....

As I turn over his letters, the old days, delightful to recall, come back again with added interest. "I sha'n't have the new story," he says in one of them, dated from Lenox on the 1st of October, 1850, "ready by November, for I am never good for anything in the literary way till after the first autumnal frost, which has somewhat such an effect on my imagination that it does on the foliage here about me,—multiplying and brightening its hues; though they are likely to be sober and shabby enough after all.

"I am beginning to puzzle myself about a title for the book. The scene of it is in one of those old projecting-storied houses, familiar to my eye in Salem; and the story . . . is a little less than two hundred years long; though all but thirty or forty pages of it refer to the present time. I think of such titles as 'The House of the Seven Gables[.]' . . .

"I write diligently. . . . I find the book requires more care and thought than 'The Scarlet Letter'; also, I have to wait oftener for a mood. 'The Scarlet Letter' being all in one tone, I had only to get my pitch, and could then go on interminably. Many passages of this book ought to be finished with the minuteness of a Dutch picture, . . . to give them their proper effect. Sometimes, when tired of it, it strikes me that the whole is an absurdity . . . but the fact is, in writing a romance, a man is always, or always ought to be, careening on the utmost verge of a precipitous absurdity, and the skill lies in coming as close as possible, without actually tumbling over." . . .

Hawthorne was a great devourer of books, and in certain moods of mind it made very little difference to him what the volume before him happened to be. An old play or an old newspaper sometimes gave him wondrous great content, and he would ponder the sleepy, uninteresting sentences as if they contained immortal mental aliment. He once told me he found such delight in old advertisements in the newspaper files at the Boston Athenaeum, that he had passed delicious hours among them. At other times he was very fastidious, and threw aside book after book until he found the right one. De Quincey was a special favorite with him. . . . In his library was an old copy of Sir Philip Sidney's "Arcadia," which had floated down to him from a remote ancestry, and which he had read so industriously for forty years that it was nearly worn out of its thick leathern cover. Hearing him say once that the old English State Trials were enchanting reading, and knowing that he did not possess a copy of those heavy old folios, I picked up a set at a book-stall and sent them to him. He often told me that he spent more hours over them . . . than tongue could tell, and . . . if five lives were vouchsafed to him, he could employ them all in writing stories out of those books. He had sketched, in his mind, several romances founded on the remarkable trials reported in the old volumes; and one day . . . he made my blood tingle by relating some of the situations he intended . . . to weave into future romances. Sir Walter Scott's novels he continued almost to worship, and was accustomed to read them aloud in his family. . . . [H]e had high praise to bestow on the novels of Anthony Trollope. "Have you ever read these novels?" he wrote. . . . "They precisely suit my taste; solid and substantial, written on the strength of beef and through the inspiration of ale, and just as real as if some giant had hewn a great lump out of the earth and put it under a glass case, with all its inhabitants going about their daily business and not suspecting that they were made a show of." . . .

. . . You ask me if all his moods were sombre, and if he was never jolly sometimes like other people. Indeed he was; and although the humorous side of Hawthorne was not easily or often discoverable, yet have I seen him marvellously moved to fun, and no man laughed more heartily in his way over a good story. . . . I remember how Hawthorne writhed with hilarious delight over Professor L[ongfellow]'s account of a butcher who remarked that, "Idees had got afloat in the public mind with respect to sassingers." I once told him of a young woman who brought in a manuscript, and said, as she placed it in my hands, "I don't know what to do with myself sometimes, I'm so filled with *mammoth thoughts*." A series of convulsive efforts to suppress explosive laughter followed. . . .

He had an inexhaustible store of amusing anecdotes to relate of people and things he had observed on the road. One day he described to us, in his inimitable and quietly ludicrous manner, being *watched*, while on a visit to a distant city, by a friend who . . . thought he needed a protector, his health being at that time not so good as usual. "He stuck by me," said Hawthorne, "as if he were afraid to leave me alone; he stayed past the dinner-hour, and when I began to wonder if he never took meals himself, he departed and set another man to *watch* me till he should return. That man *watched* me so, in his unwearying kindness, that when I left the house I forgot half my luggage, and left behind . . . a beautiful pair of slippers. They *watched* me so, among them, I swear to you I forgot nearly everything I owned." . . .

Hawthorne is still looking at us in his far-seeing way, as if he were pondering what was next to be said about him. It would not displease him, I know, if I were to begin our discursive talk to-day by telling you a little incident connected with a famous American poem.

Hawthorne dined one day with Longfellow, and brought with him a friend from Salem. After dinner the friend said: "I have been trying to persuade Hawthorne to write a story, based upon a legend of Acadie, and still current there; the legend of a girl who, in the dispersion of the Acadians, was separated from her lover, and passed her life in waiting and seeking for him, and only found him dying in a hospital, when both were old." Longfellow wondered that this legend did not strike the fancy of Hawthorne, and said to him: "If you have really made up your mind not to use it for a story, will you give it to me for a poem?" To this Hawthorne assented. . . . And so we have "Evangeline" in beautiful hexameters. . . .

Since we talked together last . . . I have met an early friend of Hawthorne's, older than himself, who knew him intimately all his life long, and I have learned some additional facts about his youthful days. Soon after he left college he wrote some stories which he called "Seven Tales of my Native Land." The motto which he chose for the title-page was "We are Seven," from Wordsworth. My informant read the tales in manuscript, and says some of them were very striking, particularly one or two Witch Stories. As soon as the little book was well prepared for the press he deliberately threw it into the fire, and sat by to see its destruction. . . .

Those early days in Salem,—how interesting the memory of them must be to the friends who knew and followed the gentle dreamer in his budding career! When the whisper first came to the timid boy . . . that he too possessed the soul of an artist, there were not many about him to share the divine rapture that must have filled his proud young heart. Outside of his own little family circle, doubting and desponding eyes looked upon him, and many a stupid head wagged in derision as he passed by. But there was always waiting for him a sweet and honest welcome by the humble hearth where his mother and sisters sat and listened to the beautiful creations of his fresh and glowing fancy. We can imagine the happy group gathered around the evening lamp! "Well, my son," says the fond mother, looking up from her knitting-work, "what have you got for us to-night? It is some time since you read to us a story, and your sisters are as impatient as I am to have a new one." And then we can hear, or think we hear, the young man begin in a low and modest tone the story of "Edward Fane's Rosebud," or "The Seven Vagabonds," or perchance . . . that tender idyl of "The Gentle Boy!" What a privilege to hear for the first time a "Twice-Told Tale," before it was even *once* told to the public! . . . [W]ith what rapture that delighted little audience must have hailed the advent of every fresh indication that genius, so seldom a visitant at any fireside, had come down . . . to bless their humble hearthstone in the sombre old town. . . .

Hawthorne seems never to have known the raw period in authorship so common to most growing writers, when the style is "overlanguaged," and when it plunges wildly through the "sandy deserts of rhetoric," or struggles as if it were having a personal difficulty with Ignorance and his big brother Platitude. It was capitally said of Chateaubriand that "he lived on the summits of syllables." . . . Hawthorne had no such literary vices to contend with. His looks seemed from the start to be

Commercing with the skies,[3]

and he marching upward to the goal without impediment. I was struck a few days ago with the untruth, so far as Hawthorne is concerned, of a passage in the Preface to Endymion. Keats says: "The imagination of a boy is healthy, and the mature imagination of a man is healthy; but there is a space of life between, in which the soul is in a ferment, the character undecided, the way of life uncertain, the ambition thick-sighted." Hawthorne's imagination had no middle period of decadence or doubt, but continued, as it began, in full vigor to the end. . . .

In 1852 I went to Europe, and while absent had frequent most welcome letters from the delightful dreamer. He had finished the "Blithedale Romance" during my wanderings, and I was fortunate enough to arrange for its publication in London simultaneously with its appearance in Boston. . . .

When I returned from abroad I found him getting matters in readiness to leave the country for a consulship in Liverpool. He seemed very happy at the thought of flitting, but I wondered if he could possibly be as contented across the water as he seemed in Concord. I remember walking with him to the Old Manse, a mile or so distant from The Wayside, his new residence, and talking over England and his proposed absence of several years. We strolled round the house, where he spent the first years of his married life, and he pointed from the outside to the windows, out of which he had looked and seen supernatural and other visions. We walked up and down the avenue, the memory of which he has embalmed in "Mosses," and he discoursed most pleasantly of all that had befallen him since he led a lonely, secluded life in Salem. It was a sleepy, warm afternoon, and he proposed that we should wander up the banks of the river and lie down and watch the clouds float above and in the quiet stream. I recall his lounging, easy air as he tolled me along until we came to a spot secluded, and oft-times sacred to his wayward thoughts. He bade me lie down on the grass and hear the birds sing. As we steeped ourselves in the delicious idleness, he began to murmur some half-forgotten lines from Thomson's "Seasons," which he said had been favorites of his from boyhood. . . .

The hedgerows of England, the grassy meadows, and the picturesque old cottages delighted him, and he was never tired of writing to me about them. While wandering over the country, he was often deeply touched by meeting among the wild-flowers many of his old New England favorites,—bluebells, crocuses, primroses, foxglove, and other flowers which are cultivated in our gardens, and which had long been familiar to him in America.

I can imagine him, in his quiet, musing way, strolling through the daisied fields on a Sunday morning and hearing the distant church-bells chiming to service. His religion was so deep and broad that he could not bear to be fastened in by a pew-door, and I doubt if he often heard an English sermon. He very rarely described himself as *inside* a church, but he liked to wander among the graves in the church-yards and read the epitaphs on the moss-grown slabs. He liked better to meet and have a talk with the *sexton* than with the *rector*. . . .

Hawthorne's first visit to London afforded him great pleasure, but he kept out of the way of literary people as much as possible. He introduced himself to nobody, except Mr. ——, whose assistance he needed, in order to be identified at the bank. He wrote to me . . . and told me he delighted in London, and wished he could spend a year there. He enjoyed floating about, in a sort of unknown way, among the rotund and rubicund figures made jolly with ale and port-wine. He was greatly amused at being told . . . "that he would never be taken for anything but an Englishman." He called Tennyson's "Charge of the Light Brigade," just printed at that time, "a broken-kneed gallop of a poem." . . .

One of his most intimate friends . . . was Francis Bennoch[.] . . . Hawthorne's letters constantly abounded in warm expressions of affection for the man whose noble hospitality and deep interest made his residence in England full of happiness. Bennoch was indeed like a brother to him, sympathizing warmly in all his literary projects, and giving him the benefit of his excellent judgment while he was sojourning among strangers. That is Bennoch's portrait near the likeness of his friend. . . .

Many and many a happy time Bennoch and Hawthorne and [I] have had together on British soil. Let me tell you a little incident that occurs to me now. I remember we went together to dine at a great house in the country, . . . where it was understood there would be no dinner speeches. The banquet was in honor of some society,—. . . but it was a jocose and not a serious club. The gentleman who gave it, Sir ——, was a most kind and genial person, and gathered about him on this occasion some of the brightest and best from London. All the way down in the train Hawthorne was rejoicing that this was to be a dinner without speech-making; "for," said he, "nothing would tempt me to go if toasts and such confounded deviltry were to be the order of the day." So we rattled along, without a fear of any impending cloud of oratory. The entertainment was a most exquisite one, about twenty gentlemen sitting down at the beautifully ornamented table. Hawthorne was in uncommonly good spirits, and, having the seat of honor at the right of his host, was pretty keenly scrutinized by his British brethren of the quill. He had, of course, banished all thought of speech-making. . . . But it became evident . . . that Hawthorne's health was to be proposed with all the honors. I glanced at him across the table, and saw that he was unsuspicious of any movement against his quiet serenity. Suddenly . . . our host rapped the mahogany, and began a set speech of welcome to the "distinguished American romancer." It was a very honest and a very hearty speech, but I dared not look at Hawthorne. I expected every moment to see him glide out of the room, or sink down out of sight from his chair. . . . I knew nothing would have induced the shy man of letters to go . . . if he had known he was to be spoken at in that manner. . . . [B]ut judge of my surprise, when he rose to reply with so calm a voice and so composed a manner, that, in all my experience of dinner-speaking, I never witnessed such a case of apparent ease.... There was no hesitation, no sign of lack of preparation, but he went on for about ten minutes in such a masterly manner, that I declare to you it was one of the most successful efforts of the kind ever made. Everybody was delighted, and, when he sat down, a wild and unanimous shout of applause rattled the glasses on the table. The meaning of his singular composure on that occasion I could never get him satisfactorily to explain, and the only remark I ever heard him make . . . was simply, "What a confounded fool I was to go down to that speech-making dinner."

. . . [W]hile Hawthorne was absent in Europe, he was anything but an idle man. On the contrary, he was an eminently busy one, in the best sense of that term; and if his life had been prolonged, the public would have been a great gainer for his residence abroad. His brain teemed with romances, and once I remember he told me he had no less than five stories, well thought out, any one of which he could finish and publish whenever he chose to. There was one subject for a work of imagination that seems to have haunted him for years, and he has mentioned it twice in his journal. This was the subsequent life of the young man whom Jesus, looking on, "loved," and whom he bade to sell all that he had and give to the poor, and take up his cross and follow him. "Something very deep and beautiful might he made out of this," Hawthorne said, "for the young man went away sorrowful, and is not recorded to have done what he was bidden to do." . . .

All sorts of adventures befell him during his stay in Europe, even to that of having his house robbed, and his causing the thieves to be tried and sentenced to transportation. In the summer-time he travelled about the country in England and pitched his tent wherever fancy prompted. . . .

It was during one of his rambles through the Manchester Exhibition rooms that Hawthorne saw Tennyson wandering about. I have always thought it a great pity that these two men of genius could not have been introduced on that occasion. Hawthorne was too shy to seek an introduction, and Tennyson was not aware that the American author was present. Hawthorne records in his journal that he gazed at Tennyson with all his eyes, and rejoiced more in him than in all the other wonders of the Exhibition. When I afterwards told Tennyson that the author whose "Twice-Told Tales" he happened to be then reading . . . had met him at Manchester, but did not make himself known, the Laureate said in his frank and hearty manner: "Why didn't he come up and let me shake hands with him? I am sure I should have been glad to meet a man like Hawthorne anywhere."

At the close of 1857 Hawthorne writes to me that he hears nothing of the appointment of his successor in the consulate, since he had sent in his resignation. "Somebody may turn up any day," he says, "with a new commission in his pocket." He was meanwhile getting ready for Italy. . . .

Released from the cares of office, and having nothing to distract his attention, his life on the Continent opened full of delightful excitement. His pecuniary situation was such as to enable him to live very comfortably in a country where, at that time, prices were moderate. In a letter . . . from a villa near Florence on the 3d of September, 1858, he describes in a charming manner his way of life. . . .

> . . . It is pleasant to feel at last that I am really away from America,—a satisfaction that I never enjoyed as long as I stayed in Liverpool, where it seemed to me that the quintessence of nasal and hand-shaking Yankeedom was continually filtered and sublimated through my consulate, on the way outward and homeward. I first got acquainted with my own countrymen there. At Rome . . . it was not much better. But here in Florence, and in the summer-time, and in this secluded villa, I have escaped out of all my old tracks, and am really remote. . . .
>
> At one end of the house there is a moss-grown tower, haunted by owls and by the ghost of a monk, who was confined there in the thirteenth century, previous to being burned at the stake in the principal square of Florence. I hire this villa, tower and all, at twenty-eight dollars a month; but I mean to take it away bodily and clap it into a romance, which I have in my head ready to be written out. . . .

I went abroad again . . . and found Hawthorne back in England, working away diligently at "The Marble Faun." While travelling on the Continent, during the autumn, I had constant letters from him, giving accounts of his progress on the new romance. He says: "I get along more slowly than I expected. If I mistake not, it will have some good chapters." Writing on the 10th of October he tells me: "The romance is almost finished. . . . If hard pushed, I could have it ready for the press in a fortnight; but unless the publishers . . . are in a hurry, I shall be somewhat longer about it. . . . To confess the truth, I admire it exceedingly at intervals, but am liable to cold fits, during which I think it the most infernal nonsense." . . .

I am glad . . . you have been reading so many of Hawthorne's books since we last met, and I do not at all wonder at the deep impression his style has made upon you. He was, indeed, a consummate artist, and I do not remember a single slovenly passage in all his acknowledged writings. . . . He was unlike any other author I have met, and there were qualities in his nature so sweet and commendable, that, through all his shy reserve, they sometimes asserted themselves in a marked and conspicuous manner. I have known rude people, who were jostling him in a crowd, give way at the sound of his low and almost irresolute voice, so potent was the gentle spell of command that seemed born of his genius.

Although he was apt to keep aloof from his kind, and did not hesitate frequently to announce by his manner that

> Solitude to him
> Was blithe society, who filled the air
> With gladness and involuntary songs,[4]

I ever found him, like Milton's Raphael, an "affable" angel, and inclined to converse on whatever was human and good in life. . . .

We met in London early in May [1860], and . . . we were frequently together. I recall many pleasant dinners with him and mutual friends in various charming seaside and country-side places. We used to take a run down to Greenwich or Blackwall once or twice a week, and a trip to Richmond was always grateful to him. Bennoch was constantly planning a day's happiness for his friend, and the hours at that pleasant season of the year were not long enough for our delights. In London we strolled along the Strand, day after day, now diving into Bolt Court, in pursuit of Johnson's whereabouts, and now stumbling around the Temple, where Goldsmith at one time had his quarters. Hawthorne was never weary of standing on London Bridge, and watching the steamers plying up and down the Thames. I was very much amused by his manner towards importunate and sometimes impudent beggars, scores of whom would attack us even in the shortest walk. He had a mild way of making a severe and cutting remark, which used to remind me of a little incident which Charlotte Cushman once related to me. She said a man in the gallery of a theatre . . . made such a disturbance, that the play could not proceed. Cries of "Throw him over" arose from all parts of the house, and the noise became furious. All was tumultuous chaos until a sweet and gentle female voice was heard in the pit, exclaiming, "No! I pray you don't throw him over! I beg of you . . . don't throw him over, but—*kill him where he is.*"

One of our most royal times was at a parting dinner at the house of Barry Cornwall. Among the notables present were Kinglake and Leigh Hunt. Our kind-hearted host and his admirable wife greatly delighted in Hawthorne, and they made this occasion a most grateful one to him. I remember when we went up to the drawing-room to join the ladies after dinner, the two dear old poets, Leigh Hunt and Barry Cornwall, mounted the stairs with their arms round each other in a very tender and loving way. Hawthorne often referred to this scene as one he would not have missed for a great deal. . . .

We sailed from England together in . . . June, as we had previously arranged, and our voyage home was, to say the least, a very unusual one. We had calm, summer, moonlight weather, with no storms. Mrs. Stowe was on board, and in her own cheery and delightful way she enlivened the passage with some capital stories of her early life. . . .

Hawthorne's love for the sea amounted to a passionate worship; and while I . . . was longing, spite of the good company on board, to reach land as soon as possible, Hawthorne was constantly saying, . . . "I should like to sail on and on forever, and never touch the shore again." He liked to stand alone in the bows of the ship and see the sun go down, and he was never tired of walking the deck at midnight. I used to watch his dark, solitary figure under the stars, pacing up and down some unfrequented part of the vessel, musing and half melancholy. Sometimes he would lie down beside me and commiserate my unquiet condition. Seasickness, he declared, he could not understand. . . .

That was a voyage, indeed, long to be remembered, and I shall always look back upon it as the most satisfactory "sea turn" I ever happened to experience. I have sailed many a weary, watery mile since then, . . . but *Hawthorne* was not on board! . . .

. . . [A]fter his return from Europe, I saw him frequently at the Wayside. . . . He now seemed very happy in the dwelling he had put in order for the calm and comfort of his middle and later life. He had added a tower to his house, in which he could be safe from intrusion, and where he could muse and write. Never was poet or romancer more fitly shrined. Drummond at Hawthornden, Scott at Abbotsford, Dickens at Gad's Hill, Irving at Sunnyside, were not more appropriately sheltered. Shut up in his tower, he could escape from all the tumult of life. . . .

His favorite walk lay near his house, indeed it was part of his own grounds, a little hillside, where he had worn a foot-path, and where he might be found in good weather, when not employed in the tower. While walking to and fro on this bit of rising ground, he meditated and composed innumerable romances that were never written, as well as some that were. Here he first announced to me his plan of "The Dolliver Romance," and, from what he told me of his design of the story as it existed in his mind, I always thought it would have been the greatest of his books. . . .

Time went on, the war broke out, and he had not the heart to go on with his new Romance. During the month of April, 1862, he made a visit to Washington with his friend Ticknor, to whom he was greatly attached. . . .

After his return home from Washington, Hawthorne sent to me, during the month of May, an article for the Atlantic Monthly, which he entitled "Chiefly about War Matters." The paper, excellently well done throughout, of course, contained a personal description of President Lincoln, which I thought, considered as a portrait of a living man, and drawn by Hawthorne, it would not be wise or tasteful to print. The office of an editor . . . is a disagreeable one sometimes, and the case of Hawthorne on Lincoln disturbed me not a little. After reading the manuscript, I wrote to the author, and asked his permission to omit his description of the President's personal appearance. As usual, for he was the kindest and sweetest of contributors, the most good-natured and the most amenable man to advice I ever knew, he consented to my proposal, and allowed me to print the article with the alterations. If you turn to the paper, you will observe there are several notes; all of these were written by Hawthorne himself. He complied with my request without a murmur, but he always thought I was wrong in my decision. He said the whole description of the interview and the President's personal appearance were, to his mind, the only parts of the article worth publishing. "What a terrible thing," he complained, "it is to try to let off a little bit of truth into this miserable humbug of a world." . . .

. . . Whenever I look at [Hawthorne's] portrait, . . . some new trait or anecdote or reminiscence comes up and asks to he made known to those who feel an interest in it. But time and eternity call loudly on mortal gossip to be brief. So this . . . morning shall be our last session over that child of genius. . . .

He began in 1862 to send me some articles from his English Journal for the magazine, which he afterwards collected into a volume and called "Our Old Home." . . . While he was engaged in copying out and rewriting his papers on England for the magazine, he was very despondent about their reception by the public. Speaking of them one day to me, he said: "We must remember that there is a good deal of intellectual ice mingled with this wine of memory." He was sometimes so dispirited during the war, that he was obliged to postpone his contributions for sheer lack of spirit to go on. . . .

Those were troublous days, full of war gloom and general despondency. The North was naturally suspicious of all public men who did not bear a conspicuous part in helping to put down the Rebellion. General Pierce had been President of the United States, and was not identified . . . with the great party which favored the vigorous prosecution of the war. Hawthorne proposed to dedicate his new book to a very dear friend, indeed, but in doing so he would draw public attention in a marked way to an unpopular name. Several of Hawthorne's friends, on learning that he intended to inscribe his book to Franklin Pierce, came to me and begged that I would . . . help Hawthorne to see that he ought not to do anything to endanger the success of his new volume. Accordingly I wrote to him just what many of his friends had said to me, and this is his reply to my letter, which bears date the 18th of July, 1863—

> . . . I find that it would be a piece of poltroonery in me to withdraw either the dedication or the dedicatory letter. My long and intimate personal relations with Pierce render the dedication altogether proper, especially as regards this book, which would have had no existence without his kindness; and if he is so exceedingly unpopular that his name is enough to sink the volume, there is so much the more need that an old friend should stand by him. . . . [I]f I were to tear out the dedication, I should never look at the volume again without remorse and shame. . . .

"Our Old Home" was published in the autumn of 1863, and although it was everywhere welcomed, in England the strictures were applied with a liberal hand. . . .

Meantime the "Dolliver Romance," which had been laid aside on account of the exciting scenes through which we were then passing, and which unfitted him for the composition of a work of the imagination, made little progress. . . .

I had frequent accounts of his ill health and changed appearance, but I supposed he would rally again soon, and become hale and strong before the winter fairly set in. But the shadows even then were about his pathway, and Cunningham's lines, which he once quoted to me, must often have occurred to him,—

> Cold's the snow at my head,
>   And cold's the snow at my feet;
> And the finger of death's at my eyes,
>   Closing them to sleep.[5]

We had arranged together that the "Dolliver Romance" should be first published in the magazine, in monthly instalments and we decided to begin in the January number of 1864. . . .

In . . . December [1863] Hawthorne attended the funeral of Mrs. Franklin Pierce, and, after the ceremony, came to stay with us. He seemed ill and more nervous than usual. He said he found General Pierce greatly needing his companionship, for he was overwhelmed with grief at the loss of his wife. I well remember the sadness of Hawthorne's face when he told us he felt obliged to look on the dead. "It was," said he, "like a carven image laid in its richly embossed enclosure, and there was a remote expression about it as if the whole had nothing to do with things present." He told us, as an instance of the ever-constant courtesy of his friend . . . that while they were standing at the grave, the General, though completely overcome with his own sorrow, turned and drew up the collar of Hawthorne's coat to shield him from the bitter cold.

The same day, as the sunset deepened and we sat together in this room, Hawthorne began to talk in an autobiographical vein, and gave us the story of his early life. . . . He said that at an early age he accompanied his mother and sister to a township in Maine, which his grandfather had purchased. That, he continued, was the happiest period of his life, and it lasted till he was thirteen, when he was sent to school in Salem. "I lived in Maine," he said, "like a bird of the air, so perfect was the freedom I enjoyed. But it was there I first got my cursed habits of solitude." During the moonlight nights of winter he would skate until midnight all alone upon Sebago Lake, with the deep shadows of the icy hills on either hand. When he found himself far away from his home and weary with the exertion of skating, he would sometimes take refuge in a log-cabin, where half a tree would be burning on the broad hearth. He would sit in the ample chimney and look at the stars through the great aperture while the flame went roaring up. "Ah," he said, "how well I recall the summer days also, when, with my gun, I roamed at will through the woods of Maine. How sad middle life looks to people of erratic temperaments. Everything is beautiful in youth, for all things are allowed to it then!"

The new year found him incapacitated from writing much on the [Dolliver] Romance. . . . On Monday, the 28th of March, Hawthorne came to town and made this house his first station on his journey to the South for health. I was greatly shocked at his invalid appearance, and he seemed quite deaf. The light in his eye was beautiful as ever, but his limbs seemed shrunken and his usual stalwart vigor utterly gone. He said to me with a pathetic voice, "Why does Nature treat us like little children! I think we could bear it all if we knew our fate; at least it would not make much difference to me now what became of me." Toward night he brightened up a little, and his delicious wit flashed out, at intervals, as of old, but he was evidently broken and dispirited about his health. Looking out on the bay that was sparkling in the moonlight, he said he thought the moon rather lost something of its charm for him as he grew older. . . . At breakfast, next morning, he spoke of his kind neighbors in Concord, and said Alcott was one of the most excellent men he had ever known. "It is impossible to quarrel with him, for he would take all your harsh words like a saint."

He left us shortly after this for a journey to Washington, with his friend Mr. Ticknor. The travellers spent several days in New York, and then proceeded to Philadelphia. Hawthorne wrote to me from the Continental Hotel, . . . announcing the severe illness of his companion. He did not seem to anticipate a fatal result, but on Sunday morning the news came that Mr. Ticknor was dead. Hawthorne returned at once to Boston, and stayed here overnight. He was in a very excited and nervous state, and talked incessantly of the sad scenes he had just been passing through. We sat late together, conversing of the friend we had lost, and I am sure he hardly closed his eyes that night. In the morning he went back to his own home in Concord.

His health, from that time, seemed to give way rapidly, and his friend, General Pierce, proposed that, as early as possible, they should go among the New Hampshire hills together and meet the spring there. . . .

I saw Hawthorne alive, for the last time, the day he started on this his last journey. His speech and his gait indicated severe illness. . . . His tones were more subdued than ever, and he scarcely spoke above a whisper. He was very affectionate in parting, and I followed him to the door, looking after him as he went up School Street. I noticed that he faltered from weakness, and I should have taken my hat and joined him to offer my arm, but I knew he did not wish to seem ill, and I feared he might be troubled at my anxiety. . . . I followed him with my eyes only, and watched him till he turned the corner and passed out of sight. . . .

Hawthorne's lifelong desire that the end might be a sudden one was gratified. Often . . . he has said to me, "What a blessing to go quickly!" So the same swift angel that came as a messenger to Allston, Irving, Prescott, Macaulay, Thackeray, and Dickens, was commissioned to touch his forehead also, and beckon him away. . . .

On [23] May we carried Hawthorne through the blossoming orchards of Concord, and laid him down under a group of pines, on a hillside, overlooking historic fields. All the way from the village church to the grave the birds kept up a perpetual melody. The sun shone brightly, and the air was sweet and pleasant, as if death had never entered the world. . . . [O]ld friends walked slowly by his side that beautiful spring morning. The companion of his youth and his manhood, for whom he would willingly at any time have given up his own life, Franklin Pierce, was there among the rest, and scattered flowers into the grave. The unfinished [Dolliver] Romance, which had cost him so much anxiety, the last literary work on which he had ever been engaged, was laid on his coffin. . . .

Notes

1. William Wordsworth, "I Wandered Lonely as a Cloud," l. 1.
2. Leigh Hunt, "To Robert Batty . . . on His Giving Me a Lock of Milton's Hair," ll. 9–14.
3. John Milton, "Il Penseroso," l. 39.
4. William Wordsworth, "Characteristics of a Child," ll. 12–14.
5. Allan Cunningham, "The Spring of the Year," ll. 4–8.

[James T. Fields], From "Our Whispering Gallery," *Atlantic Monthly* 27 (February–May 1871): 246–52, 256–57, 380, 382–89, 391, 504, 506–10, 639–40, 643–49, 651–53.

From *Concord Days* (1872)

A[MOS] BRONSON ALCOTT

⋇

Educator, philosopher, lecturer, and author, Amos Bronson Alcott (1799–1888) lived one of the purer—albeit, at times, wholly impractical—versions of Transcendentalism. After an unsuccessful stint as a teacher in Philadelphia, Alcott, who lived in Boston in the 1820s, returned there in 1834 to operate the progressive Temple School with the assistance of Elizabeth Palmer Peabody. An early defender of Emersonian idealism, an original member of the Transcendental Club founded in 1836, cofounder with Charles Lane of the utopian community Fruitlands in 1843, and the organizer of the short-lived "Town and Country Club" in 1849, Alcott was both praised and ridiculed as a conversationalist and reformer by his contemporaries, as several narratives included in this volume show. With his wife, Abigail (Abba) May, and growing family of daughters, in the 1840s he settled in various places in Concord, including the Hillside, which he sold to Hawthorne in 1852. After a series of dislocations, the Alcotts returned to Concord permanently in 1857, purchasing Orchard House next to the Wayside, which made them the Hawthornes' neighbors. Perhaps the signal success of Alcott's career was his founding of the Concord School of Philosophy in 1879, where scholarly meetings often arranged as conversations convene to this day. In 1848, Emerson expressed the sentiment that best characterizes Alcott's centrality to the Transcendentalist movement: "Alcott is a . . . fluid in which men of a certain spirit can easily expand themselves & swim at large, they who elsewhere found themselves confined. He gives them nothing but themselves. . . . Me he has served . . . in that way; he was the reasonable creature to speak to, that I wanted" (*JMN*, 11:19).

Sharing a number of friends and acquaintances, Hawthorne and Alcott met in the late 1830s. The Hawthornes and Alcotts were on cordial terms while Nathaniel and Sophia lived at the Old Manse, but when both families later settled in Concord permanently, Hawthorne tolerated Alcott's company, but he did not seek it. Whether Alcott considered Hawthorne's attitude toward him a personal slight is unclear; what is clear from occasional letters and jottings in his journals is that Alcott considered Hawthorne a great author and a decent but elusive person. For instance, writing to James T. Fields in 1870,

Alcott expressed admiration for "Hawthorne's English Note Books" as "pleasant reading for these June days. We can never have too much England from any lover of it. . . . Few of his contemporaries have observed with finer eyes than did our American Romancer. His facts are better facts than most historians, since he dealt with life and living things as only poets can" (*Letters ABA,* 515–16). Earlier, when Hawthorne decided to renovate and expand the Wayside upon his return from England, he asked Alcott for his "suggestions and counsels." Rejoicing at the overture, Alcott wrote, "I shall delight to assist him and build for him in my rustic way, restoring his arbours if he wishes" (28 June 1860; *Journals ABA,* 328). But within a few months Alcott decided that Europe had not moderated Hawthorne's antisocial impulse. On 17 February 1861 he observed,

> The snow is melting fast and the ground beginning to appear. I get glimpses of Hawthorne as I walk up the sled paths, he dodging about amongst the trees on his hilltop as if he feared his neighbor's eyes would catch him as he walked. A coy genius, and to be won as a maid is, by some bashful stratagem, and as difficult of approach as Channing, only less capricious, and having nothing of impudence in his bearing. His avoidances have a certain reasonableness, nothing sullen or morose about them, and excite a pitying affection, as if he were their unwilling victim and would gladly meet you if he dared disobey the impulse that dogs him to solitude and study. (*Journals ABA,* 335–36)

The selection that follows grew out of this last journal entry, which Alcott rewrote and expanded on several occasions: in 1864 for a sentimental obituary on Hawthorne that appeared in the *Boston Commonwealth* ("Hawthorne," 3 June 1864, 1:6–7), and then in a journal entry dated 10 June 1870 (*Journals ABA,* 411–12), prior to expanding it once more for *Concord Days.* The "Southern guest at [Hawthorne's] table" whom Alcott describes here is Rebecca Harding Davis; her recollection of the same dinner is printed above.

HAWTHORNE WAS OF THE darker temperament and tendencies. His sensitiveness and sadness were native, and he cultivated them apparently alike by solitude, the pursuits and studies in which he indulged, till he became almost fated to know gayer hours only by stealth. By disposition friendly, he seemed the victim of his temperament, as if he sought distance, if not his pen, to put himself in communication, and possible sympathy with others,—with his nearest friends, even. His reserve and imprisonment were more distant and close, while the desire for conversation was livelier, than anyone I have known. There was something of strangeness even in his cherished intimacies, as if he set himself afar from all and from himself with the rest; the most diffident of men, as coy as a maiden, he could only be won by some cunning artifice, his reserve was so habitual, his isolation so entire, the solitude so vast. How distant people were from him, the world they lived in, how he came to know so much about them, by what stratagem he got into his own house or left it, was a marvel. Fancy fixed, he was not to be jostled from himself for a moment, his mood was so persistent. There he was in the twilight, there he stayed. Was he some damsel imprisoned in that manly form pleading alway for release, sighing for the freedom and companionships denied her? Or was he some Assyrian ill at ease afar from the olives and the East? Had he strayed over with William the Conqueror, and true to his Norman nature, was the baron still in republican America, secure in his castle, secure in his tower, whence he could defy all invasion of curious eyes? What neighbor of his ever caught him on the highway, or ventured to approach his threshold?

> His bolted Castle gates, what man should ope,
> > Unless the Lord did will
> > To prove his skill,
> And tempt the fates hid in his horoscope?

Yet if by chance admitted, welcome in a voice that a woman might own for its hesitancy and tenderness; his eyes telling the rest.

> For such the noble language of his eye,
> That when of words his lips were destitute,
> Kind eyebeams spake while yet his tongue was mute.

Your intrusion was worth the courage it cost; it emboldened to future assaults to carry this fort of bashfulness. During all the time he lived near me, our estates being separated only by a gate and shaded avenue, I seldom caught sight of him; and when I did it was but to lose it the moment he suspected he was visible; oftenest seen on his hilltop screened behind the shrubbery and disappearing like a hare into the bush when surprised. I remember of his being in my house but twice, and then he was so ill at ease that he found excuse for leaving politely forthwith,—"the stove was so hot," "the clock ticked so loud." Yet he once complained to me of his wish to meet oftener, and dwelt on the delights of fellowship, regretting he had so little. I think he seldom dined from home; nor did he often entertain anyone,—once, an Englishman, when I was also his guest; but he preserved his shrinking taciturnity, and left to us the conversation. Another time I dined with a Southern guest at his table. The conversation turning on the war after dinner, he hid himself in the corner, as if a distant spectator, and fearing there was danger even there. It was due to his guest to bear the human side of the question of slavery, since she had heard only the best the South had to plead in its favor.

I never deemed Hawthorne an advocate of Southern ideas and institutions. He professed democracy, not in the party, but large sense of equality. Perhaps he loved England too well to be quite just to his native land. . . . He seemed to regret the transplanting, as if reluctant to fix his roots in our soil. His book on England, entitled "Our Old Home," intimates his filial affection for that and its institutions. If his themes were American, his treatment of them was foreign, rather. He stood apart as having no stake in home affairs. While calling himself a democrat, he sympathized apparently with the absolutism of the old countries. He had not full faith to the people; perhaps feared republicanism. . . . Of our literary men, he least sympathized with the North. . . . It is doubtful if he ever attended a political meeting or voted on any occasion throughout the long struggle with slavery. He stood aloof, hesitating to take a responsible part, true to his convictions, doubtless, strictly honest, if not patriotic.

He strove by disposition to be sunny and genial, traits not native to him. Constitutionally shy, recluse, melancholy, only by shafts of wit and flow of humor could he deliver himself. There was a soft sadness in his smile, a reserve in his glance, telling how isolate he was. Was he ever one of his company while in it? There was an aloofness, a *besides,* that refused to affiliate himself with himself, even. His readers must feel this, while unable to account for it, perhaps, or express it adequately. A believer in transmitted traits needs but read his pedigree to find the genesis of what characterized him distinctly, and made him and his writings their inevitable sequel. Everywhere you will find persons of his type and complexion similar in cast of character and opinions. His associates mostly confirm the observation.

From *Concord Days* (Boston: Roberts Brothers, 1872), 193–97.

"Bowdoin College—Nathaniel Hawthorne" (1875)

John S. C. Abbott

⫶⫶

Written to celebrate the fiftieth anniversary of Bowdoin College's class of 1825 and its most prominent member, the reminiscence that follows is among the best of the type that began to appear with increasing frequency after 1875. A classmate of Hawthorne and Longfellow, John Stevens Cabot Abbott (1805–1877) was ordained a Congregational minister in 1830, after finishing his studies in theology at Andover Theological Seminary in 1829. Abbott held pastorates in Worcester, Roxbury, and Nantucket, Massachusetts, and in New Haven, Connecticut, but he made his reputation as an author of popular histories, biographies, and devotional and instructional tracts, rather than as a preacher. His major works include *The Mother at Home* (1833), *A History of Napoleon Bonaparte* (1855), *A History of the Civil War in America* (1863–1866), and *A History of Frederick the Great* (1871).

Although Abbott borrowed some details of Hawthorne's life in Concord from Curtis's 1853 sketch printed above, his treatment of Hawthorne here, especially in its emphasis on his subject's college days, is largely original. Remarking that during the four years of their collegiate intimacy "I cannot remember that I ever heard Hawthorne *laugh*," his recollections of Hawthorne's association with himself, Cilley, Cheever, and Pierce are nonetheless positive and, in many instances, quite flattering. Following its appearance, Abbott's reminiscence became a source for other treatments of Hawthorne's time at Bowdoin. Two of the more notable such works are Joseph W. Symonds's *Nathaniel Hawthorne: An Oration Delivered before the Alumni of Bowdoin College* (1878) and George T. Packard's "The College Days of Hawthorne" (*The Christian Union* 41 [26 June 1890]: 900–1). Ramblingly nostalgic about the Bowdoin of Hawthorne's day and his place in it, both authors narrowly read Hawthorne's inner life through reference to his fictional characters. For instance, after introducing the assembled alumni to "the men whose genius and fame have become a part of our common inheritance," Symonds brings Hawthorne into his narrative this way:

> And among these, somewhat aloof from the group, in the seclusion of a
> strange experience, with a shadow resting upon his face, that might be of a

passing cloud, but does not pass, intent, absorbed, as if he had questioned guilt and sorrow for their darkest secret and was awaiting reply, or as if he were following to the utmost verge of thought the threads of somber hue on which human life is woven in woof of changeful light and shade, however memory may recall or fancy may paint him, will forever remain the noble presence of Nathaniel Hawthorne. (5–6)

. . . EMERSON HAS BEEN CREDITED with saying: "I do not love to see a distinctly-defined, clean-cut thought. I love rather to see a grand idea looming up majestic through the haze of obscurity."

Nathaniel Hawthorne was such a *man.* No one could read him. He dwelt in unrevealed recesses, which his most intimate friends were never permitted to penetrate. He entered Bowdoin College at the age of seventeen, a well-dressed, gentlemanly boy, of ordinary stature, but of unusually winning countenance and gentle manners. In a class of but about forty, nearly all dwelling in the same hall and meeting three or four times each day, in chapel or classroom, the members were thrown into the most intimate social relations.

The soft tones of voice, remarkably sweet, modest address, and courteous bearing of Hawthorne rendered him universally popular. He was an accomplished scholar, a great reader, and he soon acquired the reputation of being one of the finest writers in the class. In such an intimacy of four years I cannot remember that I ever heard Hawthorne *laugh,* though his face was often brightened by a very winning smile. He never seemed melancholy, so as to oppress one's spirits with gloom; but there was an aspect of silent pensiveness spread over his features, which arrested the eye and led one to inquire: "Who is that young man?"

In saying that Hawthorne was *popular* the word must be used a little differently from its ordinary sense. There was no one in the class who would have taken the liberty of slapping him on the shoulder. He was a lonely man, living by himself; yet there was nothing in his demeanor to repel the friendly advances of any one.

It may not be improper here to remark that the class of 1825 was to a remarkable degree composed of young men from the first families of Maine. Very many of them had found the cradle of their infancy in homes of refinement and intellectual culture. This gave such a tone to character that very seldom was there an ungraceful action witnessed or a coarse word uttered.

It was not uncommon in those days for little groups to meet and spend an hour in the evening, with wine and cigars, telling stories and singing songs. There were, of course, in a gathering of over one hundred young men in college some rude and noisy collections of this kind. Such young men had been drawn together by what has been called elective affinity. This was long before the temperance reform. When our somewhat stern but able village pastor, the Rev. Asa Mead, inquired of one of the students, Lory Odell: "Are the students in the habit of keeping ardent spirits in their rooms?" he emphatically replied, . . . "No, sir; never, never! They always drink it all up!"

There was a singular element of hilarity in the nature of Hawthorne. He was very fond of being present at these festivities; and yet he never told a story or sang a song. His voice was never heard in any shout of merriment. But the silent beaming smile would testify to his keen appreciation of the scene and to his enjoyment of the wit.

He would often sit for a whole evening, with his head gently inclined to one side, hearing every word, seeing every gesture, and yet scarcely a single word would pass his lips. But there was an indescribable something in the silent presence of Hawthorne which rendered him one of the most desired guests on such occasions.

Jonathan Cilley was probably Hawthorne's most intimate friend in the class. And yet his discrimination would lead him to say: "I love Hawthorne[;] I admire him; but I do not know him. He lives in a mysterious world of thoughts and imagination which he never permits me to enter."

In the class next above Hawthorne's there was a young man but seventeen years of age, by the name of Franklin Pierce. He was the youngest member of his class and I think the most popular young man in college. He was the son of a noble sire, was very handsome, and was always a genial, courteous, friendly gentleman. Hawthorne and Pierce were instinctively drawn together. They became intimate and life-long friends. The whispering pines of Brunswick, free from all underbrush, presented very attractive avenues for solitary or social walks. Pierce and Hawthorne almost invariably joined arm in arm in sauntering through these groves. They were alike in age, in courteous instincts, in scholarly tastes, and in purity of lip and life.

Little did they then imagine, those two lads of seventeen years, that the one was to be President of the United States, placed in that exalted station perhaps through the instrumentality of the biography which his companion would write of him; and that the other would receive, in recompense, the office of consul of Liverpool which was said to be the most lucrative position at the disposal of the Government. It was estimated to be worth to its incumbent twenty thousand dollars a year.

Even Henry W. Longfellow, prominent as he himself was in the class, knew so little of the cloistered, taciturn Hawthorne that he wrote that he remembered him in his student days only "as a shy youth, in a bright-buttoned coat, flitting across the college grounds."

Upon graduating, there seemed to be nothing attractive in life opening before Hawthorne. He could not endure the thought of either of the professions. From all the turmoil and agitations of business life he recoiled. The attempt to get a living by literature would not then have entered any one's mind. He went to Salem, . . . where he spent several years in a seclusion which could scarcely have been surpassed by that of the cloistered monk.

I must now resort to rumor, for the minute accuracy of which I cannot vouch; but the main and important facts are certainly true. The Rev. George B. Cheever went to Salem as pastor of one of the churches there. He hunted up his old classmate, Hawthorne; and found him solitary, alone forgotten in his chamber. He was sustained in his living burial by a small stipend, and the great flood of busy life rolled by him unheeded.

Mr. Cheever was not a man to shrink from grappling with the world in its sternest conflicts. He recalled . . . some of his classmate's eloquent themes in college, spoke to him words of cheer, and infused into Hawthorne's desponding spirit somewhat of the energies of his own brave heart. He urged Hawthorne to write for the press.

Thus roused and animated, he sent an article to Mr. Goodrich, the renowned "Peter Parley," who was then editing a periodical in Boston. Mr. Goodrich was delighted with the genius displayed and wrote for more. The new, laborious, brain-wearing life of authorship was commenced. Hawthorne rose slowly to fame. He was not popular with the masses; but the most cultivated scholars in the land read whatever came from his pen with the highest appreciation.

Hawthorne continued to live in the companionship of his own thoughts. He shunned all society and took long and lonely moonlight walks in the woods or along the seashore. His vivid imaginings and kindly feelings rendered him not unhappy in thus gratifying his peculiar tastes. He was not born to shine in society, but he was born to be contented and happy in solitude. His contributions to periodicals were collected and published in . . . "Twice Told Tales." . . .

In subsequent years there came from his pen those wonderful volumes which have attracted the admiration of every scholarly mind in England and America. "The Scarlet Letter," "The House of the Seven Gables," "The Marble Faun," and the "Mosses from an Old Manse" have placed Mr. Hawthorne in the first ranks of the writers of the English language.

It is not my object to enter into the details of Hawthorne's life. That would require a volume. In 1842 he entered into perhaps as congenial a marriage union as was ever formed. In the silence of the venerable old town of Concord he found a home just suited to his tastes. The loneliness of the somewhat dilapidated "Old Manse" pleased him. Always meeting one with a pleasant smile, always ready to exchange a few affable words, he still avoided all society with the village people. He was, however, beloved by his neighbors, for there was not the slightest admixture of austerity or moroseness in [his] character. . . .

In Ralph Waldo Emerson, Hawthorne found a congenial friend. One winter evening there was a tea-party [at Emerson's] of distinguished guests gathered around the great wood-fire which blazed upon the hearth. Hawthorne delighted to be a silent participant in such a gathering. Mr. Curtis . . . gives [an] account of the appearance of Mr. Hawthorne. It is so graphic and so precisely corresponds with scenes which I have often witnessed in the early youth of Mr. Hawthorne that I cannot refrain from transcribing [some of] it here. . . .

"I . . . [was] scarcely aware of a man who sat upon the edge of the circle, a little withdrawn, his head slightly thrown forward upon his breast and his bright eyes clearly burning under his black brow. . . .

"He rose and walked to the window, and stood quietly there for a long time, watching the dead, white landscape. No appeal was made to him. . . . The conversation flowed as steadily on as if every one understood that his silence was to be respected. . . .

"But there was a light in his eye which assured . . . that nothing was lost. So supreme was his silence that it presently engrossed me to the exclusion of everything else. There was brilliant discourse; but this silence was much more poetic and fascinating." . . .

There was certainly something social in the silence of Hawthorne.... [His] presence, in some nameless way, added to the enjoyment of the party. . . .

Hawthorne's reputation was now established as the most classical of American novelists. Circumstances removed him from Concord to a beautiful cottage in Lenox, amidst the mountains of Berkshire. . . . He finally returned to Concord for his permanent home. While these years were gliding away he had been for a short time a clerk in the custom-house at Boston and also surveyor of the port of Salem. During the four years of the administration of his friend, Franklin Pierce, he resided in Liverpool. Most of the business of his office of consul was conducted by his subordinates.

From Liverpool he returned with replenished resources—pecuniary as well as intellectual—to his home in Concord. . . . In the spring of 1864, as he had attained his sixtieth year, his health began to fail. Accompanied by his life-long friend, President Pierce, he undertook an excursion to the White Mountains of New Hampshire. Hawthorne seemed desponding, and expressed to his friend his conviction that his life-work was done. They reached Plymouth, and took rooms for the night at the Pemigewasset House.

Mr. Hawthorne had that day seemed unusually feeble, silent, and sad. President Pierce felt so anxious for his friend that in the middle of the night he rose and went softly into his room. Mr. Hawthorne was apparently sweetly sleeping. . . . But the sleep of Hawthorne was that final, solemn sleep which has no earthly waking. In the morning he was found dead.

The Independent (24 June 1875): 3–4.

From *A Study of Hawthorne* (1876)

GEORGE PARSONS LATHROP

⇥⇤

Born near Honolulu, Hawaii, and educated in New York and in Dresden, Germany, George Parsons Lathrop (1851–1898) enjoyed a multifaceted career as an associate editor of the *Atlantic Monthly* (1875–1877), a newspaper journalist, an author of poetry and fiction, and Hawthorne's first comprehensive biographer and editor of his works. A founder of the American Copyright League in 1883, Lathrop lobbied widely for the eventual passage of the international copyright law. Although his poetry and fiction have lapsed into obscurity, Lathrop's illustrated "Riverside Edition" of *The Complete Works of Nathaniel Hawthorne* (Boston: Houghton, Mifflin, 1883) introduced all of Hawthorne's writings to the public-at-large, and even today his *Study of Hawthorne* (1876) remains a starting point for serious biographical and critical treatments of the emergence of Hawthorne's reputation.

Lathrop married Rose Hawthorne, Nathaniel and Sophia's youngest child, in London on 11 September 1871, barely seven months after her mother's death. A rift between Julian Hawthorne and Lathrop over his use of what Julian claimed as private family papers in *A Study*, the death of the Lathrops' only child, Francis, and Lathrop's alcoholism exerted considerable pressure on their marriage. In 1891, they converted to Roman Catholicism, yet the respite religion brought to their marriage was temporary, and they formally separated in 1895. Rose moved to New York City, where, after training as a nurse, she opened a refuge for cancer victims on the Lower East Side. Prior to his death, Lathrop, who had become debilitated by alcoholism, adapted *The Scarlet Letter* for a three-act opera that Walter Damrosch produced in New York in 1896.

The influence that Lathrop's *Study of Hawthorne* exerted on Hawthorne's reputation in the nineteenth century and beyond is discussed at length in the introduction to this volume.

THIS BOOK WAS NOT DESIGNED as a biography, but is rather a portrait. And ... it is not so much this, as my conception of what a portrait of Hawthorne should be. For I cannot write with the authority of one who had known him and had been formally intrusted with the task of describing his life. On the other hand, I do not enter upon this attempt as a mere literary performance, but have been assisted in it by an inward impulse, a consciousness of sympathy with the subject, which I may perhaps consider a sort of inspiration. My guide has been intuition, confirmed and seldom confuted by research. Perhaps it is even a favoring fact that I should never have seen Mr. Hawthorne; a personality so elusive as his may possibly yield its traits more readily to one who can never obtrude actual intercourse between himself and the mind he is meditating upon. An honest report upon personal contact always has a value denied to the reviews of after-comers, yet the best criticism and biography is not always that of contemporaries.

Our first studies will have a biographical scope, because a certain grouping of facts is essential, to give point to the view which I am endeavoring to present; and as Hawthorne's early life has hitherto been but little explored, much of the material used in the earlier chapters is now for the first time made public. The latter portion of the career may be treated more sketchily, being already better known; though passages will be found throughout the essay which have been developed with some fulness, in order to maintain a correct atmosphere, compensating any errors which mere opinions might lead to. Special emphasis, then, must not be held to show neglect of points which my space and scope prevent my commenting on. But the first outline requiring our attention involves a distant retrospect.

The history of Hawthorne's genius is in some sense a summary of all New England history.

From amid a simple, practical, energetic community, remarkable for its activity in affairs of state and religion, but by no means given to dreaming, this fair flower of American genius rose up unexpectedly enough, breaking the cold New England sod for the emission of a light and fragrance as pure and pensive as that of the arbutus in our woods, in spring. The flower, however, sprang from seed that rooted in the old colonial life of the sternly imaginative pilgrims and Puritans. Thrusting itself up into view through the drift of a later day, it must not be confounded with other growths nourished only by that more recent deposit; though the surface-drift had of course its own weighty influence in the nourishment of it. The artistic results of a period of action must sometimes be looked for at a point of time long subsequent, and this was especially sure to be so in the first phases of New England civilization. The settlers in this region, in addition to the burdens and obstacles proper to pioneers, had to deal with the cares of forming a model state and of laying out for posterity a straight and solid path in which it might walk with due rectitude. All this was in itself an ample enough subject to occupy their powerful imaginations. They were enacting a kind of sacred epic, the dangers and the dignity and exaltation of which they felt most fervently. The Bible, the Bay Psalm Book, Bunyan, and Milton, the poems of George Wither, Baxter's Saint's Rest, and some controversial pamphlets, would suffice to appease whatever yearnings the immense experiment of their lives failed to satisfy. Gradually . . . the native press and new-comers from England multiplied books in a community which held letters in unusual reverence. But the continuous work of subduing a new country, the dependence upon the mother-land for general literature, and finally the excitements of the Revolutionary period, deferred the opportunity for any aesthetic expression of the forces that had been at work here ever since Winthrop stepped from the Arbella on to the shore of the New World, with noble manliness and sturdy statesmanship enough in him to uphold the whole future of a great people. When Hawthorne came, therefore, his utterance was a culmination of the two preceding centuries. An entire side of the richly endowed human nature to which we owe the high qualities of New England,—a nature which is often so easily disposed of as meagre, cold, narrow, and austere,—this side, long suppressed and thrown into shade by the more active front, found expression at last in these pages so curiously compounded of various elements, answering to those traits of the past which Hawthorne's genius revived. The sensuous substance of the early New England character had piously surrendered to the severe maxims which religion and prudence imposed; and so complete was its suppression, that all this part of Puritan nature missed recording itself, except by chance glimpses through the history of the times. For this voluntary oblivion it has been rarely compensated in the immortality it meets with through Hawthorne. Not that he set himself with forethought to the illustration of it; but, in studying as poet and dramatist the past from which he himself had issued, he sought . . . to light it up from the interior, to possess himself of the very fire which burned in men's breasts and set their minds in movement at that epoch. In his own person and his own blood the same elements, the same capabilities still existed, however modified or differently ordered. The records of Massachusetts Bay are full of suggestive incongruities between the ideal, single-souled life which its founders hoped to lead, and the jealousies, the opposing opinions, or the intervolved passions of individuals and of parties, which sometimes unwittingly cloaked themselves in religious tenets. Placing himself in the position

[163]

of these beings, then, and conscious of all the strong and various potencies of emotion which his own nature, inherited from them, held in curb, it was natural that Hawthorne should give weight to this contrast between the intense, prisoned life of shut sensibilities and the formal outward appearance to which it was moulded. . . . It is thus that his figures get their tremendous and often terrible relief. They are seen as close as we see our faces in a glass, and brought so intimately into our consciousness that the throbbing of their passions sounds like the mysterious, internal beating of our own hearts in our own ears. And even when he is not dealing directly with themes or situations closely related to that life, there may be felt in his style . . . a union of vigorous freedom, and graceful, shy restraint, a mingling of guardedness which verges on severity with a quick and delicately thrilled sensibility for all that is rich and beautiful and generous, which is his by right of inheritance from the race of Non-conformist colonizers. How subtle and various this sympathy is, between himself and the past of his people. . . .

. . . [By] reviewing that past, then trying to reproduce in imagination the immediate atmosphere of Hawthorne's youth, and comparing the two, . . . we shall best arrive at the completion of our proposed portrait. We have first to study the dim perspective and the suggestive coloring of that historic background from which the author emerges, and then to define clearly his own individual traits as they appear in his published works and Note-Books.

The eagerness which admirers of such a genius show, to learn all permissible details of his personal history, is, when freed from the vulgar and imbecile curiosity which often mars it, a sort of homage that it is right to satisfy. It is a respect apt to be paid only to men whose winning personal qualities have reached through their writing, and touched a number of grateful and appreciative hearts. But two objections may be urged against giving such details here: one is, that Hawthorne especially disapproved the writing of a Life of himself; the other, that the history of [his native New England] and the works of Hawthorne are easily accessible to any one, without intervention.

Of the first it may frankly be said . . . that Hawthorne alone could have adequately portrayed his life for us; though in the same breath it should be added that the idea of his undertaking to do it is almost preposterous. To such a spirit as his, the plan would have had an exquisite absurdity about it, that might even have savored of imposition. The mass of trivial details essential to the accurate and consecutive account of an entire life could never have gained his serious attention. . . . There is something natural and fine in this.

I confess that to me the spectacle presented by Goethe when dwelling on the minutest incidents of his childhood with senile vanity and persistence, and fashioning with avaricious care the silver shrine and crystal case in which . . . he hopes to have the reverent ages view him, is one which increases my sense of his defective though splendid personality. And yet I cannot suppress the opposite feeling, that the man of note who lets his riches of reminiscence be buried with him inflicts a loss on the world which it is hard to take resignedly. In the Note-Books of Hawthorne this want is to a large extent made good. His shrinking sensitiveness in regard to the embalming process of biography is in these somewhat abated, so that they have been of incalculable use in assisting the popular eye to see him as he really was. Other material for illustration of his daily life is somewhat meagre; and yet . . . this is perhaps a cause for rejoicing. There is a halo about every man of large poetic genius which it is difficult for the world to wholly miss seeing, while he is alive. Afterward, when the biographer comes, we find the actual dimensions, the physical outline, more insisted upon. That is the biographer's business; and it is not altogether his fault . . . that the public regard is thus turned away from the peculiar but impalpable sign that floats above the poet's actual stature. But, under this subtile influence, forgetting that old, luminous hallucination . . . we suddenly feel the want of it, are dissatisfied; and, not perceiving that the cause lies largely with us, we fall to detracting from the subject. Thus it is fortunate that we have no regular biography of Shakespeare authoritative enough to fade our own private conceptions of him; and it is not an unmixed ill that some degree of similar mystery should soften and give tone to the life of Hawthorne. . . . The contact of life and death is too unsympathetic. Whatever stuff the writer be made of, it seems inevitable that he should suffer injury from exposure to the busy and prying light of subsequent life, after his so deep repose in death. . . .

. . . [My] book makes no pretension to the character of a Life. The wish of Hawthorne on this point would alone be enough to prevent that. If such a work is to be undertaken, it should be by another hand, in which the right to set aside this wish is much more certainly vested than in mine. But I have thought that an earnest sympathy with the subject might sanction the present essay. Sympathy, after all, is the talisman which may preserve even the formal biographer from giving that injury to his theme just spoken of. And if the insight which guides me has any worth, it will present whatever material has already been made public with a selection and shaping which all researchers might not have time to bestow.

. . . I am quite alive to the difficulties of my task; and I am conscious that the work may to some appear supererogatory. Stricture and praise are, it will perhaps be said, equally impertinent to a fame so well established. Neither have I any rash hope of adding a single ray to the light of Hawthorne's high standing. But I do not fear the charge of presumption. Time, if not the present reader, will supply the right perspective and proportion.

On the ground of critical duty there is surely defence enough for such an attempt as the one now offered; the relative rank of Hawthorne, and other distinctions touching him, seem to call for a fuller discussion than has been given them. I hope to prove . . . that my aim is in no wise a partisan one. Criticism is appreciative estimation. It is inevitable that the judgments of competent and cultivated persons should flatly contradict each other, . . . and this whether they are coeval or of different dates. At the last, it is in many respects [a] matter of simple individual impression; and there will always be persons of high intelligence whom it will be impossible to make coincide with us entirely, touching even a single author. So that the best we can do is to set about giving rational explanation of our diverse admirations. . . .

What has thus far been developed in this essay, concerning Hawthorne's personality . . . has, I hope, served the end in view,—that of suggesting a large, healthy nature, capable of the most profound thought and the most graceful and humorous mental play. The details of his early life already given show how soon the inborn honor of his nature began to shine. The small irregularities in his college course have seemed to me to bring him nearer and to endear him, without in any way impairing the dignity and beauty of character which prevailed in him from the beginning. It is good to know that he shared the average human history in these harmless peccadilloes; for they never hurt his integrity, and they are reminders of that old but welcome truth, that the greatest men do not need a constant diet of great circumstances. He had many difficulties to deal with, as unpicturesque and harassing as any we have to encounter in our daily courses,—a thing which people are curiously prone to forget in the case of eminent authors. The way in which he dealt with these throws back light on himself. We discover how well the high qualities of genius were matched by those of character.

Fragmentary anecdotes have a value, but so relative that to attempt to construct the subject's character out of them is hazardous. Conceptions of a man derived only from such matter remind one of Charles Lamb's ghosts, formed of the particles which, every seven years, are replaced throughout the body by new ones. Likewise, the grossest errors have been committed through the assumption that particular passages in Hawthorne's writings apply directly and unqualifiedly to himself. There is so much imagination interfused with them, that only a reverent and careful imagination can apply them aright. Nor are private letters to be interpreted in any other way than as the talk of the hour, very inadequately representative, and often—unless read in many lights—positively untrue, to the writer. It gives an entirely false notion, for example, to accept as a trait of character this modest covering up of a noble sentiment, which occurs in a letter refusing to withdraw the dedication of "Our Old Home" to Pierce, in the time of the latter's unpopularity:—

> Nevertheless, I have no fancy for making myself a martyr when it is honorably and conscientiously possible to avoid it; and I always measure out my heroism very accurately according to the exigencies of the occasion, and should be the last man in the world to throwaway a bit of it needlessly.

Such a passage ought never to have been printed without some modifying word; for it has been execrably misused. "I have often felt," Hawthorne says, "that words may be a thick and darksome veil of mystery between the soul and the truth which it seeks." What injustice, then, that he should be judged by a literal construction of words quickly chosen for the transient embodiment of a mood!

The first and most common opinion about the man Hawthorne is, that he must have been extremely gloomy, because his mind nourished so many grave thoughts and solemn fancies. But this merely proves that, as he himself says, when people think he is pouring himself out in a tale or an essay, he is merely telling what is common to human nature, not what is peculiar to himself. "I sympathize with them, not they with me." He sympathizes in the special direction of our darker side. A creative mind of the higher order holds the thread which guides it surely through life's labyrinths; but all the more on this account its attention is called to the erratic movement of other travellers around it. The genius who has the clew begins, therefore, to study these errors and to describe them for our behoof. It is a great mistake to suppose that the abnormal or preposterous phases which he describes are the fruit of *self*-study,—personal traits disguised in fiction; yet this is what has often been affirmed of Hawthorne. We don't think of attributing to Dickens the multiform oddities which he pictures with such power, it being manifestly absurd to do so. As Dickens raises the laugh against them, we at once perceive that they are outside of himself. Hawthorne is so serious, that we are absorbed in the sober earnest of the thing, and forget to apply the rule in his case. Dickens's distinct aim is to excite us with something uncommon; Hawthorne's, to show us that the elements of all tragedies lie within our individual natures; therefore we begin to attribute in undue measure to *his* individual nature all the abnormal conditions that he has shown to be potential in any of us. But in truth he was a perfectly healthy person. . . .

This very healthiness was his qualification for his office. By virtue of his mental integrity and absolute moral purity, he was able to handle unhurt all disintegrated and sinful forms of character; and when souls in trouble, persons with moral doubts to solve and criminals wrote to him for counsel, they recognized the healing touch of one whose pitying immaculateness could make them well.

She who knew best his habitual tone through a sympathy such as has rarely been given to any man, who lived with him a life so exquisitely fair and high, that to speak of it publicly is almost irreverent, has written:—

He had the inevitable pensiveness and gravity of a person who possessed what a mend has called his 'awful power of insight'; but his mood was always cheerful and equal, and his mind peculiarly healthful, and the airy splendor of his wit and humor was the light of his home. He saw too far to be despondent, though his vivid sympathies and shaping imagination often made him sad in behalf of others. He also perceived morbidness wherever it existed instantly, as if by the illumination of his own steady cheer.

His closest friends, too, speak with delight of his genial warmth and ease in converse with them. He could seldom talk freely with more than two or three, however, on account of his constitutional shyness, and perhaps of a peculiarly concentrative cast of mind; though he possessed a ready adaptability. . . . A gentleman who was with him at Brook Farm, and knew him well, tells me that his presence was very attractive, and that he inspired great esteem among all at the farm by his personal qualities. On a walking trip to Wachusett, which they once made together, Hawthorne showed a great interest in sitting in the bar-rooms of country taverns, to listen to the talk of the attendant farmers and villagers. The manner in which he was approached had a great deal to do with his response. If treated simply and wisely, he would answer cordially;

but he was entirely dismayed, as a rule, by those who made demonstrations of admiration or awe. "Why do they treat me so?" he asked a friend, in one case of this sort. "Why, they're afraid of you." "But I tremble at *them,*" he said. "They think," she explained, "that you're imagining all sorts of terrible things." "Heavens!" he answered; "if they only knew what I *do* think about." . . .

He was simple in his habits, and fond of being out of doors, but not—after his college days—as a sportsman. While living beside the Concord, he rowed frequently, with a dreamy devotion to the pastime, and was fond of fishing; swimming, too, he enjoyed. But his chief exercise was walking; he had a vast capacity for it, and was, I think, never even seen upon horseback. At Brook Farm he "belabored the rugged furrows" with a will; and at the Old Manse he presided over his garden in a paradisiacal sort of way. Books in every form he was always eager for, sometimes, as has been reported, satisfying himself with an old almanac or newspaper, over which he would brood as deeply as over richly stored volumes of classic literature. At other times he was fastidious in his choice, and threw aside many books before he found the right one for the hour. An impression has been set afloat that he cared nothing for books in themselves, but this is incorrect. He never had the means to accumulate a library of any size, but he had a passion for books. . . .

. . . He was . . . a cordial admirer of other writers, seldom vexing himself with a critical review of their merits and defects, but applying to them instead the test of his own catholic capacity for enjoyment. The deliberate tone in which he judges his own works, in his letters, shows how little his mind was impressed by the greatness of their fame and of the genius found in them. There could not have been a more modest author, though he did not weakly underrate his work. "Recognition," he once said to Mr. Howells, "makes a man very modest."

[Attempts have] been made to show that he had little interest in animals, partly based, ludicrous as it may seem, on his bringing them into only one of his books. In his American journals, however, there is abundant evidence of his acute sympathy in this direction; at the Old Manse he fried fish for his dog Leo, when he says he should not have done it for himself; and in the Trosachs he finds a moment for pitying some little lambs startled by the approach of his party. I have already mentioned his fondness for cats. It has further been said that he did not enjoy wild nature, because in the "English Note-Books" there is no out-gushing of ecstatic description. But in fact he had the keenest enjoyment of it. He could not enter into the spectacle when hurrying through strange regions. Among the English lakes he writes:—

> To say the truth, I was weary of fine scenery, and it seemed to me that I had eaten a score of mountains and quaffed as many lakes, all in the space of two or three days, and the natural consequence was a surfeit.
>
> I doubt if anybody ever does really see a mountain, who goes for the set and sole purpose of seeing it. Nature will not let herself be seen in such cases. You must patiently bide her time; and by and by, at some unforeseen moment, she will quietly and suddenly unveil herself and for a brief space allow you to look right into the heart of her mystery. But if you call out to her peremptorily, 'Nature! unveil yourself this very moment!' she only draws her veil the closer; and you may look with all your eyes, and imagine that you see all that she can show, and yet see nothing.

But this was because his sensibility was so great that he drew from little things a larger pleasure than many feel when excited by grand ones; and knowing this deeper phase, he could not be content with the hasty admiration on which tourists flatter themselves. The beauty of a scene which he could absorb in peace was never lost upon him. Every year the recurrent changes of season filled him with untold pleasure; and in the spring, Mrs. Hawthorne has been heard to say, he would walk with her in continuous silence, his heart full of the awe and delight with which the miracle of buds and new verdure inspired him. Nothing could be more accurate or sensitive than the brief descriptions of nature in his works. But there is nothing sentimental about them; partly owing to the Anglo-Saxon instinct which caused him to seek precise and detailed statement first of all, and partly because of a certain classic, awe-inspired reserve, like that of Horace and Virgil.

There was a commendable indolence in his character. It was not a constitutional weakness, overcoming will, but the instinctive precaution of a man whose errand it was to rise to great emergencies of exertion. He always waited for an adequate mood, before writing. But these intervals, of course, were richly productive of revery which afterward entered into the creative moments. He would sometimes become deeply abstracted in imagination; and while he was writing "The Scarlet Letter" it is related by a trustworthy person that, sitting in the room where his wife was doing some sewing, he unconsciously took up a part of the work and cut it into minute fragments with the scissors, without being aware that he had done so. At some previous time, he had in the same way gradually chipped off with a knife portions of a table, until the entire folding-leaf was worn away by the process. The opinion was sometimes advanced by him that without a certain mixture of uncongenial labor he might not have done so much with the pen; but in this he perhaps underestimated the leisure in his blood, which was one of the elements of his power. Men of smaller calibre are hollowed out by the fire of ideas, and decay too quickly; but this trait preserved him from such a fate. Combined with his far-reaching foresight, it may have had something to do with his comparative withdrawal from practical affairs other than those which necessity connected him with. Of Holgrave he writes:—

> His error lay in supposing that this age more than any past or future one is des-
> tined to see the garments of antiquity exchanged for a new suit, instead of gradu-
> ally renewing themselves by patchwork; . . . and more than all, in fancying that it
> mattered anything to the great end in view whether he himself should contend for
> it or against it.

The implied opinion of the author, here, is not that of a fatalist, but of an optimist (if we must connect him with any "ism") who has a very profound faith in Providence; not in any "special providence," but in that operation of divine laws through unexpected agencies and conflicting events, which is very gradually approximating human affairs to a state of truthfulness. Hawthorne was one of the great believers of his generation; but his faith expressed itself in the negative way of showing how fragile are the ordinary objects of rever-ence in the world, how subject the best of us are to the undermining influence of very great sin; and, on the other hand, how many traits of good there are, by consequence, even in the worst of us. This, however, is a mere skeleton statement: the noblest element in his mood is that he believes with his heart. A good interpreter has said that he *feels* with his *brain,* and *thinks* with his *heart,* to show the completeness with which he mingled the two elements in his med-itations on existence. A warm, pure, living sympathy pervaded all his analysis of mankind, without which that analysis would have taken no hold upon us. It is a crude view which reckons him to have been wanting in moral enthusiasm: he had not that kind which can crush out sympathy with suffering, for the sake of carrying out an idea. Perhaps in some cases this was a fault; but one cannot dwell on the mistaken side of such a phase, when it possesses another side so full of beneficent aid to humanity. And it must be remembered that with all this susceptibility, he was not a suffering poet, like Shelley, but distinctly an endurer. His moral enthusiasm was deeper that that of any scheme or system.

His distaste for society has been declared to proceed from the fact that, when he once became interested in people, he could no longer chemically resolve them into material for romance. But this assumption is also erroneous; for Hawthorne, if he felt it needful, could bring to bear upon his best friends the same qualitative measuring skill that he exercised on any one. I do not doubt that he knew where to place his friends and acquaintance in the scale of relative excellence. All of us who have not an equal analytic power with his own can at least reverence his discretion so far as to believe that he had stand-points not open to every one, from which he took views often more essentially just than if he had assumed a more sweeping estimate. In other cases, where he bestowed more friendship and confidence than the object of them especially deserved, he no doubt sought the simple pleasure of accepting what circumstances offered him. He was not a suspicious person; although, in fear of being fooled by his fancy, he cultivated what he often spoke of to a friend as 'morose common-sense,' deeming it a desirable alloy. There was even, in many relations, an unquestioning trust on his part; for he might well be called

> As the greatest only are,
> In his simplicity sublime.[1] . . .

. . . [I]t is impossible to define Hawthorne's personality precisely. A poet's whole effort is to indirectly express this, by expressing the effect of things upon him; and we may read much of Hawthorne in his books, if we have the skill. But it is very clear that he put only a part of himself into them; that part which best served the inexorable law of his genius for treating life in a given light. For the rest, his two chapters on "The Custom-House" and "The Old Manse" show us something of his mode of taking daily affairs. But his real and inmost character was a mystery even to himself, and this, because he felt so profoundly the impossibility of sounding to the bottom any human heart. "A cloudy veil stretches over the abyss of my nature," he writes, at one time. "I have, however, no love of secrecy or darkness." At another time: "Lights and shadows are continually flitting across my inward sky, and I know neither whence they come nor whither they go; nor do I look too closely into them." A mind so conscious as his of the slight reality of appearances would be dissatisfied with the few tangible qualities which are all of himself that a man can discern: at the same time he would hesitate to probe the deeper self assiduously, for fear of turning his searching gaze too intently within, and thus becoming morbid. In other persons, however, he could perceive a contour, and pursue his study of investigation from without inward,—a more healthy method. His *instinctive* knowledge of himself, being brought into play, would of course aid him. Incidentally, then, something of himself comes to light in his investigation of others. And it is perhaps this inability to define their own natures, except by a roundabout method, which is the creative impulse of all great novelists and dramatists. I doubt whether many of the famous delineators of character could give us a very distinct account of their own individualities; and if they did, it would probably make them out the most uninteresting of beings. It would certainly be divested of the special charm of their other writing. Imagine Dickens clearly accounting for himself and his peculiar traits: would he be able to excite even a smile? How much of his own delicious personality could Thackeray have described without losing the zest of his other portraitures? Hawthorne has given a kind of picture of himself in Coverdale, and was sometimes called after that character by his friends; but I suspect he has adroitly constructed Coverdale out of the *appearance* which he knew himself to make in the eyes of associates. I do not mean that Hawthorne had not a very decisive personality; for indeed he had. But the essence of the person cannot be compressed into a few brief paragraphs, and must be slowly drawn in as a pervasive elixir from his works, his letters, his note-books. In the latter he has given as much definition of his interior self as we are likely to get, for no one else can continue the broken jottings that he has left, and extend them into outlines. We shall not greatly err if we treat the hidden depths of his spirit with as much reverence as he himself used in scrutinizing them. Curiously enough, many of those who have studied this most careful and delicate of definers have embraced the madness of attempting to bind him down in unhesitating, absolute statements. He who mastered words so completely that he learned to despise their obscurity, has been made the victim of easy epithets and a few conventional phrases. But none can ever be said to know Hawthorne who do not leave large allowances for the unknowable.

Note

1. Alfred, Lord Tennyson, "Ode on the Death of the Duke of Wellington," ll. 33–34.

From *A Study of Hawthorne* (Boston: J. R. Osgood, 1876), 7–11, 13–18, 284–88, 292–99.

From *Hawthorne* (1879)

Henry James

-)|(-

American author, theorist, and biographer of Emerson and William Wetmore Story as well as of Hawthorne, Henry James (1843–1916) admired great writers, lofty ideas, and culture steeped in tradition. Several novels of James's early and later periods—*The American* (1877), *The Portrait of a Lady* (1881), *The Bostonians* (1886), *What Maisie Knew* (1897), *The Wings of the Dove* (1902), and *The Ambassadors* (1903), for instance—have endured to become not only classics but also defining moments in the development of psychological realism in American fiction. From the outset of his prolific career, James distrusted local movements such as Transcendentalism and doubted whether young, provincial America could either inspire or support an original literary imagination. In deciding to write *Hawthorne*, James chose a figure whose life and art represented a great deal about American character that gave him pause. Although James is traditionally introduced as an American writer, his personal biography complemented his criticism. In 1876—three years before he published *Hawthorne*—James settled permanently in London; he became a British subject the year before his death.

James's *Hawthorne* is discussed at length in the introduction to this volume.

IT WILL BE NECESSARY ... to give this short sketch the form rather of a critical essay than of a biography. The data for a life of Nathaniel Hawthorne are the reverse of copious, and even if they were abundant they would serve but in a limited measure the purpose of the biographer. Hawthorne's career was probably as tranquil and uneventful a one as ever fell to the lot of a man of letters; it was almost strikingly deficient in incident, in what may be called the dramatic quality. Few men of equal genius and of equal eminence can have led on the whole a simpler life. His six volumes of Note-Books illustrate this simplicity; they are a sort of monument to an unagitated fortune. Hawthorne's career had few vicissitudes or variations; it was passed for the most part in a small and homogeneous society, in a provincial, rural community; it had few

[174]

perceptible points of contact with what is called the world, with public events, with the manners of his time, even with the life of his neighbours. Its literary incidents are not numerous. He produced, in quantity, but little. His works consist of four novels and the fragment of another, five volumes of short tales, a collection of sketches, and a couple of story-books for children. And yet some account of the man and the writer is well worth giving. Whatever may have been Hawthorne's private lot, he has the importance of being the most beautiful and most eminent representative of a literature. The importance of the literature may be questioned, but at any rate, in the field of letters, Hawthorne is the most valuable example of the American genius. That genius has not, as a whole, been literary; but Hawthorne was on his limited scale a master of expression. He is the writer to whom his countrymen most confidently point when they wish to make a claim to have enriched the mother-tongue, and, judging from present appearances, he will long occupy this honourable position. If there is something very fortunate for him in the way that he borrows an added relief from the absence of competitors in his own line and from the general flatness of the literary field that surrounds him, there is also, to a spectator, something almost touching in his situation. He was so modest and delicate a genius that we may fancy him appealing from the lonely honour of a representative attitude—perceiving a painful incongruity between his imponderable literary baggage and the large conditions of American life. Hawthorne on the one side is so subtle and slender and unpretending, and the American world on the other is so vast and various and substantial, that it might seem to the author of *The Scarlet Letter* and the *Mosses from an Old Manse,* that we render him a poor service in contrasting his proportions with those of a great civilization. But our author must accept the awkward as well as the graceful side of his fame; for he has the advantage of pointing a valuable moral. This moral is that the flower of art blooms only where the soil is deep, that it takes a great deal of history to produce a little literature, that it needs a complex social machinery to set a writer in motion. American civilization has hitherto had other things to do than to produce flowers, and before giving birth to writers it has wisely occupied itself with providing something for them to write about. Three or four beautiful talents of trans-Atlantic growth are the sum of what the world usually recognizes, and in this modest nosegay the genius of Hawthorne is admitted to have the rarest and sweetest fragrance. . . .

. . . Poet and novelist as Hawthorne was, sceptic and dreamer and little of a man of action, late-coming fruit of a tree which might seem to have lost the power to bloom, he was morally, in an appreciative degree, a chip off the old block. His forefathers had crossed the Atlantic for conscience' sake, and it was the idea of the urgent conscience that haunted the imagination of their so-called degenerate successor. The Puritan strain in his blood ran clear— there are passages in his Diaries, kept during his residence in Europe, which might almost have been written by the grimmest of the old Salem worthies. To him as to them, the consciousness of sin was the most importunate fact of life, and if they had undertaken to write little tales, this baleful substantive, with its attendant adjective, could hardly have been more frequent in their pages than in those of their fanciful descendant. Hawthorne had moreover in his composition, contemplator and dreamer as he was, an element of simplicity and rigidity, a something plain and masculine and sensible, which might have kept his black-browed grandsires on better terms with him than he admits to be possible. However little they might have appreciated the artist, they would have approved of the man. The play of Hawthorne's intellect was light and capricious, but the man himself was firm and rational. The imagination was profane, but the temper was not degenerate. . . .

. . . [In his early manhood Hawthorne subscribed] to a state of solitude which was the young man's positive choice at the time—or into which he drifted at least under the pressure of his natural shyness and reserve. He was not expansive, he was not addicted to experiments and adventures of intercourse, he was not, personally, . . . what is called sociable. The general impression of this silence-loving and shade-seeking side of his character is doubtless exaggerated, and, in so far as it points to him as a sombre and sinister figure, is almost ludicrously at fault. He was silent, diffident, more inclined to hesitate, to watch and wait and meditate, than to produce himself, and fonder, on almost any occasion, of being absent than of being present. This quality betrays itself in all his writings. There is in all of them something cold and light and thin, something belonging to the imagination alone, which indicates a man but little disposed to multiply his relations, his points of contact, with society. If we read the six volumes of Note-Books with an eye to the evidence of this unsocial side of his life, we find it in sufficient abundance. But we find at the same time that there was nothing unamiable or invidious in his shyness, and above all that there was nothing preponderantly gloomy. The qualities to which the Note-Books most testify are, on the whole, his serenity and amenity of mind. They reveal these characteristics indeed in

[176]

an almost phenomenal degree. The serenity, the simplicity, seem in certain portions almost child-like; of brilliant gaiety, of high spirits, there is little; but the placidity and evenness of temper, the cheerful and contented view of the things he notes, never belie themselves. I know not what else he may have written in this copious record, and what passages of gloom and melancholy may have been suppressed; but . . . his Diaries . . . offer in a remarkable degree the reflection of a mind whose development was not in the direction of sadness. . . . [C]ertainly, the note of depression, of despair, of the disposition to undervalue the human race, is never sounded in his Diaries. These volumes contain the record of very few convictions or theories of any kind; they move with curious evenness, with a charming, graceful flow, on a level which lies above that of a man's philosophy. They adhere with such persistence to this upper level that they prompt the reader to believe that Hawthorne had no appreciable philosophy at all—no general views that were in the least uncomfortable. They are the exhibition of an unperplexed intellect. I said just now that the development of Hawthorne's mind was not towards sadness; and I should be inclined to go still further, and say that his mind proper—his mind in so far as it was a repository of opinions and articles of faith—had no development that it is of especial importance to look into. What had a development was his imagination—that delicate and penetrating imagination which was always at play, always entertaining itself, always engaged in a game of hide and seek in the region in which it seemed to him that the game could best be played—among the shadows and substructions, the dark-based pillars and supports, of our moral nature. Beneath this movement and ripple of his imagination—as free and spontaneous as that of the sea surface—lay directly his personal affections. These were solid and strong, but, according to my impression, they had the place very much to themselves.

His innocent reserve . . . and his exaggerated, but by no means cynical, relish for solitude, imposed themselves upon him, in a great measure, with a persistency which helped to make the time a tolerably arid one—so arid a one indeed that we have seen that in the light of later happiness he pronounced it a blank. But in truth, if these were dull years, it was not all Hawthorne's fault. His situation was intrinsically poor—poor with a poverty that one almost hesitates to look into. When we think of what the conditions of intellectual life, of taste, must have been in a small New England town fifty years ago; and when we think of a young man of beautiful genius, with a love of literature and romance, of the picturesque, of style and form and colour, trying to make a career for himself in the midst of them, compassion for the young man becomes our dominant sentiment, and we see the large dry village picture in perhaps almost too hard a light. It seems to me then that it was possibly a blessing for Hawthorne that he was not expansive and inquisitive, that he lived much to himself and asked but little of his *milieu*. If he had been exacting and ambitious, if his appetite had been large and his knowledge various, he would probably have found the bounds of Salem intolerably narrow. But his culture had been of a simple sort—there was little of any other sort to be obtained in America in those days, and though he was doubtless haunted by visions of more suggestive opportunities, we may safely assume that he was not to his own perception the object of compassion that he appears to a critic who judges him after half a century's civilization has filtered into the twilight of that earlier time. If New England was socially a very small place in those days, Salem was a still smaller one; and if the American tone at large was intensely provincial, that of New England was not greatly helped by having the best of it. The state of things was extremely natural, and there could be now no greater mistake than to speak of it with a redundancy of irony. American life had begun to constitute itself from the foundations; it had begun to *be,* simply; it was at an immeasurable distance from having begun to enjoy. I imagine there was no appreciable group of people in New England at that time proposing to itself to enjoy life; this was not an undertaking for which any provision had been made, or to which any encouragement was offered. Hawthorne must have vaguely entertained some such design upon destiny; but he must have felt that his success would have to depend wholly upon his own ingenuity. I say he must have proposed to himself to enjoy, simply because he proposed to be an artist, and because this enters inevitably into the artist's scheme. There are a thousand ways of enjoying life, and that of the artist is one of the most innocent. But for all that, it connects itself with the idea of pleasure. He proposes to give pleasure, and to give it he must first get it. Where he gets it will depend upon circumstances, and circumstances were not encouraging to Hawthorne.

He was poor, he was solitary, and he undertook to devote himself to literature in a community in which the interest in literature was as yet of the smallest. It is not too much to say that even to the present day it is a considerable discomfort in the United States not to be "in business." . . . Hawthorne, beginning to write subtle short tales at Salem, was empirical enough;

[178]

he was one of, at most, some dozen Americans who had taken up literature as a profession. The profession in the United States is still very young, and of diminutive stature; but in the year 1830 its head could hardly have been seen above ground. It strikes the observer of to-day that Hawthorne showed great courage in entering a field in which the honours and emoluments were so scanty as the profits of authorship must have been at that time. I have said that in the United States at present authorship is a pedestal, and literature is the fashion; but Hawthorne's history is a proof that it was possible, fifty years ago, to write a great many little masterpieces without becoming known. He begins the preface to the *Twice-Told Tales* by remarking that he was "for many years the obscurest man of letters in America." When once this work obtained recognition, the recognition left little to be desired. . . .

I have said that Hawthorne was an observer of small things, and indeed he appears to have thought nothing too trivial to be suggestive. His Note-Books give us the measure of his perception of common and casual things, and of his habit of converting them into *memoranda*. . . . I am thankful . . . as a biographer, for the Note-Books, but I am obliged to confess that, though I have just re-read them carefully, I am still at a loss to perceive how they came to be written—what was Hawthorne's purpose in carrying on for so many years this minute and often trivial chronicle. For a person desiring information about him at any cost, it is valuable; it sheds a vivid light upon his character, his habits, the nature of his mind. But we find ourselves wondering what was its value to Hawthorne himself. It is in a very partial degree a register of impressions, and in a still smaller sense a record of emotions. Outward objects play much the larger part in it; opinions, convictions, ideas pure and simple, are almost absent. He rarely takes his Note-Book into his confidence or commits to its pages any reflections that might be adapted for publicity; the simplest way to describe the tone of these extremely objective journals is to say that they read like a series of very pleasant, though rather dullish and decidedly formal, letters, addressed to himself by a man who, having suspicions that they might be opened in the post, should have determined to insert nothing compromising. . . . They widen . . . our glimpse of Hawthorne's mind . . . by what they fail to contain, as much as by what we find in them. . . .

I know not at what age he began to keep a diary; the first entries in the American volumes are of the summer of 1835. There is a phrase in the preface to his novel of *Transformation*, which must have lingered in the minds of many Americans who have tried to write novels and to lay the scene of them in the western world. "No author, without a trial, can conceive of the difficulty of writing a romance about a country where there is no shadow, no antiquity, no mystery, no picturesque and gloomy wrong, nor anything but a commonplace prosperity, in broad and simple daylight, as is happily the case with my dear native land." The perusal of Hawthorne's American Note-Books operates as a practical commentary upon this somewhat ominous text. It does so at least to my own mind; it would be too much perhaps to say that the effect would be the same for the usual English reader. An American reads between the lines—he completes the suggestions—he constructs a picture. I think I am not guilty of any gross injustice in saying that the picture he constructs from Hawthorne's American diaries, though by no means without charms of its own, is not, on the whole, an interesting one. It is characterised by an extraordinary blankness—a curious paleness of colour and paucity of detail. Hawthorne, as I have said, has a large and healthy appetite for detail, and one is therefore the more struck with the lightness of the diet to which his observation was condemned. For myself, as I turn the pages of his journals, I seem to see the image of the crude and simple society in which he lived. I use these epithets . . . not invidiously, but descriptively; if one desires to enter as closely as possible into Hawthorne's situation, one must endeavour to reproduce his circumstances. . . . If Hawthorne had been a young Englishman, or a young Frenchman of the same degree of genius, the same cast of mind, the same habits, his consciousness of the world around him would have been a very different affair; however obscure, however reserved, his own personal life, his sense of the life of his fellow-mortals would have been almost infinitely more various. The negative side of the spectacle on which Hawthorne looked out, in his contemplative saunterings and reveries, might, indeed, with a little ingenuity, be made almost ludicrous; one might enumerate the items of high civilization, as it exists in other countries, which are absent from the texture of American life, until it should become a wonder to know what was left. No State, in the European sense of the word. . . . No sovereign, no court, no personal loyalty, no aristocracy, no church, no clergy, no army, no diplomatic service, no country gentlemen, no palaces, no castles, nor manors, nor old country houses, nor parsonages, nor thatched cottages nor ivied ruins; no cathedrals, nor abbeys, nor little Norman churches; no great Universities nor public schools[;] . . . no literature, no novels, no museums, no pictures, no political society, no sporting class[!] . . . Some such list as that might be drawn up of the absent things in American life—especially in the American life of forty years ago, the effect of which, upon an English or a French imagination, would probably as a general thing be appalling. The natural remark, in the almost lurid light of such an indictment, would be that if these things are left out, everything is left out. The American knows that a good deal remains; what it is that remains—that is his secret, his joke. . . .

The history of the little industrial and intellectual association [known as Brook Farm] which formed itself at this time in one of the suburbs of Boston has not . . . been written; though it is assuredly a curious and interesting chapter in the domestic annals of New England. It would of course be easy to overrate the importance of this ingenious attempt of a few speculative persons to improve the outlook of mankind. The experiment came and went very rapidly and quietly, leaving very few traces behind it. It became simply a charming personal reminiscence for the small number of amiable enthusiasts who had had a hand in it. There were degrees of enthusiasm, and I suppose there were degrees of amiability; but a certain generous brightness of hope and freshness of conviction pervaded the whole undertaking and rendered it, morally speaking, important to an extent of which any heed that the world in general ever gave to it is an insufficient measure. Of course it would be a great mistake to represent the episode of Brook Farm as directly related to the manners and morals of the New England world in general—and in especial to those of the prosperous, opulent, comfortable part of it. The thing was the experiment of a coterie—it was unusual, unfashionable, unsuccessful. It was, as would then have been said, an amusement of the Transcendentalists—a harmless effusion of Radicalism. The Transcendentalists were not, after all, very numerous; and the Radicals were by no means of the vivid tinge of those of our own day. . . . [T]he Brook Farm community left no traces behind it that the world in general can appreciate; I should rather say that the only trace is a short novel, of which the principal merits reside in its qualities of difference from the affair itself. *The Blithedale Romance* is the main result of Brook farm; but [it] was very properly never recognised by the Brook Farmers as an accurate portrait of their little colony.

Nevertheless, in a society as to which the more frequent complaint is that it is monotonous, that it lacks variety of incident and of type, the episode, our own business with which is simply that it was the cause of Hawthorne's writing an admirable tale, might be welcomed as a picturesque variation. At the same time, if we do not exaggerate its proportions, it may seem to contain a fund of illustration as to that phase of human life with which our author's own history mingled itself. The most graceful account of the origin of Brook Farm is probably to be found in these words of one of the biographers of Margaret Fuller: "In Boston and its vicinity several friends, for whose character Margaret felt the highest honour, were earnestly considering the possibility of making such industrial, social, and educational arrangements as would simplify economies, combine leisure for study with healthful and honest toil, avert unjust collisions of caste, equalise refinements, awaken generous affections, diffuse courtesy, and sweeten and sanctify life as a whole." The reader will perceive that this was a liberal scheme, and that if the experiment failed, the greater was the pity. . . .

It is safe to assume that Hawthorne could not on the whole have had a high relish for the very positive personality of this accomplished and argumentative woman, in whose intellect high noon seemed ever to reign, as twilight did in his own. He must have been struck with the glare of her understanding, and, mentally speaking, have scowled and blinked a good deal in conversation with her. But it is tolerably manifest, nevertheless, that she was, in his imagination, the starting-point of the figure of Zenobia; and Zenobia is, to my sense, his only very definite attempt at the representation of a character. The portrait is full of alteration and embellishment; but it has a greater reality, a greater abundance of detail, than any of his other figures, and the reality was a memory of the lady whom he had encountered in the Roxbury pastoral or among the wood-walks of Concord, with strange books in her hand and eloquent discourse on her lips. *The Blithedale Romance* was written just after her unhappy death, when the reverberation of her talk would lose much of its harshness. In fact, however, very much the same qualities that made Hawthorne a Democrat in politics—his contemplative turn and absence of a keen perception of abuses, his taste for old ideals, and loitering paces, and muffled tones—would operate to keep him out of active sympathy with a woman of the so-called progressive type. We may be sure that in women his taste was conservative.

It seems odd, as his biographer says, "that the least gregarious of men should have been drawn into a socialistic community;" but although it is apparent that Hawthorne went to Brook Farm without any great Transcendental fervour, yet he had various good reasons for casting his lot in this would-be happy family. He was as yet unable to marry, but he naturally wished to do so as speedily as possible, and there was a prospect that Brook Farm would prove an economical residence. And then it is only fair to believe that Hawthorne was interested in the experiment, and that though he was not a Transcendentalist, an Abolitionist, or a Fourierite, as his companions were in some degree or other likely to be, he was willing, as a generous and unoccupied young man, to lend a hand in any reasonable scheme for helping people to live together on better terms than the common. The Brook Farm scheme was, as such things go, a reasonable one; it was devised and carried out by shrewd and sober-minded New Englanders, who were careful to place economy first and idealism afterwards, and who were not afflicted with a Gallic passion for completeness of theory. There were no formulas, doctrines, dogmas; there was no interference whatever with private life or individual habits, and not the faintest adumbration of a rearrangement of that difficult business known as the relations of the sexes. The relations of the sexes were neither more nor less than what they usually are in American life, excellent; and in such particulars the scheme was thoroughly conservative and irreproachable. Its main characteristic was that each individual concerned in it should do a part of the work necessary for keeping the whole machine going. . . . Allowing, however, for everything that was a concession to worldly traditions and to the laxity of man's nature, there must have been in the enterprise a good deal of a certain freshness and purity of spirit, of a certain noble credulity and faith in the perfectibility of man, which it would have been easier to find in Boston in the year 1840, than in London five-and-thirty years later. If that was the era of Transcendentalism, Transcendentalism could only have sprouted in the soil peculiar to the general locality of which I speak—the soil of the old New England morality, gently raked and refreshed by an imported culture. [T]he . . . strong and deep New England conscience accompanied them on all their intellectual excursions, and there never was a so-called "movement" that embodied itself, on the whole, in fewer eccentricities of conduct, or that borrowed a smaller licence in private deportment. Henry Thoreau, a delightful writer, went to live in the woods; but Henry Thoreau was essentially a sylvan personage and would not have been, however the fashion of his time might have turned, a man about town. The brothers and sisters at Brook Farm ploughed the fields and milked the cows; but I think that an observer from another clime and society would have been much more struck with their spirit of conformity than with their *déréglements*. Their ardour was a moral ardour, and the lightest breath of scandal never rested upon them, or upon any phase of Transcendentalism. . . .

Hawthorne appears, like his own Miles Coverdale, to have arrived at Brook Farm in the midst of one of those April snow-storms which, during the New England spring, occasionally diversify the inaction of the vernal process. Miles Coverdale, in *The Blithedale Romance,* is evidently as much Hawthorne as he is any one else in particular. He is indeed not very markedly any one, unless it be the spectator, the observer; his chief identity lies in his success in looking at things objectively and spinning uncommunicated fancies about them. This indeed was the part that Hawthorne played socially in the little community at West Roxbury. . . . He put his hand to the plough and supported himself and the community, as they were all supposed to do, by his labour; but he contributed little to the hum of voices. Some of his companions, either then or afterwards, took . . . rather a gruesome view of his want of articulate enthusiasm, and accused him of coming to the place as a sort of intellectual vampire, for purely psychological purposes. He sat in a corner, they declared, and watched the inmates when they were off their guard, analysing their characters, and dissecting the amiable ardour, the magnanimous illusions, which he was too cold-blooded to share. In so far as this account of Hawthorne's attitude was a complaint, it was a singularly childish one. If he was at Brook Farm without being of it, this is a very fortunate circumstance from the point of view of posterity, who would have preserved but a slender memory of the affair if our author's fine novel had not kept the topic open. The complaint is indeed almost so ungrateful a one as to make us regret that the author's fellow-communists came off so easily. They certainly would not have done so if the author of *Blithedale* had been more of a satirist. Certainly, if Hawthorne was an observer, he was a very harmless one; and when one thinks of the queer specimens of the reforming genus with which he must have been surrounded, one almost wishes that, for our entertainment, he had given his old companions something to complain of in earnest. There is no satire whatever in the Romance; the quality is almost conspicuous by its absence. Of portraits there are only two; there is no sketching of odd figures—no reproduction of strange types of radicalism; the human background is left vague. Hawthorne was not a satirist, and if at Brook Farm he was, according to his habit, a good deal of a mild sceptic, his scepticism was exercised much more in the interest of fancy than in that of reality.

There must have been something pleasantly bucolic and pastoral in the habits of the place during the fine New England summer; but we have no retrospective envy of the denizens of Brook Farm in that other season which, as Hawthorne somewhere says, leaves in those regions, "so large a blank—so melancholy a deathspot—in lives so brief that they ought to be all summer-time." . . .

Hawthorne's . . . biographer justly quotes two or three sentences from *The Blithedale Romance*, as striking the note of the author's feeling about the place. "No sagacious man," says Coverdale, "will long retain his sagacity if he live exclusively among reformers and progressive people, without periodically returning to the settled system of things, to correct himself by a new observation from that old standpoint." And he remarks elsewhere that "it struck me as rather odd that one of the first questions raised, after our separation from the greedy, struggling, self-seeking world, should relate to the possibility of getting the advantage over the outside barbarians in their own field of labour. But to tell the truth I very soon became sensible that, as regarded society at large we stood in a position of new hostility rather than new brotherhood." He was doubtless oppressed by the "sultry heat of society," as he calls it in one of the jottings in the Note-Books. "What would a man do if he were compelled to live always in the sultry heat of society, and could never bathe himself in cool solitude?" His biographer relates that one of the other Brook Farmers, wandering afield one summer's day, discovered Hawthorne stretched at his length upon a grassy hill-side, with his hat pulled over his face, and every appearance, in his attitude, of the desire to escape detection. On his asking him whether he had any particular reason for this shyness of posture—"Too much of a party up there!" Hawthorne contented himself with replying, with a nod in the direction of the Hive. He had nevertheless for a time looked forward to remaining indefinitely in the community; he meant to marry as soon as possible and bring his wife there to live. Some sixty pages of the second volume of the American Note-Books are occupied with extracts from his letters to his future wife and from his journal[,] . . . consisting almost exclusively of descriptions of the simple scenery of the neighbourhood, and of the state of the woods and fields and weather. Hawthorne's fondness for all the common things of nature was deep and constant, and there is always something charming in his verbal touch, as we may call it, when he talks to himself about them. "Oh," he breaks out, of an October afternoon, "the beauty of grassy slopes, and the hollow ways of paths winding between hills, and the intervals between the road and wood-lots, where Summer lingers and sits down, strewing dandelions of gold and blue asters as her parting gifts and memorials!" He was but a single summer at Brook Farm; the rest of his residence had the winter-quality. . . .

From *Hawthorne* (London: Macmillan, 1887), 1–3, 10, 26–32, 40–44, 76–78, 80–83, 86–89, 91–92.

"Nathaniel Hawthorne" (1880)

George B. Loring

⊰|⊱

> Although he prepared as a physician at Harvard, George Bailey Loring (1817–
> 1891) spent the greater part of his career as a conservative politican, holding
> positions such as postmaster of Salem, chairman of the Massachusetts State
> Republican Committee, U.S. commissioner of agriculture, and U.S. minister
> to Portugal. Loring typically wrote essays on politics and agriculture, but had
> Hawthorne lived, he would have found in his former friend a clever and sen-
> sitive reader who applauded the strength implicit in Hawthorne's Calvinist
> lineage and understood more clearly than most that he consciously divided
> his public (including familial) and creative time between the real world and
> the supernatural.
>
> In 1882, Loring drew an address on the real and the supernatural in Haw-
> thorne's life and writings from the essay that follows (see "Pictures of Haw-
> thorne. *From an Address by the Hon. G. B. Loring*," *New-York Tribune* [25 April
> 1882]: 6:1). In the address as reported, he developed his subject with the ex-
> actness of a scientist and included this anecdote, likely for oratorical effect:
> "Theodore Parker once said to me he had no idea that Hawthorne understood
> his own genius or comprehended the philosophical meaning of many of the
> circumstances or characters found in his books; that his characters were true
> to Nature, in spite of himself."

WHEN . . . WE APPROACH the investigation of a character like Hawthorne's,
we start with a feeling that our vision must inevitably be limited. His horizon
is so much more vast than ours, that we hardly expect to view it, either with
the naked eye, or with any artificial aid within our reach. But we can turn with
interest and satisfaction to the circumstances under which he was developed,
and the influences by which he was surrounded. The fact that he was born in
Salem may not amount to much to other people, but it amounted to a great
deal to him. The sturdy and defiant spirit of his progenitor, who first landed
on these shores, found a congenial abode. . . . He was a stern separatist . . . and
had that liberal religious faith which made the Plymouth colony the home

[187]

of the persecuted, and gave it immortal power in controlling the religious and political systems of our land; but he was also a warrior, a politician, a legislator, a legal adviser, a merchant, an orator with persuasive speech. His piety seldom drove him to fanaticism, and he had a sound and just understanding of the wants of those about him, and of the form of government under which they were to live—an understanding so clear that whenever he surrendered as a magistrate to the heated and intolerant spirit of his times, he did it reluctantly and with mental and moral protest. He had great powers of mind and body, and forms a conspicuous figure in that imposing and heroic group which stands around the cradle of New England. The generations of the family that followed took . . . [a] prominent part in the manly adventures which marked our entire colonial period. With less religious demonstration than the first of their line on this continent, they were severe and gloomy justices, strong and successful farmers, bold and adventurous mariners, down to the time when the great author was born. It was among the family traditions gathered from the Indian wars, the tragic and awful spectre of the witchcraft delusion, the wild life of the privateer, that he first saw the light, and while he was yet a child the death of his father in a distant port was impressed upon his mind as one of the solemn mysteries of the sea. It was not a conspicuous, but it was an intimate part which his progenitors performed in that period which constitutes the romance of American history. . . . There was never a more intense Hathorne than the father of Nathaniel Hawthorne, the silent, sombre sailor, who represented all the courage and power of the family, with a busy and thoughtful mind which dwelt upon that curious and interesting family-record with a sort of superstitious awe and deep admiration. So far as any inheritance of faculties from his father's line is concerned, Hawthorne had a right to be a powerful, thoughtful, reticent, dreamy, brooding, sensible, unambitious, retiring man—and he was. . . . [H]is mother simply added to all these qualities greater intensity and more fervor from her own soul. . . .

The qualities of mind and heart, which were active in these many generations of toil, and trial, and varied experience on land and sea, strong as they were in their primitive state, were full of admirable power when . . . they entered upon a field of intellectual labor. The boy, who, in after life, was counted by some as gloomy and sombre, was abounding in a rich and mellow humor—the seafaring humor of his class. . . . It was a delicate and chaste humor which he had as a boy, and it never deserted him through his long literary life. Even his wit soared into the regions of humor, and avoided the

[188]

low association of ideas which lies at the foundation of much of the accept-
able wit of the world. . . . Hawthorne's perception was exquisitely keen also.
His eyes were as quick and sharp as were those of his ancestor with his "eye
to the wind'ard" in a gale at sea. Not a bird, not a beast, nor a flower, nor a
twig, nor cloud, nor tree escaped him, when he followed his uncle and his
men on their tramps along the shores of Sebago Lake. And so it was through
life. Strolling along the street in apparent reverie, dreaming on his tall stool at
the custom-house, pacing his solitary walk in the country, at home or abroad,
he saw all that was to be seen. . . . He admired facts and things, and reached
their philosophical meaning by instinct, and not by a process of reasoning.
He saw things, too, just as they are, whether things of the past or the present.
If any one supposes that he had a distorted and discolored view of society,
its thoughts and incidents and individuals in the early periods of our Colonial history, he must remember that no man has ever described persons and
things about him better than he did. . . . He had, moreover, the keen insight
into and understanding of human nature, which belongs to those who are
early thrown upon their own resources, and are tossed about from shore to
shore over all seas and among all peoples. We have had many essays upon the
Puritan character, many treatises of Puritan history, many pictures of Puritan
life in New England; but the secret chambers were first unlocked and opened
by him in the "Scarlet Letter," and we saw the Puritan as he was, his heaven
and his hell. We have had many bright and elaborate descriptions of Rome,
its art and architecture; but never an inside view of the artist's life there, never
a picture of the Italian genius which presides over that land of beauty and
the beast, until this great magician created the "Marble Faun." Salem in the
"House of the Seven Gables," and Concord in "Mosses from an old Manse,"
are Salem and Concord in intense reality. His pictures are not the fruits of a
diseased imagination, but they are the actual life as seen by the eye of Him
who made it. If he makes virtue as beauteous as a star, and vice as hideous
as a rayless night, so do nature and the divine law. . . . Hawthorne's pictures
may at times have been gloomy but they are always true to nature, and the
gloom is only the shadow falling upon the landscape to perfect its beauty. His
art was so guided and controlled by natural laws that all artistic design was
thoroughly hidden; and even the most fantastic of his shapes filled the places
assigned them with as much fitness and propriety as do the mountains and
the sea. For this work, he preserved his natural powers as few writers . . . have
done. He seems not to have derived great strength from books. . . . He read,

because he liked the companionship of books; they were good friends for his solitude. But, although he had the humor of Charles Lamb, and the pathos of Richter, and the penetration of Goldsmith, he had no need of their support. He knew well what he did know, but he seldom introduced his knowledge into his books—never ostentatiously or like a pedant. He never presented his knowledge of history in a novel, like Scott; he never poured out his contempt for social wrong in tales, like Dickens; he never exposed the hollow folly of society, like Thackeray; but he wrought the work of all into his marvellous volumes . . . as the consequence of that commanding vision with which he surveyed society and the acuteness with which he read the heart of man. . . .

In the performance of his literary work . . . Hawthorne's pictures are all extraordinary. They may be compared with the domestic groups of the Dutch painters, with the addition of the dreamy, misty coloring which gives such a charm to Allston's dark landscape, where some mysterious figure is used to give life to the scene. His characters, which are all strong and natural, are never left by him until the supernatural has been expressed. His grotesqueness is inimitable. . . . His Pyncheon hens, with their aristocratic attenuation, are the very expression of gallinaceous absurdity. Old Venner is a model of a fussy fixture of an active pauper. Hepzibah has not her equal as a representative of her peculiar class. Starved, and withered, and pinched, in her poor old heart for the want of human sympathy and warm human experience, she is pursed and prim in her griefs and joys, and peevish in her kindness. Never has there been seen a better delineation of an active, uneasy, protean Yankee, half speculator, and half philosopher, than Holgrave. We know of no man who, with all this universality of perception and all this quaintness of conception, deserves to be called American so truly as Hawthorne. . . . [T]he past and present of American thought, of American psychology, especially as exhibited in New England, has had no interpreter like Hawthorne, in the Puritanism of the "Scarlet Letter" and in the Yankeeism of the "House of the Seven Gables." Nor have ever before the physical features of society met with so true an artist. The stiff, formal crowd which gathered around Hester Prynne, and the busy, gossiping neighbors who came morning and evening to trade with Hepzibah in her cent-shop—the children of that day and . . . of this, are all American. . . . The beauty and grandeur and grace of art are very visible in Hawthorne, but they are often veiled in an awful mystery, as is the majesty in Michael Angelo's "Day and Night." . . .

Throughout his life, Hawthorne led a twofold existence—a real and a supernatural. As a man, he was the realest of men. From childhood to old age he had great physical powers. His massive head sat upon a strong and muscular neck, and his chest was broad and capacious. His strength was great; his hand and foot were large and well made. . . . In walking, he had a firm step and a great stride without effort. In early manhood he had abounding health, a good digestion, a hearty enjoyment of food. His excellent physical condition gave him a placid and even temper, a cheerful spirit. He was a silent man, and often a moody one, but never irritable or morose. . . . He was a most delightful companion. In conversation he was never controversial, never authoritative, and never absorbing. In a multitude, his silence was oppressive; but, with a single companion, his talk flowed on sensibly, quietly, and full of wisdom and shrewdness. He discussed books with wonderful acuteness, sometimes with startling power and with an unexpected verdict, as if Shakespeare were discussing Ben Jonson. He analyzed men, their characters and motives and capacity, with great penetration, impartially if a stranger or an enemy, with the tenderest and most touching justice of a friend. He was fond of the companionship of all who were in sympathy with this real and human side of his life. A genuine character was very attractive to him. And so in the "Scarlet Letter" he warms over the custom-house clerk and the old collector, because each was perfect in his way. . . . Men who did not meddle with him he loved, men who made no demands on him, who offered him the repose of genial companionship. His life-long friends were of this description, and his loyalty to them was chivalrous and fearless, and so generous that when they differed from him in matters of opinion he rose at once above the difference and adhered to them for what they really were; and these friends were usually remarkable for great force of one description or another. Of General Pierce, after a long discussion of his character and career, he said, with inexpressible sadness in his tone: "It is so hard for Frank to get a new idea!" Of the dedication of "Our Old Home" to General Pierce, he said, in face of the most bitter opposition, the strongest threats, the most urgent appeals: "I cannot withdraw that dedication and wound my friend. My loyalty to him is involved. I would not do it, even if the financial success of the book depended upon it." And he said this, not in the heat of passion, but with a calm, and generous courage. In his intercourse with his friends, he seldom discussed his books. Adverse criticism, he never read; and while he was encouraged by approval he never required the stimulus of flattery, nor was he disheartened by dissent. Placid, peaceful, calm, and retiring as he was, in all the ordinary events of life, he was tempestuous and irresistible when roused. An attempt on the part of a rough and overbearing sea-captain to interfere with his business as an inspector of the customs in charge of his ship, was met with such a terrific uprising of spiritual and physical wrath that the dismayed captain fled up the wharf and took refuge at the feet of him who sat at the receipt of customs, enquiring, with a sailor's emotion and a sailor's tongue, "What, in God's name, have you sent on board my ship for an inspector?" He knew no such thing as fear; was scrupulously honest; was unwavering in his fidelity; conscientious in the discharge of his duty. There may have been men of more latent power, but I have known no man more impressive, none in whom the great reposing strength seemed clad in such a robe of sweetness as he wore. I saw him on the day General Pierce was elected to the Presidency. It was a bright and delicious afternoon in late autumn. He was standing under the little shaded and embowered piazza of the "Wayside" at Concord, in the full vigor of his manhood, radiant with joy at the good fortune of his friend. . . . I have seen him fishing from the rocks of the Essex County shore at Swampscott, enjoying the bliss of absolute repose and the sweet uncertainty which attends the angler's line. I have sat with him in the dimly-lighted room on autumnal evenings, cheerful and vocal with the cricket's chirp, and have heard his wise and sensible talk, uttered in that soft, melodious tone which gave such a peculiar charm to his utterances—a tone so shy that an intruder would hush it into silence in an instant. I have strolled with him in the darkness of a summer night through the lanes of Concord, assured by his voice, which came up from the grass-grown roadside in a sort of mysterious murmur, that he was my companion still. And everywhere, and at all times, he bore about him a strong and commanding presence, an impression of unpretending power. . . .

And now . . . [from portraying Hawthorne as] a commanding and sensible man . . . standing on the earth and engaged in the toil of life, I present the other side.

It is the supernatural element in Hawthorne which has given him his high distinction. When he entered upon his work as a writer, he left this personality which I have just described entirely behind him. In this work, he allowed no interference, he asked for no aid. He was shy of those whose intellectual power and literary fame might seem to give them a right to enter his sanctuary.

In an assembly of illustrious authors and thinkers, he floated, reserved and silent, around the margin in the twilight of the room, and at last vanished into the outer darkness. . . . The working of his mind was so sacred and mysterious to him that he was impatient of any attempt at familiarity or even intimacy with the divine power within him. His love of personal solitude was a ruling passion, his intellectual solitude was an overpowering necessity. Barry Cornwall says: "A spider, my dear, the meanest thing that crawls, or lives, has its mate, or fellow; but a scholar has no mate or fellow"; and yet the isolation of the scholar is mere twilight when compared with the solitude which settles around the great creative genius. Hawthorne said himself that his work grew in his brain as it went on, and was beyond his control or direction, for nature was his guide. And so in great loneliness he toiled, conscious that no human power could guide him, and that human sympathy was of no avail. I have often thought that he understood his own greatness so imperfectly, that he dared not expose the mystery to others, and that the sacredness of his genius was to him like the sacredness of his love. That this sentiment, so natural and admirable, made him somewhat unjust to his literary associates, there can be but little doubt. For, while he applied to them the powerful test of his own genius, before whose blaze many of them withered, his retiring disposition kept him at a distance almost fatal to any estimate of their true proportions. And, even when he admired and respected the authors among whom he moved, and was proud of the companionship into which his genius had elevated him, he never got over his natural sensitiveness with regard to the demand they might make on him as a fellow-artist to open his creations to their vision, and with regard to the test that they might apply to him. For his sturdy manhood he sought intimates and companions—not many, but enough to satisfy his natural longing for a fellow; for his genius he neither sought nor desired nor expected to find companionship. For his old official friend, he had a tender affection; for the strong and practical young men with whom he had set forth in life, he had an abiding love and attachment. . . . For the throne on which he sat in the imperial realm of his own creative thought, he desired no associate; his seat there was for him alone, his reign there was supreme. And, when he retired to that lonely room which he had set apart at the height of the tower which overtopped his humble abode in Concord, and, without book or picture, alone with a solitary seat and desk, having none to commune with except nature which stood before his windows to cheer his heart, entered upon his work, his creation moved steadily and majestically on. . . .

[193]

And so, when Hawthorne died, the world felt that . . . a most brilliant star had dropped from the firmament of the heavens. The scholars and the men of genius hastened to pay tribute to his greatness. Freed at last from associations which many of the refined and thoughtful could not and would not understand, he took in an instant his recognized place among the few great masters whom God had sent on earth to teach man the glory of the place assigned him in creation. But it was the companions of his human side, who mourned for him as for a brother, and who felt that, when he passed away, the strong staff of their lives was broken. He died peacefully, under the affectionate care of the least poetical and most purely practical man of his time, and found with him his natural repose. It was the scholars and poets, however, who gathered around his grave and paid a tender tribute to those supernatural powers which they could not approach while he was on earth.

George B. Loring, "Nathaniel Hawthorne," in *Papyrus Leaves,* ed. William Fearing Gill (New York: Worthington, 1880), 250–62, 266–68.

[A Conversation about Hawthorne at the Concord School of Philosophy in 1880]

[Franklin B. Sanborn]

⭤

Over his long and varied career as a teacher in Concord, journalist, abolitionist and social reformer, prolific reporter of Transcendentalism in New England, and biographer of Emerson, Thoreau, Bronson Alcott, and others, Franklin Benjamin Sanborn (1831–1917) earned immense respect from his contemporaries. Today, however, his reputation is mixed at best. For although as a second-generation Transcendentalist he—probably more than anyone else—transmitted the intellectual fervor of the movement's founders to twentieth-century readers, Sanborn had an unfortunate tendency to rewrite history, usually to his own advantage.

That does not appear to be a problem in Sanborn's following account of the unscheduled conversation about Hawthorne that occurred in July 1880 during the second season of the Concord School of Philosophy. Here, Sanborn is on his best behavior as a journalist as he records what must have struck all in attendance as the most important public discussion of Hawthorne's life and writing held in the sixteen years since the author's death. On the platform with Sanborn, who moderated the conversation, were Bronson Alcott and Elizabeth Palmer Peabody, and both were in their best talkative moods. William Sloane Kennedy, George Parsons Lathrop, and William Henry Channing, who were in the audience, actively contributed their own anecdotes, insights, and reminiscences relating to Hawthorne to the conversation. Nothing seemed to be off limits as the conversation unfolded: Hawthorne's character, early life, relation to his parents and his own family, life in Concord and abroad, complex attitude toward American culture, and sense of personal and authorial isolation all receive detailed comment.

Sanborn appreciated the importance of what he witnessed at the Concord School of Philosophy. In the article he immediately wrote for the *Boston Herald,* from which the text that follows is drawn, he added three subtitles in bold lettering below "Nathaniel Hawthorne," his title for the piece: "Conversation about the Author of 'The Scarlet Letter' "; "His Friends Tell the Story of His Life Anew"; "Fresh Facts about the Great Romancer." Two days later Sanborn's abridged versions of the original appeared in the *Springfield Republican* (8 [3 August 1880]: 1–2) and the *New-York Tribune* (6 [3 August 1880]: 2–4). But the excitement of the moment did not end there. A year later, Kennedy, who was troubled by the disposition among the conversation's participants to separate Hawthorne's art from his inner life, published "The Seclusion and Isolation of Hawthorne," a decidedly psychoanalytic reading of the subject, in *The Californian* (4 [August 1881]: 124–26). Arguing that introspection and reflection were the sources of his genius, Kennedy said that Hawthorne wrote about the truth of life as he discovered it within himself during his most "despondent moods": "In the gleaming sunny chambers of his fantasy were many doors opening abruptly upon the dark, inane, and ghost-haunted region of despair, and if occasionally he permitted the dim phantoms to troop through the opened doors, it was . . . that he might group them, sketch them, and then wave them back" (125). According to Kennedy, the "conclusion and the moral" of his life and writings "Hawthorne would say to be this: Sedulously avoid everything that tends to destroy sympathy and love in your breast. This was the course Hawthorne himself pursued. . . . He saw the danger of isolation in time to avoid it, and in his *Dramas of Sorrow* he . . . warned others against the danger, and helped them to avoid it" (126).

THE SURPRISES AT THE Concord school of philosophy this season have been numerous and memorable. The various sessions have often been brilliant beyond expectation. While the lectures have been good, the conversations following them have often been better than the lectures themselves, even the lecturers often saying their best things unconsciously at this time. But the surprise of surprises came yesterday morning. It had been expected that Prof. Benjamin Peirce would lecture, but . . . he was too ill to fulfil his engagement. Many knew this . . . but some came to hear the conversation on Hawthorne that was to take the place of Prof. Peirce's lecture, and among them a member of the *Herald*'s staff. It was easy to foresee, on looking over the audience, that persons were present who, if they could be induced to tell what they knew of the great romancer, could impart the deepest interest to the occasion, and this they did. Mr. Frank B. Sanborn took the chair. On his right sat Miss Elizabeth P. Peabody, and on his left Mr. Alcott. In the audience were Rev. W. H. Channing, who was the pastor of Hawthorne's family while he was consul at Liverpool, and Mr. George P. Lathrop, his biographer. Mrs. Hawthorne was Miss Peabody's sister. Mr. Alcott had been Mr. Hawthorne's neighbor for three years while he lived at the Wayside, now the home of Mr. Lathrop, and Mr. Lathrop is the husband of his only daughter now living. The rest of the company was made up of persons deeply interested in Hawthorne and in his writings, and making an atmosphere fit for saying the choicest words about him.

Mr. Sanborn opened the conversation by a few general remarks, during which he read extracts from the poems of William Ellery Channing, the Concord recluse, . . . [and from his] biography of "Thoreau, the [Poet-]Naturalist," giving in each characteristic views of the author of "The Scarlet Letter." The most distinctive thing read was that Hawthorne and Thoreau were both stoics in the essential basis of their lives. Miss Peabody called up the remark of Rev. James Freeman Clarke at Hawthorne's funeral, that "he was the friend of sinners," alluding to his intense study of criminal careers. Hawthorne's wife had the temperament opposite to her husband's. There never was a more perfect match than that, because the ideal he had which he had not been able to exemplify in his own outward action, was embodied in his wife and he enjoyed her sociality, though he thought it too late for him to cure himself of exclusiveness. Society was painful to him, but he enjoyed her going out, and when they lived in Salem he used to go with her to the door and then would go away. When she returned he would sit up half the night to hear her tell of what had taken place. He enjoyed society through her, and enjoyed it when in it himself, provided he was let alone. He liked to hear everything. Now and then he would say a word, and the word would be to carry on the conversation. You felt, when with him, that you did all the talking and had had a delightful conversation. His answer was indicated by a question "Why not," and now and then he was full of meaning. Mr. W. E. Channing, said Mr. Sanborn, once told me that Hawthorne had a great habit of sitting unnoticed in bar-rooms and stage offices, and all places where people came and went. He would sit by the hour in these places listening to the conversation and observing the characters. His note books abound in descriptions of these country geniuses.

Miss Peabody said: "Yes, he also used to wander about and go to farm houses and talk with people there. He said he hadn't had the least difficulty if they didn't know his name. So also in sympathizing society, he said he never felt any shyness. Something is explained by his mother, who was a woman of no sociality. She lived when widows in New-England were expected to cherish the memory of their husbands somewhat after the Hindoo fashion, by retiring from the world. Mrs. Hawthorne was a person of very fine common sense, with a clear, strong mind, and was not the least bit of a sentimentalist, but she rather took advantage of that custom, and her surroundings not being quite to her mind, she lived in her own room, dressing in white. This custom broke up every family arrangement. Hawthorne never remembered sitting down to a meal with his mother until after he was married. His wife had the pleasure of bringing that about at Thanksgiving. Mrs. Hawthorne said to her son's wife one morning near that time, 'I want Una (the daughter, then 2 years old,) to remember her first Thanksgiving dinner with her grandmother.' Una's mother, Sophia, said to her husband, 'I'm going to have your mother laugh,' but he laughed even at the idea. He reverenced human liberty, thought every individual was a messenger out of heaven. He never directed his wife in anything, but only studied to see what she wanted, and then helped her to accomplish it. He studied his children in the same way. He felt them to be an open book in his nature. He wished to speak spontaneously, and, if they said what he did not like, he met them in the same respectful way that he would a grown-up person."

Mr. Sanborn—"Miss Peabody has spoken of Hawthorne's mother. He was a person in whom the doctrine of heredity certainly finds the most remarkable illustration. He has reproduced his ancestors and added to them the spirit of his own time. Wherever Hawthorne might appear, as was said of Sir Kenelm Digby, 'if he had dropped from the clouds in any part of the world, he would have made of himself a favorite, provided that he did not stay longer than six weeks.' In whatever part of the world he appeared, he would appear to have belonged to the nobility. He had those evident marks of descent which we shall hear more of in this country when the doctrine of heredity is established."

Miss Peabody here broke in saying: "His mother had great sensibility and a force of imagination. I often think of Goethe's mother. She could never hear anything disagreeable. There was something of that in Mrs. Hawthorne. She was not very thoroughly understood by those around her. The Hawthorne family was extremely individual. They had not so much sensibility as self-determining powers. An old sea captain met my father on the street and said: 'Well, I hear that your daughter is going to marry Hawthorne; I know'd his father. He was the sternest man that ever walked a deck.' That granite element was in Hawthorne. He had immense sternness of character. If he had not had this, he would have been swamped by this immense susceptibility, the greatest susceptibility to pain I ever saw. In the 'Gentle Boy' he describes himself. He said he was destitute of the malice that generally belongs to sensitive natures. I was struck with this, and said to him, 'Are sensitive natures malicious?' He said, 'Yes; they are wounded so easily that self-defence begins at babyhood, and when they feel antagonism in that way they are pained.'"

Mr. Kennedy here raised a point as to how far the element of shyness in Hawthorne is a key to his original productions.

Miss Peabody said: "I think it true that Hawthorne thought the social connection was the healing, and that isolation was the unpardonable sin. I have heard many strong expressions from him on this point, because I was almost the first lady acquaintance he had whom he was at all intimate with. I remember two instances of persons who made confessions to him—one a very bad man, who gave to him the whole story of his terrible life."

Mr. Sanborn here interposed a reply to Mr. Kennedy's question by alluding to a remark of Mr. [W. H.] Channing's, that Hawthorne's characters were not drawn from life. The character of Donatello was never seen by any person, and never could have been, and, in varying degrees, the same is true of these New England characters which seem on one side so familiar. They are creatures of his imagination, not drawn from the real life of the time. Hawthorne, who described nature with a photographic accuracy, seems to be incapable of reproducing any individual character without some change.

Mr. George P. Lathrop interposed, "Except in the custom-house."

Miss Peabody—"It is a story known to him, even on Salem turnpike. He disowned spontaneity which to him was reality."

Mr. Lathrop remarked: "It seems to me he separated the world of reality and the world of imagination. Not that he was incapable of describing the real world, because he showed great capacity for that, but when he went to writing a romance, he did not draw his characters from any living person. They were potentialities."

Miss Peabody said: "I cannot conceive of any one of his persons really living in the world." Miss Peabody here related the story of the original of "Aunt Hester," who was the second cousin of Stephen Higginson, and never accepted this government, and always lived on a pension from King George. "She was full of wit, and, though keeping much to herself, appeared as if her place was at the top of society. Some say that in Zenobia he described

Margaret Fuller; some that the character was Mrs. Ripley, of Concord. Hawthorne said he was astonished that anybody should think that, but when I said Zenobia reminded me of Margaret Fuller in some things, he replied, 'I should think anybody would know that I was not describing her. Many persons went to the formation of that character.' I suggested such and such a person. He laughed every time, admitting that he had got an idea from them. He had taken very peculiar characters in each instance, and they all united in Zenobia."

Here Rev. William H. Channing said: "Hawthorne told me that characters like that did usually come from living persons, and knowing how intimate I was with Margaret Fuller, he said, 'How anybody could suppose that Margaret Fuller was intended by Zenobia could not be conceived.' It is possible that one or two tints might have come from Margaret, but the whole life is moulded on an entirely different idea. The sad close of Zenobia's life was based upon an incident in Concord, but Hawthorne was actually grieved that any person could believe that he designed to give such a conception of one whom he held in such affectionate remembrance as he did Miss Fuller. But in regard to 'The Scarlet Letter,' too, I wish to say that there was a foundation in life for Dimmesdale. In the 'Blithedale Romance' enter some other characters, which sprung out of the potentialities of characters he met in actual life. I think one of the most wonderful facts about Hawthorne was his penetrating eye and sympathetic heart. There was no more keeping a secret from him than from an angel. The man read you like a book. Added to this was a wonderful tenderness." . . .

Mr. [W. H.] Channing resumed: "My first acquaintance with Hawthorne was at Brook Farm and at the old manse, but our real friendship was when he was consul at Liverpool. At his house there I first visited him, and took my first meal in England. In the intimate acquaintance that followed I discovered traits of character in him that have rarely been spoken of. The first was his boundless generosity, and the next was his clear, equable sense of justice, a latent equity, but he always tempered his justice with his generosity. I have never known a person who had more delicate sense of honor. He was as if he had already passed the veil and had met people on a higher ground; as if he comprehended what was nicest and deepest in them, by a spiritual revelation. He would sooner cut off his right hand than slander a human being." Mr. Channing here alluded to Hawthorne's consulship just before the rebellion, and his delicate relations with the British government, whereupon Mr. Sanborn related a conversation which occurred some years later at Hawthorne's own table in Concord, in which the latter said: "We are two distinct people—the North and the South. Whenever I met a man from the South in Liverpool, I always felt that he belonged to one nation and I to another."

Mr. Lathrop here added: "Hawthorne wrote a letter to his intimate friend, [Horatio] Bridge, when at Liverpool, in which he discussed the subject, using this expression: 'My heart, I think, is not large enough to take in more than my own part of the country.'" Mr. Lathrop thought this expression, while referring, no doubt, to an actual feeling, was a little despondent, and did not express his whole conviction. He had a great enthusiasm for the Union.

Mr. [W. H.] Channing again said: "As exhibiting the singular honor of the man, I will state that he stood by the Union always, and yet met the southerners just as freely as he did the northerners. I shall never forget a conversation we had once. He folded his arms and looked up and said: 'Yes. I think I would like to go home. One might as well go home and die with the Republic.' He had no hopes that we should come out of the struggle. His despair for the country hastened his death. I do not doubt that he died of a broken heart." Mr. Lathrop quoted James Russell Lowell as having said distinctly that the war shortened his life. Hawthorne saw so far ahead and had such insight that he thought the civil conflict would last for years.

Miss Peabody likened him to Hamlet, as one too finely developed for the position into which he came. Reflection predominated in him. He was one who could only suffer. He could not enter personally into the conflict.

Mr. [W. H.] Channing added on this point: He said to me: "I think it would need a good 1000 years of sleep to rest from the turmoils of this mortal life."

Mr. Alcott said: "I remember walking with Hawthorne when he was living at the Wayside, at a time when it was feared the rebel armies might reach New York and Boston. He expressed great sorrow, and seemed to be very much moved with the sentiment of patriotism." Mr. Lathrop here broke in with the remark that his wife told him that her father declared in her presence that, if the rebels attacked Boston, he and Julian would volunteer in its defence. Mr. Alcott resumed: "I infer from what he said that he wished the Union to be preserved, but did not quite see how it could be, under all circumstances, and I thought I saw a patriotism in him which, remembering what had been said about him, sympathized with the South, a fact surprising to me, because I thought it was not so. I thought he had an equal sympathy with the North, and that it was a sentiment of opinion which even allowed him for a moment to seem to support the Southern side. I remember, also, that when he sent me his book on England, I spoke to him about the dedication to President Pierce, his classmate and chum at Bowdoin College, and he said: 'How could I, as a friend, do otherwise than inscribe the book to him? I have expressed my opinions freely in it, and this is a work of friendship which I inscribe to him. Therefore it must stand.' Although some friends did, I believe, take the leaf out of the book, mine remains, and is still in the copy he gave me. What I have to say about him is reminiscences. He lived for three years in the neighboring house. There is an avenue between my house and his, inside the road. Mr. Hawthorne was a very coy and diffident person. He did not willingly seem to pass beyond the limits of his own wayside. He loved to walk on the hilltop, and the paths are still there which he made by his continued walks. I think of all his accomplishments his diffidence and coyness were the finest, and yet he was a man so magnificent in physique—an ideal Webster—that you could have said a sword belonged to him. His wife knew how to protect him from company. On his return from England he put up a lodge on top of the ancient house, approached by a pair of very steep steps. I think his temperament had a certain feature of reserve in it which made it less easy for him to unbend."

Mr. [W. H.] Channing interposed: "He was kindly in his bearing always."

Mr. Alcott resumed: "It is said that after he returned from Liverpool, honored as he was by England and this country, he was invited to dine with the Atlantic Club in Boston, where were many of the scholars of the time. There was an attempt made to get him to speak, but he was so coy even there that, while he received all his honors gracefully, he said nothing, and on his return home declared that he would never go again—a resolution which he afterward broke. I remember that, on visiting him with some distinguished persons and dining at his house, while he discharged the duties of the table with grace and elegance, he said very little, and, according to the highest rules of gentility, he withdrew and threw the conversation upon his guests. Such was his extreme diffidence. I never met him in the street during all the time he was here. In these three years he was in my house twice only. Passing by one day when we had young lady visitors, they persuaded this coy gentleman to come into my study. I found he was uneasy, and suspected he was trying to find an excuse for leaving. At last he said, 'The stove is too hot,' and retreated. Again the decoys were out to catch this fine genius. They succeeded, and the same thing occurred, but this time he said: 'The clock ticks so loud that I must retire.' Another incident shows his extreme sensibility. I had a grandson who was not very well, and was taking him in my arms and walking about the streets. Coming up the Hawthorne lane, I saw Hawthorne just before he left us for the last time standing at the gate, and I thought that, with my grandson I might venture to approach him. I addressed him, and he looked sadly. Said he: 'It seems to me your little boy is not looking well,' and he turned away as if he felt that he himself was not well; as if the suggestions of this little boy were an omen of his own illness. He went to meet his friend Mr. Ticknor, and there during Mr. Ticknor's illness, he remained until the very last, so that he was almost paralyzed by that. He went with his friend, President Pierce, and was found in his chamber asleep, a sleep from which he never waked. His funeral here was one of the most beautiful, and at the same time it was one of the most touching spectacles to see the Atlantic Club, Dr. Holmes, Mr. Emerson, Mr. Longfellow and others, accompany him to his last place where he now lies in Sleepy Hollow. Here were these distinguished men stooping over this man of genius with tears in their eyes, and in the absolute silence each took that occasion of paying his last tribute to this man of genius. He did not wish his body to be seen after death, and it was with the utmost persuasion that Mr. Hawthorne could be induced to allow his dear friends to gaze upon his noble form for the last time." Mr. Alcott concluded his remarks by reading selections from his own "Concord Days."

Mr. [W. H.] Channing here alluded to Hawthorne's remarkable speech at St. George's Hall in Liverpool, saying that not a better one was made there on that afternoon, and that there was no more kingly presence there than Hawthorne's.

Miss Peabody demurred to the use of the word diffidence. "He had," she said, "immense sensibility, and he had not had that kind of intercourse with society which gave him confidence. He felt out of place in conventional society, because he was a citizen in the company of a higher world, but he liked to see people, and the only thing I ever heard him remonstrate with his wife for was her efforts to keep people away from him." Here Miss Peabody detailed in a confidential way, with great animation and with the old-time smile of youth and middle age upon her face, the story of her first acquaintance with Hawthorne, how anxious she was to find out the author of "The Gentle Boy," how she supposed the author was an old man, who was done with the passions of the world and only contemplating them; how, finally, she made bold to invite the Hawthornes to her house, and how delighted she was when she could say to her Salem friends after their call, "I've got him." Then she

delineated the steps by which the handsome young Hawthorne was gradually thawed into the utmost geniality over Flaxman's illustrations of Homer,
Hesiod and Dante in her own home, and how he became a diner out, and
then how he waited upon the Misses Peabody home, and grew even anxious
that they should spend an evening with his own sisters, promising even to
escort them to his home and back to their own if they would consent to go, a
thing they had been longing to do for two or three years. His readiness in the
matter was both a surprise and delight to the Peabody girls. Hawthorne went
so far as to urge gently the visit on his own account. "I'll come after you," he
said; "I wish you would come. My sister Elizabeth is very witty. I want to see
her. I have not seen her in three months. We don't live at our house; we only
vegetate." "That was the first time," remarked Miss Peabody, "that he spoke
of this isolation. His conversation was very interesting. The things he would
observe in nature, the most beautiful flecks of light, were always an emblem
of something in the mind. Human nature was what he talked about through
these symbols."

Miss Peabody went on to say that she knew Hawthorne's sisters when they
were children in Salem. One of them, Elizabeth, shut herself up at 18, and
saw almost nobody for 20 years. She was a very peculiar person, and insisted
on living out of doors, summer and winter. This preserved her health. Hawthorne was very much liked as a child, and began to tell stories when he was
only 5 or 6 years old. At about his 12th year he was a great reader. He didn't
remember the time when he couldn't read. Shakespeare was familiar to him
from boyhood. He was called Oberon at Bowdoin on account of his beauty.
In those years he spent much of his time on the Kennebec river and in the
woods. He was disturbed about a profession even when a boy. He didn't want
to be a minister because he didn't know enough to teach people. He could
not be a doctor nor a lawyer. He couldn't do anything but write, and then
he added, as if in bravo, "How would it look to see Nathaniel Hawthorne's
works on the shelf?" He wrote enormously, but could not get anything published. Mr. Peabody read his stories as they appeared in the Token and other
quarters. He wrote a book called "The Story-Teller," in which there were
two characters, one resembling the late Jones Very, and the other standing for
himself. Very stood for a minister who wanted to convert the world, but had
no parish. Hawthorne stood for an idler who could only write stories. The
two set out to convert the world and went from place to place announcing,
as they approached a village, by posters, that there would be preaching, and

after the preaching a story. Mr. S. G. Goodrich, the "Peter Parley" of those days, refused to publish this book, and Hawthorne said he was like one "talking to himself in a dark place."

Mr. [W. H.] Channing added: "Hawthorne became the man he was very much through the influence of his wife. She was the influence that gave him a home which fulfilled his ideal. I considered her to be one of the most perfect women in her womanliness I have ever known. Hawthorne was a man who did not like to speak of the sublime and all the mysteries. Not that he did not in his innermost soul believe them, but that he felt they were too vast, too pure and too holy for him to be their medium."

Mr. Lathrop said: "Hawthorne's fondness for England did not exclude his devotion to his own country. I have been told that he brought his family home because he felt it to be of the utmost importance that his children should grow up in this country, and be educated as Americans. Mr. Longfellow once said to me that when Hawthorne was in the room it was like speaking in the presence of a woman. Creative genius when lodged in a man has feminine qualities. His diffidence was due to the feminine traits of genius. This quality was as natural to him as the delicate reserve of a woman is in her."

Miss Peabody said: "Mr. Channing has not overstated my sister's character. I don't think there was ever realized more completely the idea expressed in Mr. Emerson's lecture on 'Love,' that it is the union of two self-sufficing worlds. Her character had been matured by great suffering, and his by great suffering. Her's was bodily and his mental suffering. The union on that account was a very rare one. She gave him an atmosphere."

Rev. Julius H. Ward referred to Dr. G. B. Loring's sketch of Hawthorne as a man who enjoyed rollicking company, as Shakespeare is said to have done, and asked for more information about it.

Mr. [W. H.] Channing answered by an allusion to the "Tanglewood Tales," to the story of the Pygmies. Hawthorne, interpreting the symbol, says that these earth-born creatures lost their strength when lifted into a higher atmosphere, but also, ideal democrat as he was, he felt that you could force up the coarse elements of democracy by a higher ideal.

Miss Peabody here remarked: "Hawthorne said, 'The reason I am a Democrat is because the Salem people are Whigs.'"

Mr. [W. H.] Channing afterward added, on the way from the chapel to Mr. Emerson's house: "Hawthorne once said to me, when I asked him why the weird element always appeared in his works, 'Every time I sit down to write a story I design that it shall not intrude, but as soon as I dip my pen in ink the little imp that lurks in the inkstand runs up my arm and takes possession, and guides my pen.' Another point is worth remembering. I once asked him about his style, how he got it. He replied: 'It is the result of a great deal of practice. It is a desire to tell the simple truth as honestly and vividly as one can.'"

Such was the conclusion of a conversation so vivid and remarkable, that those who engaged in it were astonished when it was over, as if they had been lifted out of the real world in a dream. Mr. Lathrop, who knew the whole field, said that many points presented were new even to him. Miss Peabody, though long past her 70th year, fairly sparkled with joy as she entered into the story, and there were moments when the emotion was so deep and thrilling that one could have heard a pin drop on the floor or felt the flow of another's breath. No person who was present will ever forget the conversation, the faces, the persons, the divine spell of the hour.

[Franklin B. Sanborn,] "Nathaniel Hawthorne. Conversation about the Author of 'The Scarlet Letter.' His Friends Tell the Story of His Life Anew. Fresh Facts about the Great Romancer," *Boston Herald* 5 (1 August 1880): 1–3.

"Nathaniel and Sophia Hawthorne" (1882)

Moncure Daniel Conway

> Born in Virginia to a slaveholding family, the Unitarian minister, prolific author, and abolitionist Moncure Daniel Conway (1832–1907) might seem an unlikely advocate for the core beliefs associated with Transcendentalism. However, after first meeting Emerson in Concord in 1853, and through him being drawn into the eclectic circle that included Thoreau, Elizabeth Hoar and Elizabeth Peabody, Sanborn, the Ripleys, and the Hawthornes, Conway believed he had arrived at his intellectual and ethical home. Like Sanborn, Conway was a second-generation Transcendentalist; since they knew and outlived the principal figures involved in the movement, both enjoyed a quarter-century reign as historians of Transcendentalism and biographers of its leading figures.
>
> As Conway states in the following selection drawn from his *Emerson at Home and Abroad* (1882), he knew Hawthorne through his writings long before he met him. An unapologetic sentimentalist, especially in his account of the relationship he personally witnessed between Nathaniel and Sophia, he was sympathetic to the variety of personal trials Hawthorne endured by virtue of his lineage, the slowness with which his literary reputation emerged, and his position on the Civil War. As far as Conway was concerned, Hawthorne was the creative equal of any of the major writers and thinkers of his time, including Emerson, a conviction that is evident throughout the many reviews he wrote of Hawthorne's works as well as in his *Life of Nathaniel Hawthorne* (1890).

ON A DAY IN CONCORD I saw the two men whom Michael Angelo might have chosen as emblems of Morning and Twilight, to be carved over the gates of the New World. Emerson emerged from his modern home, and the shade of well-trimmed evergreens in front, with "shining morning face," his eye beaming with its newest vision of the golden year. Hawthorne, at the other extreme[,] . . . came softly out of his earlier home, the Old Manse—the grey-gabled mansion, where dwelt in the past men and women who have gained new lease of existence through his genius—and stepped along the avenue of ancient ash-trees, which made a fit frame around him. A superb man he was! His erect, full, and shapely figure might have belonged to an athlete, were it not for the grace and reserve which rendered the strength of frame unobtrusive. The massive forehead and brow, with dark locks on either side, the strong nose and mouth, with another soul beneath them, might be the physiognomy of a military man or political leader—some man impelled by powerful public passions; but with this man there came through the large soft eyes a gentle glow which suffused the face and spiritualised the form. No wonder such fascination held his college fellows to him! Longfellow used to talk in poetry when his early days at Bowdoin with Hawthorne were the theme; and the memory of President Pierce has lost some stains through his lifelong devotion to his early friend.

How the personages who had long before preceded him in that first home of his manhood had become his familiar friends and visitors—preferred to others separated from him by reason of their flesh and blood—no reader of "Mosses from an Old Manse" need be told. As he came down the avenue, unconscious of any curious or admiring eye resting on him, every step seemed a leap, as if his shadowy familiars were whispering happy secrets. What was this *genius loci* thinking of as he walked there? It may have been about that time he mentioned the Old Manse to a friend, and wrote: "The trees of the avenue—how many leaves have fallen since I last saw them!" It was always on the fallen leaf that Hawthorne found the sentence for his romance, but to what a beautiful new life did it germinate there!

It is an almost solemn reflection that in that same Old Manse, and in the same room, were written Emerson's "Nature" and Hawthorne's "Goodman Brown."

On the twenty-eighth birthday of the American Republic was born also this last wizard of Salem; and the spirit of the day, as well as of the place, was potent in him. . . . I know not whether it be because Beauty insists on rising from even such distant waves, but the Salem people and their homes always appeared to me to possess a peculiar charm. Here young Nathaniel could read on Gallows Hill, where the witches were hung, the tragical story of that era, to the time when the people arose and broke open the prison doors of those victims, and entered the door of the judge, whom they forced to kneel and ask pardon of outraged humanity. On the neighbouring seabeach he was wont to wander in the twilight and see—sombre Astarte shall we say?—rising from the waves, where his fathers had commanded ships of war or merchandise. From these years grew many of those mystical "Twice-

Told Tales" in which all the moonlight and starlight of New England history is garnered. When they were first read, some thought even the author's name a myth. "Nathaniel" had been suggested by the Puritan's fondness for scriptural names, and "Hawthorne" had an obvious significance; and, indeed, the letter *w*, which the author inserted in the old Wiltshire name, may have represented some conscious spiritualisation of his family tree. His ancestor who planted the American branch of Hathornes persecuted Quakers, the next persecuted witches. The best compensation for their lives was when they were turned into gloomily picturesque figures by the art of their descendant, and the blood shed by their thorns tinted the blossoms of Hawthorne. . . .

"The Celestial Railway" was the first piece by Hawthorne that penetrated our Southern region. It was copied in the newspapers . . . and much enjoyed as a satire upon the rationalistic tendencies of the North. When I became old enough to appreciate the humour of that allegory, and the "serene strength" which Emerson found in it, I was also able to recognise its reactionary spirit. And years later, recognising Hawthorne as the one American whose genius was comparable with that of Emerson for power, it was my conviction that the piece I have mentioned, and the greater part of the "Mosses from an Old Manse," belong to the earlier and unsunned time of his life. . . . A dismal day cast its last shadows on those "Mosses," and a careful eye may find them sheathing . . . roses of the fairer morning that had come upon his life.

In his earliest tales, . . . there is revealed . . . a sensitive and loving nature, thirsting for affection, faint with growing despair of finding a nature responsive to his deep heart. In 1836 Margaret Fuller wrote to a friend: "I took a two or three year old 'Token,' and chanced on a story called 'The Gentle Boy,' which I remembered to have heard was written by somebody in Salem. It is marked by so much grace and delicacy of feeling that I am very desirous to know the author, whom I take to be a lady."

Meantime in that same old town . . . was dwelling near Hawthorne the heart that held his sunbeam. A kind and intelligent physician dwelt in Salem, with his three lovely daughters, dowered only with riches of mind and heart. Of these sisters Peabody, all lived to do honour to the womanhood of America. Mary, as Mrs. Horace Mann, was able to assist her eminent husband in his educational work East and West. . . . Elizabeth, by an unwearied zeal in the pursuit of every high ideal, became a kind of saintly abbess at Concord, of whom I heard Emerson say that her recollections and correspondence would comprise the spiritual history of her time. Sophia, as the wife of Hawthorne, aided in the realisation of ideals as beautiful as any she dreamed while a favourite pupil in the studio of Allston.

It was with a certain despair that Hawthorne made his first pilgrimage to the Brook Farm community,—the wild plunge of a starved heart to find some other world. He found his millennium in a heart. He was a stranger in the land of promise, but found his ideal community, which consisted of two, whose model halls were in the most ancient and solitary mansion of Concord village. There was indeed one other member of the Old Manse community,—Poverty; but never was poor relation treated more good-humouredly.

No other! Yes, Happiness. To read Hawthorne's "Notes" of these years starts to the eyes tears that flash prismatic hues. He is still "the obscurest man of letters in America;" he is poor and without prospect of becoming otherwise; and he feels himself supremely blessed. His honeymoon never waned. He compares himself to Adam with Eve beside him, and cannot think Eden could have been very different from their garden with its Balm-of-Gilead trees and its unforbidden apples. All the four rivers of paradise were merged in [the Concord River] . . . gently streaming past, adorned with lilies . . . and reflecting the scarlet cardinal-flower, which he would have accepted as a confessor had there been any snake in his garden.

He gave his perfect happiness as a reason why he did not seek from Emerson his solution of the riddle of the universe. . . .

There is an allegorical flower growing out of a grave, so often met with in Hawthorne's pages that it can never fade from his escutcheon. . . . [T]here are some startling correspondences between the early fancies of Hawthorne and the great pessimistic systems. . . .

One day there was a Mayday festival for the children of Concord. Emerson gave the use of his woods and a Maypole. While the ladies were out there making the preparations, Hawthorne came up and said he would like to see the children dancing if he could do so without being perceived. There was found for him the hollow trunk of a tree long dead; he hid himself as the children were coming, and gazed upon them. He left unperceived. Was it a tree grown from a slip of Buddha's Bo-tree, brought over by the Puritans to represent their dogma of a curse on nature? It could not live on Emerson's farm, and its last service was to give Hawthorne his outlook on the dance of happy children in which he could not freely unite. Yet was he a charming playmate to his children and a profoundly sympathetic man; though to the last he could not part with his "horse of the night," as Emerson styled it. . . .

Emerson feared the melancholy temperament of his most distinguished neighbour, but recognised his genius and his almost magical art. So long as Margaret Fuller frequented Concord, she was an element which enabled them to mingle, but when that mediator was gone, the two shrank a little from each other by elective necessity. . . . Hawthorne may have been afraid of casting a shadow across that path of sunshine visible wherever Emerson moved, and he may also have feared to meet the unfamiliar people who sought the Sage. Here was a man whose nerves were without integument, terribly exposed to all kinds of impressions from without. If any person or thing came into real contact with his mind, it sank deeply into him, drew upon his heart's blood, and remained until it was born into some mental offspring. Every new experience was a fatality to him for good or ill. Not everyone who saw how reserved and gentle he was knew the great struggle by which a nature full of fiery forces had been brought into harmony with its ideal elements. Beneath these remained the lava soil, which must needs nurse into life every seed fallen in it.

[Hawthorne's] ancestors became his literary offspring. The genesis of "The Scarlet Letter" . . . has been shadowed forth by himself; and there is nothing more thrilling in it than the scene of Hawthorne himself, in the prosaic Custom-house pressing the faded broidered "A" to his breast till it burns. But whence came the letter and the tale? From the brow or Cain. . . . The "House of the Seven Gables" was once the doomed House of Agamemnon. Nearly all the tales of Hawthorne, even the smallest, have bloomed from seed taken . . . from the cerements of royal mummies, where they symbolised eternal ideas, albeit the bodies they receive from his genius have such an American look. That, I believe, is why they possess the unique character of seeming new and startling every time one reads them. They do not appear like literary creations, but draw the reader at once to the man in whom these things exist. His writings are over-cast with the pain of a heart held under a necessity to expose its inmost recesses to the world. . . .

It must have seemed to Nathaniel and Sophia Hawthorne a very long pilgrimage that had brought them from the Old Manse to that pretty villa, [the Wayside,] little as is the distance. It was with a sigh that Hawthorne responded to the kindness of . . . George Bancroft . . . in appointing him surveyor of the port of Salem. It ended his poverty, but also his paradise. It seemed also a farewell to his literary aims. It was during the years between 1846, when he received his appointment, and 1849, when he was removed, that he was haunted by the spirits of "The Scarlet Letter." One very intimate with him told me a pleasant story about it. One wintry day he received at his office notification that his services would no longer be required. With heaviness of heart he repairs to his humble home. His young wife recognises the change, and stands waiting for the silence to be broken. At length he falters, "I am removed from office." Then she leaves the room; soon she returns with fuel and kindles a bright fire with her own hand; next brings pen, paper, ink, and sets them beside him. Then she touches the sad man on the shoulder, and, as he turns to the beaming face, says, "Now you can write your book!" The cloud cleared away. The lost office looked like a cage from which he had escaped. The book was written; it was welcomed by the publisher, who knew how to think and write—yes, and how to be a friend—James Fields. . . .

When his old college-friend Franklin Pierce was nominated for the Presidency, Hawthorne wrote a biography of him; and when, after election, Pierce appointed him Consul at Liverpool, some, who did not know Hawthorne, regarded the proceeding as a bargain. The truth was, Hawthorne was intensely loyal to the few intimate friends of his life, and he could not be persuaded of anything against Franklin Pierce, who, indeed, had many amiable qualities. When Pierce had become exceedingly unpopular in the country, Hawthorne stood by him even to his cost, . . . dedicating "Our Old Home" to him, despite the protest of his publishers.

This man, who had inherited from an ancestry of soldiers a port and courage equal to the bravest of them, had gained from the record of their cruelties a horror of bloodshed, something like that of a Confederate soldier of my acquaintance, who, since the American war, refuses to kill a mosquito. Probably his "democratic" sympathies were largely due to his dread of the conflict to which the anti-slavery agitation was leading.

The shadow that fell upon Hawthorne's patriotic heart from the blackening sky of his country was for a time forgotten in the shadow of death that seemed to be drawing near and nearer his daughter Una. From that long illness in Rome this lovely girl seemed to recover, but not her father. He came back to England and wrote "Transformation." He went to Leamington and other pretty places, but found that he could not write well amid ornamental and social surroundings, so his dear friend Francis Bennoch found a wild and desolate seaside place, Redcar, where, in a seclusion like that of the Concord snowstorms, which protected his hours of inspiration, those exquisite creations were finished.

When he foresaw the civil war in America to be inevitable, Hawthorne said to a friend in Liverpool that he meant to "go home and die with the Republic." The war did indeed wear deeply upon his mind and health. He could not share the high hopes which sustained his nearest friends during those terrible years; he could not see beyond the black cloud a country liberated from the blight of slavery. To him the war was an overwhelming tragedy, and the inevitable end seemed to be the end of the Republic.

These forebodings found much to foster them in the earlier course of the war. Hawthorne visited Washington, and on his return wrote that strange account of his observations and reflections there which appeared in the "Atlantic Monthly" for July 1862. That paper is a notable instance of the subtlety of Hawthorne's art, which in this case has deceived even so subtle an artist as Henry James, jun. "The article," says Mr. James in his Biography of Hawthorne, "has all the usual merit of such sketches on Hawthorne's part—the merit of delicate, sportive feeling, expressed with consummate grace; but the editor of the periodical appears to have thought that he must give the antidote with the poison, and the paper is accompanied with several little notes disclaiming all sympathy with the writer's political heresies." The footnotes here mentioned are severe, and sometimes contemptuous in their rebuke of the text; but they were written by Hawthorne himself! So, at any rate, I was assured by Emerson at the time, and as also about that time I passed a night at the house of Mr. Fields with Hawthorne, feel certain that this is the case. No doubt Mr. Fields had remonstrated with Hawthorne on some sentiments in the contribution to his magazine, but the sharp criticisms were by Hawthorne on himself. . . .

Shortly after Hawthorne's return from Europe, I met him at a dinner of the Literary Club in Boston. A larger number than usual had come together to welcome him home. He was more social and talkative than I had ever supposed he could be, but was much aged in appearance. He had repaired to his Concord home, and, could he only have escaped the sounds of war, perhaps he might have tasted at the Wayside a drop of that elixir which its old Sachem was fabled to possess. But he could not find repose, and instead of dreaming, like Septimius, of endless life, said that he hoped no trumpet, however angelic, would sound over his grave short of a thousand years.

When I passed a night with him under the roof of James T. Fields, after his return from Washington, he had the expression of one who had been wandering amid ruins—the ruins of his country. Mrs. Fields had invited a little company, but after the first arrivals Hawthorne made his escape to his room. At the request of Mrs. Fields, I went to ask if he could not come down, and found him deep in Defoe's "Short Stories." He did not emerge until the next morning at breakfast-time, and then, with the amusing look of a naughty child, pleaded that he had been carried off by Defoe's wicked ghosts. He must . . . have been contemplating some phantasmal production at that time; for I remember his asking me questions about the ghost-beliefs of the negroes, among whom my early life was passed. One of these was of a negro who saw an enormous conflagration near by, but on reaching the spot found only one firecoal and heard a dog bark. Hawthorne was interested in this, and spoke in a sympathetic way about the negroes that I did not expect. But he evidently suspected that the war conflagration would end in a small ember for the negroes, and I suspect did not believe that race would be made happier than he had been by freedom and culture.

Hawthorne could see between the Old Manse and the Wayside a transformation as beautiful as that which gave Cinderella beauty for ashes: he saw his lovely and gifted children growing around him like fulfilments of what the riverside flowers had promised his early wedded happiness; and perhaps it seemed to him that it was well enough to pass away in that fulness of life. So it was. Amidst hearts that loved him he was carried to his repose in Sleepy Hollow. . . .

Hawthorne once wrote from England to a friend: "Of all things, I should like to find a gravestone in one of these old churchyards with my name upon it; although, for myself, I should wish to be buried in America." It was not very long before his name was read on an English gravestone. On March 4, 1871, when I stood beside the open grave of Mrs. Nathaniel Hawthorne in Kensal Green Cemetery, my vision wandered away to another in that little cemetery at, Concord, which, though primitive, is also consecrated by the dust of noble spirits; and the two, so sundered, seemed to represent a happy tale suddenly broken off, and ending with heaviness and pain. She was laid to rest by those who had known and loved her—Francis Bennoch, W. H. Channing, Robert

Browning, Russell Sturgis; and not far off the face of Leigh Hunt, from the marble over his grave, seemed to beam with sympathy upon the two lonely daughters of his friends. Before the coffin was lowered, these two—Una and Rose—laid upon it, the one a wreath, the other a cross, of white camelias. . . .

Moncure Daniel Conway, "Nathaniel and Sophia Hawthorne," in *Emerson at Home and Abroad* (Boston: J. R. Osgood, 1882), 207–14, 217–19, 223–25.

"My First Visit to New England" (1894)

WILLIAM DEAN HOWELLS

⸬

As a young staffer on the *Ohio State Journal,* William Dean Howells (1837–1920) undertook a literary tour of New England and New York in 1860. He called on Holmes, Lowell, and Fields in Boston; Hawthorne, Thoreau, and Emerson in Concord; and Walt Whitman in New York, where he also fell in with the Bohemians at Pfaff's Bleeker Street restaurant. After serving from 1861 to 1865 as the American consul in Venice, Howells returned to the United States, where for the next quarter century he held important editorial positions at the *Atlantic Monthly, Harper's Magazine,* and *Cosmopolitan Magazine* and emerged as one of America's most influential spokespersons for the realistic school in fiction.

Except for his visits to Thoreau and Emerson, Howells thoroughly enjoyed his tour of New England. Prior to arriving in Boston, he spent a few days in Hawthorne's native Salem, which set the tone for his journey. There, he found himself whisked back across time from the "new America" of the West to the worldly-wise America of the Puritan Northeast. Howells's description of his time in Salem reveals both his admiration of Hawthorne and his recognition of his own literary and nationalistic innocence (see *Harper's New Monthly Magazine* 89 [June 1894]: 40–41). In Boston, his conversations were uniformly positive; looking back across the decades that separated his visits with them from the memoir of the tour he first published serially in *Harper's New Monthly Magazine* (1894–1895) and then collected in *Literary Friends and Acquaintance* (1900), he felt Holmes, Lowell, and Fields recognized in him the aspiring young writers, editors, and critics that they once were. Especially eager to meet Hawthorne, "the exquisite artist, the unrivalled dreamer" (*Harper's New Monthly Magazine* 88 [May 1894]: 821), Howells accepted a letter of introduction from Lowell, though Holmes forewarned him that even if he were to meet Hawthorne, "I don't know that you will ever feel you have really met him. He is like a dim room with a little taper of personality burning on the corner of the mantel." Howells recalled that as all three affectionately expressed "the same sense of something mystical and remote" in Hawthorne, they cautioned him not to be too taken in by the Transcendentalists (*Harper's New Monthly Magazine* 89 [July 1894]: 232).

Traveling to Concord by way of Lowell, Massachusetts, Howells visited Hawthorne on 9 August 1860 and called on Thoreau and Emerson the next day. For all the joy he took from his meeting with Hawthorne, his encounters with Thoreau and Emerson verged on the unpleasant. Unlike Hawthorne, whose geniality far exceeded Howells's already inflated expectations, in person neither Thoreau nor Emerson matched the figures he so eagerly anticipated meeting. Admitting that "in those days I was a helplessly concrete young person," he reports that he was mystified by Thoreau, who launched into a reverie not over himself or his love of nature, but over John Brown—"not the warm, palpable, loving, fearful old man of my conception, but a sort of John Brown type, a John Brown ideal, a John Brown principle, which we were somehow . . . to cherish." The meeting with Emerson was nearly as disastrous. After an exchange of initial pleasantries, the conversation turned to Hawthorne, whom Emerson praised for his "personal excellence and . . . fine qualities as a neighbor," then indicted for his latest book, *The Marble Faun,* which he considered "mere mush." Confused as he was by Thoreau's Transcendental musings, Howells felt that Emerson's indifference to Hawthorne's literary merit exposed his "defective sense . . . of literature; he praised extravagantly . . . among the new things, and he failed to see the worth of much that was . . . precious beside the line of his fancy" (*Harper's New Monthly Magazine* 89 [August 1894]: 447–49).

I WONDER IF THERE IS A stage that still runs between Lowell and Concord, past meadow walls, and under the caressing boughs of way-side elms, and through the bird-haunted gloom of woodland roads, in the freshness of the summer morning? By a blessed chance I found that there was such a stage in 1860, and I took it . . . up to Concord. . . . The journey gave me the intimacy of the New England country as I could have had it in no other fashion, and for the first time I saw it in all the summer sweetness which I have often steeped my soul in since. The meadows were newly mown, and the air was fragrant with the grass, stretching in long winrows among the brown bowlders, or capped with canvas in the little haycocks it had been gathered into the day before. I was fresh from the affluent farms of the Western Reserve, and this care of the grass touched me with a rude pity[;] . . . the land was lovelier than any I had ever seen, with its old farm-houses, and brambled gray stone walls, its stony hill-sides, its staggering orchards, its wooded tops, and its thick-brackened valleys. . . .

[217]

I made phrases to myself about the scenery as we drove along; and yes, I suppose I made phrases about the young girl who was one of the inside passengers, and who, when the common strangeness had somewhat worn off, began to sing, and sang most of the way to Concord. . . .

Her fellow-passenger was in far other excitement; he was to see Hawthorne, and in a manner to meet Priscilla and Zenobia, and Hester Prynne and little Pearl, and Miriam and Hilda, and Hollingsworth and Coverdale, and Chillingworth and Dimmesdale, and Donatello and Kenyon; and he had no heart for any such poor little reality as that, who could not have been got into any story that one could respect, and must have been difficult even in a Heinesque poem.

I wasted that whole evening and the next morning in fond delaying . . . [until] I found courage to go and present Lowell's letter to Hawthorne. I would almost have foregone meeting the weird genius only to have kept that letter, for it said certain infinitely precious things of me with such a sweetness, such a grace as Lowell alone could give his praise. Years afterwards, when Hawthorne was dead, I met Mrs. Hawthorne, and told her of the pang I had in parting with it, and she sent it to me, doubly enriched by Hawthorne's keeping. But now if I were to see him at all I must give up my letter, and I carried it in my hand to the door of the cottage he called The Wayside. It was never otherwise than a very modest place, but the modesty was greater then than to-day, and there was already some preliminary carpentry at one end of the cottage, which I saw was to result in an addition to it. I recall pleasant fields across the road before it; behind rose a hill wooded with low pines, such as is made in Septimius Felton the scene of the involuntary duel between Septimius and the young British officer. I have a sense of the woods coming quite down to the house, but if this was so I do not know what to do with a grassy slope which seems to have stretched part way up the hill. As I approached, I looked for the tower which the author was fabled to climb into at sight of the coming guest, and pull the ladder up after him; and I wondered whether he would fly before me in that sort, or imagine some easier means of escaping me.

The door was opened to my ring by a tall handsome boy . . . and the next moment I found myself in the presence of the romancer, who entered from some room beyond. He advanced carrying his head with a heavy forward droop, and with a pace for which I decided that the word would be *pondering*. It was the pace of a bulky man of fifty, and his head was that beautiful head we all know from the many pictures of it. But Hawthorne's *look* was different from that of any picture of him that I have seen. It was sombre and brooding, as the look of such a poet should have been; it was the look of a man who had dealt faithfully and therefore sorrowfully with that problem of evil which forever attracted, forever evaded Hawthorne. It was by no means troubled; it was full of a dark repose. Others who knew him better and saw him oftener were familiar with other aspects, and I remember that one night at Longfellow's table, when one of the guests happened to speak of the photograph of Hawthorne which hung in a corner of the room, Lowell said, after a glance at it, "Yes, it's good; but it hasn't his fine *accipitral* look."

In the face that confronted me, however, there was nothing of keen alertness; but only a sort of quiet, patient intelligence, for which I seek the right word in vain. It was a very regular face, with beautiful eyes; the mustache, still entirely dark, was dense over the fine mouth. Hawthorne was dressed in black, and he had a certain effect which I remember, of seeming to have on a black cravat with no visible collar. He was such a man that if I had ignorantly met him anywhere I should have instantly felt him to be a personage.

I must have given him the letter myself . . . but I only remember his offering me his hand, and making me shyly and tentatively welcome. After a few moments of the demoralization which followed his hospitable attempts in me, he asked if I would not like to go up on his hill with him and sit there, where he smoked in the afternoon. He offered me a cigar, and when I said that I did not smoke, he lighted it for himself, and we climbed the hill together. At the top, where there was an outlook in the pines over the Concord meadows, we found a log, and he invited me to a place on it beside him, and at intervals of a minute or so he talked while he smoked. Heaven preserved me from the folly of trying to tell him how much his books had been to me, and though we got on rapidly at no time, I think we got on better for this interposition. He asked me about Lowell, I dare say, for I told him of my joy in meeting him and Dr. Holmes, and this seemed greatly to interest him. Perhaps because he was so lately from Europe, where our great men are always seen through the wrong end of the telescope, he appeared surprised at my devotion, and asked me whether I cared as much for meeting them as I should care for meeting the famous English authors. I professed that I cared much more, though whether this was true, I now have my doubts, and I think Hawthorne doubted it at the time. But he said nothing in comment, and went on to speak generally of Europe and America. He was curious as to the West, which he seemed to fancy much more purely American, and said he would like to see some part of the country on which the shadow, or, if I must be precise, the damned shadow, of Europe had not fallen. I told him I thought the West must finally be characterized by the Germans, whom we had in great numbers, and, purely from my zeal for German poetry, I tried to allege some proofs of their present influence, though I could think of none outside of politics, which I thought they affected wholesomely. I knew Hawthorne was a Democrat, and I felt it well to touch politics lightly. . . .

With the abrupt transition of his talk throughout, he began somehow to speak of women, and said he had never seen a woman whom he thought quite beautiful. In the same way he spoke of the New England temperament, and suggested that the apparent coldness in it was also real, and that the suppression of emotion for generations would extinguish it at last. Then he questioned me as to my knowledge of Concord, and whether I had seen any of the notable people. I answered that I had met no one but himself, as yet, but I very much wished to see Emerson and Thoreau. I did not think it needful to say that I wished to see Thoreau quite as much because he had suffered in the cause of John Brown as because he had written the books which had taken me; and when he said that Thoreau prided himself on coming nearer the heart of a pine-tree than any other human being, I could say honestly enough that I would rather come near the heart of a man. This visibly pleased him, and I saw that it did not displease him, when he asked whether I was not going to see his next neighbor Mr. Alcott, and I confessed that I had never heard of him. That surprised as well as pleased him; he . . . entered into some account of the philosopher, whom I suppose I need not be much ashamed of not knowing then, since his influence was of the immediate sort that makes a man important to his townsmen while he is still strange to his countrymen.

Hawthorne descanted a little upon the landscape, and said certain of the pleasant fields below us belonged to him; but he preferred his hill-top, and if he could have his way those arable fields should be grown up to pines too. He smoked fitfully, and slowly, and in the hour that we spent together, his whiffs were of the desultory and unfinal character of his words. When we went down, he asked me into his house again, and would have me stay to tea, for which we found the table laid. But there was a great deal of silence in it all, and at times, in spite of his shadowy kindness, I felt my spirits sink. After tea, he showed me a bookcase, where there were a few books toppling about on the half-filled shelves, and said, coldly, "This is my library." I knew that men were his books, and though I myself cared for books so much, I found it fit and fine that he should care so little, or seem to care so little. Some of his own romances were among the volumes on these shelves, and when I put my finger on the Blithedale Romance and said that I preferred that to the others, his face lighted up, and he said that he believed the Germans liked that best too.

Upon the whole we parted such good friends that when I offered to take leave he asked me how long I was to be in Concord, and not only bade me come to see him again, but said he would give me a card to Emerson, if I liked. I answered . . . that I should like it beyond all things; and he wrote on the back of his card something which I found, when I got away, to be, "I find this young man worthy." The quaintness, the little stiffness of it . . . was amusing to one who was not without his sense of humor, but the kindness filled him to the throat with joy. . . . I entirely liked Hawthorne. He had been as cordial as so shy a man could show himself; and I perceived, with the repose that nothing else can give, the entire sincerity of his soul.

Nothing could have been farther from the behavior of this very great man than any sort of posing, apparently, or a wish to affect me with a sense of his greatness. I saw that he was as much abashed by our encounter as I was; he was visibly shy to the point of discomfort, but in no ignoble sense was he conscious, and as nearly as he could with one so much his younger he made an absolute equality between us. My memory of him is without alloy one of the finest pleasures of my life. In my heart I paid him the same glad homage that I paid Lowell and Holmes. . . . This seems perhaps very little to say in his praise, but to my mind it is saying everything. . . . [A] defect of the Puritan quality, which I have found in many New-Englanders, is that, wittingly or unwittingly, they propose themselves to you as an example, or if not quite this, that they surround themselves with a subtle ether of potential disapprobation, in which, at the first sign of unworthiness in you, they help-lessly suffer you to gasp and perish; they have good hearts, and they would probably come to your succor out of humanity, if they knew how, but they do not know how. Hawthorne had nothing of this about him; he was no more tacitly than he was explicitly didactic. . . . He had just given the world the last of those incomparable works which it was to have finished from his hand; the Marble Faun had worthily followed . . . the Blithedale Romance, and the House of Seven Gables, and the Scarlet Letter, and had perhaps carried his name higher than all the rest, and certainly farther. Everybody was reading it, and more or less bewailing its indefinite close, but yielding him that full honor and praise which a writer can hope for but once in his life. . . . We are always finding new Hawthornes, but the illusion soon wears away, and then we perceive that they were not Hawthornes at all; that he had some peculiar difference from them, which . . . we shall no doubt consent must be his difference from all men evermore.

I am painfully aware that I have not summoned before the reader the image of the man as it has always stood in my memory, and I feel a sort of shame for my failure. He was so altogether simple that it seems as if it would be easy to do so; but perhaps a spirit from the other world would be simple too, and yet would no more stand at parle, or consent to be sketched, than Hawthorne. In fact, he was always more or less merging into the shadow, which was in a few years wholly to close over him; there was nothing uncanny in his presence, there was nothing even unwilling, but he had that apparitional quality of some great minds which kept Shakespeare largely unknown to those who thought themselves his intimates, and has at last left him a sort of doubt. There was nothing teasing or wilfully elusive in Hawthorne's impalpability, such as I . . . felt in Thoreau; if he was not there to your touch, it was no fault of his; it was because your touch was dull, and wanted the use of contact with such natures. The hand passes through the veridical phantom without a sense of its presence, but the phantom is none the less veridical for all that.

"My First Visit to New England. Fourth Part," *Harper's New Monthly Magazine* 89 (August 1894): 441–46.

From *Sketches from Concord and Appledore* (1895)

FRANK PRESTON STEARNS

Frank Preston Stearns (1846–1917) was the son of George Luther Stearns, the fiery reformer who supported John Brown in Kansas, belonged to Concord's "Secret Six," and helped establish the Freedmen's Bureau. The son's life took a very different direction. Educated at Sanborn's academy in Concord and then at Harvard, Stearns, who was the same age as Julian Hawthorne and on friendly terms with the Alcott girls and the Emerson children, became an authority on Italian art and published several books and articles on the subject.

Stearns's extended commentary that follows reveals his appreciation of Hawthorne's merit as a person and an artist. Devoting minimal attention to Hawthorne's Salem roots, Stearns begins with the suggestion that Hawthorne's Brook Farm experience was the impetus behind his need to find a career. Lathrop and James had already advanced the same suggestion, but Stearns's sarcastic representation of the utopian experiment elevates Hawthorne in the reader's mind as a person of good sense who mistakenly became involved with some very strange people. Further, Stearns's genteel representation of the Hawthornes' marriage, his reserved development of Hawthorne's shyness through an analogy drawn from Thoreau's characterization of how wild apple trees are grown, and his conviction that Hawthorne's allegories make a more lasting impression on readers than do many sermons they might otherwise hear all suggest that Stearns was one of the first biographers at the end of the nineteenth century to take a fresh look at Hawthorne. Stearns's view of Hawthorne is thus unburdened by the rush of critical opinions that appeared in print during the 1870s and 1880s, and it informed his later treatments of Hawthorne in *Cambridge Sketches* (1905) and *The Life and Genius of Nathaniel Hawthorne* (1906).

THE LITERARY CELEBRITIES OF Concord, with the exception of Thoreau, were not indigenous. Emerson may have gone there from an hereditary tendency[, and] ... Hawthorne ... by way of the Brook Farm experiment. How, with his reserved and solitary mode of life, he should have embarked in such a gregarious enterprise is not very clear; but the election of General Harrison had deprived him of a small government office[,] . . . his writings brought him very little, and perhaps he hardly knew what to do with himself.

All accounts agree that he joined the West Roxbury association of his own free-will, and without solicitation of any kind. He not only threw himself into this hazardous scheme with an energy that astounded his friends but he embarked in it all the money he had in the world, which was nearly a thousand dollars. He has left no notation from which we might infer what his hopes or his motives were. . . .

George Ripley and his friends do not seem to have made any definite calculation of what might be the result of their experiment. They expected, by working six hours a day and limiting themselves to the simplest and most frugal living, to have six left for literary pursuits and the enjoyment of profound conversation. Any practical farmer would have told them that this could not be done and make both ends meet at the close of the year. Any political economist would have told them that a community which disregards the advantage of division of labor, could not compete with one which recognizes that advantage. . . .

The greater number of the Brook Farm community were transcendentalists, and we have no desire to depreciate the work which the transcendentalists accomplished. They were the needful men and women of their time; the importers of fresh thought and a more elevated mental activity. . . .

Since the time of the early Christians there was never a more pure-minded and loyal-hearted congregation than that which was gathered at Brook Farm. They were really the best society of the day. George Ripley himself, one of the finest scholars and most agreeable writers of that time, afterwards found his right place as literary editor of the New York Tribune. . . . There were poets, painters, musicians in the community; especially John S. Dwight, who as the life-long editor of the "Journal of Music," also deserves a place on the roll of our public educators. George William Curtis was one of the youngest members of the community, but always one of the most brilliant. Sometimes of a rainy day there was very good cheer and entertainment in the "Hive" as they called their most commodious building, but generally the men were too drowsy and fatigued after their work was done for much intellectual activity.

It is necessary . . . to distinguish between the New England transcendentalists and the German school of philosophy, from which they are supposed to have derived their inspiration. A German critic has said of them that they were not so much philosophers as poetical rhapsodists. . . . Their business was not so much thinking, as to celebrate thinking. There was also in the composition of their creed a strong element of French naturalism, which is not easily reconciled with the teachings of the German transcendentalists. . . . It was this empirical French quality in New England transcendentalism which gave it a certain popularity, but at the same time prevented it from striking its roots deeply into the national soil. . . .

The one quality which Hawthorne had in common with the transcendentalists, except such qualities as are common to all good people, was ideality. Next to the grand structure of his head, this is the most noticeable characteristic in the pictures of him. He seems to have been attracted to them at first, and was even mistaken for a transcendentalist by Edgar A. Poe, and was attacked by that fiery Virginian in a most belligerent manner.

At Brook Farm, however, he soon began to differentiate from them, and finally acquired for them something like an aversion. Neither is this to be wondered at. Hawthorne was an artist pure and simple. He looked for ideality in human life; not in the ideas that control and direct it. He was not like Raphael and Shakespeare, men who could enjoy philosophy and make their art so much the richer and deeper for it. He saw everything in a pictorial form; facts and conditions which did not make a picture had no value for him, and reasoning was a weariness and a disagreeable effort. Nevertheless he did the best he could.

It is delightful to think of the tremendous energy with which he worked at Brook Farm. No, no one else seems to have done so much hard labor there. He was better fitted for this than many of his colleagues, having a strong, full-chested frame, and is said in his youth to have been a very swift runner and skater; but nothing indicates better the latent force that was in this quiet and usually inactive man. Many of the Brook Farm adventurers were not physically equal to a solid day's work, but this was a contingency which nobody had foreseen.

Hawthorne was one of the first to discover the futility of the experiment. Early in the following year he wrote to Miss Sophia Peabody to whom he was then engaged: "It has become quite evident to me that our fortunes are not to be found in this place;" a conclusion which he no doubt arrived at from an examination of the accounts of the association. It was Hawthorne's salvation in the difficult path of life he had chosen; a path as difficult and dangerous as that of an Alpine climber, that, poet as he was, he always looked facts sternly in the face and did not permit himself to be misled by romantic or sentimental illusions.

It had been expected that the more brilliant members of the community would be able to write magazine articles, or other remunerative literature, in their hours of leisure, and money thus obtained would go into the common fund. Hawthorne found that he could do nothing of the kind. Two or three hours' work in the sun did not quite deprive him of the use of his brains, but it left him without either fancy or imagination. He also felt the want of that external refinement which a nature like Hawthorne's requires as a fulfilment of its internal condition. The lack of nicety in the housekeeping became continually more and more unpleasant to him. The expenditures at the end of the first year were largely in excess of the receipts; in fact the inmates had eaten up nearly everything that the farm produced. His friend Franklin Pierce, who was just beginning to be prominent in politics, asked him the salutary question, "What are you gaining by this peculiar mode of life?"

His experience there served as a foundation for the "Blithedale Romance," and caused no further injury than the loss of his money. It would have required a Thackeray to have realized and described the humorous side of it—the highly practical joke of so many well-educated and cultivated people making life unnecessarily hard for themselves.

In the autumn of 1841 a reverend gentleman, the brother of Mrs. L. Maria Child, went to visit his friend at Brook Farm accompanied by his niece, who is one of the few persons now living who have a distinct memory of the place. On calling at the "Hive" they learned that only a few members of the association were present at that moment, but Mr. Ripley himself could be found in the turnip field, where they soon discovered him with two others, throwing turnips into a cart. On the approach of his friends, Mr. Ripley came forward and said, "Dr. Francis, this is really kind of you, to come such a distance to see an old fellow. You perceive I am occupied with the philosophy of 'de cart.'" This referred to some writings he had lately published on Descartes' philosophy, and made his audience laugh heartily.

Mr. Dwight then appeared and gave an interesting account of a flock of wild geese which he had discovered early in the morning marching through the cornfield. He said they looked exactly like tame geese, but as soon as he came in sight of them they flew away in a most surprising manner. Mr. Bradford, who is frequently mentioned in Hawthorne's note-book, looked sunburnt and very thin, and averred that milking the cows on a frosty morning was a chilly kind of business. Hawthorne himself had gone to Boston.... The visitors walked about the premises and were shown through the "Hive," but found it rather a dreary and comfortless building. The farm did not appear to be well kept. There was too evidently a lack of order and discipline there....

Having discovered nothing better than fool's gold at Brook Farm, Hawthorne suddenly came across the true metal in the domestic privacy of his married life at Concord. It would appear from one of Mrs. Hawthorne's letters that George Ripley was so sanguine of the success of his experiment that he had given Hawthorne a sort of guarantee for the thousand dollars which the latter had invested in it. When, at the close of the first year, Hawthorne had decided to withdraw from the association, he naturally hoped to regain a portion of his capital. Mr. Ripley was too deeply involved to accommodate him in that way, and offered instead the rent of the old Ripley mansion in Concord, which then happened to be vacant. So Hawthorne and Miss Peabody were happily married, with no immediate fund save the rent of an ancient house in the country, and no better expectations than the uncertain income from his pen.

It was a hazardous undertaking, but he was now nearly forty years old, his *fiancée* more than thirty, nor could the sharpest foresight discover any advantage from waiting longer. Emerson, in his lecture on heroism, has signalled especially the heroism of the scholar, and selected as an example the Frenchman Anquetil Duperron, who worked his passage on a vessel to India, and then worked his way, mostly on foot, through Afghanistan and Persia, learning languages as he went, in order to obtain copies of the sacred books of the Persians, which were then unknown in Europe. Were it not for fear of giving offence he might have found a finer heroism in literary genius, and selected an example from his own village.

For fifteen years Hawthorne had been like a ship detained from port by adverse winds. The handsomest and most gifted man in America had nearly reached to forty years without being married or finding a home of his own. It was a life of hardship; of social starvation almost like exile. It tested his courage, his faith in human nature, to the utmost. How difficult were the earlier years of Irving and Bryant and Longfellow. That he remained always true to himself and never lost sight of that ideal of excellence which was his guiding-star.

We are not surprised to learn that his difficulties were rather augmented than diminished by matrimony. Even in plain, rural Concord he found at the end of three years, that his expenses had exceeded his income by what seemed to him quite a formidable debt. This distressed him the more because he had not yet learned that all men must lose in some manner, and that the whole community is bound to take a share in such losses as are honestly incurred. This is what charity and philanthropy, as well as the various forms of insurance, finally result in. But Hawthorne was the last man to apply such a principle to his own case. He had continually hoped that when a balance-sheet was drawn up at Brook Farm some portion of his investment there would be returned to him; but this resource also failed him.

At last Bancroft the historian . . . heard of his situation, and had him appointed collector of the port at Salem. He was again removed from that position by President Taylor, and it has been said that his wife heroically supported him by her skill in drawing and painting until the "Scarlet Letter" could be finished and money procured from its publication. The nomination of Franklin Pierce for the presidency was a piece of good fortune for Hawthorne such as the wildest expectation could never have imagined; and at length in his fiftieth year, with the consulate of Liverpool, he finally saw the wolves driven from his door. This realistic side of his life seems to have escaped the attention of his biographers.

Yet he may be called fortunate to have lived when he did. It is easy to say that we should have appreciated Emerson and Hawthorne better than their contemporaries appreciated them, but it is one thing to recognize a genius when we meet him and a very different matter to admire him after we have been informed that he is a famous man. It is doubtful if writers in whom the ideality is so strongly marked would be received with favor at the present time either by editors or the public. The tendency to materialism would have been too strong for them. Lyceum lectures, on which Emerson depended chiefly, are not what they were; and either of them in a magazine would appear in too startling a contrast with the smooth impersonal writing of to-day. The two cardinal sins of a writer now are to have a style of his own and ideas of his own.

Complaint is frequently made that we have no great men like those of the past; but such grand individualities as Hawthorne and Webster, or even self-centred characters like Horace Greeley, are no longer possible. Everywhere, in the college, in the market, and in society, war is waged upon originality and independence of character. . . .

Most husbands are fortunate if their honeymoon lasts a month, but Hawthorne's lasted two years. It would seem as if during that space not a cloud came across his sky. He gathered flowers for his wife—water lilies, which he must have sought for in a boat, fringed gentians and the queenly "Lilium Canadensis"—and then felt that the most beautiful of them were unequal to the loveliness of her nature. After the first months, few visitors came to see them. "George Prescott," he says, "sometimes enters our paradise to bring us the products of the soil, but for weeks the snow in our avenue has been untrodden by any other guest." Mrs. Hawthorne's letters at this period are exceedingly interesting, for nowhere in her husband's writings, or in those of others, do we come so close to this rare and remarkable man. The following description of his character seems to have been a genuine case of thought transference, so much is it like his own writing in grace and purity of expression: "He loves power as little as any mortal I ever knew; and it is never a question of private will between us, but of absolute right. His conscience is too fine and high to permit him to be arbitrary. His will is strong, but not to govern others. He is so simple, so transparent, so just, so tender, so magnanimous, that my highest instinct could only correspond to his will. I never knew such delicacy of nature." . . .

With the exception of William Ellery Channing, he made no friends in Concord, though he speaks kindly of Thoreau, and compares Channing to him. It is to be suspected that this was largely on account of his political principles—or the lack of them. He had held office under a democratic administration and felt that his interests were connected with that party. Further than that, he does not appear to have distinguished between the two parties. Of his most intimate friends, one was a democrat and the other a whig. But the annexation of Texas was now in sight, and Concord was stirred again with the spirit of '75. Hawthorne . . . did not take interest in the antislavery movement, and a heated discussion of any subject must have been jarring and unpleasant to him.

It is not impossible that in this way he came into conflict with Margaret Fuller and conceived an abiding dislike to her. Miss Fuller would not have spared her eloquence in regard to what she considered a matter of principle, nor is it likely that she would have been more considerate of the respect which is due in such matters from a woman to a man.

There were not a few persons whom she offended by too much "bounce." . . . Hawthorne and his wife had not been four days in Concord before she came to them with a proposition that they should take Ellery Channing and his wife, who was her own sister, into their family as boarders. One cannot help some astonishment at this proceeding, for it is an instinct with all women to know that a newly married couple do not like to be interfered with. No word has ever been published from which we can infer how the grievance between them originated, but it is morally certain that there was a grievance of some kind, and as Hawthorne was the most inoffensive of men, it is not likely that he was responsible for it. . . .

How could it happen that Hawthorne deceived himself? Is it possible that he was in the right, and men like Emerson, Ripley, and James Freeman Clarke in the wrong? Why does he consider Miss Fuller to have had a strong, coarse nature, and to have been morally unsound? Here we enter into the deepest recesses of the author's nature.

Hawthorne was not wholly a fatalist, or he never could have conceived the character of Donatello, but he was very largely so. A man for whom a life of action is impossible, and who is thus unable to escape wholly from his own shadow, naturally comes to look on any series of events as an inevitable chain of cause and effect. He speaks somewhere of Byron's virtues and vices as being so closely interwoven that he could not have had one without the other, and if the objectionable passages in his poetry were expurgated, the life and genius of it would go with them. His story of "The Birth-mark" is an allegory of the same description. He did not agree with Shakespeare, that the best men are moulded out of faults, but believed that as we are in the beginning, so we remain essentially till the end.

He says that whenever Margaret Fuller heard of a rare virtue, she wished to possess it and adorn herself with it; so that she finally became a sort of brilliant external patchwork, dazzling to the eye, but internally quite different. There is a certain truth in this, but it is not a whole truth; for there is Socrates—a compendium of all the ancient virtues, consistent throughout, and who formed himself in the manner Hawthorne describes. It is true that in a search after rare and exceptional virtues we are apt to lose sight of the more homely kind which form the bone and sinew of human-life. But is not this effort a virtue in itself? . . . Is not the very crown of character that which we derive from failure, penitence, and self-reproach? Human nature is a mysterious labyrinth and the wisest have only found a partial clue to it.

George S. Hillard . . . came to visit Hawthorne one of the last Sundays while he remained in the Old Manse, and the two went together to spend the forenoon in Walden woods, calling on Emerson by the way to inquire what the best road might be. Emerson prudently detained them until after the townspeople were safely in their churches, and then accompanied them. It is a pleasant retrospect to think of those two mighty men, so like and yet so unlike, together with their amiable and gifted friend, going off on this Sunday excursion. Mr. Hillard was a fortunate companion for him, for no one could serve better as a mean between two extremes. At the close of Hawthorne's rehearsal of this episode, he makes this note, in commentary: "I find that my respect for clerical people, as such, and my faith in the utility of their office, decrease daily. We certainly do need a new Revelation, a new system; for there seems to be no life in the old one." . . . Was this the summary and net result of their stroll in Walden woods? . . .

[In] 1860 the Hawthorne family returned from their long residence in England and Italy. There was no little curiosity concerning them in the quiet old settlement, which was increased by the fact that nothing was seen of them for several months after they came.

If Thoreau was a recluse, Hawthorne was an anchorite. He brought up his children in such purity and simplicity as is scarcely credible,—not altogether a wise plan. It was said that he did not even take a daily paper. In the following year Martin F. Conway, the first United States representative from Kansas, went to Concord to call on Emerson, and Emerson invited Hawthorne to dine with them. Judge Conway afterwards remarked that Mr. Hawthorne said very little during the dinner, and whenever he spoke he blushed. Imagine a man five times as sensitive as a young lady in her first season, with the will of a Titan, and a mind like a crown-glass mirror, and you have Nathaniel Hawthorne. While he was in a state of observation, the expression of his face reflected everything that was going on about him; in his reflective moods, it was like looking in at the window of a dark room, or perhaps a picture-gallery; and if any accident disturbed him his look was something like a cracked pane of glass.

Moreover there was something unearthly or superterrestrial about him, as if he had been born and brought up in the planet Saturn. Wherever he went he seemed to carry twilight with him. He walked in perfect silence looking furtively about for fear he might meet some one that he knew. His large frame and strong physique ought to have lasted him till the year 1900. There would seem to be something strange and mysterious about his death, as there was in his life. His head was massive, and his face handsome without being attractive. The brow was finely chiseled, and the eyes beneath it were dark, luminous and fathomless. I never saw him smile, except slightly with his eyes. . . .

Emerson has given an account of this trait in Hawthorne's character, but he has failed to discover the mainspring of it. Who indeed can explain it? It was part of the man, and without it we could not have had Hawthorne. Perhaps the easiest solution is that of Thoreau's wild apple-tree. When the sprout from an apple-seed comes up in the grass a cow pretty soon bites it off. The next year it puts out two more shoots, and the ends of these are again nipped off. Thus it continues to grow under severe restrictions and forms at length a large thorn-bush, from which finally the tree is able to shoot up beyond the cow's reach and bears its proper fruit. So no doubt Hawthorne in his youth, being a tender plant, was greatly annoyed by brutal and inconsiderate people. A sensitive, proud and refined nature inevitably becomes a target for all the cheap wits and mischievous idlers in the neighborhood. To escape from this we may suppose that Hawthorne surrounded himself with an invisible network of reserve, behind which his pure and lofty spirit could develop itself in a harmonious manner.

This he certainly succeeded in doing. In purity of expression and a graceful diction Hawthorne takes the lead of his century. He was the romance writer of the Anglo-Saxon race; in that line only Goethe has surpassed him. Nor is it possible for pure and beautiful work to emanate from a mind which is not equally pure and beautiful. Wells of English undefiled cannot flow from a turbid spring.

In purity Emerson probably equaled him, but not in his sense of beauty. Where he surpassed Hawthorne was in manliness, and in his broad humanitarian interests. Otherwise no two men could be more unlike than these, and it would seem to be part of the irony of fate that they should have lived on the same street, and been obliged to meet and speak with each other. One was like sunshine, the other shadow. Emerson was transparent, and wished to be so, he had nothing to conceal from friend or enemy. Hawthorne was simply impenetrable. Emerson was cordial and moderately sympathetic. Hawthorne was reserved, but his sympathies were as profound as the human soul itself. To study human nature as Hawthorne and Shakespeare did, and to make models of their acquaintances for works of fiction, Emerson would have considered a sin; while the evolution of sin and its effect on character was the principal study of Hawthorne's life. One was an optimist, and the other what is sometimes unjustly called a pessimist: that is, one who looks facts in the face and sees people as they are. Hawthorne could not have felt quite comfortable in the presence of a man who asked such searching questions as

Emerson frequently did, and Emerson could scarcely have found satisfaction in conversing with one who never had any opinion to express.

A good many people claimed to have been Hawthorne's friends after his death who were sufficiently afraid of him while he was alive. He does not appear to have ever had but two very intimate friends, Franklin Pierce and George S. Hillard, both remarkably amiable and sympathetic men,— qualities to which they owed equally their successes and failures in life. Ex-president Pierce used to come to Concord and carry Hawthorne off to the White Mountains, the Isles of Shoals or Philadelphia, just as two college-students will drop their books and go off somewhere to have a good time. Once while Hawthorne was in Boston, Mr. Hillard tried to persuade him to go to Cambridge and dine with Longfellow; but he would not, and went home by the next train.

He was pro-slavery in politics, partly because his two friends were so, and partly because he disliked the abolitionists. It is not necessary to suppose that the pro-slavery people of the North in those days believed that human slavery was morally right. It is doubtful if anyone believed that. A great many considered it, as Webster did, a serious evil but a dangerous matter to interfere with (and so it proved); some were influenced by mercenary motives; and the northern Democrats, misled by the illogical doctrine of State Sovereignty, believed they had no right to interfere with it. Mr. Hillard held the first of these positions, and General Pierce the last. Very likely Hawthorne shared in both of them; but he never explained himself, and what he thought on the subject will always remain a mystery. . . .

Alcott was almost the only man in Concord who had the courage to call on Hawthorne. Sometimes they even went to walk together. How much satisfaction Hawthorne found in these visits it would be difficult to say, for the very philosophic breadth and extension of Alcott's interest were enough to make Hawthorne feel rather shy of him. Alcott's conversation about books and literature was often very fine, but even this could not have given Hawthorne much entertainment. His own library, as he states himself somewhere, was of a miscellaneous character, and contained the works of scarcely any author of repute except Shakespeare. Alcott's sense of humor and keen knowledge of human nature may have been a sort of common ground between them.

Meanwhile Hawthorne, as afterwards appeared, was making a study of Alcott to see whether he would serve his purpose as the mainspring for a new work of fiction. The manuscript plot of a romance was found among

Hawthorne's papers in which he describes a personage in general outline like his neighbor Alcott, but without his ideality and good-humor. This imaginary character was supposed to live in a retired manner, together with an old housekeeper, a boy of whom he is the legal guardian, and a huge spider in which his interest and solicitude are more especially centred. What the catastrophe of this strange story was to have been, we are not informed, but it naturally would have arisen from the unhealthy and oppressive social position in which the boy must have found himself as he advanced towards manhood. At the close of his memoranda Hawthorne says, "In person and figure Mr. Alcott—". To be selected as the mainspring of a romance is properly a compliment.

There was a certain Dutch artist who made a specialty of sheep, and painted them so well that Goethe said of him, "This painter so entered into the life of his subject that I think he must have been a sheep, and I shall become one if I continue to look at his pictures." In the same way Hawthorne had such penetrating sympathy for all living things, that he unconsciously absorbed certain qualities from those with which he was most familiar. . . .

Venomous creatures appeared to have been especially interesting to him, and he even fancied a poisonous influence in the Roman sunshine. Perhaps his liking for spiders may account for a certain cobwebby feeling which comes over one at times while reading his books. There can be no doubt of this, for when I once spoke of it, a lawyer who was present replied, "I have said the same myself; and when I was in Paris reading a French newspaper, I had a feeling as if cobwebs were being drawn across my face, and looking down to the end of the column, I saw that it was a translation from Hawthorne." But these peculiarities are like the soil which gives flavor to the grape, and the wine that comes from the grape.

If the reader thinks that in these few paragraphs Hawthorne has hardly received proper justice, he may not be far wrong. Yet how can any personal account of such a man do him justice. It may be said of him that he was a model husband, a kind father, and an exemplary citizen, and that is all. During his lifetime there were people who did him great injustice. His reserved life was looked upon as a morbid selfishness. The rare publication of his writings was supposed to arise from indolence. It was thought that he wrote the life of Franklin Pierce for the sake of a government office, and when he was actually appointed consul at Liverpool, the case was proved beyond a doubt. The anti-slavery people looked upon him as a lamentable exception to the other literary men of America, who were all on their side: they doubted if he had been born with any sense of right and wrong. What answer can be made to such accusations? . . .

But why multiply these unpleasant examples of misrepresentation? Hardly a great and good man has ever lived without suffering from it at one time or another. They originate in bad temper, in partisan malice, and those believe them who have no just criterion to distinguish truth from falsehood.

After all, what other American has accomplished a literary work equal to Hawthorne's. He was an artist, purely an artist, and of the finest quality. The raw material may be in us, but to develop it requires pains and labor. The greater the talent the more difficult is its fruition. Hawthorne's life was absorbed in this. His habitual mood was a dreamy, brooding observation. When Englishmen say that no great work of art has been produced in America; that Allston's magnificent pictures remain half-finished; that neither Emerson or Lowell has been able to write a book, but only essays; that we have no historian as good as Macaulay, and that the best of our poetry consists of ballads and other short pieces; my reply is, "The Scarlet Letter" and "The Marble Faun." These are great works of art. The most unique and original, perhaps, of the present century; and if they have not the lyrical form they are exquisitely written, and none the less poetic. . . . Mrs. Hawthorne said that during the period while her husband was occupied with the "Scarlet Letter," there were a contraction of his brow, and a look of care and anxiety in his face, which were reflected in her own nerves and made her unhappy, although she knew little of what he was writing. Both these romances are tragedies; and there is something in tragedy that places it at the top of all literature. Their subjects also indicate that he was in full sympathy with his own time, and perhaps understood the nineteenth century better than it does itself.

Emerson has been called a Greek, but Hawthorne was more Hellenic than he. This may be perceived in his version of the Greek legends in "Tanglewood Tales." His style is much like that of Isocrates. Where Webster or Emerson would use Saxon words, Hawthorne would use Greek or Latin ones, and gain in grace and flexibility what he lost in force and vigor. He would seem to have been a southerner by nature, fond of warm weather and an inactive life.

His short stories are of equal value comparatively with those that are longer and more complete. I remember in my youth being attracted by the title of one of them. It was called "The Unpardonable Sin," and described a man, who, having spent many years in search of this iniquity, finds it too heavy a burden for his soul to carry, and destroys himself one night in a lime-kiln. Next morning the lime-burner discovered a marble heart floating on the surface of the seething lime. This was the unpardonable sin,—to have a cold, unfeeling heart. Such allegories make a more lasting impression than many sermons. His note-books also are of great value, especially the American ones. He makes dramatic situations out of the simplest incidents, and we read between the lines sentences he never wrote. We remember them without in the least intending to do so, and find ourselves reflecting upon them as if they were important events. No writer since Fielding has given so faithful a picture of the time in which he lived. . . .

More than ten years after his death on a summer afternoon Mr. Alcott was entertaining some friends, and as they looked towards the Hawthorne house one of them said, "Would you be surprised, Mr. Alcott, to see Nathaniel Hawthorne some day gliding past your rustic fence as he used to do?" "No, sir, I should not," replied the old philosopher, "for while he lived he always seemed to me like an apparition from some other world. I used to see him coming down from the woods between five and six o'clock, and if he caught sight of anyone in the road he would go under cover like a partridge. Then those strange suspicious side-glances of his! They are not anywhere in his writings. I believe they were inherited from some ancestor who was a smuggler, or perhaps even an old pirate. In his investigation of sin he was expiating the sins of his progenitors." There is reason for believing that Alcott was not far wrong in this conjecture.

From *Sketches from Concord and Appledore* (New York and London: G. P. Putnam's Sons, 1895), 29–31, 33–35, 37–48, 50–67.

"Hawthorne's Last Years" (1904)

JULIAN HAWTHORNE

—)|(—

Julian Hawthorne (1846–1934) was Nathaniel and Sophia's middle child and only son. Spending his early years in Massachusetts, as his parents moved from place to place, and abroad in England and Italy during and after his father's consulship in Liverpool and Manchester, Julian enjoyed his first real sense of home when the family returned to the Wayside in Concord in 1860. For most of his formative years he was homeschooled by his parents, especially his father. An equestrian and avid walker, he inherited his appreciation of the outdoors from his father, and he came by his appreciation of art—particularly sketching—and philosophy from his mother. In Concord, where he was on cordial terms with the Alcott and Emerson children as well as with the many American literati who visited his parents, he attended Sanborn's academy before entering Harvard in 1863. Although Julian had always been a somewhat desultory student, his father's unexpected death in 1864 was a severe blow from which his academic performance never recovered, and he was asked by Harvard's administration to leave at the beginning of his senior year. After continuing his engineering studies in Dresden, Germany, he returned to America in 1870 and immediately launched a highly productive but ultimately lackluster career as a fiction writer, essayist, reviewer, historian, and biographer. *Bressant*, his first novel, appeared in 1873, and for many years he regularly contributed stories and essays to *Harper's Weekly*, *Harper's New Monthly Magazine*, *Scribner's Magazine*, and other popular journals.

In spite of his substantial literary output, Julian is primarily known today as his father's biographer and as the sometimes misguided defender of his family's honor in public arguments over the management of his parents' published and unpublished writings. Scharnhorst indexes several dozen journal and newspaper articles in print by Julian before 1900 (*Nathaniel Hawthorne*, 396); however, Julian's two most enduring works are *Nathaniel Hawthorne and His Wife* (1884) and *Hawthorne and His Circle* (1903). Yet, more than in any other of his many writings on his father, in the piece that follows, Julian expresses what having Nathaniel Hawthorne as a father meant to him. Here, Julian's memory of his relationship with his father and his father's friends appears clarified and, perhaps, purified by time; here, too, the son's reverential tone serves as an acknowledgment that he was never equal in genius to his father. In contrast to the emphasis that has always been placed on Hawthorne's Salem roots, Julian summons the reader's attention to Concord's importance in his father's life, stating, "And it was no wonder . . . that Nathaniel Hawthorne, after his tour of the world, should return at last to old Concord as to the most desirable place on this planet to live and die in" (68). Written for the centenary of Hawthorne's birth, just as he was himself approaching his father's age at the time of his death, in "Hawthorne's Last Years" Julian also stresses the social qualities of his father's personality and character. In this loving remembrance he suggests that, although his father "did not speak much," "his presence was the finest conversation" and "the few words that he uttered [always] came pointed with . . . meaning and aimed with . . . relevance" (71).

FROM GREEN, SHOWERY ENGLAND and the cool Atlantic my father returned to Concord to find it parching under the unmitigated heat of the New England summer. A few friends met him at the dock; but he took the afternoon train out of Boston and reached the Wayside before supper-time. Little Benjie, the youngest son of Uncle Horace Mann, attended us on our way from the railway station, and entertained us by his Yankee "guessing" and smart ways. And my father, who, during the voyage, had cast many a thoughtful glance back toward the east, now beheld the buff-colored old dwelling in which he was to pass the four closing years of his life. No doubt he may have said to himself that there were villas in Italy, and country-seats in England, which would better have suited him. Doubtless, too, but for his children's sake, he would have settled somewhere in Europe; he had lived in Europe so long, and it had become endeared to him by so many associations, sad as well as pleasant, and the quiet and old-fashioned ways there so well suited his age and temperament, that he could no longer feel anything homelike in America. Yet he was patriotic, and loved his country. The truth may have been, that he could have been content neither in the Old World nor in the New; whichever he had chosen, he would have regretted the other. Be that as it may, it was America that he chose; he wished his son to go to an American college, and his daughters to grow up under American conditions. There are indications that he may have entertained a hope that, after some years, circumstances would permit him to revisit the Old Home. But, if so, the hope was soon abandoned. Meanwhile he maintained a cheerful demeanor, and contemplated the Wayside with a humorous expression, half-pleased, half-rueful. He was still boy enough to feel something of those pleasurable thrills which shook the hearts of his children at their homecoming. Perhaps he would find it possible to take up the old life with fresh zest, and to do work which should have in it the spirit of the Western continent, enriched and deepened by his experience of the East. America was the nobler choice.

Concord, in those days, was after all a homely old place, and the folks were hospitable. Here were the cordial Manns, and Aunt Lizzie Peabody, and Mr. Bull, the grape-grower, and the benign light of Emerson's countenance, and white-locked, orphic Mr. Alcott, blinking as though dazzled by the light of his own inspiration; and hook-nosed, bearded, stealthy Thoreau, and Ellery Channing, stalking in, downcast and elusive, but with a substantial man inside, could you but catch him; and Judge Ebenezer Rockwood Hoar, with his lovely, spiritual sister; and other kindly people. There was none of the storied richness and automatic method of English society, which takes the individual into its comfortable current, and sweeps him along through agreeable eddies and leisurely stretches with the least possible exertion on his own part; yet it was in its way the best of society, intelligent, simple, natural, self-respecting, and quietly independent. Its members knew how to be social, and also how to let one another alone. They were mutually helpful, but not intrusive. If they happened to know that Concord was the best place in the world they did not think it necessary to proclaim the fact in and out of season. There stood the stout little town; let it speak for itself. Down by the river, where had stood the rude bridge that arched the flood, was a little gray stone obelisk, marking the spot where the British soldiers fell with the sound of the shot that was heard round the world ringing in their dying ears. A mile away was the four-square white wooden home of Emerson, toward which were turned the trusting eyes of all emancipated optimists the world over, though his fellow-townsmen knew him to be, really, simply a good neighbor and useful citizen, who had as much to thank Concord for as Concord him, and whose transcendental vagaries they regarded with kindly indulgence. Thoreau had his amiable foibles too; and Concord had fought it out with him, and overcome him, in the matter of tax-paying; but he could bear witness that in Concord grew all the flowers and sang all the birds worth mentioning in the world, and he could cause Indian arrow-heads to sprout out of the earth merely by casting his eyes downward. Judge Hoar, again, was the best judge in New England, and his venerable father, who was still living (a memorable figure, gentlemanly, mild, slender, with a rusty black body-coat and high stock, and a tall, dusty stove-pipe hat set on his pale, serene brows), would have been better than he had he not already lived his active life in a former generation. Where in the world could you buy better groceries than at Walcott and Holden's, or finer shoes than those that Jonas Hastings made in his little back shop, or a more commodious assortment of general goods than were to be found in Mr. Stacy's store[?] . . . If you spoke of farming, there were Mr. Moore's broad acres, with their thriving crops of asparagus, brought up according to the latest scientific methods, and rhubarb, and corn, and to-matoes, and other vegetables; not to speak of his many prosperous rivals. In the way of a hostelry, there was the time-honored Middlesex Hotel, with its veranda and sheds and easy-going bar-room; and on the other side of the vil-lage square was the brick town-hall, where, every week in the season, one or other of the lights of the New England lecture-platform held forth to attentive and appreciative audiences; or where balls and receptions were given upon occasion, or political meetings held as important as any in Faneuil Hall; or if you wanted medical treatment, who was better than old Doctor Bartlett?—or if a school, Master Sanborn . . . was second to no pedagogue in the world in his ability to turn country boys and girls into accomplished men and women. It was not necessary to draw attention to these excellences; they were visible and undeniable to the most careless eye. And it was no wonder, therefore, that Nathaniel Hawthorne, after his tour of the world, should return at last to old Concord as to the most desirable place on this planet to live and die in.

So my Father, clad in an old hat and coat and village-made shoes, strolled about his estate and meditated over Concord and the less notable places that he had known. He did not much affect Boston or even local society. He did not care to take a longer walk than to Walden Pond and back, or up the old turnpike along which the British had retreated a hundred years before; he confined himself for the most part to his own fields and hillside. The level meadow on the south of the road was laid out partly in young fruit-trees, and partly in corn and beans; a straight path to the brook was made, and larches were set out on both sides of it. A few old apple-trees grew to the west of the area divided by the path; and there was one Porter apple-tree that stood close to the fence, on which early and delicious fruit appeared in profusion every year. The house-enclosure was protected from the street by a hedge, and by tall spruces; there was likewise an ancient mulberry-tree, spreading its boughs over the tiny lawn in front of the library windows, and scattering it, in the season, with its crimson and purple berries. Against its low trunk a rustic seat was put up, on which my father and mother often sat in the afternoons, talking over their domestic and agricultural plans. On the hillside, terraced out years before by Alcott, more apple-trees grew; and abundant laburnums, their branches heavy with pendulous golden blossoms; and higher up, on the summit, white pines and pitch pines, and a mingled, irregular array of birch, oak, elm, and hickory, all of recent growth; a tangled little wood, with none of the grandeur and spaciousness of the forests of Walden. But there was a pleasant, quiet view from the western brow of the hill, and a seat was made there, in the Alcott style, of twisted boughs; and eastward from it, along the crest of the acclivity, my father was wont to pace to and fro by himself, mornings and afternoons, until at length a foot-path was worn into the rooty substance of the hill, a distance of some two hundred yards to the fence which enclosed Mr. Bull's estate. Many a meditative mile did he pace there; and the track formed by his recurrent footsteps remained distinct long after he had passed farther on his way, whither none might overtake him.

But the family needed more elbow-room than in the early days, and it was necessary to make the Wayside bigger. My father had long contemplated these additions; and he now called the village carpenters into consultation; and after much debate, Mr. Wetherbee and Mr. Watts submitted their plans. They thought that the requisite enlargement could be done for about five hundred dollars. Upon this basis they set to work and labored with more or less diligence for a year or thereabouts, and the bill gradually and inevitably grew until at the end it amounted to thrice the sum originally named. My father watched the operations with his hands folded behind him and his soft felt hat pulled down on his forehead; or he ascended the hill, to escape the hammering and sawing; but during that year there could be no studious repose for him in which to evolve literary imaginings. A room was added over the library; another in the rear of the dining-room; another above that, and above that still one more, the three constituting the tower, and the top room being my father's study. Besides these a large room was placed over the kitchen, with its outlook on the terraces of the hill; it had an arched roof, devised to please my mother; and the walls were painted with a color which the painter described as "a kind of blue pink." Ornamental eaves and gables were added here and there; in the place of the main entrance, which had been under the gable in the centre of the house-front, a bow window was devised;

and the entrance was put to the west, and covered with a pretty gabled porch. To me and to my younger sister the racket, the clutter, and the construction were delightful, a continuous vaudeville; and my mother was always an interested and hopeful spectator and counsellor; but my father's bearing denoted humorous resignation oftener than any other emotion. He attempted no writing; but in the evenings, after the uproar was done for the day, we would gather in the library, and he would read aloud to us; the greater part of that year was occupied with the Waverley novels, taken up one after another from beginning to end of the series. I cannot overestimate either the enjoyment or the profit that I got from those readings. My sisters sat large-eyed and rapt; my mother sewed and listened with that sympathy and apprehension which made her face always beautiful. I doubt not that the reader, too, was happy in these evenings. The tall astral lamp gave out its soft light, which glistened on the backs of the books in the surrounding bookcases; outdoors there was peace, save for the song of insects in summer, and in winter the cracklings of the frost. The two splendid hours over, I would go to bed, with a heart and mind full of adventure, chivalry, and romance.

Before the building was done another and deeper kind of disturbance came to keep my father from his work. The first great breakers of our national storm had been rolling in heavily upon the shore, and the ills which they foreboded robbed him of tranquility. It was in vain that he placed the period of his "Romance of Immortality" a century ago; the guns of Sumter and of Bull Run sounded in his ears none the less distinct for the imaginative remoteness in which he strove to seclude himself. And then, unexpectedly, and with what seemed some abruptness, his health and strength began to fail. He lost weight, his cheeks grew hollow, his hair whitened, his once firm and elastic step grew slow and uncertain. He still climbed his hill, though slowly, and paced to and fro on its summit, or sat for long periods gazing out over the meadows, or listening to the music of the pines. He would also shut himself up in his tower-study for hours each day, and the manuscripts he left behind him showed that he worked hard; his general mood in quiescence became grave, though in family intercourse he still maintained the playfulness and humor that had always marked him in my knowledge. He possibly realized better than any of us what his illness portended. "There was nothing the matter" with him; and that indefiniteness of ailment was the serious feature. He was approaching the end, and was silently adjusting himself to the prospect of death, while his mind was consciously richer both in the acquisitions of experience and in the treasures of wisdom than ever before, and . . . he feared that the wife and children whom he loved would be left inadequately provided for. My father was a wise man,—too wise to delude himself into accepting as true happiness the spiritual self-mutilation of the ascetic or self-denier; happiness, to him, meant the full freedom and energy of every faculty, employed on a stage unimpeded by unfavorable conditions either public or private. There had never been and there could never be such happiness for him in this world. He had deep and reverent religious faith, though of what precise purport I am unable to say. But when a man of great soul finds himself face to face with the end of all things earthly, he must admit that he knows nothing, and that the unsearchable ways of the Almighty may prove widely divergent from those which theory and hope have forecast. Dramatic natures, fanatics and enthusiasts, the dull and the defiant, may meet death with indifference, or with a smile or a scoff; but a man of sincerity so organic as my father could not resort to these subterfuges. He went on his way, not complainingly or grudgingly, not fearfully or fantastically, but with a grave simplicity that was impressive. In this, as in all his other manifestations, he showed courage and self-respect and a noble modesty. He had been a happy man, as this world goes; yet when at the close of his career he glanced back over its former stages, he was unable . . . to recall a moment when he would have commanded the fatal joy-bell of King Felix to be rung. Happiness would be a foolish word did we not believe that a life is to come in which the word will represent a reality and not a dream.

He took a cordial interest in his son's college experiment; and I have always been glad that he did not witness its somewhat unstimulating termination. When anxiety as to his physical condition increased, he submitted to expedients devised to restore his vigor; he made occasional visits to Boston, chatting in the old Corner Bookstore, or dining with Fields and his wife, whose hospitality and good humor refreshed him. Later he undertook little journeys away from home; to Washington and the seat of war, or, with his son, to some nearby seaside place; but he did this to please others, not with the hope in himself of any lasting benefit. In the last but one of these trips, the sudden death of Ticknor, his companion, had a disastrous effect upon him. I remember the description my mother gave of his dismayed and anguished appearance. After some weeks he was induced to make another trial of change of scene with Franklin Pierce; and I need not recount the last days, which are well-known. The news came to me, in Harvard, in the forenoon of the 19th of May; I went to speak with Professor Gurney, who had been my especial friend and counsellor in college; and he said: "It is only a few months since Thackeray, one of the best men in England, died; and now we have lost by far the best man in America." It was beautiful spring weather; but the sunlight, and the blue, and the green looked strange, like a phantasmagory thrown upon the dark.

It was during these last Concord years that I had begun to form relations with my father beyond the instinctive, unreasoning affection of childhood. He had begun to speak with me of other than childish things. He encouraged me to enter into the society of the young folks in Concord,—the dances and picnics and masqued balls and rowing and bathing parties; he got me good clothes to wear, and quietly stimulated my rather lagging interest in the social amenities of my companions. No doubt he was contemplating the future of us all with some solicitude. But I think he especially desired to steer me away from the lonely experiences of his own young manhood; and, as I have said before, he explicitly advised me against adopting the literary calling. I can hardly infer that, modest as was his estimate of his own literary achievements, he actually regretted having devoted himself to writing; but it may be that he believed it would have been better for him and his had he more cultivated intercourse with his fellow-creatures, at the age when such intercourse affects a man. He did not wish "the cursed habit of solitude" to hamper his descendant. Not only in this, but in many other ways, did his loving and wise forethought seek to guard and make easy the path of his children in the world; much of this care we did not recognize till afterward. Certainly there was no duty of husband and father that he did not fulfil, giving good measure, pressed down and running over, and yet giving it so unobtrusively and naturally as to make it appear, if possible, a mere matter of course and of routine. But, in truth, it was the love that went with the gift that with its lovely splendor dazzled out of sight all thought or consciousness of duty; and made the memory of the husband and father a more precious heritage and protector than his own wise counsel, even, could be. Forty years' contemplation of what he was has served to render him only brighter and loftier in my memory. I have known many good men since he died, and not a few men of genius; but my father's figure still stands high and apart. The world regards him as one of the great lights of American literature; a handful of surviving friends remember him as a man distinguished in their love and honor; but in my thought of him he has a quality not to be described; that is associated with the early impressions which make the name of home beautiful; with a child's delight in the glory of nature; with a boy's aspirations toward a pure and generous career; with intimate conceptions of truth, bravery, and simplicity. He did not speak much; but his presence was the finest conversation; and the few words that he uttered came pointed with a meaning and aimed with a relevance that have held them in my mind after more than half a lifetime.

"Hawthorne's Last Years," *The Critic* 45 (July 1904): 67–71.

Permissions

꘏

[Reminiscences of My Brother from His Childhood through the 1830s] by Elizabeth Manning Hawthorne is taken from Randall Stewart, "Recollections of Hawthorne by His Sister Elizabeth," *American Literature* 16 (January 1945), copyright © 1945 by Duke University Press. All rights reserved. Used by permission of the publisher.

[Childhood Encounters with Hawthorne in Salem] by [Lucy Ann Sutton Bradley] is taken from Manning Hawthorne, "A Glimpse of Hawthorne's Boyhood," *Essex Institute Historical Collections* 83 (1947), copyright © 1947 by the Essex Institute. All rights reserved. Used with permission of the Phillips Library at the Peabody Essex Museum.

[Epistolary Thoughts on Hawthorne, 1838–1886] by Elizabeth Palmer Peabody is taken from *Letters of Elizabeth Palmer Peabody: American Renaissance Woman,* ed. Bruce A. Ronda (Middletown, CT: Wesleyan University Press, 1984), copyright © 1984 by Wesleyan University Press. All rights reserved. Used with permission.

[Journal Thoughts on Hawthorne, 1838–1864] by Ralph Waldo Emerson is taken from *The Journals and Miscellaneous Notebooks of Ralph Waldo Emerson,* ed. William H. Gilman, Ralph H. Orth et al., 16 vols. (Cambridge: Harvard University Press, 1960–1982), copyright © 1960–1982 by the President and Fellows of Harvard College. Used by permission of the Ralph Waldo Emerson Memorial Association.

[First Years of Marriage at the Old Manse, 1842–1845] by [Sophia Amelia Peabody Hawthorne] is taken from Patricia Dunlavy Valenti, "Sophia Peabody Hawthorne's *American Notebooks,*" in *Studies in the American Renaissance 1996,* ed. Joel Myerson (Charlottesville: University Press of Virginia, 1996), copyright © 1996 by Joel Myerson.

[Reminiscences of a Childhood in Concord in the 1840s] by [Annie Sawyer Downs] is taken from Annie Sawyer Downs, "Mr. Hawthorne, Mr. Thoreau, Miss Alcott, Mr. Emerson, and Me," ed. Walter Harding, *American Heritage* 30 (December 1978), copyright © 1978 by Walter Harding. Used by permission of the Thoreau Society, Inc.

[On First Meeting Hawthorne in America, 1852] by [Henry Arthur Bright] is taken from *Happy Country This America: The Travel Diary of Henry Arthur Bright,* ed. Anne Henry Ehrenpreis (Columbus: Ohio State University Press, 1978), copyright © 1978 by Ohio State University Press. Used by permission of David H. Ehrenpreis.

[Vagabondizing with Hawthorne in England in 1856] by [Francis Bennoch] is taken from T. A. J. Burnett, "A Week's Vagabondage with Nathaniel Hawthorne," *The Nathaniel Hawthorne Journal 1971*, ed. C. E. Frazer Clark, Jr. (Washington, D.C.: NCR Microcard Editions, 1971), copyright © 1971 by NCR Microcard Editions. Used by permission of Bruccoli Clark.

Quote from Annie Keyes Bartlett's 26 May 1864 letter to Edward Jarvis Bartlett is used by permission of the Concord Free Public Library, Concord, Massachusetts.

Works Cited

Alcott, A[mos] Bronson. *The Journals of Bronson Alcott*. Ed. Odell Shepard. Boston: Little, Brown, 1938. Cited as *Journals ABA*.

———. *The Letters of A. Bronson Alcott*. Ed. Richard L. Herrnstadt. Ames: Iowa State University Press, 1969. Cited as *Letters ABA*.

Bridge, Horatio. *Personal Recollections of Nathaniel Hawthorne*. New York: Harper and Brothers, 1893.

Browning, Elizabeth Barrett. *The Letters of Elizabeth Barrett Browning to Mary Russell Mitford*. Ed. Meredith B. Raymond and Mary Rose Sullivan. 3 vols. [Waco, TX]: Armstrong Browning Library of Baylor University, The Browning Institute, Wedgestone Press, and Wellesley College, 1983. Cited as *Letters EBB*.

Channing, William Ellery. *Thoreau, the Poet-Naturalist*. 1873. Ed. F. B. Sanborn. Boston: Charles E. Goodspeed, 1902.

Conway, Moncure Daniel. *Emerson at Home and Abroad*. Boston: James R. Osgood, 1882.

———. *Life of Nathaniel Hawthorne*. New York: Scribner and Welford, 1890.

Emerson, Ralph Waldo. *The Journals and Miscellaneous Notebooks of Ralph Waldo Emerson*. Ed. William H. Gilman, Ralph H. Orth, et al. 16 vols. Cambridge: Harvard University Press, 1960–1982. Cited as *JMN*.

———. *The Letters of Ralph Waldo Emerson*. Ed. Ralph L. Rusk (vols. 1–6) and Eleanor M. Tilton (vols. 7–10). New York: Columbia University Press, 1939–1995. Cited as *Letters RWE*.

Fields, James T. *Hawthorne*. Boston: James R. Osgood, 1876.

———. *Yesterdays with Authors*. Boston: James R. Osgood, 1872.

Gollin, Rita K. *Portraits of Nathaniel Hawthorne: An Iconography*. DeKalb: Northern Illinois University Press, 1983.

Goodrich, S. G. *Recollections of a Lifetime; or Men and Things I Have Seen*. 2 vols. New York: Miller, Orton, and Mulligan, [1857].

Harding, Brian, ed. *Nathaniel Hawthorne: Critical Assessments*. 4 vols. East Sussex, UK: Helm Information, 1997.

Hawthorne, Julian. *Hawthorne and His Circle*. New York: Harper and Brothers, 1903.

———. *Nathaniel Hawthorne and His Wife: A Biography*. 2 vols. Boston: James R. Osgood, 1884.

Hawthorne, Nathaniel. *Centenary Edition of the Works of Nathaniel Hawthorne*. Ed. William L. Charvat, Thomas Woodson, et al. 23 vols. Columbus: Ohio State University Press, 1962–1997.

Homes of American Authors: Comprising Anecdotal, Personal, and Descriptive Sketches by Various Writers. New York: G. P. Putnam, [1853].

Howells, William Dean. *Literary Friends and Acquaintance: A Personal Retrospect of American Authorship*. New York: Harper and Brothers, 1900.

Idol, John L., Jr., and Buford Jones, eds. *Nathaniel Hawthorne: The Contemporary Reviews*. New York: Cambridge University Press, 1994.

James, Henry [Jr.]. *Hawthorne*. 1879. London: Macmillan, 1887.

———. *Notes of a Son and Brother*. New York: Charles Scribner's Sons, 1914.

Lathrop, George Parsons. *A Study of Hawthorne*. Boston: James R. Osgood, 1876.

Loring, George B. "Nathaniel Hawthorne." *Papyrus Leaves*. Ed. William Fearing Gill. New York: Worthington, 1880. 249–68.

Lowell, James Russell. *The Letters of James Russell Lowell*. Ed. Charles Eliot Norton. 2 vols. New York: Harper and Brothers, 1894. Cited as *Letters JRL*.

Marshall, Megan. *The Peabody Sisters: Three Women Who Ignited American Romanticism*. Boston: Houghton Mifflin, 2005.

McFarland, Philip. *Hawthorne in Concord*. New York: Grove/Atlantic Monthly Press, 2004.

Miller, Edwin Haviland. *Salem Is My Dwelling Place: A Life on Nathaniel Hawthorne*. Iowa City: University of Iowa Press, 1991.

Millington, Richard H., ed. *Cambridge Companion to Nathaniel Hawthorne*. New York: Cambridge University Press, 2004.

Peabody, Elizabeth Palmer. *Letters of Elizabeth Palmer Peabody: American Renaissance Woman*. Ed. Bruce A. Ronda. Middletown, CT: Wesleyan University Press, 1984. Cited as *Letters EPP*.

Reynolds, Larry J., ed. *A Historical Guide to Nathaniel Hawthorne*. New York: Oxford University Press, 2001.

Ronda, Bruce A. *Elizabeth Palmer Peabody: A Reformer on Her Own Terms*. Cambridge: Harvard University Press, 1999.

Scharnhorst, Gary. *Nathaniel Hawthorne: An Annotated Bibliography of Comment and Criticism before 1900*. Metuchen, NJ: Scarecrow Press, 1988.

Schreiner, Samuel A., Jr. *The Concord Quartet: Alcott, Emerson, Hawthorne, Thoreau and the Friendship That Freed the American Mind*. Hoboken, NJ: John Wiley, 2006.

Stearns, Frank Preston. *Cambridge Sketches*. Philadelphia: J. B. Lippincott, 1905.

———. *The Life and Genius of Nathaniel Hawthorne*. Philadelphia: J. B. Lippincott, 1906.

———. *Sketches from Concord and Appledore: Concord Thirty Years Ago; Nathaniel Hawthorne; Louisa M. Alcott; Ralph Waldo Emerson; Matthew Arnold; David A. Wasson; Wendell Phillips; Appledore and Its Visitors; John Greenleaf Whittier*. New York: G. P. Putnam's Sons, 1895.

Symonds, Joseph W. *Nathaniel Hawthorne: An Oration Delivered before the Alumni of Bowdoin College, Brunswick, Maine, July 10, 1878*. Portland, ME: Steven Berry, 1878.

Tharp, Louise Hall. *The Peabody Sisters of Salem*. Boston: Little, Brown, 1950.

Valenti, Patricia Dunlavy. *Sophia Peabody Hawthorne: A Life, Volume 1, 1809–1847*. Columbia: University of Missouri Press, 2004.

Whipple, Edwin P. *Character and Characteristic Men*. Boston: Ticknor and Fields, 1866.

Wineapple, Brenda. *Hawthorne: A Life*. New York: Alfred A. Knopf, 2003.

Index

WRITERS IN THEIR OWN TIME

Alcott in Her Own Time
Edited by Daniel Shealy

Emerson in His Own Time
Edited by Ronald A. Bosco and Joel Myerson

Hawthorne in His Own Time
Edited by Ronald A. Bosco and Jillmarie Murphy

Whitman in His Own Time
Edited by Joel Myerson